SOCIOLOGICAL METHODOLOGY
❧ 2015 ❧

AMERICAN SOCIOLOGICAL ASSOCIATION

SOCIOLOGICAL METHODOLOGY

2015

VOLUME 45

EDITOR

Tim Futing Liao

MANAGING EDITOR

Lisa Savage

EDITORIAL BOARD

Paul D. Allison	Monica McDermott
Carolyn J. Anderson	Stephen L. Morgan
Jake Bowers	Raffaella Piccarreta
Elizabeth Bruch	Daniel A. Powers
Damon M. Centola	Lyn Spillman
Roberto P. Franzosi	Tanya Stivers
Guang Guo	Katherine Stovel
Michele Ann Haynes	Jeroen Vermunt
Erin Leahey	Kazuo Yamaguchi

EDITORIAL ASSISTANT: Andrea Wilbon Hartman

An official publication by SAGE Publications, Inc. for

THE AMERICAN SOCIOLOGICAL ASSOCIATION
SALLY T. HILLSMAN, *Executive Officer*

Sociological Methodology (SM) is the only American Sociological Association periodical publication devoted entirely to research methods. It is a compendium of new and sometimes controversial advances in social science methodology. Contributions come from diverse areas and have something new and useful—and sometimes surprising—to say about a wide range of methodological topics. *SM* seeks qualitative and quantitative contributions that address the full range of methodological problems confronted by empirical research in the social sciences, including conceptualization, data analysis, data collection, measurement, modeling, and research design. The journal provides a forum for engaging the philosophical issues that underpin sociological research. Papers published in *SM* are original methodological contributions including new methodological developments, reviews or illustrations of recent developments that provide new methodological insights, and critical evaluative discussions of research practices and traditions. *SM* encourages the inclusion of applications to real-world sociological data. *SM* is published annually as an edited, hardbound book. Manuscripts should be submitted electronically to http://mc.manuscriptcentral.com/smx.

Sociological Methodology is published annually—in August—by SAGE Publications, Inc., 2455 Teller Road, Thousand Oaks, CA 91320, on behalf of the American Sociological Association, 1430 K Street NW, Suite 600, Washington, DC 20005. Send address changes to *Sociological Methodology* c/o SAGE Publications, Inc., 2455 Teller Road, Thousand Oaks, CA 91320.

Non-Member Subscription Information: All non-member subscription inquiries, orders, back issues, claims, and renewals should be addressed to SAGE Publications, 2455 Teller Road, Thousand Oaks, CA 91320; telephone: (800) 818-SAGE (7243) and (805) 499-0721; fax: (805) 375-1700; e-mail: journals@sagepub.com; http://www.sagepublications.com. **Subscription Price:** Institutions: $425 (online/print), $390 (online only). Individual subscribers are required to hold ASA membership. For all customers outside the Americas, please visit http://www.sagepub.co.uk/customerCare.nav for information. **Claims:** Claims for undelivered copies must be made no later than six months following month of publication. The publisher will supply replacement issues when losses have been sustained in transit and when the reserve stock will permit.

Member Subscription Information: American Sociological Association member inquiries, change of address, back issues, claims, and membership renewal requests should be addressed to the Executive Office, American Sociological Association, 1430 K Street NW, Suite 600, Washington, DC 20005; Web site: http://www.asanet.org; e-mail: customer@asanet.org. Requests for replacement issues should be made within six months of the missing or damaged issue. Beyond six months and at the request of the American Sociological Association the publisher will supply replacement issues when losses have been sustained in transit and when the reserve stock permits.

Abstracting and Indexing: Please visit http://sm.sagepub.com and, under the "More about this journal" menu on the right-hand side, click on the Abstracting/Indexing link to view a full list of databases in which this journal is indexed.

Copyright Permission: Permission requests to photocopy or otherwise reproduce material published in this journal should be submitted by accessing the article online on the journal's Web site at http://sm.sagepub.com and selecting the "Request Permission" link. Permission may also be requested by contacting the Copyright Clearance Center via their Web site at http://www.copyright.com, or via e-mail at info@copyright.com.

Advertising and Reprints: Current advertising rates and specifications may be obtained by contacting the advertising coordinator in the Thousand Oaks office at (805) 410-7772 or by sending an e-mail to advertising@sagepub.com. To order reprints, please e-mail reprint@sagepub.com. Acceptance of advertising in this journal in no way implies endorsement of the advertised product or service by SAGE, the American Sociological Association, or the journal editor(s). No endorsement is intended or implied. SAGE reserves the right to reject any advertising it deems as inappropriate for this journal.

Change of Address for Non-Members: Six weeks' advance notice must be given when notifying of change of address. Please send the old address label along with the new address to the SAGE office address above to ensure proper identification. Please specify the name of the journal.

International Standard Serial Number ISSN 0081-1750
International Standard Book Number ISBN 978-1-5063-2352-7 (Vol. 45, 2015, hardcover)
Manufactured in the United States of America. First printing, August 2015.
Copyright © 2015 by the American Sociological Association. All rights reserved.

Printed on acid-free paper

Reviewers

Paul Allison
Zack Almquist
Duane Alwin
Bruno Arpino
Shyon Baumann
Henning Best
Ulf Bockenholt
Kenneth Bollen
Jake Bowers
Jessica Broome
Babette Brumback
Carter Butts
Feinian Chen
Kevin Clarke
Paul Clarke
Jennifer Beam Dowd
Anette Fasang
Glenn Firebaugh
Amber Fox
Roberto Franzosi
Noah Friedkin
Markus Gangl
Steven J. Gold
Amir Goldberg
Luca Grassetti
William Greene
Justin Grimmer
Maryclare Griffin
Thomas M. Guterbock
Alex Hagen-Zanker
Shin-Kap Han
Ben Hansen
Lingxin Hao
Douglas Heckathorn

Christian Hennig
Michael Hout
Catherine Hurley
Paul A. Jargowsky
Timothy Johnson
Will Kalkhoff
ChangHwan Kim
Frauke Kreuter
Klaus Krippendorf
Maria Krysan
Danielle Lavin-Loucks
Rachel Levenstein
Kurt Lindemann
Omar Lizardo
Scott J. Long
Howard Lune
James Mahoney
Reuben May
Monica McDermott
Shaila Miranda
David Morgan
Stephen L. Morgan
Michel Mouchart
Ina V. S. Mullis
Thomas Brendan
  Murphy
Rüdiger Mutz
Andrew Noymer
Wendy Olsen
Berkay Özcan
Pamela Paxton
Eva Petkova
Raffaella Piccarreta
Art FY Poon

Daniel A. Powers
Charles Ragin
Sara Randall
Stephen Raudenbush
Craig M. Rawlings
Ho Moon-ho Ringo
Molly Roberts
Ingo Rohlfing
Matthew Salganik
Willem E. Saris
Ryan Saylor
Michael Schober
Uri Shwed
Klaas Sijtsma
Chris Skinner
Herbert L. Smith
Volker Stocké
Ross M. Stolzenberg
Judith Tanur
Luca Tardella
Roger Tourangeau
Su-Hao Tu
Stephen Vaisey
Jorre Vannieuwenhuyze
Susanne Vogl
Susanne von Below
Cuntong Wang
Michael J. White
Richard A. Williams
Raymond Wong
Shlomo Yitzhaki
Cristobal Young
Tian Zheng
Xiang Zhou

Volume 45   August 2015

SOCIOLOGICAL
METHODOLOGY

Contents

Big Data

Data Collection, Management, and Analysis

Analysis of Inequalities

Submission Information for Authors

Sociological Methodology (SM) is the only American Sociological Association periodical publication devoted entirely to research methods. It is a compendium of new and sometimes controversial advances in social science methodology. Contributions come from diverse areas and have something new and useful—and sometimes surprising—to say about a wide range of methodological topics. *SM* seeks qualitative and quantitative contributions that address the full range of methodological problems confronted by empirical research in the social sciences, including conceptualization, data analysis, data collection, measurement, modeling, and research design. The journal provides a forum for engaging the philosophical issues that underpin sociological research. Papers published in *SM* are original methodological contributions including new methodological developments, reviews or illustrations of recent developments that provide new methodological insights, and critical evaluative discussions of research practices and traditions. *SM* encourages the inclusion of applications to real-world sociological data. *SM* is published annually as an edited, hardbound book.

The content of each annual volume of the journal is driven by submissions initiated by authors; the volumes do not have specific themes. Editorial decisions about manuscripts submitted are based on the advice of expert referees. Criteria include originality, breadth of interest and applicability, and expository clarity. Discussions of implications for research practice are vital, and authors are urged to include empirical illustrations of the methods they discuss.

Manuscripts should be submitted electronically to http://mc .manuscriptcentral.com/smx. Submitting authors are required to set up an online account on the SAGE Track system, powered by Scholar One. The submission fee of $25 is payable through SAGE Track. Submission of a manuscript for review by *Sociological Methodology* implies that the article has not been previously published and that it is not under review elsewhere.

For full manuscript submission guidelines see sm.sagepub.com. For further information about the journal, visit the ASA journal page at http://www .asanet.org/journals/sm. Inquiries concerning the appropriateness of material are welcome. Prospective authors should send inquiries to soc-methodology@ psu.edu.

Sociological Methodology
2015, Vol. 45(1) ix–xi
© American Sociological Association 2015
DOI: 10.1177/0081175015598733
http://sm.sagepub.com

EDITOR'S INTRODUCTION

This is the sixth and final volume of *Sociological Methodology* under my editorship at the University of Illinois. It has been my privilege to serve as editor of this highly regarded and influential journal. In July, I will pass on the editorship to Duane Alwin of Penn State University. The American Sociological Association has recently informed me that the impact factor in 2014 of our journal was ranked fifth of 142 sociology journals. Therefore, I am doubly pleased to pass on the journal in fine shape to Duane's able hands.

In this year's volume, we feature again a symposium, "Life-course Sequence Analysis." Sequence analysis was introduced into sociology by Andrew Abbott over two decades ago, and the second-wave sequence analysis has seen a resurgence of much interest in sociology, a topic that is also close to one of my own recent research interests. The main article in the symposium—"A 'Global Interdependence' Approach to Multidimensional Sequence Analysis" by Nicolas Robette, Xavier Bry, and Éva Lelièvre—examines a method for analyzing mothers' and daughters' employment history sequences. The paper is followed by a balanced set of commentaries by Cees H. Elzinga, Wen Fan and Phyllis Moen, Anette Eva Fasang, Jacques-Antoine Gauthier, Eliza K. Pavalko, Raffaella Piccarreta, and Matthias Studer as well as a rejoinder by the authors of the main article. The commentators from institutions in five countries represent expertise in life course research and sequence analysis. Proposing a new method is never plain sailing; the symposium shows how many aspects of a method we must consider to evaluate a proposal fully, and it should give the reader an up-to-date assessment of sequence analysis in life course research.

Following the symposium are three sections, containing a total of eight chapters. The two articles in the section following the symposium both deal with some aspects of big data. Daniel Tumminelli O'Brien,

Robert J. Sampson, and Christopher Winship's chapter, "Ecometrics in the Age of Big Data: Measuring and Assessing 'Broken Windows' Using Large-scale Administrative Records," represents a second moment of ecometric analysis, with the first moment measuring the disorder of neighborhoods in things such as graffiti and litter (as in Raudenbush and Sampson's earlier work published in volume 29 of this journal). These large-scale administrative records certainly qualify as big data. Another form of big data can be found in news reports, which provide a typical unstructured text data. In "A Progressive Supervised-learning Approach to Generating Rich Civil Strife Data," Peter F. Nardulli, Scott L. Althaus, and Matthew Hayes argue for a collaborative, hybrid approach that combines machine-based and human-centric approaches to content analysis for extracting information from unstructured text. In the age of big data, these two chapters provide a timely report on what data analysts can do to utilize two different data forms.

The next section of the volume contains three chapters related to data collection, management, and analysis. Stephen L. Morgan and Emily S. Taylor Poppe, in "A Design and a Model for Investigating the Heterogeneity of Context Effects in Public Opinion Surveys," suggest that for data collection, randomized survey experiments on representative samples, when coupled with facilitative primes, can assist modeling selection into variable context effects, thus revealing heterogeneity at the population level. In research practice, the mismatch between data and methods and the difficulties caused by messy data can lead to inaccurate conclusions. In "An Introduction to the General Monotone Model with Application to Two Problematic Data Sets," Michael R. Dougherty, Rick P. Thomas, Ryan P. Brown, Jeffrey S. Chrabaszcz, and Joe W. Tidwell show how theoretical conclusions can be affected by these issues and demonstrate the general monotone model for analyzing such messy data. Ethnographers typically face the challenges of managing, presenting, and analyzing context-dependent data generated during fieldwork. In the final chapter of the section, "Beyond Text: Using Arrays to Represent and Analyze Ethnographic Data," Corey M. Abramson and Daniel Dohan introduce an interactive visual approach called *ethnoarray* for addressing these challenges.

The final section of the volume contains three chapters focused on some aspects of inequality analysis. Building on an empirical Bayes framework, Xiang Zhou, in "Shrinkage Estimation of Log-odds Ratios for Comparing Mobility Tables," proposes a shrinkage estimator for comparing mobility tables in stratification research that improves estimation efficiency by "borrowing strength" across multiple mobility tables. In "Can Non-full-probability Internet Surveys Yield Useful Data? A Comparison with Full-probability Face-to-face Surveys in the Domain of Race and Social Inequality Attitudes," Alicia D. Simmons and Lawrence D. Bobo investigate the potential usefulness of web-based surveys relying on non-full-probability sampling for the analysis of race and social inequality attitudes. The decomposition of inequality effects by race and gender is a common practice. The standard DiNardo-Fortin-Lemieux (DFL) decomposition analysis may produce biased estimates. In the final chapter of the section, "Decomposition of Gender or Racial Inequality with Endogenous Intervening Covariates: An Extension of the DiNardo-Fortin-Lemieux Method," Kazuo Yamaguchi introduces a combination of the DFL method with Heckman's two-step method for testing and eliminating bias in DFL estimation when some intervening covariates are endogenous while bringing race and gender into the center of causal analysis.

The *Sociological Methodology* team is grateful to all authors who submitted papers to the journal, whether or not their papers are published in this volume, and to the reviewers and our board members whose devoted work guaranteed the very high standard of the publications. In the past six years, my managing editor, Lisa Savage, has stuck with me through thick and thin even though she changed her regular job with a professional publisher, and I thank her for her reliability and consistency. I also thank our editorial assistant, Andrea Wilbon Hartman, for her promptness and enthusiasm in performing various kinds of editorial assistance; copy editor Stephanie Magean and the copy editors of Sage Publications for keeping up the quality of writing; and Athena Liao, who assisted in the art design that graces the cover and for her contributions to four previous cover designs. This is the fourth year in a row that we have published a symposium with an art design either directly using "data" from the symposium or indirectly reflecting its theme. This year's art design reflects the theme of life course analysis. My appreciation also goes to Jim Ballinger and Sara Sarver, who coordinated the publication process at Sage, and Janine Chiappa McKenna, Karen Edwards, and the Publications Committee of the American Sociological Association for their continuing support. We would like to acknowledge the material support from the Department of Sociology and the College of Liberal Arts and Sciences at the University of Illinois at Urbana-Champaign that houses our editorial office in the historic building of Lincoln Hall. Last but not least, I would like to express my appreciation to the American Sociological Association for the privilege of editing this highly important journal in our profession and for the opportunity to serve the discipline through this editorship.

—Tim Futing Liao

Sociological Methodology
2015, Vol. 45(1) 1–44
© American Sociological Association 2015
DOI: 10.1177/0081175015570976
http://sm.sagepub.com
⑤SAGE

⅋ 1 ⅋

A "GLOBAL INTERDEPENDENCE" APPROACH TO MULTIDIMENSIONAL SEQUENCE ANALYSIS

*Nicolas Robette**

Xavier Bry[†]

Éva Lelièvre[‡]

Abstract

Although sequence analysis has now become a widespread approach in the social sciences, several strategies have been developed to handle the specific issue of multidimensional sequences. These strategies have distinct characteristics related to the way they explicitly emphasize multidimensionality, interdependence, and parsimony. In this context, the authors introduce an original approach based on structural links between the dimensions, combining optimal matching analysis, multidimensional scaling, canonical partial least squares, and clustering, an approach the authors call globally interdependent multiple sequence analysis (GIMSA). The authors then apply GIMSA to mother-daughter employment histories in France and discuss the value of this method.

*University of Versailles-Saint-Quentin/Laboratoire Printemps, Guyancourt, France
[†]University of Montpellier 2, Montpellier, France
[‡]Institut National d'Études Démographiques, Paris, France

Corresponding Author:
Nicolas Robette, University of Versailles-Saint-Quentin/Laboratoire Printemps, 47 Boulevard Vauban, 78280 Guyancourt, France
Email: nicolas.robette@uvsq.fr

Keywords

sequence analysis, multidimensional sequences, optimal matching, life course, career, intergenerational transmission

1. INTRODUCTION

Since the mid-1970s, life-course analysis has become a major field of interest in the social sciences. Longitudinal micro-individual data, such as panels or retrospective surveys, have become more available, and at the same time statistical methodology has undergone a profound evolution. In this context, event-history analysis, which can be viewed as adding a diachronic dimension to traditional regression models, rapidly became established as the dominant approach: It aims at modeling the duration in a given situation or the risk for experiencing a given event. However, during the past decade, a large corpus of more descriptive sequence analysis methods has been disseminated. Their main goal is to identify patterns and resemblances among sets of diverse sequences (made up of a series of successive states), most often resulting in typologies of ideal-typical sequences. Nowadays, sequence analysis provides a powerful means to describe and better understand the unfolding of many social processes.

Most of the sequence analysis techniques currently used in the social sciences are related either to algorithmic methods (Abbott and Tsay 2000) or to correspondence analysis methods (Grelet 2002).[1] All have particularities, advantages, and drawbacks, although they usually give quite similar results (Robette and Bry 2012; Robette and Thibault 2008). Optimal matching (OM) analysis (OMA) is by far the most widespread sequence analysis technique. It has the major conceptual advantage of jointly addressing the different temporal aspects of a sequence: the moment of a transition, the duration of a stage, and the order within the sequence.

OMA was initially developed in molecular biology and introduced into the social sciences by Andrew Abbott in the 1980s (Abbott and Forrest 1986). The principle is based on the notion of similarity between pairs of sequences. The dissimilarity between two sequences is measured in terms of the "cost" of transforming one into the other. The transformation is performed using three types of basic operation: (1) insertion (inserting an element into the sequence), (2) deletion (deleting an element), and (3) substitution (replacing one element by another). A cost is associated with each operation; the distance between two sequences is thus defined as the minimum cost of the operations required to transform one into the other. Matching the entire set of sequences creates a matrix of pairwise distances, which is then used to group together those that are most similar (e.g., using clustering techniques) and so to obtain a typology.[2]

Although OMA has been applied to a wide range of social objects (e.g., see Abbott and Barman [1997] for pattern searching focusing on sequences of atypical types), it has also received some criticism (Elzinga 2003; Wu 2000); some innovative developments have emerged as a consequence (see Aisenbrey and Fasang [2010] for a review; see Biemann [2011] for a recent example).

Although sequence analysis of work careers and social trajectories in general is now well established (Brzinsky-Fay and Kohler 2010), notable previous developments have tended to explore the possibility not only of considering a single dimension of the life course (e.g., employment) but also of integrating combinations of statuses pertaining to other dimensions of the life course, such as housing and family, and introducing multidimensional sequence analysis (Pollock 2007). In this paper, we examine another aspect of life-course analysis: that of patterns of transmission from one generation to the next. Although social mobility, for instance, is more usually studied in terms of cross-sectional comparison of the father's position at a given period compared with that of the son, we here consider the entire histories of both generations. More precisely, we study women's involvement in paid employment for two successive generations marked, in France, by massive female entry into the labor force. Our aim here is to identify the way specific work profiles in one generation were followed by others in the next, rather than the possible similarity of mothers' and daughters' work careers. Each generation's involvement in paid activity has been shaped by their specific historical context, and the same profile is unlikely to recur. A relevant question can be asked: What are the main female lineage patterns, in terms of school-to-work transition and employment history, that underlie the macro trends in work and family (Barrère-Maurisson 1992)?

To this end, we first review the methods already available for multidimensional sequence analysis, and we then introduce a new approach based on structural links between the parents' and children's sequences, combining OMA, multidimensional scaling (MDS), canonical partial least squares (PLS), and clustering, an approach we call globally interdependent multiple sequence analysis (GIMSA). We then apply GIMSA to mother-daughter employment histories in France and discuss its benefits for summarizing complex sequence data such as linked life courses.

2. HANDLING MULTIDIMENSIONAL SEQUENCES

In the early days of sequence analysis in the social sciences, the successive elements composing sequences were hard to simplify into a unique and limited set of states: Methodological adjustments were needed to capture the diversity and complexity of individual social statuses. In other words, to make a detailed study of careers as sequences, various dimensions must be considered. For example, in their seminal article about the careers of musicians in Germany during the baroque and classical eras, Abbott and Hrycak (1990) combine position (e.g., vocalist or instrumentalist) and sphere (e.g., court or church). Likewise, the occupational status variable of Stovel, Savage, and Bearman (1996) is a combination of position and branch size, Blair-Loy (1999) combines job code and organization size, and Han and Moen (1999) mix work status, organization, and occupation.

Later, sequence analysis applications focused on life courses and the need to handle simultaneously their various dimensions became a key concern. Conjugal, parental, occupational, and residential histories unfolded in an interdependent way (Courgeau and Lelièvre 1992), and scholars explored the methodological repercussions of this theoretical construct. Pollock (2007) introduced multiple sequence analysis, which was subsequently systematized by Gauthier et al. (2010) and renamed multichannel sequence analysis (MCSA).[3]

The various multidimensional sequence typology-building strategies found in the literature can be summarized into four groups. The first strategy involves the creation of a new state variable that combines the simple states composing each dimension (Aassve, Billari, and Piccarreta 2007; Chaloupkova 2010; Dijkstra and Taris 1995; Elzinga 2003; Elzinga and Liefbroer 2007; Lesnard 2008). For instance, in the case of conjugal and parental histories, possible combined states would include "single with no child," "married with no child," and "married with one child." This may quickly lead to a large alphabet, that is, a set of very numerous states. Hence, in the case of four dimensions with three simple states in each, the combined variable would potentially have 3 × 3

$\times$ 3 $\times$ 3 = 81 states. Such an extended alphabet may be impractical when aiming to set substitution costs specifically tailored for each pair of combined states. However, this drawback can be easily circumvented by setting a constant substitution cost or by using transition likelihood between the states (Lesnard 2008).[4]

The second strategy is a more refined approach that avoids the need for a large extended alphabet: It is based on combining the substitution costs of the various dimensions. For instance, the substitution of "single with no child" and "married with one child" will be equivalent to a combination of the substitution cost between "single" and "married" and the substitution cost between "no child" and "one child." A possible combination is the sum (or average) of the costs defined for each dimension (Blair-Loy 1999; Gauthier et al. 2010; Pollock 2007; Salmela-Aro et al. 2011; Stovel et al. 1996), for example, the sum (or average) of the substitution cost between "single" and "married" and the substitution cost between "no child" and "one child." We can also imagine a more refined linear combination of the different dimensions (Abbott and Hrycak 1990), for instance, by applying weights to these dimensions (Gauthier et al. 2010:34). If there is a unique substitution cost for each dimension and it is identical between the dimensions, substituting two multidimensional states is equivalent to counting the number of dimensions that differ (Robette 2010). For example, replacing "single with no child" with "married with one child" will cost 2, while replacing "single with no child" with "married with no child" will cost 1. Moreover, this second strategy may be seen as a particular case of the first one, so substitution costs can be set simply and efficiently.

The third strategy consists of computing a dissimilarity matrix independently for each dimension and then summarizing them into a single distance matrix by linear combination (Blanchard 2005; Han and Moen 1999).

The fourth strategy uses distinct typologies of sequences that can be built for each dimension and then compared (Blanchard 2005), for example, with cross-tabulation.[5]

These four strategies can be systematically compared and classified according to three criteria: (1) multidimensionality, (2) parsimony, and (3) interdependence (see Table 1).[6] By *multidimensionality*, we refer to the fact that an approach in which the contribution of each dimension to the overall results may or may not be explicit (i.e., unequivocal) and flexible (i.e., parameterizable by the analyst). The first strategy takes the

Table 1. Taxonomy of Strategies to Handle Sequences with Various Dimensions

Strategy	Multidimensionality	Parsimony	Interdependence
(1) Combining states	No	Yes	Local
(2) Combining costs	Yes	Yes	Local
(3) Combining distance matrices	Yes	Yes	No
(4) Combining typologies	Yes	No	Global

multiple dimensions into account, as do the other three; still, by hiding dimensions in a single combined state variable, it is the only one that does not emphasize multidimensionality: For instance, it is not possible to have specific parameters for each dimension, to give more importance to a particular dimension by weighting it, or to assess the impact of each dimension on the results.

By *parsimony*, we refer to the fact that an approach may or may not lead to a limited and manageable number of ideal types[7]: Combining typologies produced for each dimension (as is done with strategy 4) may lead to an uncomfortably large number of clusters.

By *interdependence*, we refer to the fact that the relationship between dimensions may be masked (strategy 3) or taken into account locally (as in strategies 2 and 3)—that is, the focus is on the dependency between dimensions at *each point in time*—or globally (as in strategy 4)—that is, the focus is on the dependence between dimensions through *sequences as wholes*.

Local interdependence implies an emphasis on contemporaneousness. Indeed, with strategies 1 and 2, dimensions associated with a given sequence are synchronized. Once defined at a given time point in a given sequence, a multidimensional situation "remains the same throughout the alignment procedure" (Gauthier et al. 2010:9): The various dimensions shift jointly. Technically, the synchronization of the dimensions means that they have to be defined with the same time window—that is, the same starting and ending points (whether these are ages or dates)—and the same time clock (e.g., one year or one month by time point). This also implies the use of a unique dissimilarity measure (e.g., OM).

Global interdependence releases the emphasis on contemporaneousness; it is the overall shape of a dimension that is related to the others. In strategy 4, pairwise comparisons are made separately for each dimension in a first step, and then the relationships between the patterns of each dimension are examined. As distance matrices are computed independently for each dimension, distinct dissimilarity measures can be used, for example, a metric focusing on timing (such as Hamming distance) for one dimension and a metric based on order (such as the longest common subsequence [LCS] metric; see Elzinga 2008) for another dimension. Different time windows and clocks can also be used.

Strategy 3 also allows for different dissimilarity measures, time windows, and clocks. However, by simply adding distances matrices, the relationships between dimensions are not adequately handled. For instance, with two-dimensional sequences, if two individuals have a dissimilarity of 1 for a dimension and are identical for the second, they will have the same global distance as two individuals who are identical on the first dimension and have a dissimilarity of 1 on the second.

It is important to keep in mind that these criteria—multidimensionality, parsimony, and local and global interdependence—may or may not be desirable, depending on theoretical or data issues. There is no better strategy *per se* and the choice of one or the other should be grounded on sociological and empirical criteria.

Recently, a few sequence analysis papers took into account one of the key elements shaping life courses in Elder's paradigm (Giele and Elder, 1998), for example, the fact that individual life courses are embedded into social relationships, which means that "linked lives" are studied. Most applications have dealt with the transmission of histories between parents and children (Falcon 2012; Fasang and Raab 2014; Liefbroer and Elzinga 2012; Robette, Lelièvre, and Bry 2012), although a few papers have focused on husband and wife histories (Lelièvre and Robette 2010; Lesnard 2008; Robette, Solaz, and Pailhé 2009).

To assess the strength of transmission between parents and children, Liefbroer and Elzinga (2012) left typologies to one side and analyzed the dissimilarities between the sequences of the relatives themselves. However, one might argue that in some cases, perfect similarity between the sequences of parents and children is not appropriate evidence of transmission processes. Indeed, the median age at parenthood, for instance, may be about 20 for the parents' generation and about 25 for that of their children. So, parents and their children may be viewed as having dissimilar sequences, strictly speaking, although they actually have perfectly equivalent histories given the structural changes to the historical context in which their lives unfolded. Moreover, a given amount of dissimilarity may have distinct reasons (e.g., a two-year difference in age at marriage may be judged equivalent whether it be two years earlier or two years later, although it does not have the same meaning), which remains invisible in this "dissimilarity approach."

Some have adopted the second of the strategies presented earlier, that is, the combination of substitution costs (Fasang and Raab 2014; Robette et al. 2009). This strategy has the advantage of allowing the identification of contrasting patterns (i.e., groups of dyads in which parents' and children's sequences are distinct but often associated) in the case of an intergenerational transmission study (Fasang and Raab 2014). This strategy is especially appropriate when it is meaningful to synchronize the sequences of each dimension within a dyad (e.g., to compare the timing and pace of transitions of parents and children) or to characterize the situation of the dyad at a given point in time (*local interdependence*). This is not always the case, however. For instance, sometimes the various dimensions may differ substantially in nature. An alternative objective may be to study the relationship between the parents' overall career and their children's school-to-work transition. In this example, parents' career sequences could span over 45 years, from ages 14 to 60 (with years as time units), and the alphabet (i.e. the set of possible states) would be based on an occupational classification; when children's school-to-work sequences could stretch for only 3 years after leaving school (with months as time units), and the alphabet would then be composed of employment statuses (e.g., education, unemployment, part-time employment, and full-time employment). Technically, the difference in sequence length can be handled with missing values. Nevertheless, in this hypothetical example with such different time windows and clocks, this would become at the very least inelegant—even impractical—and would certainly obscure the results. More important, from a substantive point of view, "pasting" one sequence onto the other and locally aligning them is pointless here: What we want to examine is rather the overall shapes of the separate dimensions—and the patterns in them—and the relationship between these patterns (*global interdependence*).[8]

Our objective here is to propose an approach that is parsimonious and takes into account multidimensionality as well as global interdependence between parents' and children's sequences. In effect, parents' sequences and those of their children can be of very different nature,

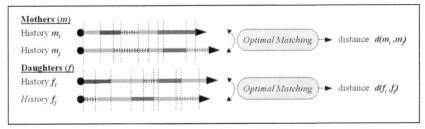

Figure 1. Step 1 of globally interdependent multiple sequence analysis.

reflecting the norms of their time, and our focus is on the relationship between sequences as wholes rather than on their synchronization in terms of age. Thus our approach presents a unique combination of the criteria defined above, well suited for the study of intergenerational transmission of life-course patterns, and it provides a useful complement to the existing strategies.

To facilitate the statistical presentation of our approach, we build on the study of the transmission of patterns of employment history between mothers and daughters, which we then empirically explore.

3. THE GIMSA APPROACH

The method we call the GIMSA approach breaks down into several steps. Let us consider that each unit of analysis is composed of one sequence for a mother and one for her daughter: a set of paired trajectories.

At the first step (Figure 1), OM, or any other standard sequence dissimilarity measure, is used to calculate distances associated with each pair of mother's and daughter's histories. This stage gives us two symmetric distance matrices $M = (m_{ij})_{i,j}$, where $m_{ij} = d(m_i, m_j) = d(m_j, m_i)$ (respectively $F = [f_{ij}]_{i,j}$, where $f_{ij} = d[f_i, f_j] = d[f_j, f_i]$) in which the diagonal is zero.

Whether GIMSA is highly sensitive to a given kind of sequence pattern depends very much on this first stage. Indeed, some sequence metrics may be more suited to capturing patterns in terms of durations or timing, whereas others may rely more on the order, on reversals, or on repetitions. The specificities of the major sequence dissimilarity measures used in the social sciences are discussed and tested with empirical and simulated data in Aisenbrey and Fasang (2010), Robette

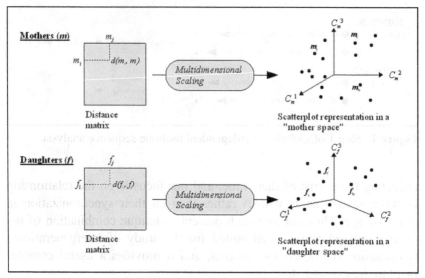

Figure 2. Step 2 of globally interdependent multiple sequence analysis.

and Bry (2012), and Studer (2012). It should be kept in mind that in the end, most of these measures, when applied to empirical data, lead to relatively similar results. The OM algorithm is presented briefly in the introduction to this paper; for a more detailed presentation, see for instance MacIndoe and Abbott (2004).

Moreover, different dissimilarity measures may be chosen for the various dimensions, emphasizing global interdependence.

In the second step (Figure 2), we use MDS (Kruskal and Wish 1984). According to Piccarreta and Lior (2010), MDS is

> a factorial technique that provides a visual representation of a dissimilarity matrix. Sequences are projected in a low dimension factorial space in such a way that the distance between cases in this space resembles as much as possible the original dissimilarity between them. (p. 166)

Here, the matrix m (respectively f) of distances between the mothers' careers (and respectively their daughters') is converted into a spatial representation by MDS, that is, represented as a scatterplot of points in a multidimensional "mother space" (or "daughter space") with respect to a system of principle components C_m^1, C_m^2, and so on (or C_f^1, C_f^2, etc.). For a brief mathematical presentation of the metric MDS that we

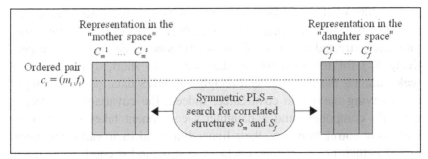

Figure 3. Step 3 of globally interdependent multiple sequence analysis.

use, see Appendix A.[9] The sequence of components C_m^1, C_m^2, and so on (or C_f^1, C_f^2, etc.) provides a hierarchical breakdown of the heterogeneity of the mothers' (or daughters') histories, in the sense that each component complements the preceding ones in an optimal manner. At the end of this stage, each mother-daughter pair is described both by the coordinates of the mother's history in the mothers' space and those of the daughter's history in the daughters' space.

The choice of the number of components[10] to be kept for the next stage may follow several criteria. The quality of MDS results against their dimensionality can be assessed with indicators such as eigenvalues or with a stress function. We may also opt for a close examination of whether a given dimension reveals a clear structure in sequence data (i.e., whether the order of sequence dyads in this dimension can be easily interpreted in a sociologically relevant way). More generally, the selection of the relevant number of components is a trade-off between two extremes: On one hand, it may be desirable to keep a maximum amount of sequence data information (i.e., to keep many components); on the other hand, noise reduction is important to prevent overinterpretation. Here again, Piccarreta and Lior (2010) provided a helpful guideline for this step of GIMSA.

We next look for structural links between the mothers' and daughters' histories (Figure 3). Although standard factor analysis techniques deal with a single set of variables, we need to study simultaneously several sets of variables (i.e., to take into account the relationship between two groups of variables). A few methods have been specifically designed to suit this partitioning of the data. Among them, we use the symmetric (or canonical) PLS method (Bry 1996; de Jong, Wise, and

Ricker 2001), which seeks structures *common to* the variability of the mothers' histories and that of the daughters' histories.[11] These structures are extracted under the form of components denoted $S_m^{\ k}$ (respectively S_f^k) for the mothers (or daughters). In short, symmetric PLS seeks, among the mothers' and daughters' MDS data, pairs of components having maximum covariance. Indeed, the covariance between a mother's component and a daughter's component takes into account both their correlation (i.e., their linear link) and their variances, interpreted as their principal component–type structural strength. For a quick mathematical presentation of symmetric PLS, see Appendix B.

Because a noise reduction step has been performed at the previous stage of GIMSA, here we keep all the components produced by PLS computation.

Finally, the Euclidean coding of the mothers' and daughters' histories, restricted to "common" components $S_m^{\ k}$ and S_f^k, provides a base for clustering the mother-daughter pairs (Figure 4). A Euclidean distance matrix between these pairs is calculated from the PLS components and will be used as an input for clustering.

Because one dimension of the dyads (e.g., mothers' sequences) may be more diverse than the other, the results may become excessively driven by this dimension, thus masking the daughters' heterogeneity. That is why the weighting issue should be considered at this stage. Indeed, it is essential to give the same importance to the encodings of mothers' and daughters' careers in the calculation of the distance. Two options may be considered. In the first option, PLS components are merely standardized, which is equivalent to weighting each with the inverse of its variance. Doing so makes them all equally important, whatever their original variance. In contrast, the second option consists of giving an equivalent weighting to all the original PLS components of mothers (respectively daughters), chosen to make the variances of mothers' components comparable to those of daughters. In this way, the PLS components of mothers (or daughters) keep their relative importance. For such weights, the inverse of the first eigenvalue of mothers' (or daughters') MDS may be used, or the inverse of the number of distinct sequences among the whole set of mothers' (or daughters') sequences.

The distance matrix is submitted to a hierarchical clustering analysis with Ward's criterion[12] (although other clustering techniques can potentially be used). This gives a typology of pairs based on structures

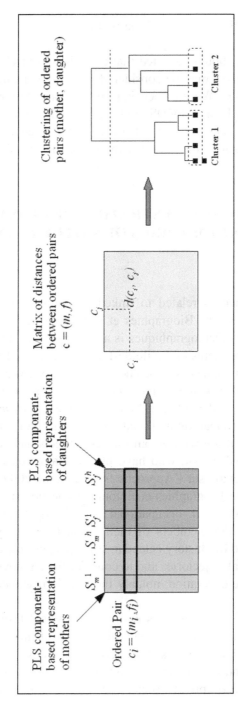

Figure 4. Step 4 of globally interdependent multiple sequence analysis.

common to the discrepancies of the mothers' histories and to those of their daughters.

Once again, it should be noted that at each step of GIMSA, several technical alternatives may be considered (e.g., *k*-means instead of hierarchical clustering). We are focusing on the combination of sequence analysis, data reduction (MDS and PLS), and clustering, and it is assumed that at each step, each of them is applied coherently and in a substantive way (or in the way that the researcher considers as "satisfactory" when not optimal).

4. AN EMPIRICAL ILLUSTRATION OF GIMSA: EMPLOYMENT HISTORIES OF MOTHERS AND DAUGHTERS

4.1. *Data*

To analyze sequences related to linked individuals, appropriate data must be available. The Biographies et Entourage survey from Institut National d'Études Démographiques is a retrospective life-event history survey of 2,830 residents of the Île-de-France[13] area aged 50 to 70 years and those of their contact circles. The sample interviewed was representative of the population in the Île-de-France region in 2000, the year the survey data were collected. The "contact circle" (*entourage*) includes family members (lineal kin and relations by marriage) across four generations, plus all those with whom the respondents have cohabited and any others, related or not, who have played major roles in their lives (Groupe de Réflexion sur l'Approche Biographique 2009; Lelièvre and Vivier 2001). The Biographies et Entourage questionnaire recorded all stages in the residential, occupational, and family trajectories of the respondents and the members of their contact circles, year by year, using an extended life history calendar. It is thus possible to reconstitute detailed individual trajectories and to consider the employment histories of more than one generation, notably the female respondents and their mothers.[14]

We thus have a respondent's entire occupational history, including periods of economic inactivity (with all periods of more than one year being included). Each stage is characterized by the occupation declared by the respondent, his or her employment status, a description of the employer (public or private sector, economic branch, location, firm size), and the proportion of time spent at work. The employment histories of the female respondents in the Biographies et Entourage survey can be summarized as sequences of employment statuses, year by year, between the ages of 14 (end of mandatory schooling for the cohorts studied) and 50 (the age of youngest respondents at the time of the survey). To demonstrate GIMSA's capacity to handle different types of paired sequences, in the application presented here, we will restrict our attention to the way in which the transition from school to work unfolds and how employment histories begin. We therefore gather the successive employment statuses of each female respondent from the completion of education to 15 years later. This gives a set of 1,413 sequences, all lasting 15 years, and each state has four categories representing the four employment statuses (i.e., education, inactivity, part-time employment, full-time employment). The time window is defined from an initial event,[15] not in terms of age or calendar year as is usually the case.

Less precision was required for the employment histories of the respondents' parents, but it is possible to reconstruct parents' employment statuses and job types, as well as any career interruptions and their nature. Again, for the purpose of our application, we here use the successive occupational statuses of the respondents' mothers from ages 14 to 60. So we have a set of 1,413 sequences, all lasting 47 years, and an alphabet comprising the five following states: (1) education, (2) inactivity, (3) self-employment, (4) lower level occupation, and (5) higher level or intermediate occupation. We therefore choose a 15-year life span for the respondents with four different statuses and a 47-year occupational career for their mothers with five distinct statuses.

4.2. *Applying Standard Sequence Analysis and GIMSA*

As a preliminary exploration, we used standard sequence analysis (not yet GIMSA) to build separate typologies of employment histories for the female respondents and their mothers. We wanted to distinguish female respondents finely according to the timing of the transitions in their early employment histories, when family formation competes strongly with their working career, and distinguish between women who leave school for the job market but shift to inactivity after a very short time, and those who establish a career before they stop working. As a result, we used the Hamming distance for dissimilarity measure, as it emphasizes timing. The choice of costs is an important aspect for sequence analysis techniques related to OM (Lesnard 2010), as is the case for Hamming distance. For our study, substitution costs were set at the same value regardless of the elements replaced. Using data-driven costs based on transition likelihoods was considered, but this leads to almost identical results (see Robette and Bry [2012] for a systematic comparison). Deriving costs from a theoretical hierarchy of statuses would be possible as well (e.g., replacing education with part-time employment would cost 1, whereas replacing education with full-time employment would cost 2). But we believe that these situations are more different in nature than in intensity and that there is no perfectly satisfying way of quantifying the difference between them.[16] Besides, for mothers, the focus is on the shapes their occupational careers have taken (always working vs. inactive, etc.), on the transitions that compose them, on whether they are characterized by stability or mobility between labor force and inactivity, and so on. For this reason, we chose a dissimilarity measure which favors order over timing, that is, the LCS metric (Elzinga 2008).

Distance matrices were computed[17] and used as input for clustering (here hierarchical clustering analysis with Ward criterion). To choose appropriate numbers of clusters, we computed several validation indicators (Milligan and Cooper 1985): Hubert's gamma (Hubert and Arabie 1985) and Hubert's C.[18] Both indicated six clusters for female respondents and four for mothers (see state distribution plots in Appendixes F and G in the online journal at http://sm.sagepub.com/supplemental.[19]). The clusters of female respondents' employment histories can be summarized as follows: mostly in full-time jobs, mostly in part-time jobs, full-time jobs and then shift to inactivity about 10 years after completing education, shift from part-time to full-time jobs between 3 and 8 years after completing education, mostly inactive, and full-time jobs interrupted by an inactivity spell around 5 to 10 years after completing education. The four patterns of mothers' occupational histories that are clustered can be crudely defined by the status held during most of the career[20]: inactivity, lower level occupations, self-employment, and higher level or intermediate occupations.

The aim now is not to identify the influence of the mother's employment history on that of her daughter but to see whether we can identify preferential dyads among the lineages, that is, recurrent sequences conditioned by the social cohesion between mother and daughter: an internal *structure* of transmission in the lineage concerning employment patterns.

We could stop here and simply cross-tabulate the typology of daughters' sequences with that of their mothers as determined above, producing a contingency table of $6 \times 4 = 24$ cells. Still, a 24-cluster distribution is hard to describe,[21] and some groupings would be needed; this result clearly lacks parsimony. Although some cells have small numbers, not one is empty (Table 2), and there is no straightforward rule to allocate less frequent combinations of mother and daughter clusters to fuller cells. This is particularly problematic when the aim is to give an exhaustive description of the population under study. Moreover, such a grouping would be based on the specific characteristics of the daughter's (respectively, the mother's) individual employment histories, whose correlations would then be identified *ex post:* The characteristics underlying mother-and-daughter dyads would be hidden. At least, this strategy shows that mothers' and daughters' sequences are significantly associated.[22] But we need to use a method that specifically and parsimoniously focuses on the linked characteristics of the two histories.

In our approach, we are not interested in synchronizing mothers and daughters (i.e., locally aligning mothers' and daughters' sequences within dyads), and the interdependence between mothers' and daughters' histories is not focused on employment statuses at a given point in time. Indeed, the daughter's situation at a given age is unlikely to be linked to her mother's situation at the same age, but rather it is the mother's whole employment history that is considered as part of the daughter's social background. The question of interest is more to identify underlying intergenerational transmission at work at the individual lineage level: the individual translation of the global trend (the massive entry into the labor force) concomitant with the baby boom. Besides, given the very different time windows (one is defined according to an initial event and lasts 15 years, whereas the other is defined according to age and lasts 47 years), synchronizing mothers' and daughters' sequences would be technically impractical.[23] For these reasons, the second strategy identified earlier (i.e., MCSA; Gauthier et al. 2010) would not be well suited to handle this application. Rather, our objective is better approached by building a typology of pairs of mother-daughter employment histories that captures in detail the correspondence between some patterns of the daughter's history and some of her mother's *taken as wholes*, that is, emphasizing *global interdependence* and illustrating intergenerational transmission. Thus, we now apply

Table 2. Cross-tabulation of Mothers' Typology and Daughters' Typology

		Mothers			
Number of Dyads	Mostly Inactive	Mostly Low	Mostly Self	Mostly High/Intermediate	Total
Daughters					
Mostly FT	437	223	162	76	898
Mostly PT	24	8	10	8	50
From FT to inactivity	93	38	33	11	175
From PT to FT	20	10	13	3	46
Mostly inactive	129	24	23	10	186
Interruption	30	15	10	3	58
Total	733	318	251	111	

Source: Biographies et Entourage survey (2000).

Note: The reference population was the 1,413 female respondents and their mothers. FT = full-time employment; low = lower level occupations; high/intermediate = higher level or intermediate occupations; PT = part-time employment.

18

Table 3. Eigenvalues and Stress Functions for Mothers' and Daughters' Multidimensional Scaling Dimensions

Dimension	Results for Mothers		Results for Daughters	
	Eigenvalue	Stress	Eigenvalue	Stress
1	1.000	.467	1.000	.373
2	.600	.253	.282	.203
3	.322	.119	.199	.136
4	.127	.094	.132	.134
5	.087	.080	.076	.151
6	.068	.081	.057	.166
7	.055	.087	.042	.177
8	.051	.095	.033	.187
9	.039	.103	.030	.197
10	.030	.109	.025	.204

Source: Biographies et Entourage survey (2000).
Note: The reference population was the 1,413 female respondents and their mothers.

GIMSA to the mothers' and daughters' employment histories from the Biographies et Entourage survey.[24]

For the first step of GIMSA, we use the dissimilarity matrices that were computed earlier for the separate typologies. We recall that two different dissimilarity measures are at work: Hamming distance for daughters and the LCS metric for mothers.[25]

Mothers' and daughters' dissimilarity matrices are then both submitted to MDS. To choose the number of MDS components to retain for the next stage of GIMSA, we look at eigenvalues and a stress function (Table 3). The stress function indicates that the first five dimensions are the most important for mothers and the first four dimensions for daughters. The situation is less clear cut for eigenvalues, but they seem to point to four or five dimensions for mothers and four or five for daughters.

Using MDS sequence plots (Piccarreta and Lior 2010), the first four mothers' dimensions are easy to interpret as follows[26]: the first dimension contrasts inactivity with full-time employment, the second contrasts low-level occupations with other occupations, the third contrasts high-level and intermediate occupations with self-employment, and the fourth ranks mothers according to the length of their studies. Interpretation is less straightforward for daughters: Although the first dimension clearly contrasts full-time jobs with inactivity and the second and third ones contrast part-time jobs with the other statuses, the meaning of the dimensions that follow remains unclear.

During the third stage of GIMSA, canonical PLS is computed on the MDS components (five for mothers and four for daughters), which leads to two sets of four components.[27] For the last stage of GIMSA, all these components are weighted according to the first option mentioned above—that is, PLS components are weighted with the inverse of their variance (see section 3, step 4)—and a Euclidean distance matrix is computed and used as input for clustering (here hierarchical clustering analysis with the Ward criterion). Hubert's gamma and Hubert's C both reach a local optimum for 10 clusters. Furthermore, these criteria are only guidelines, as the creation of a taxonomy in the social sciences should be guided above all by background theories, heuristic views, and a balance between parsimony and cluster homogeneity: "Classifications so produced can never be true or false, or even probable or improbable; they can only be profitable or unprofitable" (Williams and Lance 1965). Eventually, we opt for a 10-cluster solution.

4.3. Results

The typology of mother-daughter dyads resulting from this approach comprises 10 clusters, as shown in Table 4. This typology reveals a large diversity of employment and occupational histories, for mothers as well as for daughters. This diversity seems well-balanced between the two.

Compared with the fourth strategy, the GIMSA typology leads to a smaller number of clusters (10 vs. 24 clusters). Nevertheless, as the fourth strategy builds clusters of mothers and daughters independently, its final typology comprises more homogeneous clusters. Indeed, this typology explains 59.6 percent of the discrepancy in daughters' sequences (respectively, 50.3 percent of mothers'), whereas the GIMSA typology explains 45.6 percent (respectively, 39.5 percent). However, the difference is not massive. Besides, the six patterns of "unidimensional" daughters' sequences can be found in the GIMSA typology (see again Table 2 for the pattern labels of "unidimensional" sequence analysis, i.e., the fourth strategy), as well as the four patterns of "unidimensional" mothers' sequences. Moreover, some new patterns appear with GIMSA (e.g., "from inactivity to low" among mothers).

In addition, GIMSA seems more efficient than the fourth strategy to describe the matrix of distances between mother-daughter dyads.

Table 4. Typology of Mother-Daughter Employment Histories

Cluster	Main Features of the Dyads		n	Percent
	Mothers	Daughters		
1	Inactivity (or early shift from low to inactivity)	FT	276	19.5
2	Self-employment	FT	224	15.9
3	Inactivity	From FT to inactivity (shift after 5–10 years)	211	14.9
4	Low	FT	173	12.2
5	From inactivity to low	FT	157	11.1
6	Inactivity	Inactivity	100	7.1
7	High/intermediate	Mostly FT	95	6.7
8	Inactivity	Interruption (back to work about 10 years after completing education)	81	5.7
9	Diverse	Mostly PT employment	55	3.9
10	Diverse	Shift from PT to FT (after around 5–10 years)	41	2.9
Total			1,413	100.0

Source: Biographies et Entourage survey (2000).
Note: The reference population was the 1,413 female respondents and their mothers. FT = full-time employment; low = lower level occupations; high/intermediate = higher level or intermediate occupations; PT = part-time employment.

21

Indeed, the GIMSA typology in 10 clusters explains a slightly smaller share of the discrepancy of this distance matrix than the typology in 24 clusters of the fourth strategy (37.0 percent vs. 41.5 percent), but with a much lower number of clusters. Moreover, a GIMSA typology in 24 clusters would explain 50.9 percent of the discrepancy, that is, significantly more than the fourth strategy. This is explained by the fact that with the fourth strategy, the linking of mothers and daughters is made from severely reduced information, that is, in our example, a typology in 4 (respectively, 6) clusters, which explains only 50.3 percent (respectively, 59.6 percent) of the discrepancy of mothers' (or daughters') sequences, as we have just seen. On the other side, with GIMSA, the linking of mothers and daughters is made from the MDS components, which retain a larger share of information: the 5 (or 4) MDS components of mothers (or daughters) explain 69.5 percent (or 73.4 percent) of the discrepancy of mothers' (or daughters') sequences. And this share could be further increased keeping more MDS components without a loss of parsimony in the final typology.

Finally, the balance between the number of clusters and the homogeneity of these clusters (i.e., the parsimony issue) seems favorable to GIMSA,[28] as can be shown by close examination of the 10 clusters[29] (see state distribution plots in Appendix C[30]; a cross-tabulation of the GIMSA typology and the fourth strategy's typology is given in Appendix D).

Continuous inactivity is the most common pattern among mothers (characterizing 4 of 10 clusters, which together represent 47 percent of the sample), while a transition from school to continuous full-time employment is the most common among daughters (also 4 clusters, 59 percent of the sample). These clusters of female respondents' transition to continuous full-time employment account for 4 of the 5 largest clusters. In these, mothers are continuously inactive or shift to inactivity early in their life courses (cluster 1), they are self-employed (cluster 2), they hold lower level occupations (cluster 3), or they stay inactive for a while and then shift to lower level occupations (cluster 4). Clusters 2 and 4 on one side, and cluster 5 on the other, contrast sharply in terms of the daughters' sociodemographic profiles (see Appendix E). Indeed, whereas female respondents in clusters 2 and 4 tend to belong to older cohorts, have few qualifications and lower level occupations at the time of the survey, and are often only children, the daughters in cluster 5 belong to younger cohorts, are often the eldest children, and have the highest level occupations. They have relatively low levels of qualifications, however, which suggests upwardly mobile careers.[31]

The transmission of continuous inactivity is unusual, as it is found in cluster 6, which represents only 7 percent of the sample. Continuous inactivity is here associated with high fertility, as these respondents have the highest number of children at the time of the survey. Nevertheless, inactivity appears in other forms among daughters' early careers: In cluster 3, they shift from full-time employment to inactivity 5 to 10 years after completing education, whereas in cluster 8 they interrupt their careers for given periods, which may vary in duration but almost never end later than 10 years after completing education. Like cluster 6, cluster 3 is characterized by the high fertility rates of the female respondents; these women also often belong to older cohorts and have low levels of qualifications.

There is one cluster of upper-class mothers: They hold higher level or intermediate occupations, and their daughters, whose transition is to continuous full-time employment, work during most of their first 15 years after completing education (cluster 7). Here, female respondents are relatively young, often hold higher level or intermediate occupations at the time of the survey, and have high levels of qualifications, which emphasizes the fact that intergenerational transmission of high social status is observed on the side of female lineages as well.

Last, the two smallest clusters contrast female respondents whose early careers comprise part-time employment: In cluster 9, they work part-time almost continuously, but shift from part-time to full-time after 5 to 10 years in cluster 10. Their mothers have heterogeneous occupational careers. Female respondents in cluster 9 are the youngest of the sample, and they are relatively young in cluster 10 as well, which reflects the historically late appearance of part-time employment in France in the 1980s (Maruani 2000). These women are also highly qualified, which reflects the fact that part-time employment for these cohorts initially developed among well-educated women, whatever their mothers' careers.

To highlight an interesting point in these results, we can see that although mothers' inactivity is often linked to daughters' inactivity (and mothers' activity to daughters' full-time employment), there are also significant patterns where the daughters of inactive mothers have full-time early employment careers: Transmission does not automatically mean that mother and daughter follow identical paths.

4.4. *Robustness Checks*

Applying GIMSA implies a series of methodological choices, and it is important to assess the influence of these choices on the results. In the first step of the process, as stated in section 3, dissimilarity measures must be chosen. These are numerous, and they have already been widely discussed in the social science literature: It is beyond our scope to investigate the characteristics and impact of one metric or another. More important, one of the advantages of GIMSA is that it allows a choice of metrics that specifically fit the theoretical questions and data limitations under study, in a separate way for each dimension.

The second step of GIMSA is an operation to reduce noise by retaining only a small number of MDS components. To assess the impact of this noise reduction step, we replicated the previous analysis retaining 20 MDS components for mothers and daughters (instead of 5 and 4, respectively); noise reduction should be much weaker in this case. So we built a new 10-cluster typology, which we then compared with the previous one. The Rand index (Saporta and Youness 2002) is relatively high (.649), which means the typologies are rather similar. However, looking more closely at the new typology, we can observe some differences. First, a very large group emerges, made of daughters with transition to full-time employment and heterogeneous mothers (they are inactive and/or in lower level occupations). On the other hand, several very small clusters emerge, highlighting very marginal patterns: Mothers who studied for many years, mothers who shift from inactivity to higher level occupations, and two groups with daughters who return to education a few years after completing initial education. These rare patterns are of limited interest compared with more regular profiles: The noise reduction step, via the selection of a smaller number of MDS components, seems to improve significantly the substantive quality of the results.

The third step of GIMSA does not imply any choices, as all PLS components are retained. The fourth step includes an important operation: the weighting of the two dimensions of dyads, so that their influence may be balanced in the building of the typology. As explained in section 3, several weighting schemes are possible. In our empirical application, we chose to weight PLS components by the inverse of their variance (w1). We replicated the analysis, applying three alternative weighting schemes: no weighting at all (w0), mothers' (or daughters')° PLS

Table 5. Rand Indices for Various Weighting Schemes

	w0	w1	w2	w3
w0	.000			
w1	.850	.000		
w2	.869	.860	.000	
w3	.775	.804	.821	.000

components weighted by the inverse of the number of distinct mothers' (or daughters') sequences in the sample (w2), or by the inverse of the first mothers' (or daughters') MDS eigenvalue (w3). The 10-cluster typologies are compared with the Rand index, as shown in Table 5.

All the Rand indices are high, ranging from .775 to .869, suggesting rather similar typologies: The results are robust to different schemes of weighting. When we examine more carefully the various typologies, a few comments may be added. First, the typology with no weighting comprises many clusters in which daughters have comparable patterns; variety is significantly higher on the mother's side. Thus the balance between mothers' and daughters' dimensions is not satisfying, which emphasizes the added value of using a weighting strategy. Moreover, every major pattern comes to light whether w1, w2, or w3 is used. The differences concern small clusters and minority patterns, which are more or less aggregated according to the weighting scheme. Although w1 distinguishes two clusters with part-time employed daughters, w2 gives only one but contrasts three patterns with daughters who shift from full-time jobs to inactivity according to the age of the shift. The w3 index identifies three groups with daughters in part-time work: one where women shift from full-time to part-time, another with the opposite shift, and the last one with continuous part-time employment.

5. CONCLUSION

In this paper, we examined the intergenerational pattern of women's careers within lineages, pairing the employment histories of mothers and daughters. Using the rich data from the Biographies et Entourage survey, from which we can track respondents' employment and occupational careers and also those of their mothers, we applied an approach we called GIMSA to make a typological analysis of mother-daughter employment histories, a method that combines standard sequence analysis (e.g., OMA), MDS, canonical PLS, and clustering techniques.

We intentionally devised an application example more suited for discussion of the methodology than its substantive sociological output. Nevertheless, the first results presented here are promising. They open perspectives for studying long-term trends and understanding specific intrafamily features and continuities that contribute to the overall macro changes in women's involvement in paid activity. The typologies obtained shed light on intergenerational transmission, leaving aside a mechanical determinism and showing the relative multiplicity of career pathways open to children starting from similar parental background in terms of their mother's labor market participation: Some never employed mothers have daughters with incomplete careers, but the daughters of other mothers always work full-time, and so on. The differences depend on characteristics such as educational background, cohort, or birth order among siblings.

From a methodological point of view, GIMSA provides a flexible way to uncover patterns of dyads of sequences. It is parsimonious and takes multidimensionality into account; that is, each dimension's contribution remains explicit and can be specifically parameterized. Moreover, GIMSA emphasizes *global interdependence* between sequences within dyads; that is, the relationship between *sequences taken as wholes*. It presents very few constraints about the data. Sequences within the dyads do not have to be synchronized or to have the same nature: They may have completely different alphabets, time windows, and time units, and distinct aspects of temporality (e.g., order vs. timing) can be emphasized separately for each dimension. Besides the theoretical advantages that this flexibility provides, it also means that the quality of the data does not have to be comparable between the dimensions; detailed information about respondents' histories and cruder material about their parents can be used together. Combining OMA with Euclidean tools, GIMSA offers a straightforward and computationally efficient multidimensional approach to sequence pattern mining, complementary to existing strategies such as MCSA (Gauthier et al. 2010). The choice of one method or the other will depend on theoretical and data issues. Although MCSA is best suited to analyze the interdependence between various dimensions at each point in time (i.e., *local interdependence*), GIMSA favors *global interdependence*.

GIMSA may be used for distinct purposes, as may clustering approaches in general. Indeed, when performing an in-depth exploration of the data, we tend, on one hand, to split the data into a large number of clusters to identify homogeneous patterns and to reflect the diversity embedded in the sequences. On the other hand, to summarize the heterogeneity of the sequences, it is preferable to use a smaller number of clusters, which renders further analysis manageable, as we did in this paper. This simplification of the data is not specific to GIMSA; it is a procedure that users undertake according to its relevance with their research question.

Nevertheless, GIMSA focuses on a specific kind of data, for example, linked life courses. This method allows users to identify patterns of sequences, but it does not provide the degree of association between the various dimensions of the sequence data. It will find clusters whatever the degree of association between dimensions. To avoid drawing conclusions from weakly associated dimensions, it may be best to use strategy 4 and an association index (see note 22) prior to GIMSA, to assess whether pattern searching is relevant or not. Moreover, once GIMSA has been performed, one may complement it with intracluster homogeneity measures (e.g., average intracluster sequence dissimilarity). Indeed, in a given typology, a cluster may result from a strong association between dimensions, and sequences will then be homogeneous within each dimension; another cluster may present only a weak association, and it is then probable that sequences will be considerably more homogeneous in one dimension than in the other. According to this view, sequence homogeneity measures, as well as sequence plots, are useful guidelines to identify variations in the strength of the link between dimensions.

We could argue that sequence analysis has not produced any blockbuster applications yet, as Abbott (2000) stated some years ago. In any event, blockbuster applications are rare whatever the methodological approach, and the relevant issue is whether sequence analysis helps better understand some parts of the social world. For more than 25 years, sequence analysis has played a very positive role in helping understand the complexity of life courses and careers. From this angle, GIMSA provides an additional element in the inherited toolbox. As illustrated by our application, GIMSA may offer a different viewpoint on social mobility. Indeed, mobility is often analyzed by comparing social positions at a given point in time. But this gives only a partial view of an individual's position, which could be better captured by examining his or her trajectory (or a part of it). That is why comparing multiple sequences instead of single states or events may be a fruitful avenue for research on social mobility and intergenerational transmission. For instance, it is conceivable to explore the global interdependence between siblings' and parents' life courses or careers all together, whether trajectories have different time windows or not (e.g., with children's sequences focusing on school-to-work transition and parents' on the whole career).

The range of potential applications for GIMSA thus extends well beyond intergenerational social mobility studies and intergenerational transmission in general. They can be classified on the basis of several dichotomies. First, the entities associated with the sequences under study can be human (individuals) or nonhuman (e.g., nations or firms). Second, the various dimensions that make up the multidimensional sequences can characterize a single entity (e.g., an individual) or more entities, as in this paper where one dimension characterizes the mother and another dimension characterizes her daughter. The latter case can be extended to the relationship between parents and children in general but also to siblings or to peer groups such as friends or colleagues, for instance. In addition, the various dimensions of the sequences may correspond to trajectories whose nature is either similar (as is the case here, where the careers of mothers and their daughters are analyzed) or different (e.g., when comparing family and employment histories). From the perspective of temporality, the various dimensions of the sequences can describe contemporaneous trajectories, in terms of age or historical period, or asynchronous ones. In our example, the dimensions are asynchronous, insofar as they describe the school-to-work transition for daughters and the entire career for mothers. Again, the dimensions may or may not have the same time unit (year, month, etc.) and/or the same length. Note that in the case of contemporaneous dimensions, MCSA is probably more appropriate than GIMSA. Finally, the sequences may have two dimensions, as in this paper, or a larger number. In the latter case, canonical PLS should be replaced by an alternative factor analysis technique, such as multiple factor analysis (Escofier and Pagès 1994).

APPENDIX A

MDS

Given the matrix of distances $\|\xi_i - \xi_j\|$ between n points $\{\xi_i; i = 1, n\}$ in a Euclidean space, MDS provides a means to rebuild the image of the unit scatterplot on the basis of its principal components:

- Finding the scalar product matrix of vectors centered on their centroid:

Centering vectors on their centroid, let $\xi = \frac{1}{n} \sum_{i=1}^{n} \xi_i$ and $x_i \overset{\text{def}}{=} \xi_i - \xi \; \forall i = 1, n$. We then have

$$
\forall i, j = 1, n : \|\xi_i - \xi_j\|^2 = \|x_i - x_j\|^2 = \|x_i\|^2 + \|x_j\|^2 - 2\langle x_i | x_j \rangle
$$
$$
\Leftrightarrow \langle x_i | x_j \rangle = \frac{1}{2} \left(\|x_i\|^2 + \|x_j\|^2 - \|x_i - x_j\|^2 \right)
$$
(A1)

In view of the Koenig equality applied to $\{x_i; i = 1, n\}$ with centroid $\bar{x} = 0$, we also have

$$
\forall i = 1, n : \sum_{j=1}^{n} \frac{1}{n} \|x_i - x_j\|^2 = \|x_i - 0\|^2 + \sum_{j=1}^{n} \frac{1}{n} \|x_j - 0\|^2.
$$
(A2i)

Let $D_0 = \sum_{j=1}^{n} \frac{1}{n} \|x_j\|^2$ and $D_i = \sum_{j=1}^{n} \frac{1}{n} \|x_i - x_j\|^2$. From equation (A2$_i$), we have

$$
\forall i = 1, n : \|x_i\|^2 = D_i - D_0.
$$
(A3)

Summing up equation (A2$_i$) over i and dividing by n, we get

$$
\frac{1}{n^2} \sum_{j=1}^{n} \|x_i - x_j\|^2 = 2D_0 \Leftrightarrow D_0 = \frac{1}{2n^2} \sum_{j=1}^{n} \|x_i - x_j\|^2.
$$
(A4)

So, from equations (A4) and (A3), we draw every $\|x_i\|^2$, and then, from equation (A1), every $\langle x_i | x_j \rangle$.

- Finding the principal components: Let S be the matrix $\left(\langle x_i | x_j \rangle \right)_{i,j=1,n}$. Let λ_k denote the kth eigenvalue in decreasing order and v_k be the associated unit norm eigenvector. Then, the principal components f^k of $\{x_i; i = 1, n\}$ are

$$
f^k = \sqrt{n \lambda_k} v_k.
$$

APPENDIX B

Symmetric PLS

Given the two data matrices $X(n,p)$ and $Y(n,q)$ containing respectively p and q numeric variables describing the same n statistical units, the purpose of symmetric PLS is to extract two sequences of uncorrelated components $\{f^k, k = 1, K\}$ and $\{g^k, k = 1, K\}$, such that, $\forall k$

- f^k (or g^k) belongs to the space spanned by X's (or Y's) columns;
- f^k (or g^k) captures as much as possible of X's (or Y's) variance unaccounted for by previous components; and
- f^k and g^k are as correlated as possible.

Such components are extracted through the following algorithm.

- Rank 1 components:

Let $f^1 = Xu_1$ with $\|u_1\| = 1$; $g^1 = Yv_1$ with $\|v_1\| = 1$.
    Vectors u^1 and v^1 are the solutions of the following program:

$$\mathbf{Q}(X,Y): \max_{\substack{u \in P, u'u = 1 \\ v \in q, v'v = 1}} cov(f,g) \quad \Leftrightarrow \quad \max_{\substack{u \in P, u'u = 1 \\ v \in q, v'v = 1}} \langle Xu | Yv \rangle_P \text{ where } P = \frac{1}{n}I$$

$$L = v'Y'PXu - \lambda(u'u - 1) - \mu(v'v - 1)$$

$$\underset{u}{\triangledown} L = 0 \quad \Leftrightarrow \quad X'PYv = 2\lambda u(1); \underset{v}{\triangledown} L = 0 \quad \Leftrightarrow \quad Y'PXu = 2\mu v(1')$$

With u' (1) and v' (1') we obtain

$$u'X'PYv = 2\lambda u'u = 2\lambda; v'Y'PXu = 2\mu v'v = 2\mu$$

$$\Rightarrow cov(f,g) = 2\lambda = 2\mu \overset{\text{def.}}{=} \sqrt{\eta},$$

which implies that η is the maximum value. In addition we see that

$$(1,1') \quad \Rightarrow \quad X'PYY'PXu = \eta u(2); Y'PXX'PYv = \eta v(2').$$

So, the solution vector u (or v) is the eigenvector characterized by (2) (or [2']) associated with the largest eigenvalue.

- Rank $k > 1$ components:

Rank k component f^k (or g^k) must be uncorrelated to the former rank ones $f^1, \ldots f^{k-1}$ (or $g^1, \ldots g^{k-1}$). To ensure that, we define

$$X_0 = X; Y_0 = Y \text{ and } \forall k > 1: X_k = \Pi_{(f^k)^\perp} X_{k-1}, Y_k = \Pi_{(g^k)^\perp} Y_{k-1}.$$

To put it more statistically, X_k (or Y_k) is made of the residuals of X_{k-1} (or Y_{k-1}) regressed on f^k (or g^k). We then look for

$$(u_k, v_k) = \text{sol. of } \mathbf{Q}(X_{k-1}, Y_{k-1}).$$

APPENDIX C

State Distribution Plots of the Clusters

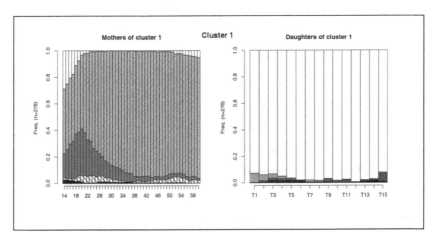

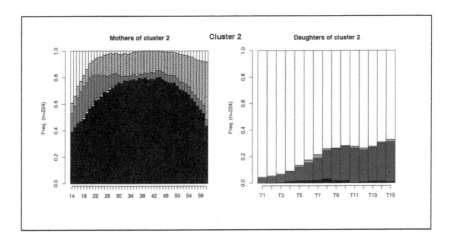

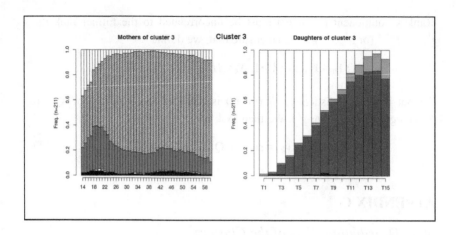

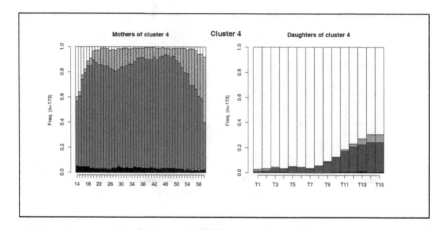

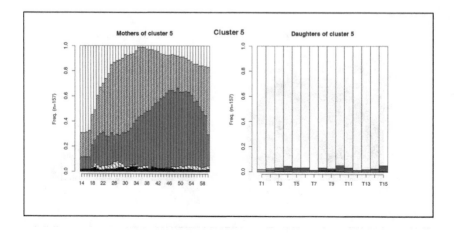

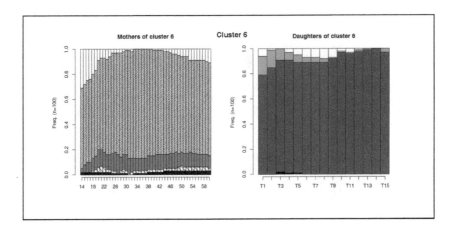

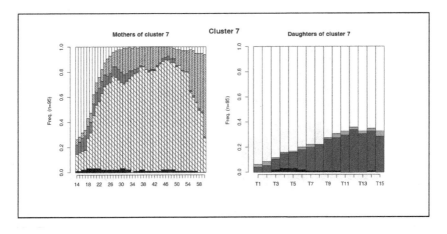

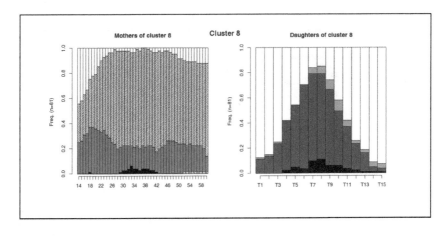

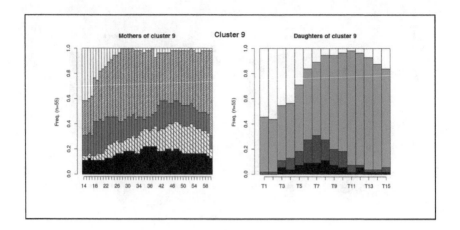

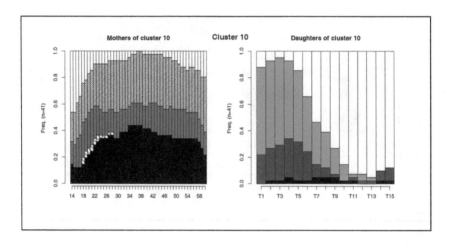

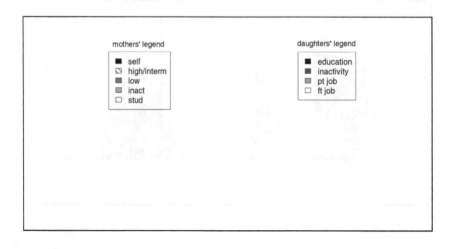

APPENDIX D

Cross-tabulation of GIMSA Typology and Fourth Strategy's Typology

Fourth Strategy's Typology (Daughters || Mothers)	GIMSA Typology										Total
	1	2	3	4	5	6	7	8	9	10	
Mostly FT || Mostly inactive	248	22	48	3	74	0	0	35	0	7	437
Mostly PT || Mostly inactive	0	0	1	0	0	0	0	1	22	0	24
From FT to inactivity || Mostly inactive	0	2	78	1	0	6	5	0	0	1	93
From PT to FT || Mostly inactive	13	0	0	0	1	0	0	0	0	6	20
Mostly inactive || Mostly inactive	0	1	45	0	0	78	0	3	0	1	129
Interruption || Mostly inactive	0	1	0	0	0	1	0	26	1	1	30
Mostly FT || Mostly low	6	4	3	136	72	0	0	2	0	0	223
Mostly PT || Mostly low	0	0	2	0	0	0	0	0	5	1	8
From FT to inactivity || Mostly low	0	1	14	23	0	0	0	0	0	0	38
From PT to FT || Mostly low	0	0	0	2	1	0	0	0	0	7	10
Mostly inactive || Mostly low	0	0	14	0	0	10	0	0	0	0	24
Interruption || Mostly low	0	0	0	0	0	0	0	13	2	0	15
Mostly FT || Mostly self	3	140	1	7	7	0	0	1	2	1	162
Mostly PT || Mostly self	0	0	0	0	0	0	0	0	10	0	10
From FT to inactivity || Mostly self	0	26	4	0	0	1	1	0	0	1	33
From PT to FT || Mostly self	0	0	0	1	0	0	0	0	0	12	13
Mostly inactive || Mostly self	0	21	0	0	0	2	0	0	0	0	23
Interruption || Mostly self	0	6	0	0	0	0	0	0	0	4	10
Mostly FT || Mostly high/intermediate	6	0	0	0	2	0	64	0	4	0	76

(continued)

Appendix D.

(continued)

Fourth Strategy's Typology (Daughters || Mothers)	GIMSA Typology										
	1	2	3	4	5	6	7	8	9	10	Total
Mostly PT || Mostly high/intermediate	0	0	1	0	0	0	0	0	7	0	8
From FT to inactivity || Mostly high/intermediate	0	0	0	0	0	2	9	0	0	0	11
From PT to FT || Mostly high/intermediate	0	0	0	0	0	0	3	0	0	0	3
Mostly inactive || Mostly high/intermediate	0	0	0	0	0	0	10	0	0	0	10
Interruption || Mostly high/intermediate	0	0	0	0	0	0	1	0	2	0	3
Total	276	224	211	173	157	100	95	81	55	41	1,413

Source: Biographies et Entourage survey (2000).

Note: The reference population was the 1,413 female respondents and their mothers. The GIMSA is more parsimonious than strategy 4 (which is one of its advantages), but it cannot be seen as a means to simplify the combinations of the contingency table produced with strategy 4. This is a completely different method, which leads to a different clustering. Looking at the two typologies, one notices that some of their clusters are very similar, while some patterns are visible in only one method or the other. For instance, GIMSA distinguishes, among daughters whose mothers are mostly inactive, between those who are mostly inactive (cluster 6) and those who shift from full-time employment to inactivity (cluster 3), while strategy 4 lumps them together (row 5). On the contrary, GIMSA groups daughters whose mothers have lower-level occupations (cluster 4), whether they are mostly employed full-time (row 7) or they shift from full-time to inactivity (row 9). FT = full-time employment; GIMSA = globally interdependent multiple sequence analysis; low = lower level occupations; high/intermediate = higher level or intermediate occupations; PT = part-time employment.

APPENDIX E

Descriptive Variables Distribution by Cluster

Characteristic						Cluster						
		1	2	3	4	5	6	7	8	9	10	Total
Daughter's year of birth	1930–1939	32.6	40.6	37.9	37	29.3	37	25.3	29.6	16.4	31.7	33.8
	1940–1945	28.3	23.2	28	24.9	26.1	34	28.4	37	30.9	24.4	27.7
	1946–1950	39.1	36.2	34.1	38.2	44.6	29	46.3	33.3	52.7	43.9	38.5
Daughter's occupation at the time of the survey	Inactive	12	16.5	42.7	20.2	10.8	61	18.9	13.6	10.9	19.5	22.4
	Self-employed	.7	2.2	1.4	1.2	2.5	1	3.2	3.7	1.8	2.4	1.8
	Intermediate occupation	27.9	12.1	9	8.1	14	4	31.6	25.9	25.5	22	16.8
	Higher level occupation	28.3	24.1	13.7	23.1	36.3	11	28.4	24.7	30.9	17.1	24.1
	Clerical and sales	29.3	41.5	31.3	43.4	33.8	21	17.9	27.2	23.6	34.1	32.2
	Manual worker	1.8	3.6	1.9	4	2.5	2	0	4.9	7.3	4.9	2.8
Daughter's qualification	None	8	9.4	11.8	7.5	5.1	31	0	4.9	14.5	14.6	9.8
	< Baccalaureate	38	56.7	54	66.5	57.3	27	26.3	43.2	18.2	41.5	47.1
	Baccalaureate	21.4	16.5	20.9	15.6	19.7	19	28.4	23.5	16.4	9.8	19.5
	> Baccalaureate	32.6	17.4	13.3	10.4	17.8	23	45.3	28.4	50.9	34.1	23.6
Daughter's number of children	0	23.6	10.7	1.4	12.7	20.4	1	10.5	4.9	14.5	22	12.6
	1	26.1	14.3	11.4	20.2	30.6	6	23.2	21	14.5	19.5	19.2
	2	31.9	42	42.2	42.8	29.3	20	38.9	50.6	40	29.3	37
	3 or more	18.5	33	45	24.3	19.7	73	27.4	23.5	30.9	29.3	31.1

(continued)

Appendix E.

(continued)

Characteristic		Cluster										Total
		1	2	3	4	5	6	7	8	9	10	
Daughter's birth order	Only child	5.4	12.1	7.6	27.7	8.9	2	9.5	6.2	10.9	17.1	10.5
	Eldest	29	26.3	35.1	34.1	35	25	26.3	30.9	30.9	22	30.3
	In between	38.4	36.2	38.4	18.5	28.7	50	37.9	45.7	34.5	39	35.6
	Youngest	27.2	25.4	19	19.7	27.4	23	26.3	17.3	23.6	22	23.6
Daughter's father's occupation	Farmer	8	12.5	10	9.2	8.9	9	9.5	6.2	9.1	4.9	9.3
	Self-employed	14.1	12.9	18.5	16.8	17.8	11	17.9	18.5	9.1	12.2	15.4
	Intermediate occupation	20.3	17.4	17.5	24.3	21.7	22	11.6	13.6	21.8	29.3	19.5
	Higher level occupation	12	11.6	12.8	13.3	7	15	13.7	12.3	10.9	7.3	11.8
	Clerical and sales	15.2	9.8	12.3	11.6	10.8	12	12.6	13.6	14.5	14.6	12.5
	Manual worker	26.1	29.5	21.8	19.7	27.4	23	27.4	27.2	30.9	29.3	25.5
	Inactive	4.3	6.2	7.1	5.2	6.4	8	7.4	8.6	3.6	2.4	6

Source: Biographies et Entourage survey (2000).

Note: The reference population was the 1,413 female respondents and their mothers. For example, 32.4 percent of daughters belonging to cluster 1 were born between 1930 and 1939.

Acknowledgment

The authors thank the anonymous reviewers for their useful comments.

Notes

1. For an extensive review of these two sets of methods, see Robette and Bry (2012).
2. For a detailed presentation of the different stages of a sequence analysis by OM, see, for example MacIndoe and Abbott (2004).
3. The same kind of problems have been considered for more atypical sequences, for example, activity patterns from diary data (Wilson 1998) or activism careers (Blanchard 2005).
4. That is, the frequency of transition between the states (or a function of it).
5. It should be noted that some authors have compared several of these approaches using the same data set (Blanchard 2010). Furthermore, Piccarreta and Lior (2010) used MDS to sort one-dimensional index plots according to a second dimension; however, the scope of our review focuses on the dominant view, that is, on typological approaches.
6. These criteria are inspired by Gauthier et al. (2010).
7. More precisely, one typology may be considered more parsimonious than another if it keeps the same amount of information with fewer clusters or if it keeps more information with the same number of clusters. In practical terms, parsimony is a balance between the amount of information and the number of clusters, and the decisions it implies are not always straightforward.
8. Another example could be the dyad of sequences formed by the current workday or workweek, as gathered in time-use surveys (Lesnard and Kan 2011), and past occupational career.
9. Other MDS techniques exist, such as nonmetric MDS (Shepard 1962) or Bayesian MDS (Oh and Raftery 2001). We follow Piccarreta and Lior's (2010) approach by applying metric MDS to sequence dissimilarity measures. Another application of MDS to sequence analysis may be found in Halpin and Chan (1998).
10. The number of retained components may be different for mothers and daughters.
11. Although symmetric (or canonical) PLS can deal with only two sets of variables, in this case it is probably still the most powerful method (Bry 1996). In cases of three sets of variables or more, alternative factor analysis techniques such as multiple factor analysis or STATIS may be used (Escofier and Pagès 1994).
12. Ward's criterion is known to produce homogeneous and compact clusters (Nakache and Confais 2004). It has been widely and successfully applied with sequence analysis.
13. The Île-de-France region comprises the Paris metropolitan area plus the outer suburbs and was home to 19% of the French population in 2000.
14. In our survey, the interviewees are the children's generation, and no siblings were interviewed; each mother is thus present only once in our sample.
15. Completing education at ages that range from 14 to 28 years.
16. Added to that, in our survey, part-time employment covers jobs at 80% of full-time hours, as well as jobs at 50% or even less.

17. These analyses were done using R software (R Development Core Team 2013) and the TraMineR package (Gabadinho et al. 2011).
18. These computations were done using the WeightedCluster package (Studer 2012) in R.
19. Colored index plots are available at http://nicolas.robette.free.fr/publis_eng.html.
20. Despite the choice of a dissimilarity measure emphasizing order.
21. The 24-state distribution plots are available from the authors.
22. To test the association between the typologies, we first perform a Pearson's chi-square test ($p = .0008624$. However, because some cell counts are lower than 5, Fisher's exact test is best suited ($p = .0004998$). Both tests show that the typologies are significantly associated.
23. From a strictly practical view, using MCSA here would imply adding 32 "nonresponse" states within every daughter's sequence. And it is not clear where these states should be added (at the beginning, at the end, or somewhere in the middle), because of the difference in the definition of the time windows. Although it is not technically impossible, the interpretation of the results would be blurred: to what extent would these results be driven by the reshaping of daughters' sequences? But our major argument for using GIMSA to analyze the data remains the difference between local and global interdependence.
24. The R program of the GIMSA application process is given in Appendix H in the online journal.
25. As mentioned before, this characteristic of GIMSA emphasizes global interdependence.
26. The figures are available from the authors.
27. That is, min(5, 4, 1,413).
28. It would be all the more so in the case of more than two dimensions.
29. Automatic clustering procedures for empirical data are hierarchical; this means that each cluster could be further divided into several subclusters, which are distinct and more homogeneous than the main cluster. Thus a typology is based on a delicate choice between the aggregated profile of the whole sample and the idiosyncrasy of individual cases.
30. Colored index plots are available at http://nicolas.robette.free.fr/publis_eng.html.
31. Social origin as measured by the occupation of a daughter's father is not significantly associated with the clusters. This may be explained by the fact that the occupation of a daughter's mother is taken into account in the dyads that lead to the clusters, combined with the importance of homogamy in France (Vanderschelden 2006).

References

Aassve, Arnstein, Francesco C. Billari, and Raffaella Piccarreta. 2007. "Strings of Adulthood: A Sequence Analysis of Young British Women's Work-family Trajectories." *European Journal of Population* 23:369–88.

Abbott, Andrew. 2000. "Reply to Levine and Wu." *Sociological Methods and Research* 29:65–76.

Abbott, Andrew, and Emily Barman. 1997. "Sequence Comparison via Alignment and Gibbs Sampling: A Formal Analysis of the Emergence of the Modern Sociological

Article." Pp. 47–87 in *Sociological Methodology*, Vol. 27, edited by Adrian E. Raftery. Boston: Blackwell.

Abbott, Andrew, and John Forrest. 1986. "Optimal Matching Methods for Historical Sequences." *Journal of Interdisciplinary History* 16:471–94.

Abbott, Andrew, and Alexandra Hrycak. 1990. "Measuring Resemblance in Sequence Data: An Optimal Matching Analysis of Musicians' Careers." *American Journal of Sociology* 96:144–85.

Abbott, Andrew, and Angela Tsay. 2000. "Sequence Analysis and Optimal Matching Methods in Sociology." *Sociological Methods and Research* 29:3–33.

Aisenbrey, Silke, and Anette E. Fasang. 2010. "New Life for Old Ideas: The 'Second Wave' of Sequence Analysis Bringing the 'Course' Back into the Life Course." *Sociological Methods and Research* 38:420–62.

Barrère-Maurisson, Marie-Agnès. 1992. *La Division Familiale du Travail. La Vie en Double*. Paris: Presses Universitaires de France.

Biemann, Torsten. 2011. "A Transition-oriented Approach to Optimal Matching." Pp. 195–221 in *Sociological Methodology*, Vol. 41, edited by Tim Futing Liao. Hoboken, NJ: Wiley-Blackwell.

Blair-Loy, Mary. 1999. "Career Patterns of Executive Women in Finance: An Optimal Matching Analysis." *American Journal of Sociology* 104:1346–97.

Blanchard, Philippe. 2005. "Multi-dimensional Biographies. Explaining Disengagement through Sequence Analysis." Presented at the Third ECPR Conference, Budapest, Hungary.

Blanchard, Philippe. 2010. Analyse Séquentielle et Carrières Militantes. Retrieved December 11, 2014 (http://halshs.archives-ouvertes.fr/hal-00476193/).

Bry, Xavier. 1996. *Analyses Factorielles Multiples*. Paris: Economica Poche.

Brzinsky-Fay, Christian, and Ulrich Kohler. 2010. "New Developments in Sequence Analysis." *Sociological Methods and Research* 38:359–64

Chaloupkova, Jana. 2010. "The De-standardisation of Early Family Trajectories in the Czech Republic: A Cross-cohort Comparison." *Czech Sociological Review* 46: 427–51.

Courgeau, Daniel, and Eva Lelièvre. 1992. *Event History Analysis in Demography*. Oxford, UK: Clarendon.

de Jong, Sijmen, Barry M. Wise, and N. Lawrence Ricker. 2001. "Canonical Partial Least Squares and Continuum Power Regression." *Journal of Chemometrics* 15: 85–100.

Dijkstra, Wil, and Toon Taris. 1995. "Measuring the Agreement between Sequences." *Sociological Methods and Research* 24:214–31.

Elzinga, Cees H. 2003. "Sequence Similarity: A Nonaligning Technique." *Sociological Methods and Research* 32:3–29.

Elzinga, Cees H. 2008. "Sequence Analysis: Metric Representations of Categorical Time Series." Technical Report, Department of Social Science Research Methods, Vrije Universiteit, Amsterdam, the Netherlands.

Elzinga, Cees H., and Aart C. Liefbroer 2007. "De-standardization of Family-life Trajectories of Young Adults: A Cross-national Comparison Using Sequence Analysis." *European Journal of Population* 23:225–50.

Escofier, Brigitte, and Jérôme Pagès. 1994. "Multiple Factor Analysis (AFMULT Package)." *Computational Statistics and Data Analysis* 18:121–40.

Falcon, Julie. 2012. "Behind the Black Box: The Effect of Intragenerational Social Mobility on Intergenerational Social Mobility." Presented at the Lausanne Conference on Sequence Analysis, Lausanne, Switzerland.

Fasang, Anette E., and Marcel Raab. 2014. "Beyond Transmission: Intergenerational Patterns of Family Formation among Middle-class American Families." *Demography* 51:1703–28.

Gabadinho, Alexis, Gilbert Ritschard, Nicolas S. Müller, and Matthias Studer. 2011. "Analyzing and Visualizing State Sequences in R with TraMineR." *Journal of Statistical Software* 40:1–37.

Gauthier, Jacques-Antoine, Éric D. Widmer, Philipp Bucher, and Cédric Notredame. 2010. "Multichannel Sequence Analysis Applied to Social Science Data." Pp. 1–38 in *Sociological Methodology*, Vol. 40, edited by Tim Futing Liao. Hoboken, NJ: Wiley-Blackwell.

Giele, Janet Z., and Glen H. Elder. 1998. "Life Course Research: Development of a Field." Pp. 5–27 in *Methods of Life Course Research: Qualitative and Quantitative Approaches*, edited by J. Giele and G. Elder. London: Sage Lrd.

Grelet, Yvette. 2002. "Des Typologies de Parcours. Méthodes et Usages." *Document Génération* 92 20:1–47.

Groupe de Réflexion sur l'Approche Biographique. 2009. Biographies d'Enquêtes: Bilan de 14 Collectes Biographiques. Paris: INED. (http://grab.site.ined.fr/fr/editions_en_ligne/biographies_enquetes/).

Halpin, Brendan, and Tak Wing Chan. 1998. "Class Careers as Sequences: An Optimal Matching Analysis of Work-life Histories." *European Sociological Review* 14:111–30.

Han, Shin-Kap, and Phyllis Moen. 1999. "Clocking Out: Temporal Patterning of Retirement." *American Journal of Sociology* 105:191–236.

Hubert, Lawrence, and Phipps Arabie. 1985. "Comparing Partitions." *Journal of Classification* 2:193–218.

Kruskal, Joseph B., and Myron Wish. 1984. *Multidimensional Scaling*. Beverly Hills, CA: Sage.

Lelièvre, Eva, and Nicolas Robette. 2010. "A Life Space Perspective to Approach Individual Demographic Processes." *Canadian Studies in Population* 37:207–44.

Lelièvre, Eva, and Géraldine Vivier. 2001. "Evaluation d'Une Collecte à la Croisée du Quantitatif et du Qualitatif: l'Enquête Biographies et Entourage." *Population* 56:1043–73.

Lesnard, Laurent. 2008. "Off-scheduling within Dual-earner Couples: An Unequal and Negative Externality for Family Time." *American Journal of Sociology* 114:447–90.

Lesnard, Laurent. 2010. "Setting Cost in Optimal Matching to Uncover Contemporaneous Socio-temporal Patterns." *Sociological Methods and Research* 38:389–419.

Lesnard, Laurent, and Man Yee Kan. 2011. "Investigating Scheduling of Work: A Two-stage Optimal Matching Analysis of Workdays and Workweeks." *Journal of the Royal Statistical Society, Series A: Statistics in Society* 174:349–68.

Liefbroer, Aart C., and Cees H. Elzinga. 2012. "Intergenerational Transmission of Behavioural Patterns: How Similar Are Parents' and Children's Demographic Trajectories?" *Advances in Life Course Research* 17:1–10.

MacIndoe, Heather, and Andrew Abbott. 2004. "Sequence Analysis and Optimal Matching Techniques for Social Science Data." Pp. 387–406 in *Handbook of Data Analysis*, edited by M. Hardy and A. Bryman. London: Sage Ltd.

Maruani, Margaret. 2000. *Travail et Emploi des Femmes*. Paris: La Découverte.

Milligan, Glenn W., and Martha C. Cooper. 1985. "An Examination of Procedures for Determining the Number of Clusters in a Data Set." *Psychometrika* 50:159–79.

Nakache, Jean-Pierre, and Josiane Confais. 2004. *Approche Pragmatique de la Classification*. Paris: Editions Technip.

Oh, Man-Suk, and Adrian E. Raftery. 2001. "Bayesian Multidimensional Scaling and Choice of Dimension." *Journal of the American Statistical Association* 96:1031–44.

Piccarreta, Raffaella, and Orna Lior. 2010. "Exploring Sequences: A Graphical Tool Based on Multi-dimensional Scaling." *Journal of the Royal Statistical Society, Series A: Statistics in Society* 173:165–84.

Pollock, Gary. 2007. "Holistic Trajectories: A Study of Combined Employment, Housing and Family Careers by Using Multiple-sequence Analysis." *Journal of the Royal Statistical Society, Series A: Statistics in Society* 170:167–83.

R Development Core Team. 2013. "R: A Language and Environment for Statistical Computing." Vienna: R Foundation for Statistical Computing. Retrieved December 11, 2014 (http://www.R-project.org).

Robette, Nicolas. 2010. "The Diversity of Pathways to Adulthood in France: Evidence from a Holistic Approach." *Advances in Life Course Research* 15:89–96.

Robette, Nicolas, and Xavier Bry. 2012. "Harpoon or Bait? A Comparison of Various Metrics to Fish for Life Course Patterns." *Bulletin of Sociological Methodology* 116: 5–24.

Robette, Nicolas, Eva Lelièvre, and Xavier Bry. 2012. "La Transmission des Trajectoires d'Activité: Telles Mères, Telles Filles?" Pp. 395–418 in *De la Famille à l'Entourage*, edited by E. Lelièvre and C. Bonvalet. Paris: INED.

Robette, Nicolas, and Nicolas Thibault. 2008. "Comparing Qualitative Harmonic Analysis and Optimal Matching: An Exploratory Study of Occupational Trajectories." *Population-E* 64:621–46.

Robette, Nicolas, Anne Solaz, and Ariane Pailhé. 2009. "Work and Family over the Life-cycle: A Typology of Couples." Presented at the Twenty-sixth IUSSP International Population Conference, Marrakech, Morocco.

Salmela-Aro, Katariina, Noona Kiuru, Jari-Erik Nurmi, and Mervi Eerola. 2011. "Mapping Pathways to Adulthood among Finnish University Students: Sequences, Patterns, Variations in Family- and Work-related Roles." *Advances in Life Course Research* 16:25–41.

Saporta, Gilbert, and Genane Youness. 2002. "Comparing Two Partitions: Some Proposals and Experiments." Pp. 243–48 in *Compstat: Proceedings in Computational Statistics*. Heidelberg, Germany: Physica-Verlag.

Shepard, Roger N. 1962. "The Analysis of Proximities: Multidimensional Scaling with an Unknown Distance Function, II." *Psychometrika* 27:219–46.

Stovel, Katherine, Michael Savage, and Peter Bearman. 1996. "Ascription into Achievement: Models of Career Systems at Lloyds Bank, 1890–1970." *American Journal of Sociology* 102:358–99.

Studer, Matthias. 2012. "Étude des Inégalités de Genre en Début de Carrière Académique à l'Aide de Méthodes Innovatrices d'Analyse de Données Séquentielles." Thèse SES 777, Faculté des Sciences Économiques et Sociales, Université de Genève.

Vanderschelden, Mélanie. 2006. "Homogamie Socioprofessionnelle et Ressemblance en Termes de Niveau d'Études: Constat et Évolution au fil des Cohortes d'Unions." *Economie et Statistique* 398–99:33–58.

Williams, W. T., and G. N. Lance. 1965. "Logic of Computer-based Intrinsic Classifications." *Nature* 207:159–61.

Wilson, Clarke. 1998. "Activity Pattern Analysis by Means of Sequence-alignment Methods." *Environment and Planning A* 30:1017–38.

Wu, Lawrence L. 2000. "Some Comments on 'Sequence Analysis and Optimal Matching Methods in Sociology: Review and Prospect.'" *Sociological Methods and Research* 29:41–64.

Author Biographies

Nicolas Robette is a lecturer in the Department of Sociology at the University of Versailles-Saint-Quentin and a researcher at Laboratoire Printemps (UVSQ-CNRS, UMR 8085). His main research interests include quantitative methods such as sequence analysis in the social sciences and life-course analysis.

Xavier Bry is a lecturer in statistics at the University of Montpellier 2 and a researcher at Institut de Mathématiques et de Modélisation. He recently published (with P. Redont, T. Verron, and P. Cazes): "THEME-SEER: A Multidimensional Exploratory Technique to Analyze a Structural Model Using an Extended Covariance Criterion" in the *Journal of Chemometrics*.

Éva Lelièvre is a senior researcher in demography at Institut National d'Études Démographiques, where she heads the research unit Mobilité, Logement, et Entourage. Her field of expertise covers the dynamics of individual trajectories, intergenerational relationships, and family networks, with a special interest in the interactions within individual life courses between family, work, residential mobility, and health.

Sociological Methodology
2015, Vol. 45(1) 45–100
© American Sociological Association 2015
http://sm.sagepub.com

COMMENT: ON THE ASSOCIATION BETWEEN SEQUENCES IN GIMSA

Cees H. Elzinga*

*VU University, Amsterdam, The Netherlands
Corresponding Author: Cees H. Elzinga, c.h.elzinga@vu.nl
DOI: 10.1177/0081175015587275

In my comment on Robette, Bry, and Lelièvre (this volume, pp. 1–44), I will refer to the paper and its authors alike by the abbreviation "RBL." Focusing on the situation that occurs when sequences pertain to at least two different domains,[1] the data are split into at least two distinct sets of sequences $\{X = \{x_i\}, Y = \{y_i\}, \ldots\}_{i=1}^{n}$. Gauthier et al. (2010) provided a clear analysis of the strategies, and the limitations thereof, to handle such complex data. Because these (split) sequences pertain to the same unit of analysis (a single entity such as an individual or related entities such as parents and children, siblings, or therapist-patient dyads), they are, in the framework of the life-course paradigm, somehow associated. Such associations can be studied in two different ways. The first relates state durations and transitions from different sequences. The second studies the association between the sequences by considering them as entities and as patterns, and it then unveils the association between the patterns. When, for example, the historical or institutional context of the split sequences is very different, relating state durations and transitions across sequences is meaningless, and hence the latter approach is the only sensible one. RBL present a new method to do exactly that: to unveil associations between patterns that are difficult to align across different epochs or different cultural or institutional contexts. RBL offer this explanation: "What we want to examine is rather the overall shapes of the separate dimensions—and the patterns in them—and the relationship between these patterns."

Because RBL claim that their globally interdependent multiple sequence analysis (GIMSA) proposal is a useful complement to the existing methods of sequence analysis, it is worthwhile to look at some of the tools that have already been proposed to tackle the problem of assessing the association of patterns. Therefore, it is interesting to summarize some concepts from Piccarreta and Elzinga (2013). Our goal was to propose methodology to assess the strength of association between sequences without first labeling them by applying some clustering technique. We started from the general notion that association is to be quantified as a reduction of the variance in one variable as a result of conditioning upon a particular value or class of the other variable (Guttman 1941)—that is, association means that the prediction of a particular pattern in one domain is improved when we know the pattern in the other domain. To apply this principle to patterns spatially represented in the form of a distance matrix, we first postulated a very general principle: global monotonicity. To state this principle, we denote the distance between the patterns of objects i and j in channel X by $d(x_i, x_j)$. We then say that two channels are associated precisely when for objects $\{i, j, k, \ell\}$ it is true that

$$d(x_i, x_j) > d(x_k, x_\ell) \Leftrightarrow d(y_i, y_j) > d(y_k, y_\ell). \tag{1}$$

If global monotonicity holds, it implies that objects showing near patterns in one domain will tend to show near patterns in the other domain *and* that remote patterns in one domain are connected to remote patterns in the other domain. The simplest way to measure association between distance matrices is Mantel's coefficient: Pearson's r between the off-diagonal elements of the two distance matrices. Mantel's coefficient presupposes a linear relation between the elements of the pertaining distance matrices; to accommodate for nonlinear relations, it could be replaced by a rank-based coefficient such as Kendall's τ.

A more sophisticated way to measure global association was proposed in Escoufier (1973) (see also Robert and Escoufier 1976) in the form of a generalized Pearson's r. Instead of the cosine between vectors, it calculates a generalized cosine between two matrices. In Piccarreta and Elzinga (2013), we showed that for distance matrices $\mathbf{D}_X$ and $\mathbf{D}_Y$, this coefficient R_V is easily evaluated through the use of the doubly centered matrices $\tilde{\mathbf{D}} = \mathbf{H}\mathbf{D}^2\mathbf{H}$, where $\mathbf{H} = \mathbf{I} - n^{-1}\mathbf{1}\mathbf{1}'$:

$$R_V(\mathbf{D}_X, \mathbf{D}_Y) = \frac{trace(\tilde{\mathbf{D}}_X \tilde{\mathbf{D}}_Y)}{\sqrt{trace(\tilde{\mathbf{D}}_X)trace(\tilde{\mathbf{D}}_Y)}}. \tag{2}$$

However, we argued that global association might be too gross an assumption and instead proposed to assume what we called the weaker "local monotonicity": local monotonicity holds if, for some positive constants c_X and c_Y,

$$d(x_i, x_j) > c_X \Rightarrow d(y_i, y_j) > c_Y. \tag{3}$$

This implies that objects that are close in one channel are close in the other channel, but objects that are remote in one channel are no longer supposed to be remote in the other channel too. We called this type of association "local" because we no longer require that the type of pattern association is the same for all objects: only "neighboring" objects will show similar pattern associations. Therefore, we proposed to use a coefficient that quantifies precisely this kind of association:

$$R(\mathbf{D}_X | \mathbf{D}_Y) = 1 - \frac{\sum_i d(x_i, m_i)}{\sum_i d(x_i, \bar{m})}, \tag{4}$$

wherein m_i denotes the medoid of a neighborhood of i in the Y domain, and $\bar{m}$ denotes the medoid of *all* X sequences.

Essentially, the analysis that we proposed involves the implementation of a series of two mappings:

$$(X, Y) \overset{1}{\mapsto} (\mathbf{D}_X, \mathbf{D}_Y) \overset{2}{\mapsto} c \in \mathsf{R}.$$

Mapping 1 independently generates distance matrices $\mathbf{D}_X$ and $\mathbf{D}_Y$ from the sets of sequences X and Y, and mapping 2 generates a single real number c, the numerical strength of association. For mapping 1, we could use several different metrics, and for mapping 2, we proposed particular formulas. This results in the same steps that are involved in, for example, evaluating the association between two personality traits, measured by different tests.

A slightly more involved analysis was proposed in Blanchard (2005); it has one extra step—the assignment of labels from two distinct label sets $\mathcal{L}_X$ and $\mathcal{L}_Y$ to the sequences from X and Y:

$$(X, Y) \overset{1}{\mapsto} (\mathbf{D}_X, \mathbf{D}_Y) \overset{2}{\mapsto} (L_X, L_Y) \overset{3}{\mapsto} c \in \mathsf{R}$$

To actually assign the labels, the sets X and Y are partitioned through a cluster analysis of the distance matrices, and the same label is assigned to objects in the same cluster. Cross-tabulating the frequencies of the label sets then allows a detailed analysis of the association, if any, between the labels (e.g., see Agresti 2002). Such cross-tabulation of typologies is in fact shown in RBL's Table 2, and a significant association between the clusters (i.e., between the labels) was found by RBL.[2]

Remarkably, RBL state that their Table 2 "clearly lacks parsimony." I wonder: since when is a simple two-way, six-by-four table with well-chosen row and column labels not a parsimonious way of summarizing data? Most of us have seen bigger tables.

Interestingly, inspection of RBL's Table 2 reveals that correlation is weak, as expected, and local in the sense of the above discussion as roughly 60 percent of the daughters end up in full-time employment, regardless of their mothers' careers: "remote mothers" have "close daughters."

Unfortunately, RBL confuse a 24-cluster solution with a cross-tabulation of $6 \times 4 = 24$ cells; the latter is based only on $6 + 4 = 10$ clusters. RBL reject their Table 2 as an instrument to study association between mothers' and daughters' careers: "But we need to use a method that specifically and parsimoniously focuses on the linked characteristics of the two histories." Apparently, they are after a kind of association or linkage that is beyond Guttmann's concept of reduction of variation. However, what this concept amounts to, is not explained in RBL.

Let us therefore have a look at the GIMSA approach:

$$(X, Y) \overset{1}{\mapsto} (\mathbf{D}_X, \mathbf{D}_Y) \overset{2}{\mapsto} (\mathbf{D}'_X, \mathbf{D}'_Y) \overset{3}{\mapsto} \mathbf{D}_{X \oplus Y} \overset{4}{\mapsto} \mathcal{L}_{X \oplus Y}$$

In the first mapping, the sequences X and Y are mapped onto distance matrices $\mathbf{D}_X$ and $\mathbf{D}_Y$. Because partial least square (PLS) requires vector spaces, the second mapping approximates $\mathbf{D}_X$ and $\mathbf{D}_Y$ by the multidimensional scaling (MDS)–generated $\mathbf{D}'_X$ and $\mathbf{D}'_Y$. Strangely, RBL report this step as a "noise reduction" step, but they fail to present us with a "noise model" that would allow us to estimate noise and remove it from matrices $\mathbf{D}_X$ and $\mathbf{D}_Y$. MDS is a good method to explore data (e.g., see Borg and Groenen 2005) or summarizing them in favor of clear visual rendering, as in Piccarreta and Lior (2010), but it is not an unsupervised noise filter. Later on, in their section 4.4 on robustness checks, RBL report a reanalysis with MDS-generated 20-dimensional distances instead of 4- or 5-dimensional distances. RBL report a Rand index between the original typology and the new one, obtained through the use of the 20-dimensional representation. The Rand index quantifies the agreement between clusterings C_1 and C_2 of n objects as

$$Rand(C_1, C_2) = \frac{a + b}{\binom{n}{2}}.$$

In the above expression, a is the number of pairs of objects that both C_1 and C_2 assign to the same cluster, and b is the number of pairs that, both in C_1 and C_2, end up in different clusters. Hence, the Rand index calculates the fraction of pairs that are dealt with in the same way by both clusterings. RBL report a value of .649, implying that the clustering from a 20-dimensional representation decides differently in more than 35 percent of the pairs. To me, this means that the typologies are quite different,[3] not "rather similar." Therefore, the effect of distorting the sequence space through an MDS-generated vector space is impossible to judge.

However, GIMSA's mapping 2 can easily be avoided by selecting a sequence-matching methodology that generates a sequence representation in a vector space. Such metrics have been proposed by Elzinga and Wang (2013) (see also Elzinga and Studer 2015) and are available in the TraMineR software that RBL used. Hence, the GIMSA analysis could be improved and simplified to the scheme

$$(X, Y) \overset{1}{\mapsto} (\mathbf{D}_X, \mathbf{D}_Y) \overset{3}{\mapsto} \mathbf{D}_{X \oplus Y} \overset{4}{\mapsto} \mathcal{L}_{X \oplus Y}.$$

Mapping 3 arises through the application of symmetric PLS. Unfortunately, RBL do not explain why *symmetric* PLS is used instead of the usual "asymmetric" version.[4] After all, if there is an association between mothers' and daughters' careers, it is difficult to imagine that daughters' careers would shape mothers' trajectories. However, this too is easily remedied, and some indication of the fit of such a generalized principal component analysis model would then be welcomed.

However, what is more important in mapping 3 is that in the construction of $D_{X \oplus Y}$, the association between mothers' and daughters' principal components is supposed to be linear and implicit in the composition of the "joint" principal components that arose in the PLS algorithm. Linearity, a most rigid version of global monotonicity, probably is a false assumption, and association, if any, does not become apparent in RBL's Table 4: it merely lists frequent patterns. So, RBL's claim that their Table 4 renders the linkage between mothers' and daughters' lives better than their Table 2—essentially the proposal made by Blanchard (2005)—is false.

In conclusion, RBL's claim that GIMSA is a valuable and versatile addition to the toolbox of sequence analysts does not survive. On the contrary, it veils association by hiding it in a multilinear model that is not theoretically underpinned, other than through references to the concept of "linked lives." Furthermore, the paper contains serious flaws, some of which I already commented on. To mention just one more: RBL's critique of the proposal of Han and Moen (1999) and Blanchard (2005) to add metrics ("the relationships between dimensions are not adequately handled") is false and based on a misconception of multidimensional geometry—sums of metrics are metrics again and pairs of points are not fully identified by their distance alone; we need some directions too.

Notes

1. To avoid confusion, I reserve the term *dimension* for the description of geometric objects and prefer to use *domain* or *channel* to refer to different facets of the life-course.
2. See RBL's note 22.
3. If we would have two classification methods to assign children to educational programs or patients to therapies and the Rand index between the two methods would equal .65, we would justly see a national uproar. To get both methods accepted, we would need a Rand index that exceeds .90.
4. A very accessible survey of PLS methodology is found in Abdi (2010).

References

Abdi, Hervé. 2010. "Partial Least Squares Regression and Projection on Latent Structure Regression (PLS Regression)." *Wiley Interdisciplinary Reviews: Computational Statistics* 2:97–106.

Agresti, Alan. 2002. *Categorical Data Analysis*. 2nd ed. New York: Wiley Interscience.

Blanchard, Philippe. 2005. "Multidimensional Biographies. Explaining Disengagement Through Sequence Analysis." Presented at the 3rd ECPR Conference 2005, Budapest, Hungary.

Borg, Ingwer, and Patrick J. F. Groenen. 2005. *Modern Multidimensional Scaling: Theory and Applications*. 2nd ed. New York: Springer.

Elzinga, Cees H., and Matthias Studer. 2015. "Spell Sequences, State Proximities, and Distance Metrics." *Sociological Methods and Research* 44(1):3–47.

Elzinga, Cees H., and Hui Wang. 2013. "Versatile String Kernels." *Theoretical Computer Science* 495:50–65.

Escoufier, Yves. 1973. "Le Traitement des Variables Vectorielles." *Biometrics* 29(4):751–760.

Gauthier, Jacques-Antoine, Eric D. Widmer, Philipp Bucher, and Cédric Notredame. 2010. "Multichannel Sequence Analysis Applied to Social Science Data." Pp. 1–38 in *Sociological Methodology*, vol. 40, edited by Tim Futing Liao. Hoboken, NJ: Wiley-Blackwell.

Guttman, Leon. 1941. "An Outline of the Theory of Prediction." Pp. 261–62 in *The Prediction of Personal Adjustment, Bulletin 48*, edited by Paul Horst. New York: Social Science Research Council.

Han, Shin-Kap, and Phyllis Moen. 1999. "Clocking Out: Temporal Patterning of Retirement." *American Journal of Sociology* 14:111–30.

Piccarreta, Raffaella, and Cees H. Elzinga. 2013. "Mining for Associations between Life Course Domains." Pp. 190–220 in *Contemporary Issues in Exploratory Data Mining, Quantitative Methodology Series*, edited by J. J. McArdle and G. Ritschard. New York: Routledge.

Piccarreta, Rafaella, and Orna Lior. 2010. "Exploring Sequences: A Graphical Tool Based on Multi-dimensional Scaling." *Journal of the Royal Statistical Society, Series A, Statistics in Society* 173(1):165–84.

Robert, Paul, and Yves Escoufier. 1976. "A Unifying Tool for Linear Multivariate Statistical Methods: The RV-coefficient." *Applied Statistics* 25(3):257–65.

Author Biography

Cees H. Elzinga is a full professor of pattern recognition at VU University in Amsterdam, where he served as a chair of the Sociology Department and as vice dean and faculty educational programs manager. His research interests pertain to kernel algorithms for string and graph comparison and their application to topics such as social demography and life-course research. His publications have been included in *Theoretical Computer Science, Information Sciences*, and *Pattern Recognition Letters* as well as in *Sociological Methods and Research, Demography*, and the *European Journal of Population.*

COMMENT: CAPTURING LINKED LIVES—A PROMISING NEW METHOD

Wen Fan*
Phyllis Moen*

*University of Minnesota, Minneapolis, MN, USA
Corresponding Author: Phyllis Moen, phylmoen@umn.edu
DOI: 10.1177/0081175015587277

1. INTRODUCTION

A key principle of the life-course paradigm is the notion of *linked lives*, that lives are lived interdependently, with sociohistorical influences expressed through networks of shared relationships (Elder, Johnson, and Crosnoe 2003). Although this principle is central to network and life-course analysis and has received increasing attention in the conventional regression framework (e.g., the actor-partner interdependence model, the multilevel p_2 model; for an overview, see Card, Selig, and Little [2011]; Kenny, Kashy, and Cook [2006]), it has been less developed in sequence analysis. This is unfortunate, because, since its inception in sociology in the 1980s, sequence analysis has been a new way of understanding and capturing individual lives over time (Abbott 1995; Abbott and Tsay 2000). Robette, Bry, and Lelièvre (this volume, pp. 1–44; hereafter RBL) make a significant contribution by developing a method for simultaneously detecting life-course patterns for those whose lives are linked (e.g., mothers and daughters in the illustrative case). RBL's innovative globally interdependent multiple sequence analysis (GIMSA) has considerable potential to address important questions that are of central interest to many life-course scholars (and sociologists more generally) about lives lived in tandem *and* over time.

In this comment, we focus on the contributions of GIMSA and also broach three issues, all of which are substantive but have methodological implications: temporality, analytic weight, and variability. We also briefly discuss issues related to validity and estimation uncertainty.

2. CONTRIBUTIONS

Not only life-course scholarship but sociology itself is to a large degree about discovering identifiable patterned social relationships over time. But the "over time" component has been little theorized or empirically assessed. Consider, for example, the large body of stratification research linking parents' occupational status (at no set age or when the child is 16 years old) with the subsequent occupational status of the adult child (often at no set age). Or consider studies of parental poverty or unemployment when a child is a preschooler or adolescent. This flies in the face of the dynamic and complex life paths of both generations and the relationships between them. GIMSA as a method provides the means of capturing the dynamic patterning of lives, but it also encourages its users to theorize these patterns and intergenerational transmissions both over and in time, considering and measuring their multidimensionality and the degree of contemporaneous of their interdependence while modeling them in a parsimonious way.

GIMSA is thus an important addition to the toolkit of sequence analysis that raises issues about the clocks and calendars of lives and relationships over time. For example, what matters across generations? Is it the ordering of events, their durations, or their timing (in either the parents' or the children's biographies)? What is the role of social change and historical time? RBL point out that part-time work was not widespread in France until the 1980s, yet it was prominent in some daughters' lives. They note that "in effect, parents' sequences and those of their children can be of very different nature, reflecting the norms of their time, and our focus is on the relationship between sequences as wholes rather than on their synchronization in terms of age."

3. TEMPORALITY, ANALYTIC WEIGHT, AND VARIABILITY

3.1. *Temporality*

A key component rarely fleshed out in the linked-lives principle has to do with temporality. One person's behavior could affect another person instantaneously or within a short time frame ("local interdependence"), or it could be that it is the whole history of one person that really matters ("global interdependence"). GIMSA seems to have been developed with the latter logic in mind. This obviously corresponds well with the value of sequence analysis as a holistic approach. Nevertheless, it does not appear to allow the examination, for example, of how a given transition in one person's life is tied to temporal patterns in another's life. And yet understanding these unfolding processes as turning points, contingencies, and so on, is exactly what the linked-lives formulation asks us to do.

Not requiring synchronization is a key advantage of GIMSA, which provides more latitude in addressing sequences involving different generations. However, it opens up other questions, such as the choice of the time dimension. RBL purposefully chose two different time clocks (mothers' from ages 14 to 60, daughters' from the completion of education to 15 years later) to demonstrate the power of GIMSA. Future users will also need to make decisions regarding which temporal dimensions to use. Are results sensitive to alternative time scales? If so, how should one decide which to use? Are there formal tests to discriminate alternative typologies?

A related issue is the vague temporal order, exacerbated by the lack of transparency in partial least square (PLS). Even in the example provided, there should be some overlap between the two life-courses. For example, assume that one daughter finishes her education when her mother is 45 years old. The mother's sequence after age 50, therefore, is not expected to affect her daughter's first 5 years (i.e., completion of education to 5 years later). In other words, not every year should "count" when identifying shared patterns.

3.2. *Analytic Weight*

It is not entirely clear about the analytic weight, or the relative status, of the two sequences. Lives could be linked in a variety of ways; for example, directionality could be one way or mutual. This is a distinction that needs to be clarified in life-course analysis. In this case, given the ages analyzed, the focus is unidirectional, from mothers to daughters. According to RBL, "the daughter's situation at a given age is unlikely to be linked to her mother's situation at the same age, but rather it is the mother's whole employment history that is considered as part of the daughter's social background."

But this will not always be the case when the years considered overlap for both members of a dyad. In addition, the canonic PLS treats mother and daughter as symmetric, and what GIMSA draws on is *shared* information. It is hard to see the social meanings (how lives are linked) underlying the criteria used by PLS to detect common structures.

3.3. *Variability*

We are pleased that RBL point out that the sequence of one dimension of the dyad could be more heterogeneous than the other. This observation is not merely a methodological nuisance but has a substantive basis. Changing life-courses are exhibiting dual trends of individualization and standardization (relevant when studying parent-child dyads); women typically have more variable life-courses than men (relevant for couple dyads). Therefore, choices of weights could be consequential and should be considered as a routine robustness test, just as RBL do in their analysis.

4. VALIDITY AND UNCERTAINTY

RBL clearly and succinctly lay out the processes of implementing GIMSA step by step. They also conduct several robustness tests to examine sensitivity. Questions remain, however, regarding validity and the comparative advantage of this method. For example, how well does it perform as compared with multichannel sequence analysis (Gauthier et al. 2010), at least for contemporaneous sequences such as those of couples? Future studies could be conducted to systematically evaluate the behavior of GIMSA under alternative scenarios.

We have a related comment about uncertainty. This is not a limitation unique to GIMSA but is shared by almost all classification methods. Given the multiple stages involved in GIMSA—optimal matching, multidimensional scaling, PLS, and clustering—how to quantify uncertainty seems particularly relevant. Uncertainty from one stage can easily become magnified in the next. Understanding the magnitude of this problem is important for future users.

5. CONCLUSION

We see a wide range of application potential for GIMSA that would stimulate theory building and capture identifiable patterned dynamics in relationships. This would be valuable for tracking the career trajectories of dual-earner couples as well as corresponding life trajectories of parents and children. Such analysis could shed light on within-couple inequalities as well as the intergenerational transmission of advantage and disadvantage, even in times of rapid social change. There has been a surge of interest in studies of couples' conjoint careers (e.g., Moen 2003) and of multiple generations (e.g., Mare 2011). GIMSA seems to be a good candidate for understanding these intricate relationships, at least as an exploratory tool. Similarly, it could be used to study how multiple dimensions of lives—work, family, residence, health— interrelate with one another. (RBL briefly note that this extension requires a replacement of PLS with multiple factor analysis. As we commented, however, temporality and analytic weights could be even more complicated and critical for $s \geq 3$ cases.) Nevertheless, GIMSA is an important and useful first step.

References

Abbott, Andrew. 1995. "Sequence Analysis: New Methods for Old Ideas."*Annual Review of Sociology* 21:93–113.

Abbott, Andrew, and Angela Tsay. 2000. "Sequence Analysis and Optimal Matching Methods in Sociology: Review and Prospect." *Sociological Methods and Research* 29(1):3–33.

Card, Noel A., James P. Selig, and Todd Little. 2011. *Modeling Dyadic and Interdependent Data in the Developmental and Behavioral Sciences*. New York: Routledge.

Elder, Glen H., Jr., Monica Kirkpatrick Johnson, and Robert Crosnoe. 2003. "The Emergence and Development of Life Course Theory." Pp. 3–19 in *Handbook of the Life Course*, edited by J. T. Mortimer and M. J. Shanahan. New York: Kluwer.

Gauthier, Jacques-Antoine, Eric D. Widmer, Philipp Bucher, and Cédric Notredame. 2010. "Multichannel Sequence Analysis Applied to Social Science Data." Pp. 1–38 in *Sociological Methodology*, vol. 40, edited by Tim Futing Liao. Hoboken, NJ: Wiley-Blackwell.

Kenny, David A., Deborah A. Kashy, and William L. Cook. 2006. *Dyadic Data Analysis*. New York: Guilford.

Mare, Robert D. 2011. "A Multigenerational View of Inequality." *Demography* 48(1): 1–23.

Moen, Phyllis. 2003. *It's about Time: Couples and Careers.* Ithaca, NY: Cornell University Press.

Author Biographies

Wen Fan is a PhD candidate in sociology at the University of Minnesota. Her research interests focus on social determinants of health-related outcomes over the life-course, especially how these outcomes vary across socioeconomic status, historical moments, work and family contexts, and organizational as well as institutional arrangements. Her dissertation examines the link between education and health, using China's Cultural Revolution (1966–1976) to better theorize and identify effects of education.

Phyllis Moen, after 25 years at Cornell University, accepted a McKnight Presidential Endowed Chair and a professorship in sociology at the University of Minnesota in 2003. She has published numerous books and articles on careers, retirement, health, gender, policy, and families as they are institutionalized, transforming, and intersecting over the life-course. Moen is currently writing a book on boomers.

COMMENT: WHAT'S THE ADDED VALUE?

Anette Eva Fasang*

*Humboldt University of Berlin and WZB Berlin Social Science Center, Berlin, Germany
Corresponding Author: Anette Eva Fasang, anette.fasang@wzb.eu
DOI: 10.1177/0081175015587276

In the past decade, numerous technical innovations of sequence analysis have been introduced in the social sciences. Recently, scholars have voiced increasing concerns that the development of appropriate theoretical concepts to guide these innovations has lagged behind (Blanchard, Bühlmann, and Gauthier 2014). There is some irony in this, considering that the original motivation for sequence analysis in the social sciences was strongly rooted in theoretical concerns about how we treat process and temporality, as formulated in Andrew Abbott's (1992) notes on narrative positivism. In this comment, I take Robette, Bry, and Lelièvre's (RBL) globally interdependent multiple sequence analysis (GIMSA) (this volume, pp. 1–44) as one of the recent technical propositions, and I argue

(1) for establishing stronger theoretical foundations for new sequence analysis techniques and (2) for more carefully scrutinizing their added value in addition to existing techniques. I first consider possibilities for theorizing processes of global interdependence in linked life-courses more thoroughly and then raise doubts about the added value of GIMSA over the more straightforward technique of multichannel sequence analysis (MCSA) to answer similar questions of regularities in dyadic sequences. These doubts are based on robustness checks conducted on RBL's data that show a high sensitivity of the results to different weighting strategies of the partial least square (PLS) components (step 3 of GIMSA). Furthermore, a systematic comparison of GIMSA and MCSA shows that for the example application, the same results are easily obtainable with MCSA, a procedure that involves fewer steps and fewer potentially consequential decisions by the researcher.

1. THEORETICAL CONSIDERATIONS ON GLOBAL INTERDEPENDENCE IN LINKED LIFE-COURSES

GIMSA is introduced as a new approach for studying intergenerational regularities as "process outcomes" of life-course trajectories rather than "point in time outcomes" such as occupational prestige at age 36 or "trend outcomes" such as the gender wage gap over time (Abbott 2005). Why should we care about global interdependence in process outcomes? To date, intergenerational transmission or inheritance is generally defined as similarity in point-in-time outcomes that exists if parents and their children show the same behavior, usually measured at a specific age. The focus on point-in-time outcomes potentially obscures intergenerational regularities in parent and child behavior, if they are similar in one outcome but not in another that are both part of the same process—for example, if parents and children have the same age of first birth but differ widely in completed fertility. In addition, the focus on similarity is conceptually too narrow and unsatisfactory for three reasons.

First, it neglects global similarity—that is, behavior that is similar in some way but not exactly the same. One example would be if children's family formation is a delayed and protracted version of their parents' family formation. As also noted by RBL, given changing macrostructural contexts from one generation to the next, the same behavior of parents and children might not carry the same implications in different contexts. For instance, giving birth at age 17 was not unusual in the 1960s but is considered early today. Looking for simple one-on-one similarity between parents and their children is of little use, when even the same outcomes do not necessarily carry the same information about a person's location within a population. Rather, we need to ask, which form can intergenerational inheritance or transmission possibly take given profound macrostructural change from one generation to the next?

Second, a narrow focus on similarity neglects systematic regularities beyond some form of "global" resemblance—that is, patterns of systematic contrast between parents and their children. In critiquing the conventional focus on transmission as similarity, we therefore recently proposed the concept of intergenerational patterns of family formation (Fasang and Raab 2014). Intergenerational patterns denote regularities in family formation trajectories as process outcomes, where specific parents have specific children, but parents and children are not necessarily the same—*global interdependence* in RBL's terminology. Using MCSA, we showed among other groups of transmission a "contrast pattern" of family formation for middle-class American families.

Third, a narrow focus on similarity fails to encompass intergenerational regularities cutting across life domains, such that mothers' employment trajectories might be linked to their daughters' family formation. For instance, daughters of mothers who tried to combine work and family under difficult conditions in the 1960s might choose either work or family because they shy away from a having-it-all model that they observed as difficult to realize. On the basis of the life-course paradigm (Elder, Johnson, and Crosnoe 2003), global regularities that cut across life domains in multidimensional and linked lives are theoretically plausible, but at present we know next to nothing about them.

Developing appropriate methodology for studying such "global" intergenerational regularities in process outcomes beyond simplistic similarity of parents and children in point-in-time outcomes is therefore much needed. GIMSA is motivated by this challenge, and I very much welcome the authors' efforts. However, if GIMSA is to be fruitful in future research, I believe more elaborated theoretical considerations are necessary rather than allusions to the possible general importance of global interdependence, as suggested by RBL. They do not explain why global and not local interdependence is more likely in their example of mothers' and daughters' employment trajectories, nor do they clarify which substantive content of global interdependence is theoretically likely in the study population. This theoretical "aimlessness" is visible in their difficulty to make sense of the rather confusing results of a 10-group typology without a clear takeaway message.

In fairness, developing more careful theoretical arguments about expected globally interdependent regularities is not a flaw of GIMSA as a methodological tool but a collective task for future research. As a starting point, this requires (1) specifying conditions under which global, local, or no interdependence is likely in dyadic sequences and (2) drawing on established sociological theory to specify hypotheses about which substantive content patterns of global interdependence will take, rather than just "fishing for patterns" (Wu 2000).

2. WHAT'S THE ADDED VALUE OF GIMSA?

Despite my enthusiasm for recognizing the importance of global interdependence in process outcomes, I have reservations about the added value of GIMSA. First, I am concerned about the large number of decisions that must be made in the multistep approach. Second, given this complicated implementation, I am not convinced that GIMSA provides sufficient added value over the more straightforward approach of MCSA to study global regularities in dyadic sequences. These concerns are amplified by the chosen example in RBL of mothers' and daughters' employment trajectories in France, which seems ill-suited to demonstrate a potential added value of GIMSA.

2.1. *Example Application*

A good empirical example to demonstrate new methods should explicate the added value of the method over other approaches with accessible and straightforward results that could clearly not have been obtained in any other way. Mothers' and daughters' employment patterns, however, are precisely not a straightforward case of global interdependence. Arguably two main sources of differences in mothers' and daughters' employment trajectories in the second half of the twentieth century in France will be (1) a delay of daughters' employment onset due to educational expansion and (2) more frequent interruptions in daughters' employment careers as they strive to combine work and family while entering the labor market in greater numbers than their mothers. These are mainly timing differences of delay and interruption. Issues of timing, however, are a form of local interdependence, as also noted by RBL. Rather than choosing a cross-domain application (e.g., of mothers' employment and daughters' family formation) the difference in the example application merely lies in longer observation periods for the mothers and a slightly different alphabet of employment states, which are both driven by data restrictions, not by substantive consideration. These weaknesses of the example application are apparent in the confusing detailed results that in my opinion struggle to demonstrate an added value of GIMSA, particularly without prior theoretical considerations about which patterns might be expected. However, an unconvincing choice of example is not necessarily a flaw of the method itself, which leads to my core concerns about GIMSA.

2.2. Complicated Multistep Procedure

GIMSA proceeds in four steps, each of which requires nontrivial decisions by the researcher. Thorough robustness checks would require one to modify multiple parameters in each decision step: dissimilarity measure to determine sequence similarity, multidimensional scaling (MDS), canonical PLS, and clustering. In practice, it is easy to lose track of what one is actually doing in such a procedure and what might possibly be generating the final results. When replicating this study with the data and code provided by RBL, I found that the results were highly sensitive to different strategies for weighting the PLS components before generating the distance matrix for the clustering. Weighting the PLS components, RBL argue, is important to ensure that the results are not merely driven by different degrees of heterogeneity in the sequences in the two dimensions (here mothers and daughters). RBL conduct several robustness checks, keeping the number of clusters fixed at 10 groups for each weighting approach. They report considerably stable typologies—when the number of clusters is fixed at 10. However, under different weighting scenarios, cluster cutoff criteria support very different cluster solutions that do not justify retaining 10 groups for each scenario—panels A to D of Figure 1. In practice, the applied user, whose choice of clusters is guided by cluster cutoff criteria, would arrive at different numbers of clusters with vastly different substantive conclusions, depending on which weighting of the PLS component was chosen. Figure 1 visualizes cluster cutoff criteria (Studer 2013) for different weighting strategies of the PLS components. Panel A on the left side in Figures 2, 3, and 4 shows three cluster solutions supported by these cutoff criteria after GIMSA. Panel B on the right side in Figures 2, 3, and 4 compares them with results obtained with different specifications of MCSA that are discussed below.

Specifically, in scenario 1 without weighting the PLS components, cluster cutoff criteria in panel A of Figure 1 support a 4-cluster solution,

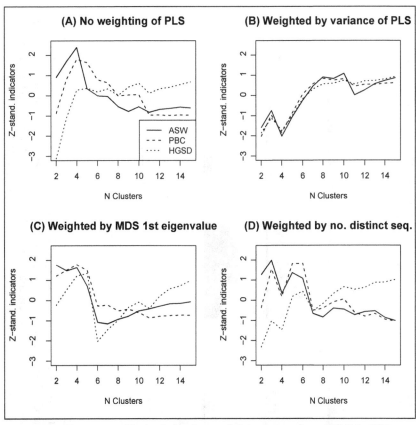

Figure 1. Cluster cutoff criteria by four weighting scenarios of PLS in RBL.
Note: ASW = average silhouette width; PBC = point biserial correlation; PLS = partial least square; HGSD = Hubert's gamma (Sommer's *D*); RBL = Robette, Bry, and Lelièvre.

in which all groups of daughters look very similar. The mothers are divided into 4 groups depending on the one state that dominated their lifetime employment (clusters in Figure 2A). We can conclude that there are 4 distinct groups of mothers (average silhouette width [ASW] = .42), but there are no systematic intergenerational links between mother and daughter trajectories. Scenario B as reported in RBL, weighting by the variance of the PLS components, yields 10 clusters as the best solution, supported by a much lower ASW of .20, meaning that this is a much less discriminant grouping (Figure 1B). However, we might conclude that there is some complex global interdependence between the mother and daughter trajectories as reported in RBL.

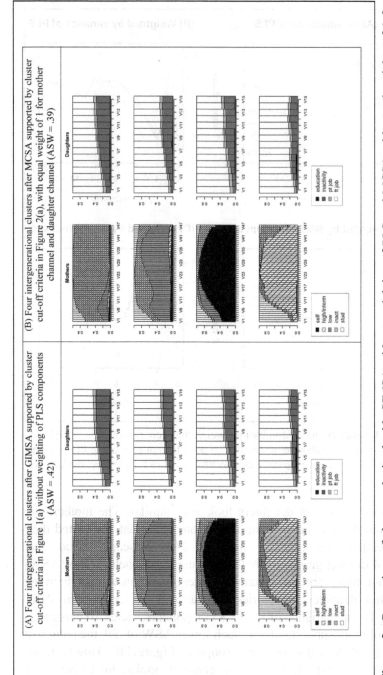

Figure 2. Comparison of clusters obtained with GIMSA without weighting of PLS and MCSA with equal weights of 1 for mothers and daughters. (A) Four intergenerational clusters after GIMSA supported by cluster cut-off criteria in Figure 1A without weighting of PLS components (ASW = .42). (B) Four intergenerational clusters after MCSA supported by cluster cutoff criteria in Figure 5A, with equal weight of 1 for mother channel and daughter channel (ASW = .39).

Note: ASW = average silhouette width; ft = full-time; GIMSA = globally interdependent multiple sequence analysis; inact = inactivity; interm = intermediate; MCSA = multichannel sequence analysis; PLS = partial least square; pt = part-time; stud = student.

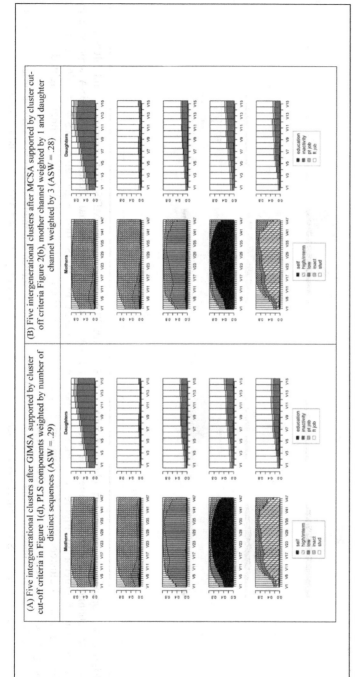

Figure 3. Comparison of clusters obtained with GIMSA with PLS weighted by number of distinct sequences and MCSA with daughter channel weighted three times the mother channel. (A) Five intergenerational clusters after GIMSA supported by cluster cutoff criteria in Figure 1D, PLS components weighted by number of distinct sequences (ASW = .29). (B) Five intergenerational clusters after MCSA supported by cluster cutoff criteria Figure 5B, mother channel weighted by 1 and daughter channel weighted by 3 (ASW = .28).

Note: ASW = average silhouette width; ft = full-time; GIMSA = globally interdependent multiple sequence analysis; inact = inactivity; interm = intermediate; MCSA = multichannel sequence analysis; PLS = partial least square; pt = part-time; stud = student.

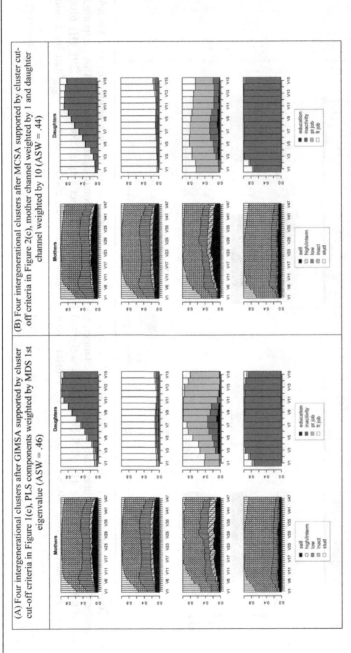

Figure 4. Comparison of clusters obtained with GIMSA with PLS weighted by MDS first eigenvalue and MCSA with daughter channel weighted 10 times the mother channel. (A) Four intergenerational clusters after GIMSA supported by cluster cut-off criteria in Figure 1(c), PLS components weighted by 1 and daughter channel weighted by 10 (ASW = .44). (B) Four intergenerational clusters after MCSA supported by cluster cutoff criteria in Figure 5C, mother channel weighted by 1 and daughter channel weighted by 10 (ASW = .44).

Note: ASW = average silhouette width; ft = full-time; GIMSA = globally interdependent multiple sequence analysis; inact = inactivity; interm = intermediate; MCSA = multichannel sequence analysis; PLS = partial least square; pt = part-time; stud = student.

Weighting by the MDS first eigenvalue in scenario C yields either 2 clusters at an ASW of .47 or 4 clusters at an ASW of .46, which again is a much more discriminant grouping than for the originally proposed 10 clusters (Figure 1C). The 4 clusters in this case are strongly patterned by the dominant state of the daughters (Figure 4A): one group that goes from full-time to inactivity, one working full-time, one working part-time, and a predominantly inactive group. The 4 mother clusters are very similar. Again we would conclude that there is no intergenerational interdependence in the mother and daughter sequences (Figure 4A). In scenario D, when weighting by the number of distinct sequences, either a 3-cluster (ASW = .31) or a 5-cluster (ASW = .29) solution is supported by the cutoff criteria (Figure 1D). The 5-cluster solution shows two groups, in which the mother is inactive, one in which daughters move from full-time work to inactivity and one in which daughters work full-time throughout (Figure 3A). This does suggest some global interdependence in intergenerational employment patterns for mother-daughter dyads in which the mother was mostly inactive.

In sum, two of these weighting scenarios of the PLS components support no global interdependence, while two support different substantive contents of global interdependence. What am I to conclude from these different results, derived by varying just one among many choices necessary in GIMSA? This is particularly so because I lack any concrete theoretical rationale about which extent and substantive content of global interdependence I might be looking for. These results may simply reflect the ill-suited example application, if in this case there is no interdependence, or if local and not global interdependence is the dominant link between mothers' and daughters' employment. Possibly, in an example application in which strong global interdependence exists, GIMSA would consistently find it. The foregoing example, however, does draw attention to the potential pitfalls of methodological procedures involving many steps with many decisions to be made. This in turn warrants careful consideration of whether we can obtain the same results in a more simple and straightforward way.

2.3. *Added Value to MCSA*

Next to cross-tabulating separate cluster solutions for the mother and daughter sequences (see RBL), MCSA is the most obvious alternative to uncover patterns of global interdependence (Fasang and Raab 2014;

Gauthier et al. 2010; Pollock 2007). In MCSA, two members of a dyad—for example, a mother and daughter—are treated as two separate channels of an intergenerational dyadic sequence. MCSA is more straightforward to apply and can identify patterns of global interdependence in fewer analysis steps, and thus fewer possibly consequential decisions are necessary from the researcher. The researcher specifies channel-specific substitution costs and weights attached to each channel and executes the MCSA that generates a pairwise distance matrix, which is entered into a cluster analysis. Compared with GIMSA, all decisions related to the MDS and PLS are omitted. RBL argue that MCSA is not practical for uncovering patterns of global interdependence because it requires sequences of equal length on both dimensions. A simple and straightforward way to deal with sequences of unequal length is to insert a missing value state to fill the gap between the shorter and longer sequence dimensions.

After filling in the remaining time of the daughter sequences with a missing value state, I used MCSA on mothers' and daughters' employment histories with constant substitution costs of 2 and indel costs of 1 as a standard choice (MacIndoe and Abbott 2004). Depending on how the mother and the daughter sequences were weighted, I found substantively the same results as in different weighting scenarios of the PLS in GIMSA (Figures 2–4). Three weighting scenarios that place different emphasis on the longer and shorter sequence dimension were tested: equal weights of one for the mother and daughter channel, weighting the daughter channel 3 times the mother channel, and weighting the daughter channel 10 times the mother channel (see cluster cutoff criteria in Figure 5). Figures 2 to 4 show systematic comparisons of typologies supported by the cluster cutoff criteria in Figures 1 and 5 obtained with GIMSA and MCSA.

Figure 2 shows a four-group typology supported for GIMSA without weights of the PLS components (Figure 1A) and MCSA with equal weights of 1 for the mother and daughter channel. The correlation between the two cluster solutions is .86, and the clusters in the two panels would lead to the same substantive conclusion: there is strong patterning into four groups in the mother generation and no intergenerational global interdependence.

This might result from the longer observation periods and correspondingly higher potential variation in the mother sequences that are roughly three times as long as the daughter sequences. To account for this different sequence length and the resulting greater possible variation

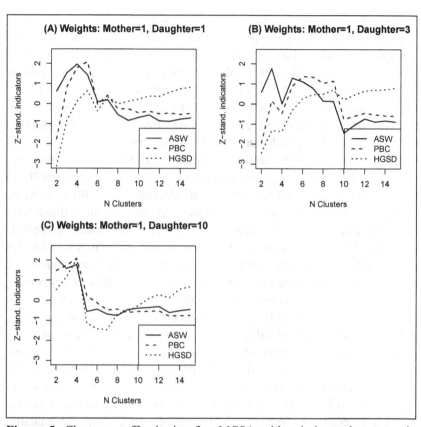

Figure 5. Cluster cutoff criteria after MCSA with missing value states in daughter sequences in different weighting scenarios of the two channels.
Note: ASW = average silhouette width; PBC = point biserial correlation; HGSD = Hubert's gamma (Sommer's *D*); MCSA = multichannel sequence analysis.

for mothers, I repeated MCSA, weighting the daughter channel three times the mother channel. Figure 3 compares the five-cluster solution supported by the cutoff criteria for this MCSA with GIMSA weighting the PLS by the number of distinct sequences. The results support some global intergenerational dependence, such that dyads in which mothers were mainly inactive are split into a group in which the daughters were consistently employed full-time and a group in which the daughters were employed full-time but then became inactive. Again, in this comparison, GIMSA and MCSA would lead to the exact same substantive conclusions.

Figure 4 compares GIMSA weighted by the MDS first eigenvalue and MCSA when weighting the daughter sequences 10 times the mother sequences. I find four identical clusters supported by the cutoff criteria in Figures 1 and 5 that are driven mainly by differences in the daughter sequences. Finally, allowing for 10 clusters after MCSA weighting the daughter sequences three times the mother sequences shows 10 groups (not presented here) that correspond closely to what is found with GIMSA and presented by RBL. Note that these 10 groups are, however, not supported by the cluster cutoff criteria after MCSA, although there is some support for a 9-cluster solution (Figure 5B).

The bottom line is that in this application, MCSA with missing value states for the shorter sequences yields the same substantive results as GIMSA, while requiring fewer necessary decisions from the researcher. Therefore, MCSA is more applicable and transparent without any apparent disadvantage compared with GIMSA in this example application. Attaching simple numerical weights to the two channels in MCSA is more intuitive than the complex weighting of the PLS components by MDS eigenvalues, variances, and the number of distinct sequences. Weighting of the channels also allows researchers to account for unequal sequence length by placing higher weights on the shorter channel filled with a missing value state. It is straightforward to include different alphabets of states in the two channels in MCSA. Because transformation costs can be defined separately for each channel, different rationales for sequence similarity in the two dimensions are easy to implement. When gaps are filled with missing value states, it is also possible to consider dimensions with different time units. Technically, MCSA easily extends to triads and beyond if a researcher wants to examine multigenerational patterns by including additional channels. In contrast to RBL, I therefore find the simple procedure of filling in gaps with missing value states in MCSA more practical—not less—and less error prone compared with the four-step procedure of GIMSA.

I want to conclude by emphasizing my enthusiasm for the attention given to improving the methods for analyzing patterns of global interdependence in linked life-course sequences. Furthermore, I do not want to jump to conclusions. There might be sociologically important and interesting empirical cases in which GIMSA has added value over MCSA. For instance, with different time units and extremely unequal sequence length, GIMSA might indeed be more useful. For the reasons outlined above, on the basis of the example of mothers' and daughters' employment trajectories in France, I am not (yet) convinced that GIMSA provides sufficient added value to cross-tabulations of separate cluster solutions or MCSA to make the complicated multistep procedure worthwhile.

To push the analysis of dyadic sequences forward, a useful step in future research would certainly be a simple test to decide whether there are associations—any dependence—in two sequence dimensions at all before continuing to disentangle whether these are local or global. More generally, if sequence analysis is to do more for us, we need to push rigorous theorizing and to gather more empirical applications, including systematic replications and reproductions of previous work. One important task for researchers is to delineate the complementary added value of different sequence analysis techniques for specific research questions among themselves as well as in comparison with adjacent methods, such as group-based trajectory modeling or latent class models. Methods are tools for meeting ends, but they are not ends in themselves. We should therefore judge them by their applicability and usefulness in helping us address sociologically important questions.

Acknowledgments

I thank Marcel Raab for fruitful discussions related to this commentary and Zachary Van Winkle for editing and proofreading.

References

Abbott, Andrew. 1992. "From Causes to Events: Notes on Narrative Positivism." *Sociological Methods and Research* 20(4):428–55.

Abbott, Andrew. 2005. "The Idea of Outcome in U.S. Sociology." Pp. 393–426 in *The Politics of Method in the Human Sciences*, edited by G. Steinmetz. Durham, NC: Duke University Press.

Blanchard, Philippe, Felix Bühlmann, and Jacques-Antoine Gauthier, eds. 2014. *Advances in Sequence Analysis: Theory, Method, Applications*. New York: Springer.

Elder, Glen H., Monica Kirkpatrick Johnson, and Robert Crosnoe. 2003. "The Emergence and Development of Life Course Theory." Pp. 3–19 in *Handbook of the Life Course*, edited by J. T. Mortimer and M. J. Shanahan. New York: Kluwer Academic/Plenum.

Fasang, Anette E., and Marcel Raab. 2014. "Beyond Transmission: Intergenerational Patterns of Family Formation among Middle-class American Families." *Demography* 51(5):1703–28.

Gauthier, Jacques-Antoine, Eric D. Widmer, Philipp Bucher, and Cédric Notredame. 2010. "Multichannel Sequence Analysis Applied to Social Science Data." Pp. 1–38 in *Sociological Methodology*, vol. 40, edited by Tim Futing Liao. Hoboken, NJ: Wiley-Blackwell.

MacIndoe, Heather, and Andrew Abbott. 2004. "Sequence Analysis and Optimal Matching Techniques for Social Science Data." Pp. 387–406 in *Handbook of Data Analysis*, edited by A. Bryman and M. Hardy. London: Sage Ltd.

Pollock, Gary. 2007. "Holistic Trajectories: A Study of Combined Employment, Housing, and Family Careers by Using Multiple-sequence Analysis." *Journal of the Royal Statistical Society, Series A, Statistics in Society*, 170(1), 167–83.

Studer, Matthias. 2013. "Weighted Cluster Library Manual: A Practical Guide to
    Creating Typologies of Trajectories in the Social Sciences with R." *LIVES Working
    Papers*, 24.
Wu, Lawrence L. 2000. "Some Comments on 'Sequence Analysis and Optimal
    Matching Methods in Sociology: Review and Prospect.'" *Sociological Methods and
    Research* 29(1):41–64.

Author Biography

Anette Eva Fasang is a professor of microsociology at Humboldt University of Berlin
and head of the demography and inequality research group at the WZB Berlin Social
Science Center. She obtained her PhD from Jacobs University Bremen and completed
postdoctoral research at Yale University and Columbia University. Her research interests include social demography, stratification, life-course sociology, family demography, and methods for longitudinal data analysis.

COMMENT: HOW TO MAKE
A LONG STORY SHORT

Jacques-Antoine Gauthier*

*University of Lausanne, Lausanne, Switzerland
Corresponding Author: Jacques-Antoine Gauthier, jacques-antoine.gauthier@unil.ch
DOI: 10.1177/0081175015588093

Using sequence analysis, along with two types of scaling techniques and
eventually cluster analysis, Robette, Bry, and Lelièvre (this volume, pp.
1–44; hereafter RBL) provide a methodological approach to elegantly
address several key issues of the multidimensionality of social phenomenon over time, such as the timing of life events, the historical location
of individuals, and the interdependencies that may develop between them.
One of the main challenges tackled by RBL in this paper is to address the
issue of assessing models of intergenerational transmission, using temporally distal life trajectories of varying length by identifying "preferential
dyads among the lineages, that is, recurrent sequences conditioned by the
social cohesion between mother and daughter: an internal *structure* of
transmission in the lineage concerning employment patterns."

While the paper has obviously many virtues—as evidenced by its publication in *Sociological Methodology*—the symposium organized around

it offers the opportunity to discuss more openly some of its features, taken as general questions in the field of sequence analysis. Let us consider the following three dimensions: (1) validation, (2) epistemology of sequences, and (3) the link between a formal model and the social sciences.

The first point concerns the complexity of the proposed procedure characterized by a four-step analytical strategy—optimal matching analysis (OMA), multidimensional scaling (MDS), partial least squares (PLS), and cluster analysis—each of them being sensitive to various parameter settings. According to the authors, "one of the advantages of GIMSA [globally interdependent multiple sequence analysis] is that it allows a choice of metrics that specifically fit the theoretical questions and data limitations under study, in a separate way for each dimension." Some years ago, the sole cost-setting issue within OMA gave rise to a lively debate (cf. Levine 2000). Despite the fact that RBL explicitly claim that they do not want to discuss each metric separately, one still may wonder if there is not a need for some quantitative validations to support the demonstration and serve as a first delineation of the range of application of GIMSA. For instance, when no comparison is available, how can we assess the relevance of choosing the longest common subsequence to compare mothers' trajectories and dynamic Hamming distance for daughters as a guarantee that timing will be central in the former case and provide order in the latter?

In line with the above statement, one may regret that no comparison is made between GIMSA and one or the other strategies presented in section 2—for example, multichannel sequence analysis (MCSA)—using the data set at hand or some simulated data. This would have given space to a more practical discussion on the ability of selected approaches to reveal various relational structures in the data, be it interindividual and/or temporal. Indeed, the choice of strategy 4 (cross-tabulation) to make the comparison presented in the paper is debatable, as it is probably the least parsimonious, and it is less able to capture the actual interdependencies of trajectories at the dyadic level (Gauthier et al. 2010). From a methodological perspective, the ability to assess the type and strength of the relations between "channels" is of central importance in multidimensional sequence analysis and calls for exploration and validation.

The next validation issue concerns RBL's statement that "in the case of contemporaneous dimensions, MCSA is probably more appropriate than GIMSA." A simple comparison of the output provided by both approaches would have provided an empirical answer. In MCSA-like approaches, the sequence comparison is made channel-wise (the unit of analysis being the mother-daughter's dyad), so a systematic sequence length difference between channels is probably not so much a problem and could easily be empirically addressed. Moreover, there is a very simple and parsimonious alternative way to address this issue by considering mother and daughter trajectories as consecutive in a single sequence (the length being equal to that of the mother's sequence plus that of the daughter). Coding the data this way conserves the integrity of each dyad, as well as the proper timing of each of the individual trajectories. Applied to the data provided by the authors, the results stemming from this latter approach are quite similar to those stemming from GIMSA and could provide a nice basis for a methodological comparison.

The second point relates to the epistemology of sequence analysis as developed by Abbott (2001:183). In this perspective, one of the most promising features of sequence analysis lies in its capacity to capture the narrative dimension of social processes in particular when using quantitative longitudinal data. Using two steps of data reduction, GIMSA does indeed efficiently concentrate the information contained in the data, but by doing so, it loses to a certain extent its temporal patterning—the *story* it contains—giving less space to the underlying process under study. Hence, we could expect some more exploration concerning the ability of GIMSA to capture and conserve time-varying patterns caused by recursion, alternation, and/or repetition of statuses in individual life-courses. In other words, there is a risk that the measure of global interdependence provided by GIMSA might eventually go a step back to a variable-based approach. This may artifactually result in reducing life-courses to *stage processes*, limiting the opportunities to conceptualize and analyze social processes as *careers* and *interactional fields* (Abbott 1992). In the data used by the authors, the small size of the alphabet available to build sequences reduces drastically the possibility of observing such variations. For instance, among the 18 types of mother and daughter employment histories, only 2 are characterized by internal variation over time (one transition).

In conclusion, although the explicit aim of the paper is chiefly methodological, there is a need to systematically discuss the specific added value of approaches such as that proposed by GIMSA for research in sequence analysis in the social sciences. We must consider the point raised by Lesnard (2006:10) when he underlies the fact that axiomatic approaches may be of little relevance to social scientists, even if they contribute undeniably to formal developments of sequence analysis. In biology, for instance, the development of sequence analytical methods is directly linked to the theoretical and empirical knowledge concerning the organizational principles of nucleic acids and proteins. As a generalized example of a new and efficient emerging methodological approach, GIMSA offers an interesting basis for a discussion on this issue in the frame of the symposium dedicated to it.

References

Abbott, Andrew. 1992. "From Causes to Events: Notes on Narrative Positivism." *Sociological Methods and Research* 20(4):428–55.

Abbott, Andrew. 2001. *Time Matters: On Theory and Method.* Chicago: University of Chicago Press.

Gauthier, Jacques-Antoine, Eric D. Widmer, Philipp Bucher, and Cédric Notredame. 2010. "Multichannel Sequence Analysis Applied to Social Science Data." Pp. 1–38 in *Sociological Methodology*, vol. 40, edited by Tim Futing Liao. Hoboken, NJ: Wiley-Blackwell.

Lesnard, Laurent. 2006. "Optimal Matching and Social Sciences." Série Des Documents de Travail Du CREST(01). Retrieved January 23, 2015 (http://halshs.archives-ouvertes.fr/halshs-00008122/).

Levine, Joel H. 2000. "But What Have You Done for Us Lately?" *Sociological Methods and Research* 29(1):34–40.

Author Biography

Jacques-Antoine Gauthier is a senior lecturer at the Life Course and Inequality Research Centre at the University of Lausanne. His current research focuses on modeling and analyzing longitudinal data on life-courses. The central issue of his research concerns the time-related construction of individual life trajectories, notably when experiencing major transitions such as conjugality and parenthood. A second field of research focuses on the range of applications of sequence analyses (costs and multidimensionality issues) and on the visualization of their results.

COMMENT: BRIDGING THE GAP BETWEEN LIFE-COURSE CONCEPTS AND METHODS

*Eliza K. Pavalko**

*Indiana University, Bloomington, IN, USA
Corresponding Author: Eliza K. Pavalko, epavalko@indiana.edu
DOI: 10.1177/0081175015587279

Robette, Bry, and Lelièvre (RBL; this volume, pp. 1–44) provide a powerful new tool related to globally interdependent multiple sequence analysis (GIMSA) and bring us closer to fully investigating the central questions of life-course research—how lives unfold over time, both in a historical context and in their interdependence with others. A long-standing challenge of the life-course perspective has been to match empirical analysis with the complexity suggested by life-course concepts and theory. These new developments in sequence methodology move us much closer to closing that gap.

Life-course research defines trajectories as sequences of roles and transitions (Elder, Johnson, and Crosnoe 2003). Trajectories provide a dynamic understanding of the broader patterns of events across the life-course, and the broader trajectory, although composed of transitions, provides important context for understanding any single transition. Our understanding of a job transition, for example, becomes far deeper when we also know the broader context of the work career in which it is embedded. Although trajectories have been a central theoretical concept since the early development of the life-course perspective, previous researchers in the field had few quantitative tools for their analysis. The analysis of transitions, on the other hand, fit well with event-history analysis, and so much of the early quantitative analysis of the life-course was dominated by the study of transitions.

The application of methods designed for DNA sequencing to sociological data and questions in the 1980s and 1990s provided a critical breakthrough for the analysis of life-course trajectories (Abbott 1995). Sequence methods, particularly optimal matching, allow us to distill complex information on the order and timing of multiple events to identify a smaller set of ideal types, or sequences. More recently, multidimensional sequence techniques have been developed, allowing the identification of multiple dimensions simultaneously (Gauthier et al. 2010). Because many of the most salient life-course questions focus on the interplay between different domains such as family and work, this is another important step toward modeling the full complexity of the life-course.

RBL's paper marks yet another significant advance in bridging the gap between life-course concepts and methods of analysis. By allowing the identification and comparison of sequences between dyads, GIMSA extends a trajectory approach to the analysis of linked lives. The life-course perspective argues that "lives are lived interdependently and socio-historical influences are expressed through this network of shared relationships" (Elder et al. 2003), but the ability to examine trajectories among dyads of persons from different contexts presents unique challenges. Most important, because of the different contexts for dyad members, constructing one set of sequences that apply to dyad members may be less meaningful than constructing parallel sequences and looking for patterns of regularity between them. As RBL point out, in the case of intergenerational comparisons, the different historical contexts in which parent and child grew up and the changing nature of the transition to adulthood mean that sequences for one generation would likely not apply well to those from another generation. Data limitations, particularly for intergenerational comparisons, may also mean that different types of data are available for parents and children. Having the flexibility to construct parallel sequences for different members of the dyad, from which regularities can be identified, is important for addressing these issues.

A trajectory approach has great potential to expand our understanding of the intergenerational transmission of socioeconomic status and other resources. The ability to compare sequences, such as the entire transition to adulthood or a work career, is particularly valuable for questions about women's employment because of the greater likelihood of movement in and out of the labor force. However, the ability to map career sequences is also important for contemporary cohorts of men and women because of the changing nature of labor-force mobility. A wealth of questions about intergenerational transmission of other resources or behaviors could be further enlightened by sequence comparisons, including family formation (Fasang and Raab 2014), health or health behaviors, or intergenerational transfers of time and money. The application of these methods also extends well beyond intergenerational relationships. For example, the ability to compare sequences between couples could inform a wide range of questions about family, gender, and work, while comparisons of sibling trajectories would allow even clearer understanding of family and individual influences on the life-course.

These new developments in sequence methodologies bring us much closer to closing the gap between the life-course vision to understand lives dynamically, contextually, and interdependently with the methods for doing so. Their flexibility, however, will also encourage further elaboration of life-course theory. The ability to construct different trajectories for dyad members and search for regularities between them challenges us to clearly define the boundaries of various trajectories and identify the key information that distinguishes one trajectory from another. All sequence methods would also benefit from greater theoretical attention to the appropriate time frame for a given sequence, including attention to the duration of the sequence and where the sequence falls in the life-course. In many cases, these decisions are determined by data availability, but the flexibility offered by these new methodological developments provides both greater latitude and a greater need for theoretical guidance.

References

Abbott, Andrew. 1995. "Sequence Analysis: New Methods for Old Ideas." *Annual Review of Sociology* 21:93–113.

Elder, Glen H., Jr., Monica Kirkpatrick Johnson, and Robert Crosnoe. 2003. "The Emergence and Development of the Life Course." Pp. 3–22 in *Handbook of the Life Course*, edited by J. T. Mortimer and M. J. Shanahan. New York: Plenum.

Fasang, Anette Eva, and Marcel Raab. 2014. "Beyond Transmission: Intergenerational Patterns of Family Formation among Middle-class American Families." *Demography* 51(5):1703–28.

Gauthier, Jacques-Antoine, Eric D. Widmer, Philipp Bucher, and Cédric Notredame. 2010. "Multichannel Sequence Analysis Applied to Social Science Data." Pp. 1–38 in *Sociological Methodology*, vol. 40, edited by Tim Futing Liao. Hoboken, NJ: Wiley-Blackwell.

Author Biography

Eliza K. Pavalko is the Allen D. and Polly S. Grimshaw Professor of Sociology at Indiana University. Her primary research interests focus on relationships among paid work, unpaid work, and health across the life-course and on intersections of individual aging and social change. Recent work has examined these issues through attention to cohort shifts in women's paid employment and health, caregiving, employment and workplace policies, and the health effects of work hours for midlife men and women.

COMMENT: IMPLYING SEQUENCES USING SCORES—SOME CONSIDERATIONS

*Raffaella Piccarreta**

*Bocconi University, Milan, Italy
Corresponding Author: Raffaella Piccarreta, raffaella.piccarreta@unibocconi.it
DOI: 10.1177/0081175015587281

The joint analysis of more domains is surely of great interest, and in my opinion it will become one of the most discussed topics in forthcoming research on sequence analysis.

Robette, Bry, and Lelièvre (RBL; this volume, pp. 1–44) consider a procedure to jointly analyze only *two* domains, and they apply it to the particular case when the trajectories in the two domains have different lengths. The results obtained with the new procedure are compared with those provided by the approach (called strategy 4 in the paper) that involves analyzing the association between the clusters determined on the basis of the two domain-specific dissimilarity matrices. Thus, the sequences here are simplified using clusters. The new method proceeds along the same direction, because the sequences in each domain are *substituted* by a set of multidimensional scaling (MDS) scores, and the suitability of the procedure strongly depends (in the first place) on the suitability of this substitution. Partial least squares (PLS) is then applied to the sets of MDS scores, and cluster analysis is finally applied to the PLS scores. Hence, compared with strategy 4, clusters are based not on the original dissimilarities but rather on a "double" transformation of the dissimilarity data. Clearly, each step involves a substantial compression of the information: the initial passage from sequences to dissimilarities is followed by passages from dissimilarities to MDS scores, from MDS scores to PLS scores, and finally from PLS scores to clusters. The PLS factors are evidently reasonable only if the dissimilarities describe the sequences well and if MDS factors describe the dissimilarities well.

Clearly it is not easy, perhaps impossible, to monitor this process carefully and to have a clear understanding of the impact of each step on the final results. This situation also occurs because of the large number of choices (and consequently of possible solutions) needed to apply the technique (choosing the dissimilarity measures for the two domains, choosing the MDS technique, choosing the number of MDS dimensions, etc.).

In addition to these considerations, a more "philosophical" issue arises here. We participated in a heated debate in the literature on the proper choice of a dissimilarity criterion. RBL seem to be convinced that moving further, and substituting the original sequences with MDS scores—thus converting the object of interest from sequences to real vectors—is a natural and acceptable step. Instead, the different methods introduced in the literature to jointly analyze more domains attempt to combine information relative to the domains by properly extending the techniques developed for the case when one domain is studied. So, for example, strategy 1 is based on the combination of the alphabets, strategy 2 on the combination of costs, and strategy 3 on the combination of the dissimilarity matrices. Actually, I think that proposing a reasonable and effective extension is the main methodological difficulty in this field.

Nonetheless, the quality of a procedure can surely be also evaluated on the basis of the quality of its results. We therefore move to a substantial discussion of the application, which surely constitutes the core of the paper, focusing specifically on the comparison with the results obtained using strategy 4. After having transformed the two sets of sequences into two MDS vectors, a PLS is applied. As is well known, the aim of PLS is to determine a projection subspace in which the relation between the two sets of MDS factors "is maximal." From this point of view, the clusters obtained using the procedure will emphasize at best the relations among the two domains (as summarized by their MDS scores), if they exist. Even so, association cannot be "created" using such a procedure, and consequently we will typically end up with a set of clusters having very clear and well-matching structures and a set of residual clusters that will possibly be homogeneous only with respect to one of the two domains.

In this sense, we can expect this procedure to summarize efficiently the most relevant tendencies observed in the cross-tabulation of the domain-specific clusters (strategy 4). Actually, RBL claim that

> GIMSA [globally interdependent multiple sequence analysis] is more parsi-monious than strategy 4 . . . but it cannot be seen as a means to simplify the combinations of the contingency table produced with strategy 4. This is a completely different method, which leads to a different clustering.

I disagree with this statement. To understand why, observe in Table 2 (in the paper) that the first daughters' cluster (mostly full-time employment, in the first row of Table 2) is split into four subclusters according to the trajectories characterizing mothers. These subclusters are recovered by GIMSA clusters 1, 4, 2, and 7 (see Appendix D in the paper and Figure 1 below). Next, the second daughters' cluster (mostly part-time employment [PT], in the second row of Table 2 in the paper) is almost entirely included in the ninth GIMSA cluster; thus, the "mostly PT" daughters are grouped together irrespective of their mothers' characteristics (which are actually described as "diverse" in Table 4 in the paper). Following the same reasoning, we can easily understand from Appendix D that the GIMSA procedure substantially proposes an aggregation of the combinations in Table 2 into a reduced number of clusters, and as such it provides us with a reorganization of the combinations of the clusters obtained separately.

In my opinion, this is not a limit of the procedure. Indeed, it can be very useful (even if alternative criteria could be used) to rationalize the results of strategy 4. Also, it does not require the specification of very detailed domain-based partitions, and it is directly focused on a combined partition highlighting the relations between the domains. Nonetheless, this aspect of the procedure must be kept in mind to better understand and interpret its results, and the labels of the GIMSA should be given accordingly. With respect to this point, I think that

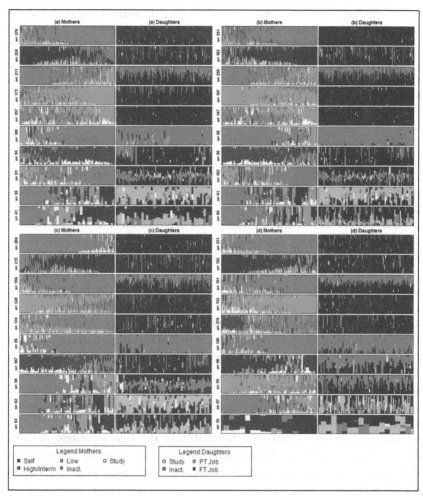

Figure 1. Index plots of the partitions obtained by applying clustering analysis (Ward criterion): (a) to the partial least squares scores on the basis of the two sets of five (for the mothers' domain) and four (for the daughters' domain) multidimensional scaling (MDS) factors; (b) to the canonical correlation analysis scores on the basis of the two sets of five (for the mothers' domain) and four (for the daughters' domain) MDS factors; (c) to the whole set of MDS (standardized) factors (five plus four); and (d) to a reduced set of four MDS (standardized) factors (two for each domain).

the index plots (reported in Figure 1 here) should be used instead of the state distributions plots to describe and label the clusters, because in the latter plots, it is not possible to understand clearly whether a given state having a low frequency characterizes a small number of

Table 1. Proportions of Discrepancy in Each Domain Explained by the Partitions Obtained Using Different Criteria

	(a) MDS/PLS	(b) MDS/CCA	(c) MDS	(d) Reduced set of MDS
Mothers	.395	.359	.440	.443
Daughters	.456	.477	.374	.508

sequences dominated by it or instead is only rarely present in some of the trajectories in the cluster.

Last but not least, if we accept the simplification of sequences through MDS scores completely, PLS is only *one* of the methods that can be used to obtain combined clusters. For the sake of exemplification, in Figure 1, the index plots are reported relative to the 10-cluster partitions obtained by applying hierarchical clustering analysis (with Ward criterion) to (a) the PLS scores on the basis of the two sets of MDS factors (five factors for the mothers' domain and four for the daughters' domain)—that is, the approach used in the paper; (b) the scores obtained by applying canonical correlation analysis (CCA) to the two sets of MDS factors; (c) the whole set of the MDS (standardized) factors; and (d) a reduced set of MDS (standardized) factors (the first two MDS factors for each domain). As is evident from Figure 1, the solutions obtained using the first three approaches lead to rather similar results, whereas the last approach leads to clusters a bit more homogeneous with respect to the mothers' domain (even if the fifth cluster is quite heterogeneous).

To quantify and summarize the quality of the four solutions, we can refer to the proportions of the discrepancy in each domain explained by the obtained partitions (a criterion also considered in the paper), reported in Table 1.

It is interesting to observe that, besides any qualitative consideration based on the interpretation of the obtained clusters, the last approach, focused only on the first two MDS factors, performs better than the others. This suggests that an "optimal" or reasonable choice at an intermediate step of the procedure proposed in the paper does not necessarily lead to an optimal final solution.

In the end, the point here is clear: "Can sequences be so easily substituted by the MDS scores?" Of course, in some applications this substitution can be perfectly reasonable and can lead to good results. Nonetheless, a new method is being proposed here, and in addition to its performance in one or more applications, our attention should be focused on its theoretical implications. Actually, if the answer to the question is yes, all the problems concerning the analysis of sequences vanish. All the multivariate analysis techniques become available, and we can skip all the sequence-based procedures introduced in the literature to maintain the level of simplification of the trajectories as low as possible. (Think, for example, of discrepancy analysis, or the problem of predicting sequences.)

Author Biography

Raffaella Piccarreta is a research scientist at Bocconi University in Milan, Italy. She holds a PhD in statistics, and her research areas include multivariate data analysis, sequence analysis, and dissimilarity data. She has produced several articles on sequence analysis, focusing specifically on clustering algorithms, classification trees, and graphical tools. Her recent research has been focused on the study of the interplay of different domains, on the development of methods to explain and predict life-courses, and on multiway multidimensional scaling. Current research projects include an analysis of the early track of the work career in Italy and a study of the impact of family formation patterns on HIV infection in sub-Saharan countries.

COMMENT: ON THE USE OF GLOBALLY INTERDEPENDENT MULTIPLE SEQUENCE ANALYSIS

Matthias Studer*

*VU University, Amsterdam, The Netherlands
Corresponding Author: Matthias Studer, matthias.studer@unige.ch
DOI: 10.1177/0081175015588095

This comment will focus on the use of three strategies identified by Robette, Bry, and Lelièvre (this volume, pp. 1–44; hereafter RBL)—namely, globally interdependent multiple sequence analysis (GIMSA), multichannel sequence analysis (MCSA), and FS, the so-called fourth strategy (clustering sequences separately and analyzing their relationship afterward). I address more specifically the question of their usefulness for analyzing the relationships between different kinds of trajectories. Meanwhile, I identify possible directions for future research and propose some new tools.

While giving sequence analysis (SA) courses or answering TraMineR-related questions, I have noticed frequent confusion about the goal of cluster analysis (CA), which I would like to clarify here. Because the

Table 1. Joint and Marginal Distributions of Two Ordinal Variables, x and y

	x_1	x_2	x_3	Total
y_1	$\frac{1}{6}$	$\frac{1}{6}$	$\frac{1}{6}$	$\frac{1}{2}$
y_2	$\frac{1}{6}$	$\frac{1}{6}$	$\frac{1}{6}$	$\frac{1}{2}$
Total	$\frac{1}{3}$	$\frac{1}{3}$	$\frac{1}{3}$	1

three aforementioned strategies are based on CA, this discussion is also relevant for our topic.

CA aims to reveal the structure of data by looking at patterns of answers—that is, configurations of the values taken by the included variables. However, this is very different from looking at the relationships among the included dimensions.

Let me briefly present the difference between the two, using a simple example. Suppose we want to analyze two ordinal variables, say x and y, with the joint and marginal distributions shown in Table 1.

In this example, patterns are identified by looking at the joint distribution. For this reason, a six-cluster solution would be a good one according to most indices of clustering quality (e.g., Studer 2013), even if there is no association between x and y. In order to interpret the relationship between x and y, we usually look at the conditional distributions, which tell us whether each value of x is associated with a different distribution of y. We may be able to deduce the association by comparing the joint distribution with the marginal ones. However, this soon becomes a difficult task when using CA, because CA may well regroup cells irrespective of their rows and columns. In that case, we would lack a reference model (such as statistical independence) to determine whether there is an association and to interpret the form of this association.

Using CA to analyze the relationship between two (or more) variables is also risky because the reduction of information made by CA can potentially lead to wrong conclusions. For instance, suppose that we retained a two-cluster solution according to the gray scale in our previous example. We could well think that higher values of x imply higher values in y, which is wrong here. Following a similar reasoning, CA can hide a significant association between two (or more) variables.

Hence, a good clustering is not a sign of a relationship between the variables, but rather it is a sign of homogeneous and well-separated configurations of answers. In other words, clustering cannot be used to test or to interpret the form of an association. This is why we should always use a proper test to confirm an association identified using CA.

Table 2. Standardized Pearson Residuals of the Contingency Table of Daughters' (Rows) and Mothers' (Columns) Trajectories

	Mostly Inactive	Mostly Low	Mostly Self	Mostly High or Intermediate
Mostly FT	−3.19	2.77	.36	1.12
Mostly PT	−.56	−1.12	.42	2.18
From FT to inactivity	.36	−.27	.40	−.82
From PT to FT	−1.16	−.13	1.89	−.34
Mostly inactive	5.12	−3.37	−2.07	−1.35
Interruption	−.02	.63	−.11	−.78

Note: Residuals less than −1.96 can be interpreted as underrepresentation and those higher than 1.96 as overrepresentation of a configuration (Agresti 1990). FT = full-time; PT = part-time.

Does this mean that CA is useless? Of course not. CA can be used to build a typology involving several indicators (or subdimensions) of a given dimension. Because these indicators measure a unique dimension, a typology can be useful to regroup them in only one construct in subsequent analysis. In this case, we make the assumption—and we should justify it sociologically—that these indicators are intrinsically related. Furthermore, in this case, the relationship between the indicators is not the primary interest, or it is analyzed separately. For all these reasons, CA is of interest when looking at one concept or dimension, without being primarily interested in the relationship between the variables or indicators.

What does it imply for SA, GIMSA, MCSA, and FS? For the SA case, Abbott (1992) justified on a theoretical ground the need to analyze trajectories and processes as a whole in order to take their internal logic into account without making too many assumptions on the generating process. However, if important relationships between different moments of the trajectories have been identified using CA, I would still recommend using a specific test to confirm the relation.

In FS, sequences are clustered separately before analyzing the relationship. Hence, the relationship can then be analyzed safely using any categorical data analysis methods.[1] RBL use, for instance, a crosstable to comment on the results (see Table 2 in their article). As noted by RBL, we observe a significant but weak (Cramer's v = .094) relationship between the two kinds of trajectories. A more detailed interpretation of the results can be made by looking at standardized Pearson residuals of the crosstable, as presented in Table 2.

We observe some kind of "inactivity transmission," because daughters with mothers who follow "mostly inactive" trajectories have more chances to be "mostly inactive" themselves. Furthermore, as noted by

RBL, daughters following "mostly part-time" trajectories have more often than expected in the independence case mothers with "mostly high or intermediate" trajectories.

MCSA and GIMSA cannot be used to describe how two (or more) sequences are interrelated, nor can it be used at a local or at a global level. The obtained frequencies of the clusters are difficult to interpret, because we lack the marginal distributions or a reference model that would allow us to interpret the association. In other words, in GIMSA, we do not know what would be the result of the analysis without an association between daughters' and mothers' trajectories, making it very difficult to interpret the relationship between the two.[2]

However, MCSA is useful when a trajectory is measured using different subdimensions—that is, when these subdimensions are studied as a unique concept. For instance, trajectories of hierarchical job positions and firm sizes could be grouped to analyze professional careers. Here again, the relationship between the sequences is not of primary interest.

GIMSA could be of interest if the trajectories under study are different subdimensions of the same concept and if we are not interested in the relationships between these trajectories. Rightly, RBL claim that they are interested in finding the frequent patterns of mother-daughter trajectories, not their relationships. However, when interpreting the results, they soon start interpreting the relationships between the two trajectories by saying that "mothers' inactivity is often linked to daughters' inactivity (and mothers' activity to daughters' full-time employment." As we have shown earlier, such a statement cannot be made safely using CA, and hence GIMSA.

In order to analyze a relationship globally (i.e., without being interested in the local or contemporaneous interdependencies), several other strategies are available. Let me illustrate them using the mother-daughter example. We can cluster mothers' trajectories and look at how much the mother clusters explain the discrepancy of daughters' trajectories using discrepancy analysis (Studer et al. 2011). Here again, we find a significant but weak association (pseudo-R^2 of about 1 percent).

Finally, we can have a more precise understanding of how daughters' trajectories differ according to the typology of mothers' trajectories by looking at the "sequences of typical states" (Studer 2012). Figure 1 presents the "sequences of typical states," visualizing the differences between two or more groups of trajectories. It presents at each time point the typical states of a subpopulation (here according to mothers' trajectories) using implicative statistics, which assess the statistical relevance of a rule of the form "A implies B."[3]

The "mostly inactive" graph in Figure 1 presents at each time point t the relevance of the rule "Having a mostly inactive mothers' trajectory

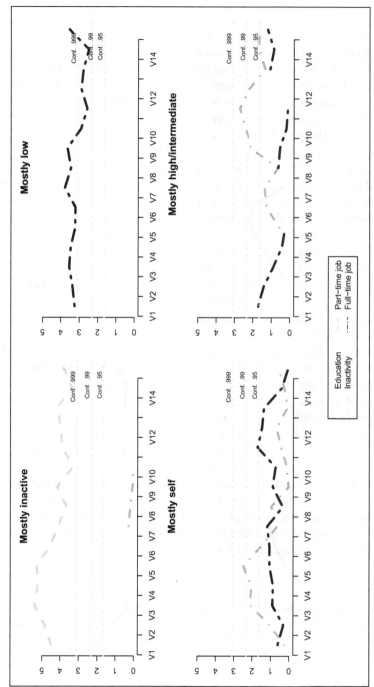

Figure 1. A sequence of typical states of daughters according to the typology of mothers' trajectories.

implies being in state A at time t." The horizontal dashed lines present the confidence thresholds. A rule is considered statistically significant at the 5 percent level if it exceeds the 95 percent confidence horizontal line.[4] Here, we can see that having a mostly inactive mothers' trajectory implies being inactive, and this rule is significant for the whole daughters' trajectory. Interestingly, some rules are significant for only a given period. Having "mostly high or intermediate" mothers' trajectories implies being in education in the beginning of the trajectories (but not later) and being in part-time employment afterward (as noted already by RBL).

This "sequence of typical states" figure can be extended to analyze local relationships. We can look at the typical states of sequence B at time t (daughters) according to the state of sequence A at time t (i.e., mothers). Such a method should allow the study of how the relationship among trajectories evolves over time.

Before concluding, I would like to discuss one final issue. If we use CA to cluster different dimensions and cross-tabulate them with a factors of interest such as cohort, we presuppose an interaction effect. But the relationship might also result from a direct effect. A more parsimonious approach would start by analyzing direct effects and include the interaction term only if it is relevant.

For instance, RBL's Appendix E analyzes how transmission patterns are related to factors such as the daughter birth cohorts. RBL found that the "inactivity transmission" pattern was more frequent in older daughters' birth cohorts than in younger ones. By doing so, they presume an interaction effect between daughters' and mothers' trajectories and daughters' birth cohorts. But this relation may well hide a direct effect.[5] GIMSA does not allow studying the direct effects—because we have only a joint typology— whereas FS (clustering sequences separately) allows this to happen.

In conclusion, I want to clarify a common confusion about the purpose of CA that may well affect GIMSA as well. CA should not be used to interpret or test a relationship, and the same applies to GIMSA. Even if some workarounds are available, we still need a proper method to do it, on a global as well as a local level.

Funding

The author disclosed receipt of the following financial support for the research, authorship, and/or publication of this article: This comment benefited from the support of a postdoctoral fellowship and from the Swiss National Centre of Competence in Research LIVES—Overcoming Vulnerability: Life Course Perspectives, both granted by the Swiss National Science Foundation. The author is grateful to the foundation for its financial assistance.

Notes

1. However, as noted by RBL, the simplification conducted by CA could potentially lower or increase the strength of the association.
2. For this reason, we cannot interpret the relationship even if GIMSA is based on the covariance between the MDS coordinates.
3. It does so by measuring the gap between the expected and the observed number of counterexamples (Gras 1979; Gras et al. 1996; Suzuki and Kodratoff 1998). If we observe many fewer counterexamples than expected under the independence assumption, the rule is considered to be strongly implicative. This gap and its significance are computed using adjusted residuals of a contingency table with continuity correction (Agresti 1990; Ritschard 2005). In order to improve the readability of the graphs, we use here the opposite of the implicative index, which is highly negative for significant rules. The index $I(A \to B)$ measuring the relevance of the rule that "A implies B" reads as follows:

$$I(A \to B) = -\frac{n_{\bar{B}A} + 0.5 - n_{\bar{B}A}^e}{\sqrt{n_{\bar{B}A}^e (\frac{n_{B.}}{n})(1 - \frac{n_{.A}}{n})}},$$

where $n_{\bar{B}A}$ is the observed number of counterexamples, $n_{\bar{B}A}^e$ the expected number of counterexamples in the independence assumption case, $n_{B.}$ the number of times that B is observed, $n_{.A}$ the number of times that A is observed, and n the total number of cases.
4. Confidence is computed using a normal distribution (Ritschard 2005). Rules with a negative implicative index are not represented because they have no meaningful interpretation.
5. Three kinds of effects should be considered. First, "inactivity" trajectories may have been more frequent among older mothers (who thus have older daughters), implying that the configuration "inactive mother"-"inactive daughter" is more frequent. Second, we may apply the same reasoning to daughters' "inactivity" trajectories. Finally, the "rate" of transmission of the inactivity trajectories may have been stronger in older cohorts.

References

Abbott, Andrew. 1992. "From Causes to Events: Notes on Narrative Positivism." *Sociological Method and Research* 20(4):428–55.

Agresti, Alan. 1990. *Categorical Data Analysis*. New York: John Wiley.

Gras, R. 1979. "Contribution à l'Étude Expérimentale et à l'Analyse de Certaines Acquisitions Cognitives et de Certains Objectifs Didactiques." PhD dissertation, University of Rennes, France.

Gras, Régis, Saddo Ag Almouloud, Marc Bailleul, Annie Laher, Maria Polo, Harrisson Ratsimba-Rajohn, and André Totohasina. 1996. "L'Implication Statistique: Nouvelle Méthode Exploratoire de Données." *Recherches en Didactique des Mathématiques*. Grenoble, Switzerland: La Pensée Sauvage.

Ritschard, Gilbert. 2005. "De l'Usage de la Statistique Implicative dans les Arbres de Classification." Pp. 305–14 in *Actes des Troisièmes Rencontres Internationale ASI Analyse Statistique Implicative*, Vol. 2, edited by Régis Gras, Filippo Spagnolo, and Jérôme David. Palermo, Italy: University of Palermo.

Studer, Matthias. 2012. "Étude des Inégalités de Genre en Début de Carrière Académique à l'Aide de Méthodes Innovatrices d'Analyse de Données Séquentielles." PhD dissertation, Faculty of Economics and Social Sciences, University of Geneva.

Studer, Matthias. 2013. "WeightedCluster Library Manual: A Practical Guide to Creating Typologies of Trajectories in the Social Sciences with R." LIVES Working Papers 24. Lausanne, Switzerland: NCCR LIVES.

Studer, Matthias, Gilbert Ritschard, Alexis Gabadinho, and Nicolas S. Müller. 2011. "Discrepancy Analysis of State Sequences." *Sociological Methods and Research* 40(3):471–510.

Suzuki, Einoshin, and Yves Kodratoff, Y. 1998. "Discovery of Surprising Exception Rules Based on Intensity of Implication." Pp. 10–18 in *Principles of Data Mining and Knowledge Discovery*, edited by J. M. Zytkow and M. Quafafou. Berlin, Germany: Springer.

Author Biography

Matthias Studer is a postdoctoral researcher in the Department of Sociology at VU University Amsterdam and a member of the Swiss NCCR program LIVES Overcoming Vulnerability: Life Course Perspectives. He is one of the TraMineR developers, and he has published articles on sequence analysis in the *Journal of Statistical Software* and *Sociological Methods and Research*. His field of interest includes life-course research, social policies, and gendered career inequalities.

REJOINDER: POSITIVISM AND BIG-GAME FISHING

*Nicolas Robette**
Xavier Bry[†]
Éva Lelièvre[‡]

[*]University of Versailles-Saint-Quentin/Laboratoire Printemps, Guyancourt, France
[†]University of Montpellier 2, Montpellier, France
[‡]Institut National d'Études Démographiques, Paris, France
Corresponding Author: Nicolas Robette, nicolas.robette@uvsq.fr
DOI: 10.1177/0081175015587511

Far better an approximate answer to the right question, which is often vague, than the exact answer to the wrong question, which can always be made precise.

—Tukey (1962)

The publication of our article in *Sociological Methodology* was the successful conclusion of a long "sequence" involving one journal's refusal to referee it (for not being in its field), a presentation at the RC33 conference of the International Sociological Association in 2012, and submission to *Sociological Methodology*, followed by rounds of revisions. The symposium concerning the article has thus gone much further than we would have hoped when we started the work in 2009. Indeed, we are grateful for the opportunity we have had to interact with specialists in sequence analysis (and life-course analysis) and in this way construct a necessarily partial and temporary status report on the progress made using this family of techniques. We do not have the space in this rejoinder to discuss all the criticisms and observations we have received. However, certain patterns emerged, and we shall try to address the most "robust." We must first point out and rectify a few misunderstandings.

1. IT ALL DEPENDS

The first misunderstanding concerns the contrast between local and global interdependence, which we explain in section 2 of the article. This contrast as we see it is a "conceptual" one, in the sense that it concerns the way the interdependence between the dimensions of the sequences is "grasped" and recorded by statistical techniques. It therefore precedes the chain of analysis. For example, to study the life-courses of two spouses after they formed a couple, it is appropriate to consider these life-courses as being simultaneous (because they develop jointly within each couple) and to compare the couples from point to point. This is a case of local interdependence, and multichannel sequence analysis (MCSA) is particularly appropriate. One of us has indeed used MCSA in exactly this sort of case (Pailhé, Robette, and Solaz 2013). But if we now turn to the study of homogamy on the basis of the two spouses' past life-courses leading to their forming a couple, their alignment from point to point makes little sense, and this is a case of global interdependence, to be analyzed with globally interdependent multiple sequence analysis (GIMSA).

Fasang, in her commentary (this volume, pp. 56–70), appears to understand this distinction between local and global interdependence in a different sense, concerning the interpretation of results. That is, subsequent to the analysis chain, a question arises: are the dimensions of the sequences substantively linked in a general manner or at certain specific points in their development? This recalls the event/sequence dichotomy or, in

Billari's (2001) terms, that between the atomistic and the holistic approach.

Under our definition of the distinction between local and global interdependence, the comparison between MCSA and GIMSA is less relevant because the two techniques do not address the same problem. That is why in the article, we compare GIMSA and strategy 4, both of which address global interdependence.[1]

The fact that Fasang's comparison of MCSA and GIMSA on the basis of our application leads to similar results does not imply that the two techniques are interchangeable and that one might reasonably choose the simpler one. This comparison reveals rather the existence of deeper structural patterns in the analyzed data (as is often the case with empirical data in the social sciences).

2. INFLEXIBILITY GOES BEFORE A FALL

The difference between MCSA and GIMSA, therefore, is "conceptual." But it is also practical: GIMSA analyzes dimensions of multidimensional sequences of varying length, with different time windows (e.g., age vs. calendar years) and time units (years, months, etc.), and uses different metrics for each dimension so as to emphasize a particular aspect of time (order, duration, date).[2] MCSA can just about cobble together the data formatting, aligning differing dimensions of length, time windows, and time units, by using missing value states, for example (cf. Fasang, this volume, pp. 56–70), but the sociological significance of this "forced" alignment remains questionable.[3] Last but not least, MCSA uses a single metric.

GIMSA's practical flexibility, pointed out by a number of commentators—especially by Pavalko (this volume, pp. 73–76) and by Fan and Moen (this volume, pp. 51–56)—is one of the elements in its added value (disputed in other commentaries). It involves a series of choices, seen by some as a weakness, in the sense that users are no longer perfectly "controlling" what they are doing, and the "robustness" of the method is allegedly weakened by this. We cover robustness issues in section 4, but here we shall merely note that this concerns a debate between flexibility and simplicity similar to that about optimal matching (OM) analysis some years ago, a debate in which it is not for us to take sides.[4]

Each of GIMSA's steps has an unmistakable and indispensable role, with a varying latitude of decision:

- Choosing a dissimilarity measure is indeed necessary when tracking patterns, because these emerge from similarity groups. Can methods that allow only one dissimilarity measure be viewed as more robust because they preclude choice? It all depends on whether this dissimilarity measure is indeed unique for theoretical reasons. Failing that, the fact that GIMSA can support various possible choices of dissimilarity measure should be viewed as an asset, not as a drawback: it should lead researchers to justify their choices of one measure over another or to use several measures and compare their outputs, looking for discrepancies as well as invariants across them.

- Multidimensional scaling (MDS) involves no real decision. It simply translates the dissimilarity into the closest Euclidean distance and outputs the corresponding coordinates of units.

- Canonical partial least squares (PLS) searches both spaces for principal "directions of matching." This also involves no choice other than the number of retained directions. This choice is a necessary compromise between the richness of the description of the matching (in terms of dimensions) and its quality: the more dimensions we retain, the less strong the matching. Now, any method concerned with matching should have the following two concerns: (1) providing the ability to tune the demanded level of matching quality and (2) keeping the dimensions of noise (i.e., dimensions carrying structurally weak information) away from those considered in the matching. PLS is one of the simplest ways to achieve that, because it involves no tuning parameter.[5] Any regularized type of canonical correlation analysis could also be used here,[6] on the condition that the regularization be based on the structural strength of the components so as not to find correlations between noisy (i.e., non-information-bearing) features. This is the value of PLS.

- The clustering step seems to us the one that involves questionable choices. It is also the only noncompulsory step in GIMSA: after identifying the structural "dimensions of matching" (previous step), we could analyze them in terms of life-history events by correlating them with all kinds of life-history descriptors and thus without having to perform clustering. Clustering is rightly famous for the many arbitrary choices it demands. This echoes the fuzziness of its root question: what is similar to what, how, and in what respect? But here, the final clustering is but one of the many ways to interpret the dimensions of matching. Ideally, these dimensions should be analyzed in a number of alternative ways, to extract the maximum amount of the information they capture.

GIMSA's flexibility means that it is a particularly suitable instrument for studying linked lives, but like sequence analysis in general, its potential field of application goes beyond life-course analysis. Consequently, we would invite colleagues to disinhibit their "sociological imagination" as Mills (1959) recommended, and include data that are perhaps richer than they habitually use.

3. GUILTY BY ASSOCIATION?

The second misunderstanding concerns the aims of GIMSA and the analysis of multidimensional sequences generally. As Studer (this volume, pp. 81–88) astutely points out, the cluster analyses we habitually use are not designed to analyze the degree of association between dimensions and are not suited to do so. We obviously agree with this: GIMSA, like MCSA, is a pattern search technique—no more, no less. We plead guilty to the sloppy use of vocabulary (noted by Studer), particularly in the description of the results of the application, in which we tended to overuse "link" terminology. The clustering step cannot, and therefore should not, be interpreted as a way of finding connections, but rather it should be seen as a way of broadly summarizing the connections teased out by the PLS components submitted to clustering. This clustering step is only secondary anyway: GIMSA is mainly the combination of the first three steps (see above). Here too, we make no claim to be doing any more than fishing for patterns of dyads of sequences.[7] This remark may disarm some of the criticisms made of GIMSA, for it can easily be seen that they are indeed expressed in terms of the degree of association between dimensions.

4. WHAT IS "PATTERN SEARCHING" IN SOCIAL SCIENCES ABOUT?

This misunderstanding evokes more serious differences of opinion about how to envisage the use of statistics in social sciences. When Andrew Abbott introduced OM into the world of social sciences in the 1980s, this took its place within a broader discussion of what he called "general linear reality" (Abbott 2001b; Robette forthcoming). He saw the "methodological framework" of the social sciences as being structured by a set of dichotomies: quantitative versus qualitative, positivism versus interpretation, and so on (Abbott 2001a:28). These dichotomies possess "elective affinities," of which the most profound associates positivism with analysis and narrative with interpretation. Abbott sought to break down these affinities by reintroducing a narrative dimension into positivism. This meant proposing an alternative to the "paradigm of variables" that dominates quantitative empiricism and its implicit presuppositions (Abbott 2001b; Fabiani 2003). The analysis of sequences provides a set of tools for developing this alternative, among which Abbott singled out OM. In 2000, an article by Abbott and Tsay in *Sociological Methods and Research* was followed by comments by Levine and by Wu. Levine (2000) took up a firm position in favor of general linear reality, reproaching OM mainly for not meeting the standards of stochastic models. Wu (2000), a specialist in event-history analysis, adopted the same point of view and also formulated more targeted criticisms of particular aspects of the method, such as the sociological meaning of the operations of substitution, insertion, and deletion of elements within sequences and the inclusion of the order of the events in the sequences. In response to all these criticisms, Abbott corrected what he saw as miscomprehensions about the workings of OM and more particularly resituated the method within the dichotomy of general linear reality versus narrative-descriptive methods: any assessment of OM against the bases of mainstream statistical methods *de facto* invalidates most of the criticisms (Abbott 2000):

> OM algorithms are not models, nor are they premised on models. That is the foundation of their difference from standard methodologies. They simply look for patterns or regularities. The type of regularity they seek can be varied by varying the structure and parameters of the algorithm. But the algorithms do not rest, ultimately, on an idea of how the data are generated. (p. 67)

And yet in this symposium, just as more broadly in the assessments of research on the basis of sequence analyses, the criticisms have often been founded on principles close to criteria of scientificness calqued on those of the experimental sciences—on an "instrumental positivism" as defined by Bryant (1989), who called it

> "instrumental" insofar as it is the available research instruments that mark out the object of research, and "positivist" because this self-imposed constraint of sociologists reflects their desire to submit to an analytical rigor similar to that they attribute to the natural sciences. (p. 64, retranslated)

For example, in his comment, Elzinga (this volume, pp. 45–51) considers that a degree of agreement of .65 between two clusterings is not satisfactory, contrary to what we state in our article. According to his view, one cannot settle for a value below .9. He illustrates this with some amusing and revealing examples: the allocation of children to one educational program or another and of patients to one therapy or another. But that is precisely the point: we are social scientists, not policymakers or doctors; decision making is far beyond our scope. In quantitative sociological research, it is common practice to use a significance threshold of 5 percent. This is merely a statistical habit: who would undergo vision correction surgery if medical engineering tolerated a similar degree of error? Many commonly accepted rules for statistical choices in our disciplines are social constructs, traditions based on no real theoretical foundations. These choices can be only contextual and often empirical, and any normative aspiration is founded on a poor understanding of the particular epistemology of the social sciences (Passeron 1991). The general problem of thresholds is easy to understand: just try to answer the question "How many grains of sand make a sand pile?"

This "instrumental positivism" recurs in the matter of the number of classes of typology produced by sequence analysis. Again and again, the referees of articles we have submitted to various journals (and here *Sociological Methodology* is no exception) have come back with remarks such as "there is no 'numerical' or 'statistical' criterion mentioned to motivate the choice of a cluster solution." Lurking in the background is the idea that there is a "true" solution, or at least a "best" solution, which statistical tools are intended to reveal.

However, any automatic classification procedure will place all the individuals in a study population into mutually exclusive groups. So any of the possible solutions is "true." As for which is the "best," no general answer can be given, even for a single set of data: it all depends on the research question, the interpretability of the results and their value for advancing current sociological themes, the use to be made of the typology, and so on.[8] As Williams and Lance (1965), cited in our article, asserted, a typology is not true or false; it is profitable or unprofitable. They added,

> To define an optimum method we should have to formalize the situation sufficiently to estimate, and thence to maximize, the expected profitability. The purpose of such methods is not to displace the intuitive taxonomist, but to suggest to him potentially fruitful lines of investigation. (p. 160)

To base the choice of number of classes on a statistical criterion is less a guarantee of scientificness on the researcher's part than an abdication of responsibility.

But our view does not appear to be widely shared: as Aisenbrey and Fasang (2010) noted, the "validation" of sequence analysis results is repeatedly criticized. They suggested that a remedy might be to use cutoff criteria based on the dispersion of within- and between-cluster distances and to take the best solution to be the number of classes at the point at which the ratio of within- to between-cluster distances falls below .5 for the first time.[9] But what is the theoretical basis for this threshold? It is merely a heuristic. Furthermore, there are many cutoff criteria, and they do not necessarily lead to the same conclusions, so it is easy for cunning researchers to choose the criteria that suit them best so as to satisfy their peers while preserving their own choices. The whole apparatus of validity tests, robustness checks, sensitivity tests, and "noise models" may well have some use, but mainly for improving one's chances of being published in the leading journals by aping the experimental sciences' criteria of scientificness. The wisest thing to do when taking an exploratory, heuristic, and nonconfirmatory approach would be to (1) use as many instruments as possible that seem to be technically suited to identifying the patterns one wishes to discover (e.g. correlations, partitions), with a wide range of values for their tuning parameters, and (2) compile and critically interpret the similarities and differences between the results obtained, so as to sort out the more robust patterns from the weaker ones (those depending most on the observation instrument), or even from pure artifacts via meta-analysis.

When Benzécri (1973) developed correspondence analysis from 1962 to 1965, he was hoping to "discover the hidden properties, higher in the natural hierarchy of causes than those that are obvious, which control the obvious ones" (p. 48). In his view, therefore, "since the realities of this world are things created by God, the statistician's work is to work back from the facts to the essence of things, the shape the Creator gave them" (Cibois 1981:339). Those using this technique immediately set aside these philosophical foundations. But one may well wonder whether, driven out by the door, these ideas have not slipped back in through the open window of mainstream statistics in its quest for the "true" or the "best" solution.[10]

With correspondence analysis, Benzécri also intended to introduce into France a way of doing and seeing statistics similar to the data analysis practiced by English-speaking researchers (Cibois 1981), which Rouanet and Lépine (1976) described as follows:

> It designates not really a set of techniques, let alone an "established doctrine," but rather "a certain idea of statistics" whereby it is legitimate in principle (even if in practice problems arise) to examine the data in order to interpret them, whatever the intentions and procedures of their collection may have been, without the need to confine oneself to a model or restrictive hypotheses. (pp. 137–38)

It is within this legacy, we believe, that pattern search techniques such as sequence analysis should be placed.

5. WHAT ARE YOU GOING TO DO FOR US PRESENTLY?

Once these misunderstandings have been cleared up, we may attempt now to summarize the encouraging prospects for research into sequence analysis outlined by the comments in this symposium.

First, as has been argued, the automatic classification of multidimensional sequences is not a tool for examining the degree of association between dimensions. However, the question of the association between dimensions is a central one, and there are already some ideas for research in that direction. Elzinga (this volume, pp. 45–51) suggests using distance matrices of the various dimensions, analyzing their association from Mantel, Kendall, or R_v coefficients and another coefficient based on the notion of "local monotonicity" (see also Piccarreta and Elzinga 2013). Studer (this volume, pp. 81–88) mentions Cramer's V and standardized Pearson residuals (to analyze the contingency table of typologies for each dimension), discrepancy analysis (see also Studer et al. 2011), and "sequences of typical states" based on implicative statistics (see also Studer 2012). Taken together, these techniques already provide a copious toolbox, which we should use and test more widely.

Nearly 30 years after OM analysis was introduced into the social sciences, the question of comparing metrics remains open. A number of studies of systematic comparison have shown that many existing metrics gave closely similar results, although some metrics do stand out (Robette and Bry 2012; Studer and Ritschard 2014). Indeed, the recent subsequence vector representation metrics seem particularly effective when focusing on the order of elements within sequences (Elzinga and Studer 2015; Elzinga and Wang 2013). We should bear in mind that the choice of metric, although it certainly does not fundamentally alter the results, is no trivial matter, and it may be instructive to test a number of metrics on one set of data before proceeding with analyses.[11]

Piccarreta's point is also important: "Can sequences be so easily substituted by the MDS scores?" (this volume, p. 80). Abbott and De Viney (1992) appear to say yes in their article on policy adoption sequences (see also Halpin and Chan 1998). MDS applied to the matrix of distances between national sequences enables them to identify two main structuring factors, interpreted as the timing of pension program adoption and the timing of health insurance adoption. These two factors are then analyzed separately as dependent variables. However, MDS provides only a Euclidean approximation of a dissimilarity that is not necessarily Euclidean. Any Euclidean metric is perfectly rendered by the full set of MDS components,[12] whereas a non-Euclidean metric is rendered only approximately. So the question is, what information is lost by substituting MDS components for the distance matrix originally chosen; that is, what is the "non-Euclidean share" of this distance? Thorough research would be needed into ways of finding the Euclidean within the non-Euclidean. The use of MDS for sequence analysis probably deserves wider investigation (Piccarreta and Lior 2010) before we adopt it as a matter of routine.

Finally, one last prospect for research is the connection between the local and global (here in Fasang's sense), that is, event and sequence. As Fan and Moen point out in their comment, one might, for example, ask "how a given transition in one person's life is tied to temporal patterns in another's." The path toward combining the standard tools of event-history analysis and those of sequence analysis appears at first blush to be a stony one in both technical and epistemological terms, but it may not be totally impassable. Studer's (2012) "sequences of typical states" may well supply another line of enquiry. Let us bet that this is the direction that will be taken by the most stimulating innovations in sequence analysis in the years ahead.

Notes

1. However, by producing mother and daughter clusterings independently, strategy 4 cannot find the "channels of information" in which the mother-daughter link is strongest; that is, it cannot explore the content of the mother-daughter similarity, which is partial. But it is instructive to look further into these partial similarities restricted to certain "channels of information" (unknown and requiring further research). That is precisely what GIMSA does in its partial least squares stage.
2. In our application, the two dimensions are substantively different, because with mothers we are examining their occupational careers (in terms of social class) and

with daughters their school-to-work transitions (in terms of employment). These are of differing lengths, one defined by age and the other by an initial event (i.e., leaving school), and two different metrics are used. Ideally, we would have preferred to have the information in months for the daughters, but we make do with the same time unit for both dimensions (namely, years). But the aim of our paper was to present briefly a new methodology we had built up, not to investigate a sociological issue in depth.

3. Gauthier (this volume, pp. 70–73) proposes an alternative, namely, placing the dimensions in a single sequence end to end. There too the substantive meaning of this formatting is dubious. Furthermore, this approach involves using a single alphabet for all dimensions.

4. Although we tend toward the view that flexibility is a virtue, both intellectually and methodologically.

5. The PLS components may admittedly lack certain forms of association, but that is true of any methodology. PLS looks for linear correlations between strong (less noisy) dimensions and finds them. Furthermore, nonlinear extensions of this PLS stage may perfectly well be envisaged via the reproducing kernel Hilbert space technology.

6. In the test carried out by Piccarreta (this volume, pp. 76–81), canonical correlation analysis provides almost the same results as PLS because the "denoising" has been done previously, and not all the MDS components are used. But it may be preferable to keep all the MDS components and apply PLS to them.

7. This also implies that we make no causal hypothesis about possible links between dimensions (such as "dimension A causes dimension B"). That is why we use symmetric PLS rather than asymmetric PLS.

8. A 24-cluster solution may be instructive at an exploratory stage but will turn out to be hard to reconcile with the characterization of classes by logistic regression and the summary presentation of results for a scientific journal article. Furthermore, it may be useful to remember that good practice advises closely studying various partitions of the same classification.

9. They add that another validity criterion is met when the groupings found with sequence analysis relate to variables as theoretically expected. This reflects a use of sequence analysis restricted to validating hypotheses and therefore not open to the possibility of "discovery." We think an exploratory stage ("fishing for patterns") is yet necessary before comparing patterns with any "well-established theory," in order for the currently admitted theory to be given a chance to evolve under the pressure of observations.

10. How much our scholarly practices and habits of thought in the social sciences owe to this deep, long-standing infusion of experimental science epistemology in our university courses, handbooks, editorial boards, and so on—even among those of us who attempt to deny the fact—is worthy of a study in itself.

11. At this step, as at others, it is more appropriate to choose on the basis of the researcher's own intelligence than on statistical validation criteria (see above).

12. MDS is a noise reduction method only if not all the components it provides are retained. This is therefore a secondary property and a relatively accessory one.

References

Abbott, Andrew. 2000. "Reply to Levine and Wu." *Sociological Methods and Research* 29:65–76.

Abbott, Andrew. 2001a. *Chaos of Disciplines*. Chicago: University of Chicago Press.

Abbott, Andrew. 2001b. *Time Matters: On Theory and Method*. Chicago: University of Chicago Press.

Abbott, Andrew, and Stanley De Viney. 1992. "The Welfare State as Transnational Event: Evidence from Sequences of Policy Adoption." *Social Science History* 16(2): 245–74.

Abbott, Andrew, and Angela Tsay. 2000. "Sequence Analysis and Optimal Matching Methods in Sociology." *Sociological Methods and Research* 29(1):3–33.

Aisenbrey, Silke, and Anette E. Fasang. 2010. "New Life for Old Ideas: The 'Second Wave' of Sequence Analysis Bringing the 'Course' Back into the Life Course." *Sociological Methods and Research* 38(3):420–62.

Benzécri, Jean-Paul. 1973. *L'Analyse des Données*. Paris, France: Dunod.

Billari, Francesco. 2001. "Sequence Analysis in Demographic Research." *Canadian Studies in Population* 28(2):439–58.

Bryant, Christopher. 1989. "Le Positivisme Instrumental dans la Sociologie Américaine." *Actes de la Recherche en Sciences Sociales* 78(1):64–74.

Cibois, Philippe. 1981. "Analyse des Données et Sociologie." *L'Année Sociologique* 31: 333–48.

Elzinga, Cees H., and Matthias Studer. 2015. "Spell Sequences, State Proximities, and Distance Metrics." *Sociological Methods and Research* 44(1):3–47.

Elzinga, Cees H., and Hui Wang. 2013. "Versatile String Kernels" *Theoretical Computer Science* 495:50–65.

Fabiani, Jean-Louis. 2003. "Pour en Finir avec la Réalité Unilinéaire. Le Parcours Méthodologique de Andrew Abbott." *Annales. Histoire, Sciences Sociales* 58(3):549–65.

Halpin, Brendan, and Tak Wing Chan. 1998. "Class Careers as Sequences: An Optimal Matching Analysis of Work-life Histories." *European Sociological Review* 14(2): 111–30.

Levine, Joel H. 2000. "But What Have You Done for Us Lately? Commentary on Abbott and Tsay." *Sociological Methods and Research* 29(1):34–40.

Mills, Charles W. 1959. *The Sociological Imagination*. New York: Oxford University Press.

Pailhé, Ariane, Nicolas Robette, and Anne Solaz. 2013. "Work and Family over the Life Course: A Typology of French Long-lasting Couples Using Optimal Matching." *Longitudinal and Life Course Studies* 4(3):196–217.

Passeron, Jean-Claude. 1991. *Le Raisonnement Sociologique: L'Espace Non-poppérien du Raisonnement Naturel*. Paris, France: Nathan.

Piccarreta, Raffaella, and Cees H. Elzinga. 2013. "Mining for Associations between Life Course Domains." Pp. 190–98 in *Contemporary Issues in Exploratory Data Mining*, edited by J. J. McArdle and G. Ritschard. New York: Routledge.

Piccarreta, Raffaella, and Orna Lior. 2010. "Exploring Sequences: A Graphical Tool Based on Multi-dimensional Scaling." *Journal of the Royal Statistical Society, Series A* 173(1):165–84.

Robette, Nicolas. Forthcoming. "Du Prosélytisme à la Sécularisation. Le Processus de Diffusion de l'"Optimal Matching Analysis."" In *Andrew Abbott, Sociologue de Chicago*, edited by M. Jouvenet and D. Demazière. Paris, France: Editions de l'EHESS.

Robette, Nicolas, and Xavier Bry. 2012. "Harpoon or Bait? A Comparison of Various Metrics in Fishing for Sequence Patterns." *Bulletin of Sociological Methodology* 116(1):5–24.

Rouanet, Henry, and Dominique Lépine. 1976. "A Propos de 'l'Analyse des Données' Selon Benzécri: Présentation et Commentaires." *L'Année Psychologique* 76(1): 133–44.

Studer, Matthias. 2012. "Étude des Inégalités de Genre en Début de Carrière Académique à l'Aide de Méthodes Innovatrices d'Analyse de Données Séquentielles." PhD dissertation, Faculté des Sciences Économiques et Sociales, Université de Genève.

Studer, Matthias, and Gilbert Ritschard. 2014. "A Comparative Review of Sequence Dissimilarity Measures." *LIVES* Working Papers 33. Lausanne, Switzerland: NCCR LIVES.

Studer, Matthias, Gilbert Ritschard, Alexis Gabadinho, and Nicolas Müller. 2011. "Discrepancy Analysis of State Sequences." *Sociological Methods and Research* 40(3):471–510.

Tukey, John W. 1962. "The Future of Data Analysis." *Annals of Mathematical Statistics* 33(1):1–67.

Williams, W. T., and G. N. Lance. 1965. "Logic of Computer-based Intrinsic Classifications." *Nature* 207(4993):159–61.

Wu, Lawrence L. 2000. "Some Comments on 'Sequence Analysis and Optimal Matching Methods in Sociology: Review and Prospect.'" *Sociological Methods and Research* 29(1):41–64.

Author Biographies

The author biographies can be found on p. 44 of this volume.

Sociological Methodology
2015, Vol. 45(1) 101–147
© American Sociological Association 2015
DOI: 10.1177/0081175015576601
http://sm.sagepub.com
$SAGE

$\mathcal{G}$ 2 $\mathcal{E}$

ECOMETRICS IN THE AGE OF BIG DATA: MEASURING AND ASSESSING "BROKEN WINDOWS" USING LARGE-SCALE ADMINISTRATIVE RECORDS

Daniel Tumminelli O'Brien[*†]
Robert J. Sampson[†]
Christopher Winship[†]

Abstract

The collection of large-scale administrative records in electronic form by many cities provides a new opportunity for the measurement and longitudinal tracking of neighborhood characteristics, but one that will require novel methodologies that convert such data into research-relevant measures. The authors illustrate these challenges by developing measures of "broken windows" from Boston's constituent relationship management (CRM) system (aka 311 hotline). A 16-month archive of the CRM database contains more than 300,000 address-based requests for city services, many of which reference physical incivilities (e.g., graffiti removal). The authors carry out three ecometric analyses, each building on the previous one. Analysis 1 examines the content of the measure, identifying 28 items that constitute two independent constructs, private neglect and public denigration. Analysis 2 assesses

---

*Northeastern University, Boston, MA, USA
†Harvard University, Cambridge, MA, USA

Corresponding Author:
Daniel Tumminelli O'Brien, Northeastern University, 1135 Tremont Street, Boston, MA 02120, USA
Email: d.obrien@neu.edu

the validity of the measure by using investigator-initiated neighborhood audits to examine the "civic response rate" across neighborhoods. Indicators of civic response were then extracted from the CRM database so that measurement adjustments could be automated. These adjustments were calibrated against measures of litter from the objective audits. Analysis 3 examines the reliability of the composite measure of physical disorder at different spatio-temporal windows, finding that census tracts can be measured at two-month intervals and census block groups at six-month intervals. The final measures are highly detailed, can be tracked longitudinally, and are virtually costless. This framework thus provides an example of how new forms of large-scale administrative data can yield ecometric measurement for urban science while illustrating the methodological challenges that must be addressed.

Keywords

ecometrics, urban sociology, big data, computational social science, physical disorder, broken windows, 311 hotlines

The global move toward digital technology has instigated a marked shift in the practice of science over the past two decades. Surveys and experiments are now often conducted through Internet platforms, Global Positioning System devices and other sensors allow us to track patterns of movement and behavior, and computer processing technology has supported the development of new forms of statistical analysis. A recent consequence of this "digital revolution" is the availability of large-scale administrative data that might prove useful in research. Many public agencies and private companies systematically collect information on services and clients and compile it in digital databases. Some of these are more detailed versions of familiar data (e.g., crime reports) while others (e.g., cell phone records or citizen requests for governmental services) are novel. These "big" or *next-generation data* offer the opportunity to paint a comprehensive picture of cities, which has the potential to transform theoretical models of urban governance and social behavior (Lazer et al. 2009).

Despite considerable excitement at this prospect, big data have not yet become commonplace in contemporary social science research, in part, it seems, because researchers do not entirely know what to make of them. Without a clear understanding of how these new data sources contribute to our ongoing debates and the questions facing our fields, some analysts might reasonably consider their promise as being overblown. There is thus a need for methodologies that can connect big data with the current practice of social science.

We offer one such "proof of concept" in the present paper, using a database of more than 300,000 citizen-generated requests for public services in Boston, Massachusetts, to measure the conditions of urban neighborhoods across space and time. Building on the methodology of ecometrics (Raudenbush and Sampson 1999), we construct and assess a measure of physical disorder, one of the most widely used and popular concepts in urban sociology, criminology, and public policy. Although the idea of disorder has a long history in sociology, it has received increased attention in recent decades because of the influential "broken windows" theory of crime and urban decline (Raudenbush and Sampson 1999; Ross, Mirowsky, and Pribesh 2001; Skogan 1992; Wilson and Kelling 1982), making it an ideal test case for assessing the potential for ecometrics based on large-scale administrative data.

1. AN ECOMETRIC APPROACH TO DISORDER

Fifteen years ago, Raudenbush and Sampson (1999) proposed a systematic approach to the measurement of neighborhood social ecology, what they termed "ecometrics." They encouraged researchers to borrow three tools developed by psychometricians for the measurement of behavior: (1) item-response models, which call for the use of scales whose multiple items vary in their difficulty, allowing greater precision in measurement across neighborhoods; (2) factor analysis, which can be used to address the interrelation between items and to identify one or a few latent constructs that the items reflect; and (3) generalizability theory, which requires criteria for ensuring that a given measurement of a neighborhood is reflective of the "true" score on the characteristic of interest, and not overly influenced by either stochastic or confounding processes. These guidelines, along with the illustrative examples that accompanied them, provided researchers with a step-by-step methodology for developing survey and observational protocols that could measure ecometrics, an approach that has been implemented by hundreds of researchers in dozens of cities.

The advent of large administrative data represents a new opportunity for ecometric study. The gigabytes and terabytes of data being collected by both public and private sector entities are a rich, low-cost resource for measuring the characteristics of neighborhoods, but using them in this manner poses clear methodological and substantive challenges. Administrative data are not collected according to any research question or plan, and thus, in their raw state, lack some of the characteristics expected of researcher-collected data. These challenges are well suited to the techniques common to ecometric study, which can act as a guide to both what is missing or occluded in such data sets, as well as how a researcher might address such issues.

We focus here on one of the most influential concepts in the urban sciences: that of *physical disorder*, including the iconic "broken window," the accumulation of litter, the presence of graffiti, or other indications that a neighborhood is poorly maintained and monitored. Such incivilities are often associated with elevated crime rates (Raudenbush and Sampson 1999; Wilson and Kelling 1982) and lower mental, physical, and behavioral health among residents (Burdette and Hill 2008; Caughy, Nettles, and O'Campo 2008; Furr-Holden et al. 2012; Mujahid et al. 2008; O'Brien and Kauffman 2013; Wen, Hawkley, and Cacioppo 2006), attracting attention from a variety of disciplines (Caughy, O'Campo, Patterson 2001; Cohen et al. 2000; O'Brien and Wilson 2011; Taylor 2001). The importance of physical disorder as a neighborhood characteristic is such that it was also one of the two test cases that Raudenbush and Sampson (1999) used to illustrate their methodological approach to ecometrics.

Physical disorder is traditionally measured either through surveys or detailed neighborhood audits (e.g., Raudenbush and Sampson 1999; Taylor 2001), but the effort and cost associated with such protocols have made whole-city assessments challenging and precise longitudinal tracking nearly impossible. Modern technology used by city agencies, however, is now recording similar information in real time. These databases have the potential to supplement traditional ecometric protocols. One such database is a result of a recent policy innovation called the constituent relationship management (CRM) system. Colloquially known as a mayor's hotline or a 311 hotline, these systems provide constituents with a variety of channels for directly requesting services from the city government, using phone, Internet, or smartphone applications that communicate requests to the appropriate department. The resultant database is a detailed documentation of constituent needs, leading some of its initial implementers to refer to it as "the eyes and ears of the city"—Jane Jacobs (1961) meets "big data," as it were. Many of the requests refer to individual instances of physical disorder, such as graffiti or abandoned housing, giving the database the ability to reflect their prevalence across neighborhoods.

Although the potential impacts of big data on science have been overhyped (Pigliucci 2009) and there have been highly visible failures of prediction based on large-scale data (Lazer et al. 2014), CRM databases offer a number of possibilities as an alternative or supplement to expensive new data collection, especially in a time of declining research support.

For one, the systems receive hundreds of cases every day, each attributed to a particular address or intersection, giving researchers considerable flexibility in how they might geographically divide cities. CRM also lends itself to the longitudinal tracking of physical disorder, a major advance considering that no whole-city protocol to date has been conducted more than once in a five-year period. Furthermore, the databases differentiate among dozens of case types, allowing greater precision in defining the events that constitute disorder than has previously been possible.

CRM databases were not created for the purposes of disorder research, however, and they have three weaknesses that any methodology must address. First, the substantive content of the databases is noisy, and it is not immediately apparent what they can measure or how they can do so. Some cases, such as requests for graffiti removal, are clear examples of physical disorder, but others, such as scheduling a bulk item pickup, are not. Second, there may be some aspect of data collection that creates systematic biases in measurement. For instance and quite importantly, CRM systems may suffer from skewed reporting in the incidence of disorder across neighborhoods. Last, there is no information about what scale of geographical analysis the databases can support (e.g., census block groups [CBGs] or tracts) or what time spans.

Whereas Raudenbush and Sampson (1999) forwarded criteria for survey- and observation-based measurement across geographical units, CRM databases make clear the need for a new set of guidelines for the use of administrative data in the creation of ecometrics. In the present study, we used the CRM database from Boston to illustrate the multiple analytic steps in the formulation of original ecometrics. This process is reported in three parts, each analysis requiring its own distinct logic, data sources, and analytical approach. Analysis 1 examines the *content* within a CRM database that reflects physical disorder, and it uses correlational analyses to identify an underlying factor structure. Analysis 2 then addresses the *validity* of any measure extracted from the CRM database by assessing biases in reporting through original data collection involving neighborhood audits. A method is then developed for using auxiliary measures from within the CRM database to estimate these biases and to help account for over- or underreporting. Analysis 3 then examines the *reliability* of these composite measures by identifying the spatial and temporal ranges at which their measurement is consistent. In each case, we spell out the assumptions in our analysis that arise from the use of administrative data.

2. ANALYSIS 1: OPERATIONALIZING PHYSICAL DISORDER

When Raudenbush and Sampson (1999) developed their methodology for ecometrics, they emphasized the development of item-response models and their examination through factor analysis, an approach that had been in common use in the field of psychometrics for decades. When conducting a neighborhood audit, for example, a protocol might measure a variety of items that collectively capture an overall pattern. A factor analysis based on their intercorrelations would then help determine which of these items in fact measured the desired construct, while also testing whether they reflected one or multiple constructs regarding the neighborhood's ecology. The challenge with next-generation data, however, is that it is not immediately apparent what they can measure. Traditionally, research measures are derived from protocols written by the researchers themselves, and their items are based on an underlying theoretical construct. Administrative data are not endowed with an a priori theoretical organization of this sort. CRM databases, for example, are by-products of systems intended to transmit the needs of constituents to the appropriate government agencies, and their organization reflects this function, rather than a deliberate intent to measure neighborhood characteristics. Nonetheless, with thousands of requests spanning more than 150 case types, CRM databases offer a rich store of information for measuring neighborhood characteristics. But before factor analysis can be considered, it falls to researchers to use existing theory to identify those specific items that are likely to be relevant.

Physical disorder is typically defined as any aspect of a neighborhood's visual cues that reflect a "breakdown of the local social order" (Skogan 1992:2), though this has come to mean two different things in practice. Raudenbush and Sampson's (1999) measure focused specifically on the publicly visible artifacts of physical incivilities that denigrated the public space according to the broken windows theory, such as graffiti and various forms of litter indicating illegal or typically problematic behavior (e.g., used condoms, empty beer bottles, hypodermic needles). A variety of other researchers have expanded this definition to include any item that might be evidence that "spaces are not being kept or used properly" (Taylor 2001:5). This had led to a variety of protocols that also include items that, although not the result of flagrant incivilities, reflect an overall pattern of neglect, including deteriorating or abandoned housing, unkempt lawns or vegetation, and litter of all kinds (Caughy et al. 2001; Cohen et al. 2000; Furr-Holden et al. 2008; O'Brien and Wilson 2011; Ross and Mirowsky 1999; Rundle et al. 2011; Skogan 1992; Taylor 2001). One important consequence of this approach is that it extends measurement to elements of the neighborhood that are technically private but whose appearance and use are a visible part of the local scenery, like front porches, lawns, and the facades of houses. Despite this distinction, factor analyses on such protocols often identify a single factor, though Ross and Mirowsky (1999) found evidence for two latent constructs they referred to as disorder and decay, approximating the dichotomy described here.

To make the greatest use of the CRM database, we identify case types that reflect either private neglect or public denigration. Some will correspond directly to items in previous methodologies, such as a report of an abandoned house or a request for graffiti removal. But others will be novel, either because they are too uncommon to be measured through one-time neighborhood audits (e.g., cars illegally parked on a lawn) or because they are more likely to be experienced in private spaces (e.g., rodent infestation). This latter opportunity to "look" at the conditions inside houses could potentially add a new dimension to the measurement of disorder, one that has been hinted at in previous protocols that examine visible deterioration but has not been completely accessible. Altogether, it is possible to construct a battery of "items" that offers a greater breadth and depth than any previous measure of physical disorder. The second stage of the analysis will then use factor analysis to explore the dimensionality of these items. Given their large number, it seems feasible that they will describe not a unitary construct but one with multiple aspects that are related but distinct.

2.1. *The CRM Database*

Boston's CRM system received 365,729 requests for service via its three channels (hotline calls, Internet self-service portals, and smartphone applications) between March 1, 2010, and June 29, 2012; of those, 334,874 had geographic references. March 1 was chosen as the start date because that is when a standardized data entry form was implemented.

The requests for service included 178 different case types. A subset of types reflected examples of physical disorder arising from either human negligence or denigration of the neighborhood (e.g., illegal dumping, abandoned bicycles). Other case types either did not indicate physical disorder (e.g., general request, bulk item pickup) or indicated deterioration that was not the fault of local residents (e.g., streetlight outage).

Each case record included the date of the request, the address or intersection where services were to be rendered, as well as the case type. These locations came from a master geographical database of the addresses and intersections of Boston that was based on the city's tax assessment and roads data, with each address keyed to the appropriate census geographies (from the 2005–2009 American Community Survey [ACS], the most recent census with socioeconomic data when the database was built). The main measures for this analysis were counts of events that occurred in a neighborhood, which we operationalize as the CBG. CBGs are smaller than the more typically used census tract (average population $\asymp$ 1,000 vs. 4,000), but the volume of CRM calls enables measurement and analysis at this finer scale. Boston contains 543 CBGs with a substantial population.

2.2. Defining Physical Disorder from Case Types

An initial examination of the 178 case types produced a list of 33 that might be evidence of human neglect or denigration in public spaces (see Table 1). Counts were tabulated for each of these 33 case types for each CBG over the period covered by the database. As a first step to identifying an underlying factor structure, an exploratory factor analysis was run on the 33 count variables (Tabachnick and Fidell 2006). The final solution produced five factors with eigenvalues > 1. These factors, whose constituent types and loadings are listed in Table 1, might be described as follows:

- *Housing issues*, including 11 items referring to poor maintenance by landlords (e.g., poor heating, chronic dampness) and the presence of pests (e.g., bedbugs).
- *Uncivil use of space*, including seven items that reflect how private actions can negatively affect the public sphere (e.g., illegal rooming house, poor condition of property, abandoned building).
- *Big-building complaints*, including three different case types regarding problems with the upkeep of big buildings such as condominiums.

Table 1. Counts of Case Types That Reflect Human Neglect or Denigration of the Neighborhood, Including the Factors and Loadings from an Exploratory Factor Analysis

Case Type	Count	Factor Loading	Case Type	Count	Factor Loading
Housing issues			Big-building complaints		
Bedbugs	871	.49	Big buildings enforcement	236	.68
Breathe easy	590	.53	Big buildings online request	274	.72
Chronic dampness/mold	442	.44	Big buildings resident complaint	209	.60
Heat—excessive, insufficient	2,175	.62	Graffiti		
Maintenance complaint—residential	687	.54	Graffiti removal	8,826	.83
Mice infestation—residential	796	.59	PWD graffiti	847	.50
Pest infestation—residential	330	.52	Trash		
Poor ventilation[a]	26	—	Abandoned bicycle	144	.45
Squalid living conditions[a]	128	—	Empty litter basket[b]	802	.30
Unsatisfactory living conditions	8,948	.85	Illegal dumping	2,292	.87
Unsatisfactory utilities—electrical, plumbing	174	.41	Improper storage of trash (barrels)	4,756	.91
Uncivil use of space			Rodent activity	3,287	.40
Abandoned building	238	.36	No factor (discarded)		
Illegal occupancy	642	.42	Illegal auto body shop	105	—
Illegal rooming house	471	.47	Illegal posting of signs	236	—
Maintenance—homeowner	180	.41	Illegal use	137	—
Parking on front/back yards (illegal parking)	336	.42	Overflowing or unkempt Dumpster[a]	526	—
Poor conditions of property	2,438	.80	Pigeon infestation	82	—
Trash on vacant lot	432	.57			

Note: For factor analysis, n = 544 census block groups. An iterated principal-factors estimation was used with a promax rotation. PWD = Public Works Department.

[a]Items did not load on initial factor analysis but were added on the basis of content similar to factor or one or more of its constituent items.

[b]Item loaded at >.3 on both the trash and graffiti factors. It was maintained on the trash factor for reasons of content.

- *Graffiti*, including two different case types regarding graffiti, one generated by constituents, the other by the Public Works Department.
- *Trash*, including five items related to incivilities regarding trash disposal: illegal dumping, improper storage of trash barrels, empty litter baskets, abandoned bicycles, and rodent activity. (The last item, not itself an incivility, is a consequence of poor trash storage.)

Five items did not load on any factor and were discarded before the foregoing analyses. Four other items that loaded at <.4, though, were maintained on the basis of conceptual similarity: abandoned buildings loaded at .36 on the factor of uncivil use, requests to empty a litter basket loaded at >.3 on both trash and graffiti and was maintained on the former factor on the basis of its substantive content, and two items were added to the housing factor because they were conceptually identical to the definition of the factor and likely did not load in the factor analysis because of their low frequency.

2.3. *Exploring the Dimensions of Physical Disorder*

New measures were created from these five factors to evaluate their higher order factor structure. We accomplished this by summing counts for each of the constituent case types for each CBG over the period covered by the database. These measures had substantial outliers and were all log-transformed before analysis. Correlations between them were all significant (except for uncivil use and graffiti), although they were modest if they are considered to be manifestations of a superordinate construct (see Table 2); only two bivariate correlations were above $r = .4$ (housing issues and uncivil use of space, graffiti and trash), and two others were above $r = .3$ (housing issues and big-building complaints). Given both content and the pattern of correlations, the five factors appear to suggest two main groupings: *denigration of the public space*, composed of trash and graffiti, and poor care or *negligence for private space*, composed of big-building complaints, housing, and uncivil use of space.

Confirmatory factor analysis, via structural equation modeling, was used to compare this two-factor structure with a one-factor structure in which all five measures were loaded together on an overarching measure of physical disorder. The two-factor model was superior by all measures. It had better fit (comparative fit index [CFI] = .82 vs. .61,

Table 2. Descriptive Statistics for and Correlations between Five Submeasures of Physical Disorder

Measure	1	2	3	4	5
1. Housing	—	.47***	.34***	.18***	.20***
2. Uncivil use of space	—	—	.10*	.04	.33***
3. Big-building complaints	—	—	—	.14**	.21***
4. Graffiti	—	—	—	—	.45***
5. Trash	—	—	—	—	—
Median	17.5	5	0	7	10
Range	0–183	0–49	0–18	0–216	0–279

Note: $N = 544$ census block groups. All variables were log-transformed before correlations.
*$p < .05$. **$p < .01$. ***$p < .001$.

standardized root mean square residual [SRMR] = .07 vs. .10, $\Delta\chi^2_{df=1}$ = 89.27, $p < .001$) and accounted for 42 percent, as opposed to 26 percent, of the variation across factors. The model estimated the correlation between the two factors at $r = .38$ ($p < .001$). Although the two-factor model was stronger, note that it still had a poor fit. Because the hypothesis in question was the efficacy of a one- or two-factor model, there were no assumptions that the components of each were completely independent. We thus took the exploratory step of examining modification indices, leading to the addition of a covariance between uncivil use of space and trash to the model, greatly improving fit (CFI = .95, SRMR = .05, $\chi^2_{df=5}$ = 24.26, $p < .001$). The final parameter estimates for this model are presented in Figure 1.

Analysis 1 thus suggests that the CRM database is at least in principle capable of measuring two distinct but related aspects of physical disorder: *private neglect* and *public denigration*. This result provides a more nuanced measurement than existing scales of physical disorder, particularly with the ability to go beyond elements visible from the street and to access conditions within buildings. Many previous protocols for measuring disorder have combined items from each of these categories (e.g., abandoned or deteriorating housing with graffiti), and thus it is not surprising that the two constructs are correlated. It may also explain why previous longitudinal work has found that such items become uncoupled across time (Taylor 2001). It is important to note that correlational constructs of this sort reflect a shared process, but it is not clear what this process actually is. It is possible, for example, that

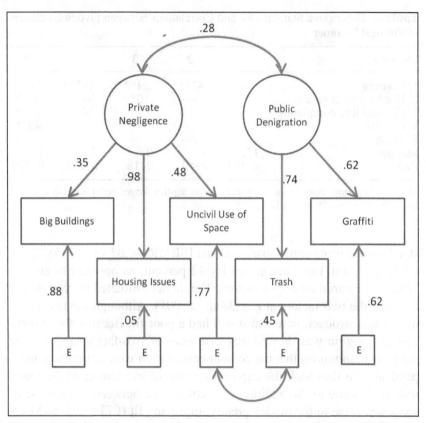

Figure 1. Estimated relationships between categories of physical disorder with standardized parameters from best-fitting confirmatory factor analysis. *Note:* Comparative fit index = .95, standardized root mean square residual = .05, n = 543 census block groups. All parameters significant at $p < .001$.

housing issues and uncivil use of private space are generated by the same behavioral tendencies, but it is equally feasible that one of these causes the other, or even that they are mutually reinforcing. These are questions that go beyond the scope of our analysis and thus are ripe for future study. For present purposes, the reliable co-occurrence of these elements across neighborhoods provides two different sets of measures we subject to an ecometric analysis: two of a generalized sort, *private neglect* and *public denigration*, and five lower level categories that are more specific, *housing, uncivil use of space, big-building complaints, graffiti*, and *trash*.

3. ANALYSIS 2: VALIDITY AND BIAS IN ADMINISTRATIVE DATA

Although it is tempting to treat the CRM database as the "eyes and ears of the city," and thereby a direct reflection of neighborhood conditions across space and time, its accuracy in this regard cannot be assumed, because each case in the database is in fact the coincidence of two events: the issue itself and the decision of a resident or passer-by to report it. This fact suggests that assumptions must be imposed to analyze the data. In guiding this process, we invoke a simple behavioral model for the distribution of calls defined not only by the probability of an issue in a given space (P_1), but also the probability that it will be reported (P_2).[1] If P_2 varies across neighborhoods, it could in turn create systematic biases in any measure based on the CRM system. To illustrate, in regions where residents are not inclined to make such calls, an issue might sit unnoted for a lengthy period, or even indefinitely, creating a gap or false negative in the database. Conversely, the residents of some neighborhoods might be highly vigilant, generating multiple reports for a single issue, leading to false positives that exaggerate the actual prevalence of disorder. This variation in P_2 might be referred to as the *civic response rate*, which we thus account for to establish validity for the measures identified in analysis 1.

In pursuing this goal, we develop a methodology that accounts for the local civic response rate, producing final measures that more accurately reflect neighborhood conditions. We focus particularly on issues in the public domain, such as streetlight outages, as these are likely to be the most vulnerable to such biases, because the responsibility for reporting them belongs to no specific individual but to the neighborhood as a whole. Developing this methodology entails three steps that use data from the CRM system and a series of neighborhood audits.

First, there must be an independent or "objective" measure of response rate that captures the propensity of a neighborhood's residents or visitors to report a given issue. We use two such measures, one identifying streetlight outages and the other evaluating sidewalk quality.

Second, it is necessary to create a measure of civic response rate that is based on measures from within the CRM system. This is critical because such a measure would allow the continual estimation of response rate, and in turn the production of valid measures of disorder, in lieu of regular neighborhood audits. In the next subsection, we develop the theoretical basis for how particular patterns in the CRM database might be reflective of the civic response rate. By examining the multivariate relationships between these internal measures and the objective measures of response rate, it is possible to construct a new measure from within the CRM system that can be used as an adjustment factor.

Third, we develop an equation that combines counts of cases with the adjustment factor to calculate final measures of physical disorder. This requires a measure of objective physical disorder, against which it is possible to calibrate the adjustment factor, determining how heavy its influence should be. This is done through an additional neighborhood audit that assessed loose litter on streets and sidewalks, an item that has been central to measures of physical disorder. In sum, this process produces a complete methodology for translating a raw database of CRM calls into a measure of physical disorder across a city. To conclude, we examine the construct validity of the measures produced by this methodology, comparing it with a series of other demographic, economic, and social indicators traditionally associated with disorder.

3.1. *Sources of the Civic Response Rate*

Reporting rates in the CRM database for public issues can be seen as having two distinct elements. The first entails knowledge of the CRM system and a willingness to use it. The second is a decision to take action or responsibility for the public space. To the former, a large part of the battle for any public service agency is informing residents of available services and making them comfortable with using them. The CRM system also requires direct interaction between constituents and the government, something that those from disadvantaged or minority groups are sometimes less inclined toward, either because they distrust the government in general or because they do not expect the requested services to actually be delivered (Putnam 1993; Verba, Schlozman, and Brady 1995). The sum of these effects might be described as *engagement*, or the likelihood that a person would use the CRM system in any case. Given the evidence that such patterns cluster demographically, it is likely to vary across neighborhoods, potentially contributing to measurement bias.

Knowing of and being willing to use the CRM system is not sufficient for using it to report a public issue, however. When calling in a report about something like graffiti or illegal dumping, an individual is taking responsibility for the public space, something that might have a different set of motivations than a call addressing personal needs (e.g., a request for a bulk item pickup). There are a number of mechanisms that may cause this *concern for public space* to vary systematically across neighborhoods. First, such variation may be the result of differences in the cognitive perception of disorder. One striking finding of citywide neighborhood surveys is that residents' ratings of local disorder vary within the same neighborhood and only moderately correlate with observational measures such as video or research ratings (Franzini et al. 2008; Sampson and Raudenbush 2004; Taylor 2001). This would indicate that individuals and communities vary in their definition of "disorder," something that might play an important role in how likely they are to feel compelled to report such issues. At the same time, it reveals that survey reports by definition are not "objective" measures of disorder either.

A second mechanism may be the variation across individuals in the level of personal responsibility they feel for the public space. For example, homeowners tend to be more engaged with public maintenance (O'Brien 2012), likely because of the long-term investment they have made by purchasing a house (Fischel 2005). Consistent with this, our preliminary analysis of the CRM data indicated that homeowners are four times more likely to report public issues than renters (O'Brien 2015). A third mechanism may be that the accumulation of physical disorder inclines residents to see the act of reporting new issues as useless, as such action will be unable to overcome the consistent generation of such problems (Ross et al. 2001). The truth may involve any one of these mechanisms, or some combination thereof, but the point stands that concern for public space could contribute to cross-neighborhood variations in the rate of reporting actual instances of physical disorder.

There are two features of the CRM database that will prove useful in the development of measures that reflect engagement and concern for public space. First, as noted, CRM case records indicate the type of services requested. From these, there is a subset that identifies issues in the public space. This subset overlaps with, but is not equivalent to, the subset of case types regarding physical disorder. Second, users of the CRM system are able to register, creating an account for tracking their reports.[2] Reports made by a registered user are then attributed to the individual's account using an anonymous code, making it possible to determine how often an individual uses the system and to approximate the individual's home location. Although this ignores those individuals who have used the system but not established accounts, the information still provides insights into an individual's calling patterns that we would not otherwise have.

The most direct way to measure engagement would be to tabulate the number of individuals who do and do not know about the CRM system. This can be approximated as the proportion of neighborhood residents who have accounts with the CRM system. A less direct approach would be to identify case types whose need might be even across the city, that is, for which P_1 would be constant across neighborhoods. In these cases, measuring their geographic distribution would then provide access to P_2, the likelihood of using the system. For example, we might expect the need for general requests, which entail questions about city services and other government-related items, to be driven solely by interest and engagement with government. Another example would be requests for sanitation services to pick up bulk items. It is reasonable to assume that residents of all neighborhoods have a similar need for this service, as it is not determined by external, neighborhood processes. A third example of an evenly distributed issue is the need for snowplows during a snowstorm, when all neighborhoods should have a roughly equal need for snowplows, controlling for certain infrastructural characteristics (e.g., the total road length, dead ends). We then have four candidate measures of a neighborhood's engagement: *total registered users, general requests, bulk item pickups*, and *snowplow requests*.

Measuring concern for public space requires a focus on reports that document a case of public deterioration and, in turn, a constituent's decision to take action regarding it. This requires a list of case types that indicate a public issue. It is not possible to use any one of these types as a benchmark, as done with general requests, bulk item pickups, and snow plow requests, because the very issue at hand is whether public issues are uniformly distributed across the city. Instead, we focus on the other two techniques described for engagement. First, it is possible to identify a subset of users who have made one or more reports of a public issue. This could be used to tabulate the number of individuals in each neighborhood who have used the CRM system for such a purpose. Additionally, some of these "public reporters" make a disproportionate number of reports. Given their zeal for neighborhood maintenance, these individuals might be referred to as "exemplars." Public issues in a neighborhood with either a greater number of average or exemplar public reporters would be expected to instigate reports to the CRM system more often and more quickly. Second, it is possible to measure the proportion of reports of public issues that were made by registered users. This would indicate how consistently such calls are part of a sustained relationship between a resident and government services. This amounts to three measures of concern for public space: (1) *public reporters*, (2) *exemplars*, and (3) *proportion of calls made by registered users*. Importantly, none of these measures is fully independent of engagement itself. For example, regardless of one's inclination to report a streetlight outage, he or she must first know that the CRM system exists. Consequently, the analysis that follows allows these measures to load on one or both of these constructs.

3.2. Estimating the Civic Response Rate from the CRM Database

To be concurrent with the neighborhood audits (described below), the current analysis uses only CRM reports from 2011, amounting to 161,703 cases with geographic reference across 154 case types. This analysis incorporates two new ways of using the CRM database. First, similar to the identification of case types reflecting physical disorder in analysis 1, 59 case types were identified as reflecting issues in the public space (e.g., streetlight outage, pothole repair, graffiti removal; a complete list appears in Appendix A). Such a report indicates a concern for the maintenance of the public space on the part of the reporter. Other case types reflected personal needs rather than public concerns (e.g., general request, bulk item pickup). Second, all individuals who have registered with the CRM system have anonymous ID codes that are appended to each of their reports. In 2011, there were 29,439 constituent users, accounting for 38 percent of all requests for service.[3] The ID codes make it possible to construct a database of users with variables describing each individual's pattern of reporting across time and space. This two-part database of calls and users was used to calculate the measures hypothesized to reflect a CBG's civic response rate.[4]

The call database was used to measure four of the seven proposed measures. Bulk item pickups (*bulk items*) and *general requests* were measured as the number of such requests occurring within a CBG. *Proportion of public issues reported by registered users* was measured as the number of public issues reported in a CBG attributed to a registered user divided by the total number of public issues reported in the CBG. *Snowplow requests* were first tabulated as a count for each CBG but were then adjusted for the total population, road length, and the length of dead-end roads.[5]

The other three measures were calculated from the database of registered users, which included three main pieces of information: (1) the total number of calls a user had made, (2) the total number of calls a user had made regarding a public issue, and (3) an estimate of the user's home location, based on the locations at which he or she requested services.[6] In 2011, 46 percent of registered users were public reporters. Of these, 87 percent reported two or fewer public issues, though there were those who were considerably more active (18 made more than 100 reports). Given this distribution, *total users* were measured as the number of registered users whose estimated locations fell within the CBG, *average public reporters* were measured as the number of a CBG's total users who had reported one or two public issues during 2011, and *exemplars* were measured as those who had reported three or more public issues.

3.3. *Objective Measures from Neighborhood Audits*

Objective neighborhood conditions were assessed through two separate audits. One identified streetlight outages and the level of street garbage in 72 of Boston's 156 census tracts (46 percent) between June 1 and August 31, 2011. In total, 4,239 street segments were assessed, and 244 streetlight outages were identified, each attributed to the nearest address. Garbage was rated for each street block on a five-point scale, with higher scores indicating more and larger piles of garbage. More detail on this protocol is provided in Appendix B in the online journal.

In the second audit, a consulting group hired by the City of Boston's Public Works Department assessed the quality of all of the city's sidewalks between November 2009 and April 2012. The unit of analysis was each continuous stretch of sidewalk that ran from intersection to intersection ($n = 27,388$). For each sidewalk, the assessors noted the proportion of panels that required replacement because they were cracked or broken, and they subtracted this from the total. This generated a 0-to-100 measure of *sidewalk quality* (with 100 indicating a sidewalk with no panels requiring replacement).

Streetlight outages and sidewalks were each cross-referenced with the CRM database to identify reports regarding them. For streetlight outages, we sought to identify the date on which each was reported. This was defined as the earliest case of an outage reported on the street segment in question that was fixed by the city after the date an auditor noted the outage.[7] This was then used to create a series of dichotomous measures indicating whether the outage had been reported by a constituent within a certain time window (e.g., one month).[8] For sidewalks, all requests for sidewalk repair were joined to the nearest sidewalk polygon from the same road. We were able to exclude those created by city employees because an additional code was included with such cases. The count of constituent reports for every sidewalk was then tabulated. Of the 27,388 sidewalk polygons, 1,168 generated requests for repair (4 percent, range = 1–19 requests).

Because the three audits described events or conditions on a single street segment within a neighborhood, multilevel models were run to create CBG-level measures (Raudenbush et al. 2004). These models controlled for microspatial characteristics of the street (e.g., zoning), and the second-level residuals were then used as CBG-level measures. Three outcome measures for these models were determined: the likelihood of a sidewalk generating one or more requests; the likelihood of a streetlight outage being reported within one month; and the continuous five-point measure of garbage. See Appendix C in the online journal for more detail on these models and the specification of outcome measures.

Two deviations from this approach are important to note. First, the number of outages per CBG was small for a multilevel model (244 outages in 127 CBGs), so the models were run instead with tracts as the second level (n = 56 tracts with outages). Each CBG then took the measure for its containing tract. Second, because sampling for the garbage audit occurred at the tract level, CBGs varied in the number of street segments that were rated. In order to be certain that neighborhood-level measures were reliable, the ensuing analysis was limited to the 196 CBGs with 10 or more street segment measures (see also Raudenbush and Sampson 1999).

3.4. *Evaluating the Proposed Model of Civic Response Rate*

Descriptive statistics for both objective measures of response rate and CRM-based measures proposed to estimate response rate, as well as the correlations among them, are reported in Table 3. All tabular variables had skewed distributions, with a long tail of CBGs that used the system extensively, leading us to log-transform them before correlational and regression analyses. As hypothesized, all variables indicating use of the system (general requests, bulk item pickups, all users, users reporting public issues, exemplary reporters) were strongly correlated ($r = .36$– $.93$, all p values $< .001$). Because of the very high correlation between all users and average users reporting public issues ($r = .93$ in the full sample and $r = .95$ in the subsample with values for all measures), the two were deemed to be the same measure. The "all users" measure was thus dropped from all proceeding analyses to avoid issues of multicollinearity.

Requests for sidewalk repairs and propensity to report streetlights were modestly correlated ($r = .18$, $p < .05$). Each also shared stronger correlations with those measures from the CRM database intended to measure concern for the public space (public reporters, exemplars, percentage of public issues reported by registered users) than those intended to measure engagement (general requests, bulk item pickups, all users). The reverse was true for requests for snowplows, as predicted. They were significantly positively correlated with the sidewalk measure ($r = .14$, $p < .05$) but not the streetlight outage measure ($r = -.12$, ns) and they had a stronger correlation with measures of engagement than with concern for public space.

Structural equation modeling was used to determine how well the proposed constructs fit the data. The model analyzed those 195 CBGs with a measure for propensity to report streetlights. The best-fitting model, depicted in Figure 2, had good fit (CFI $= .95$, SRMR $= .06$, $\chi^2_{df=9} = 25.44$, $p < .01$), and it was quite similar to the model proposed in the introduction to this section. The measures derived from the CRM system did indeed separate into the two proposed latent constructs, engagement and concern for public disorder. It is notable, however, that the two objective measures of civic response rate loaded on the latent construct of concern for public space (sidewalks: $\beta = .34$, $p < .001$; streetlight outages: $\beta = .18$, $p < .05$) but not on engagement.

As with the models in analysis 1, the novelty of the various measures required that we take a partially exploratory approach, tweaking the theoretically based model to specify the best fit. Consequently, there were four alterations that bear mentioning:

Table 3. Descriptive Statistics for and Correlations between Proposed Indicators of Response Rate

	General Requests	Bulk Item Pickups	Registered Users	Average Public Reporters	Exemplars	Percentage Public Issues by Users	Snow Plowing	Sidewalk Repairs	Streetlight Outages	Total Population
General requests[a]	—	.37***	.67***	.61***	.53***	.02	.26***	.18***	.01	.30***
Bulk item pickups[a]	.37***	—	.78***	.68***	.36***	-.24***	.43***	.19***	-.09	.07
All registered users[a]	.69***	.78***	—	.93***	.62***	-.07+	.44***	.28***	.04	.27***
Registered users reporting public issues[a]	.68***	.68***	.95***	—	.60***	.03	.42***	.30***	.13+	.26***
Exemplary reporters of public issues[a]	.51***	.40***	.66***	.64***	—	.16***	.29***	.28***	.09	.25***
Percentage of public issues reported by registered users	.04	-.25***	-.08	.05	.22**	—	-.36***	.07+	.18*	.09*
Requests for snow plowing[b]	.31***	.49***	.51***	.48***	.35***	-.36***	—	.14***	-.12	-.00
Propensity to request sidewalk repairs[b]	.13+	.08	.18*	.26***	.26***	.15*	.14+	—	.18*	.09*
Propensity to report streetlight outages within 1 month[b]	.01	-.09	.04	.13+	.09	.18*	-.12+	.18*	—	-.01
Total population	.25***	.00	.17*	.14+	.16*	.04	.04	.00	-.01	—
Mean (SD)	47.13 (34.07)	56.28 (36.28)	53.49 (30.68)	21.37 (13.33)	3.06 (2.99)	.44 (.09)	.00 (1.00)	.00 (.37)	.00 (.60)	1,153 (565)
Range	1–461	0–199	2–232	0–104	0–29	.17–0.76	-3.29–2.64	-.89–1.18	-1.01–2.22	246–4,719

Note: $N = 541$ for all measures except propensity to report streetlight outages within one month ($n = 195$). Descriptive statistics reported for all census block groups (CBGs); correlations including all CBGs with measures on both variables reported above the diagonal, correlations for those CBGs with values for all measures ($n = 195$) reported below the diagonal. See text for more details on the derivation of each measure.

[a]Log-transformed before correlations to account for skewed distribution.

[b]Deviation from regression equation controlling for key variables; see text for more details.

$+ p < .10.$ $* p < .05.$ $** p < .01.$ $*** p < .001.$

121

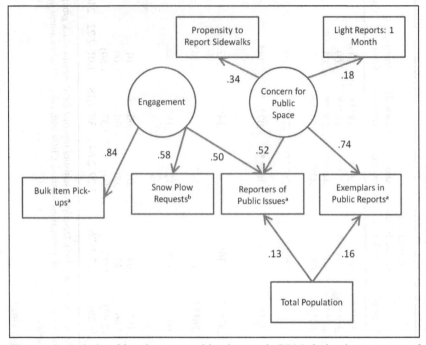

Figure 2. Relationships between objective and CRM-derived measures of response rate with standardized parameters from the best-fitting structural equation model.

Note: Comparative fit index = .95, standardized root mean square residual = .06, *n* = 195 census block groups with measures on all variables. All parameters are significant at $p < .05$. CRM = constituent relationship management
[a]Log-transformed before analysis.
[b]Controlled for total population, total street length, and dead-end length before analysis.

1. With the removal of the measure of all users, it was necessary to have average reporters of public issues load on both latent constructs (engagement: $\beta = .50, p < .001$; concern for the public space: $\beta = .52, p < .001$).

2. The measure of general requests was also removed because its strong correlation with other variables made the factor structure unstable.

3. The percentage of public calls from registered users was discarded because doing so strengthened the model's fit.

4. Total population was used as a control variable predicting average reporters of public issues ($\beta = .13, p < .05$) and exemplars ($\beta = .16, p$

< .01). Modification indices for the final model suggested that no significant bivariate relationships had been omitted.

3.5. *Evaluating the Adjustment Factor*

The results of the previous model suggest that the estimate of the civic response rate, and therefore the desired adjustment factor, is based on measures of concern for the public space. A composite measure for each CBG was created using the parameter estimates from Figure 2. We then established the efficacy of this measure as an adjustment factor by examining how well it improved the relationship between the raw measures from analysis 1 and objective measures of physical disorder, as indicated by street garbage. The analysis was performed in two parts. First, the raw counts of case types in each category (log-transformed to better approximate normality) were entered into five separate regressions predicting the level of street garbage in a CBG. Second, an adjustment factor was created for each count as an interaction with the civic response rate, which was then added to the corresponding regression.[9] This analysis was limited to residential neighborhoods (excluding regions dominated by institutions, parks, or downtown areas), as the predictive relationship between local behavior and loose litter would be most clear in these areas; in other areas, litter would be subject to dynamics that would not necessarily influence other components of physical disorder such as graffiti in the same way (n = 135 residential CBGs).

The first set of regressions found that all but one of the raw measures (graffiti) significantly predicted levels of street garbage (complete details are shown in Table 4). The strongest relationships were with housing (B = .63, p < .001) and uncivil use of space (B = .38, p < .001). Big buildings (B = .21, p < .05) and trash (B = .18, p < .05) had more moderate relationships. The fit of all five regressions increased significantly with the introduction of the adjustment factor (again see Table 4), with the strongest improvement occurring for trash (ΔR^2 = .06, p < .01) and graffiti (ΔR^2 = .05, p < .05). Notably, the variance explained more than doubled for both trash and graffiti, which had the weakest initial relationships with street garbage.

Table 4. Comparison of Results from Regressions Using the Five Categories of Physical Disorder Derived from the CRM Database to Predict Objective Measures of Garbage, with and without the CRM-based Adjustment Factor

	Housing (B)	Uncivil Use (B)	Big Buildings (B)	Graffiti (B)	Trash (B)
Raw measure	.63***	.38***	.21*	.13	.18*
R^2	.40***	.14***	.05*	.02	.03*
Raw measure	.62***	.39***	.27**	.29**	.33**
Adjustment factor	−.13+	−.19*	−.20*	−.27*	−.29**
Total R^2	.42***	.18***	.08**	.07*	.09**
ΔR^2	.02*	.04*	.03*	.05*	.06**

Note: N = 135 census block groups classified as residential and with measures of garbage for 10 or more street segments. All CRM-based variables were log-transformed before regressions. CRM = constituent relationship management.
$+p < .10.$ $*p < .05.$ $**p < .01.$ $***p < .001.$

3.6. Construct Validity for the Composite Measures

As a last step, we evaluated the construct validity of these final measures by examining their relationship with other popular indicators of neighborhood conditions, drawn from three different data sources: median income, homeownership, and measures of ethnic composition from the U.S. Census Bureau's ACS (2005–2009 estimates); survey measures of perceived physical disorder and collective efficacy (i.e., social cohesion and social control between neighbors) from the Boston Neighborhood Survey (BNS; 2008–2010 estimates, n = 3,428)[10]; and reports of gun-related incidents from Boston's 911 call record in 2011. Because the time points of these data sources vary, we analyze their relationship to the CRM-based measure for the most concurrent year: 2010 for the ACS and BNS and 2011 for 911. As before, we focus the analysis on residential neighborhoods, but in this case we analyze at the broader spatial scale of census tracts rather than block groups (n = 121 residential census tracts). We do so because the interpretation of the analysis depends in important ways on comparison with findings from previous studies, particularly Raudenbush and Sampson (1999), which were conducted on census tracts and clusters of tracts. In addition, because of the smaller sample size of the BNS compared with the Chicago study, the BNS has greater between-neighborhood reliability for tracts than for block groups. For the sake of brevity, we conducted this analysis on the higher order measures of private neglect and public denigration. Results for the five lower order measures as well as block groups are available upon request from the authors.

The measure of private neglect was lower where there was higher median income ($r = -.59$, $p < .001$), homeownership ($r = -.36$, $p < .001$), and collective efficacy ($r = -.38$, $p < .001$) and higher where there were greater black ($r = .61$, $p < .001$) and Hispanic ($r = .27$, $p < .001$) populations. It also co-occurred with gun-related incidents ($r = .68$, $p < .001$). Furthermore, it was higher where residents perceived more disorder ($r = .44$, $p < .001$). The measure of public denigration had largely similar relationships with these measures: it was lower in areas with more homeowners ($r = -.49$, $p < .001$), collective efficacy ($r = -.48$, $p < .001$), and a higher median income ($r = -.39$, $p = .001$). Public denigration was higher where there was a greater Hispanic population ($r = .41$, $p < .001$) and more gun-related incidents ($r = .27$, $p < .01$). It was also higher where residents perceived more disorder ($r = .48$, $p < .001$). The one unexpected finding was that it held no correlation with the proportion of black residents ($r = -.05$, *ns*).

These validation correlations are lower than those reported by Raudenbush and Sampson (1999:31) for survey-reported disorder. For example, public denigration correlates with perceived disorder at .48 in Boston but .71 in Chicago. However, at least four factors differ between studies beside the method (observation vs. CRM for non-survey-based indicators of disorder)—the items in the measure, city, reliability of the surveys, and time period—making direct comparability difficult. It should be noted, though, that the correlations for structural characteristics are similar; for example, the correlation between physical neglect and income in Boston is −.59, and in Chicago the correlation of observed disorder with poverty is .64. And the correlations for residential stability are −.36 in Boston and −.25 in Chicago. Moreover, the CRM correlations are on par with previous comparisons between perceived and objective disorder in other studies (Brown, Perkins, and Brown 2004; Franzini et al. 2008; Sampson and Raudenbush 2004; Taylor 2001).

Overall, the results suggest that it is possible to construct a measure from within the CRM database that adjusts counts of case types to better reflect neighborhood conditions, though there are differences between the two classes of physical disorder that should be noted. In particular, private neglect had a stronger relationship with street garbage, with two of its constituent metrics (housing and uncivil use) surpassing the threshold of about 15 percent shared variance typically seen between domains of physical disorder (Taylor 2001). The relationships between the indicators of public denigration and street garbage were a bit weaker, but the correlations with other indicators of disorder were of similar magnitude, even stronger in cases. This could be owed to one of two possible explanations. The first is that issues of trash storage and graffiti are in fact less linked to patterns of litter than expected. The second is that these issues are more susceptible to reporter bias and potentially in ways that audits of natural patterns in deterioration, such as streetlight outages and sidewalk cracks, might not fully capture. The same norms that lead to garbage-laden streets might also be responsible for diminished motivation to report graffiti or other issues in the public space. If this is so, then the assumption that a neighborhood's civic response rate, P_2, is consistent for a given neighborhood across all case types is called into question. Future validation efforts should carefully evaluate the most effective measures both for objective comparison and internal adjustment, as these might differ depending on the particular set of conditions that are intended to be the focus, a theme we return to below.

4. ANALYSIS 3: ASSESSING RELIABILITY ACROSS SPACE AND TIME

Analyses 1 and 2 have provided a methodology for measuring physical disorder using the CRM system, but without a guideline for how such measures should be bounded in space and time. Thus far, measures have been developed for CBGs over the entire available time course (two years and four months). It is desirable, however, to assess measures for smaller time windows, allowing researchers to examine local conditions at more precise intervals, and facilitating longitudinal analysis. In addition to CBGs, it would be appropriate to determine the optimal time window for census tracts, the unit at which most urban research is conducted.

Determining an "optimal" time window for measurement requires a balance of two contrasting dimensions: smaller time windows are more precise but are more sensitive to random events. To do this, we must examine how consistent the multiple measures of a single neighborhood are for different time intervals (using the intraclass correlation coefficient [ICC]) and the ability to statistically distinguish between neighborhoods (using the reliability coefficient, λ); these characteristics can be assessed using multilevel models. The goal is to identify the smallest time interval for which measures within a neighborhood are sufficiently consistent and not overly sensitive to error or stochastic processes. Because the measures of interest are in fact composites that combine counts of cases with the measures of concern for the public space, the establishment of reliability requires two steps. First, we must identify a time interval for which all of the constituent measures (e.g., instances of housing issues) attain a desired threshold for reliability and ICC. Once the appropriate time interval for the constituent measures is determined, it must be confirmed that the same time interval is appropriate for the composite measure. Note, however, that step 1 is not possible for the measure of exemplar reporters, as they are defined by their behavior over the course of a complete year. For this reason, exemplars will always be calculated as the number of public reporters in a region obtaining exemplar status over the previous 365 days.

The last question we seek to answer is that of longitudinal tracking. If the final time intervals are small enough, it would be possible to examine patterns of change across time. The multilevel models can assess the slope for a measure at both the global and neighborhood levels. If the reliability for the slope is high enough, the model is capable of discerning varying trajectories across neighborhoods, which could then be used in subsequent analyses.

4.1. *Creating Measures for Spatiotemporal Windows*

The temporal analysis utilizes the complete CRM database, including all requests for service received between March 1, 2010, and June 29, 2012. All requests are categorized by case type and include the date of the request and the address or intersection where services were to be rendered, allowing all requests to be geocoded to the appropriate census geographies.

The focal variables are those that constitute the composite measures of physical disorder, including both the raw counts of cases that reflect the five categories of physical disorder, and the measures of response rate. Drawing from analysis 1, the five categories of physical disorder were housing, uncivil use of space, big buildings, graffiti, and trash. On the basis of analysis 2, the response rate was calculated as the number of individuals reporting public issues, divided into two counts: those who made two or fewer calls in a year's time and those who made three or more calls in a year's time (i.e., exemplars).

Measures for each variable, excepting exemplars, were created for all CBGs and tracts for eight temporal windows—one, two, and three weeks, and one, two, three, four, and six months. For each, the original database was split into intervals of the given size, starting with March 1, 2010, and ending with the last complete interval. A count was then produced for each interval for each element in the given level of analysis (i.e., block group or tract).[11]

4.2. *Multilevel Models*

Hierarchical linear modeling (Raudenbush et al. 2004) was used to compare the consistency of counts within a CBG over time. A natural-log link was used to account for the Poisson distributions of all outcome variables. The first-level equation predicted the outcome for a given time point relative to other measures for that region, and it included the number of time intervals elapsed since the start of the database, to estimate the rate and direction of change over time, and dummy variables controlling for seasonal effects, based on the month of the midpoint of the given time interval. The equation takes the following form:

$$Y_{jk} = \beta_{0k} + \beta_{1k} * time_{jk} + \beta_{2k} * season_{jk} + r_{jk}$$

$$r_{jk} \sim N(0, \sigma^2).$$

The second-level equation was an intercepts-only model, estimating the average level of a measure for a neighborhood across time. In addition, the parameter relating time to changes in a measure, β_1, was allowed to vary across CBGs, permitting the model to estimate different trajectories of change for different CBGs:

$$\beta_{0k} = \gamma_{00} + \mu_{0k}$$

$$\beta_{1k} = \gamma_{10} + \mu_{1k}$$

$$\mu_{0k} \sim N(0, \tau_0)$$

$$\mu_{1k} \sim N(0, \tau_1),$$

where τ_0 is the measure of variation in the outcome measure between CBGs and τ_1 is a measure of variation between CBGs in the linear relationship between time and the outcome variable. Furthermore, σ^2 is a measure of the variation in the outcome measure within CBGs (i.e., differences within a CBG across time).

The ICC is then calculated as the proportion of variation that lies between groups:

$$\text{ICC} = \frac{\tau_0}{\sigma^2 + \tau_0}.$$

Reliability is calculated as

$$\lambda_0 = \frac{\tau_0}{\tau_0 + \sigma^2/n},$$

where n is the number of observations per CBG. As we can see, this measure grows both with a greater ICC and also with more observations.

Variation across CBGs in the linear relationship between time and the outcome measure is assessed in two ways. First, the significance of the magnitude of τ_1 is assessed using a χ^2 test. Second, its reliability is measured as

$$\lambda_1 = \frac{\tau_1}{\tau_1 + \sigma^2/SS_{\text{Time}}},$$

where SS_{Time} is the sums of squares for the measure of time.

4.3. *Comparing Spatiotemporal Windows*

The reliabilities and ICCs from the multilevel models described above are reported in Table 5 (CBGs) and Table 6 (tracts). As expected, the proportion of variation attributable to differences between both CBGs and tracts (measured by the ICC) increased monotonically as time windows became larger, because of both greater consistency and fewer measures per neighborhood. As would also be expected, ICCs were higher when comparing tracts than CBGs.

The six measures varied in their consistency. Of the measures of physical disorder, housing, graffiti, and trash had the strongest reliabilities and highest ICCs. These differences seem largely attributable to the frequency of these categories. For example, there were three times as many events reflecting housing issues than uncivil use of space. With

Table 5. ICCs and Reliabilities (λ) for Level (Intercept) and Cross-time Change (Slope) in Measures of Public Denigration and Private Neglect across Census Block Groups for Various Time Windows

	Intercept		Slope	Intercept		Slope	Intercept		Slope
	ICC	λ	λ	ICC	λ	λ	ICC	λ	λ
	Housing			Uncivil use			Big buildings		
1 week	.13	.91	.36	.02	.78	.31	.01	.46	.10
2 weeks	.23	.91	.36	.03	.78	.30	.02	.46	.10
3 weeks	.31	.91	.35	.05	.78	.30	.03	.46	.10
1 month	.39	.91	.36	.07	.78	.30	.03	.46	.11
2 months	.56	.91	.37	.13	.78	.29	.04	.46	.10
3 months	.65	.91	.37	.19	.77	.30	.10	.46	.09
4 months	.72	.91	.37	.25	.78	.29	.19	.46	.12
6 months	.77	.90	.33	.39	.74	.25	.31	.48	.01
	Graffiti			Trash			Public reporters		
1 week	.07	.87	.51	.05	.88	.48	.20	.96	.47
2 weeks	.13	.87	.51	.09	.88	.48	.32	.96	.40
3 weeks	.18	.87	.51	.13	.88	.48	.39	.96	.35
1 month	.24	.87	.51	.17	.88	.48	.47	.96	.30
2 months	.38	.87	.51	.30	.88	.48	.63	.95	.21
3 months	.47	.86	.51	.41	.88	.45	.68	.95	.03
4 months	.56	.87	.51	.47	.88	.47	.75	.95	.04
6 months	.60	.84	.05	.63	.86	.39	.80	.93	.01

Note: N's vary on the basis of the number of time intervals possible for the 28-month period in the database, nested in 541 census block groups. All ICCs are significant at *p* < .001. ICC = intraclass correlation coefficient.

a lower frequency, counts of the latter would be more stochastic and therefore less consistent at smaller time intervals. Interestingly, counts of public reporters, though far fewer in number than actual calls, featured greater consistency within a region than any of the measures of physical disorder.

All ICCs in Tables 5 and 6 were significant at $p < .001$. The intent here, however, is not to find significant between-region variation but to identify spatiotemporal windows at which a single measure is indicative of a region's "actual" value on that measure. The ICC, in that case, is used as an evaluation of how strongly a single measure of a neighborhood correlates with all other measures of that neighborhood. If we elect .7 as a threshold for a reliable neighborhood-level measure, then there

Table 6. ICCs and Reliabilities (λ) for Level (Intercept) and Cross-time Change (Slope) in Measures of Public Denigration and Private Neglect across Census Tracts for Various Time Windows

	Intercept		Slope	Intercept		Slope	Intercept		Slope
	ICC	λ	λ	ICC	λ	λ	ICC	λ	λ
	Housing			Uncivil use			Big buildings		
1 week	.30	.97	.44	.06	.92	.38	.02	.68	.26
2 weeks	.46	.97	.45	.12	.92	.37	.04	.68	.27
3 weeks	.56	.97	.45	.17	.92	.37	.07	.68	.26
1 month	.64	.97	.46	.22	.92	.37	.09	.68	.27
2 months	.78	.97	.46	.35	.92	.36	.12	.68	.27
3 months	.84	.97	.44	.46	.91	.40	.24	.68	.24
4 months	.88	.97	.45	.55	.92	.37	.40	.68	.29
6 months	.90	.96	.36	.75	.90	.31	.41	.70	.01
Composite[a]	.78	.92	—	.64	.84	—	.20	.43	—
	Graffiti			Trash			Public reporters		
1 week	.18	.95	.71	.14	.96	.68	.43	.99	.48
2 weeks	.31	.95	.71	.25	.96	.67	.59	.99	.39
3 weeks	.39	.95	.71	.32	.96	.67	.67	.99	.34
1 month	.49	.95	.71	.40	.96	.67	.73	.98	.28
2 months	.64	.95	.72	.59	.96	.67	.84	.98	.06
3 months	.73	.95	.72	.67	.96	.62	.88	.98	.07
4 months	.79	.95	.71	.74	.96	.66	.90	.98	.05
6 months	.86	.94	.77	.86	.95	.55	.93	.98	.00
Composite[a]	.53	.77	—	.59	.82	—	—	—	—

Note: N's vary on the basis of the number of time intervals possible for the 28-month period in the database, nested in 156 census tracts. All ICCs are significant at $p < .001$. ICC = intraclass correlation coefficient.

[a]A combination of the raw count and the measures of concern for the public space, calculated for 6-month windows only. See text for more details on construction.

are acceptable spatiotemporal windows available for all of the measures apart from big buildings. For those measures with greater consistency, the options are many: housing, for example, could be measured at two-month intervals for tracts or four-month intervals for CBGs. For others, like uncivil use, there is a need for six-month intervals at the tract level, and no time interval satisfies this criterion for CBGs.

The slope reliabilities in Tables 5 and 6 indicate the ability of the model to distinguish between the trajectories of different regions over time. Variation in slopes across CBGs and tracts were significant at $p <$ .05 (or some lower threshold) in nearly all models, with the exception of those for big buildings and those for public reporters of intervals longer than four months. This variation was somewhat more discernible in tract-level models.

We then examined whether these cross-time consistencies hold for the composite measures. For the sake of simplicity, this was done for all variables using six-month windows for tracts. Note that the generation of the composite measures requires the incorporation of the number of exemplars, measured for the full year preceding the last day of the given time window. Consequently, the first time window analyzed must be that which ends at or after the end of the 12th month of the available database, diminishing the number of measurements per tract. For this reason, this analysis does not examine change over time.

Similar to the above examples, multilevel models were run to examine the consistency of the composite measures across space and time. The reliabilities and ICCs from these are reported in the bottom row of Table 6. Across the board, reliabilities and ICCs were lower for the composite measures, but not alarmingly so. All measures (other than big buildings) maintained ICCs of about .6 or higher, and housing had an ICC greater than .7. Reliabilities were typically about .8.

Last, we replicated the analysis for the two higher order constructs, private neglect and public denigration. The statistical advantage is that the combination of multiple measures amplifies the number of cases in the average time interval, thereby enabling higher reliabilities and ICCs at smaller time windows. This is particularly important when considering a measure such as big buildings, which has a low reliability when measured on its own but might be fruitfully incorporated into a more comprehensive description of the neighborhood.

Reliabilities and ICCs for these higher order counts were higher than their constituent categories. For each, the criterion of ICC = .7 was attained at six-month intervals for CBGs and two-month intervals for tracts. (Complete results are available on request from the authors.) This remained largely consistent when they were combined with measures of concern for the public space to create composite measures, though the consistency in public denigration for small time windows was somewhat diminished. For tracts with two-month intervals, public denigration had an ICC of .44 and a reliability coefficient of .88. Private neglect had an ICC of .65 and a reliability coefficient of .94. For CBGs with six-month intervals, public denigration had an ICC of .51 and a reliability coefficient of .76. Private neglect had an ICC of .68 and a reliability coefficient of .87.

5. SUMMARY AND IMPLICATIONS

In the present study, we sought to demonstrate how a citizen-initiated administrative database might act as "the eyes and ears of the city" in the spirit of Jane Jacobs (1961) while providing a low-cost, real-time measure of physical disorder. To accomplish this goal, we needed to address three major issues: (1) the lack of interpretable constructs, (2) the potential that the raw database might not objectively or accurately reflect real-world conditions, and (3) the need for criteria for reliability when bounding measures in space and time. Creating a set of theoretically guided factors first required an item-response model, in this case 28 case types that reflected deterioration or incivilities within a neighborhood. The subsequent factor analysis revealed five separate categories of physical disorder. It is worth noting that these constructs were extant in the data but that it was necessary to distinguish them from the noise surrounding them. Skipping forward to analysis 3, once these measures were fully developed, criteria for reliability were established both for one-time measures and cross-time trajectories using multilevel modeling.

In between these two steps, analysis 2 addressed the question of validity, which is a perhaps underappreciated concern for ecometric study. Neighborhood audit protocols are developed and administered to measure specific things as accurately as possible, meaning that they have an inherent validity for those items that they assess. In contrast, administrative data are the by-product of processes whose idiosyncrasies might bias their reflection of ground truth. The CRM database is the product of constituent reports and is therefore vulnerable to inconsistencies in reporting across neighborhoods. Because the nature of the bias was known, however, it was possible to account for it. The final methodology used indicators of civic response rate, derived from the CRM database itself, to systematically adjust raw measures to better reflect objective conditions. Reaching this point entailed considerable work, including two independent data collections and a lengthy set of analyses. Nonetheless, that investment of cost and effort would be necessary for any traditional protocol for measuring disorder, and in our case laid the groundwork for a methodology that can be reproduced at little cost both within Boston across time and in other cities with their own CRM systems. It is also worth noting that cities frequently conduct audit studies, so it is reasonable to assume that there will be an ongoing stream of potential sources of data from which to derive validation measures.

The final product was a multidimensional measure of physical disorder that is not only nearly costless to the researcher but also more comprehensive and precise than other measures currently available. Furthermore, the programming code published along with this paper (at the Boston Area Research Initiative's Web site, http://www.bostonar earesearchinitiative.net/data-library.php) facilitates reproduction of the measure wherever similar databases exist. Given these apparent upsides to the use of administrative data, it seems appropriate to forward the following new, three-step process for carrying ecometrics into the age of big data:

1. *Extract constructs* by identifying item-specific models that are reflective of the theoretical concept of interest and then examining their underlying factor structure
2. *Validate the measure* by identifying and adjusting for any bias the information source might impart to the data and examining in conjunction with external data.
3. *Establish reliability* in the measure's ability to track information across space and time.

With this methodology in hand, the opportunity before ecometric urban science is considerable, as there is a veritable trove of information on cities that sits largely untapped, of which CRM databases are but one example. Cities collect and now make available many other data points—such as tax assessments, building permits, zoning decisions, restaurant inspections, environmental assessments, housing code violations, pedestrian flows, and bicycle collisions, to name a few— each providing its own insights on the social and physical ecology of neighborhoods. Going further, there are private databases, such as Twitter, cell phone records, and Flickr photo collections, that are also geocoded and might be equally informative in building innovative measures of urban social processes. These various resources could be used to develop new versions of traditionally popular measures, as we have done here, or to explore new ones that have not been previously accessible. An illustration of the latter comes from our own analysis, in which a by-product of validation has provided two unanticipated behavioral measures—one related to civic engagement and the other capturing attitudes toward disorder in the public space. The potential of new forms of large-scale data underscores the central inspiration of this paper: as the volume of data on urban areas continues to grow and diversify, such data provide new and distinctive ways to measure neighborhood characteristics, often in ways previously unforeseen. These advances can be appropriated to shed light on some of the most salient themes in urban science, from the structure and function of the social organization, to the role of cognition and culture in generating local patterns, to the nascent examination of relationships between neighborhoods and the higher order social structure of the city.

Apart from its implications for ecometric science more broadly, the current methodology represents an advance for the direct measurement of physical disorder in urban neighborhoods. It incorporates a broad range of phenomena and is the first physical disorder measure to divide these items into independent subcategories, suggesting new avenues for research. For example, do the five subcategories relate differently to a neighborhood's other social and demographic characteristics? If so, do they each reflect a different set of processes occurring within the neighborhood? Furthermore, what is the source of the higher order constructs suggested by analysis 1, private neglect and public denigration? Is it that their constituent types are all manifestations of the same social and behavioral patterns, or do they share other causal relationships that reinforce their correlation? It is crucial that we not overinterpret this single case and inappropriately reify these particular constructs. It will be necessary to confirm their consistency with data from other time points and cities, something that is likely to be possible with the continued proliferation of CRM systems throughout North America and Western Europe.

In addition, the measures enable a variety of analytical approaches that could prove useful in the extension of research surrounding "broken windows" and other theories of neighborhood well-being. All of the measures describe neighborhood conditions at the level of census tracts, and some can be used for CBGs. Future work could likely find ways to measure and interpret patterns of disorder for streets or even individual buildings. The measures can also be tracked across time, allowing analyses that evaluate not only what a neighborhood's current level of physical disorder is, but whether it is on an upward or downward trajectory.

Finally, the CRM data are continuously generated as part of administrative operations. A new study with up-to-date data requires only a download and some data manipulation. In an effort to assist others in initiating such work, we will be publishing the computer code for constructing the measures developed in the current paper (along with the data, at the Boston Area Research Initiative's Web site, http://www .bostonarearesearchinitiative.net/data-library.php). As CRM systems become more numerous around the world, typically in the form of 311 hotlines, this sort of measurement is becoming possible in a variety of cities. Some of these cities have established common standards for publishing CRM data, meaning that the data are not only being made readily available but are compatible in ways that would support cross-city comparisons.

6. BALANCING LIMITATIONS AND OPPORTUNITIES

We have thus far focused predominantly on the opportunity presented by "big data," but we must also take stock of the limitations that they carry and the challenges to be addressed. Indeed, the methodology presented here is only a first step—an illustration of what is possible—and future work will need to refine it further, particularly in terms of the validation process. We would likewise stress that traditional, well-established methods of urban data collection, such as community surveys and social observation (Sampson 2012), will continue to play an essential role in any future analysis. Claims to the contrary are merely "big data hubris," as aptly put by Lazer et al. (2014). Each approach has its pros and cons, the balancing of which will depend on the research question. Surveys and observation are expensive and cannot realistically be carried out in real time, for example, but they can be calibrated to be representative of the population. In contrast, the CRM data analyzed here are cheap and in principle can be measured at very fine grained geographic scales and almost in real time, but issues of reliability and what the data are really measuring remain.

For example, complaints about big buildings were not particularly common in our database, making it difficult to measure that construct reliably. Techniques that aggregate cases at higher levels, by increasing the geographical range or the temporal window or, as we did here, combining multiple related constructs, will be critical. Future research is needed to examine these issues, especially in a context that can directly compare and contrast different methodologies of data collection, such as systematic social observation. Perhaps another factor is more important: although our validation process is promising, we still cannot be entirely certain that we have directly accessed the intended information, especially for those things that occur within private spaces or out of public observation. In particular, our measures of public denigration were not as closely correlated with other indicators of urban social structure as might be expected from past research. It may be, as we noted earlier, that the techniques for measuring and accounting for bias in this case were not sufficient to fully calibrate public denigration.

Another potential weakness is our working assumption that reporting bias is consistent across case types. Our data here seem to suggest that the situation is more nuanced, as reporting rates for streetlight outages and broken sidewalks were only moderately correlated. This finding points to important improvements for future versions of the measure, while also highlighting the need to tailor the validation process to the specific measure of interest. In some cases, like the ones presented here, there is a need to adjust for biases inherent in the data, and the objective measures necessary for doing so will need to be carefully constructed and measured.

In other cases, however, such a process of construct validation or bias adjustment may be less necessary or not applicable, even though reliability assessment by temporal and geographic scale remains at issue. For example, building permits and zoning approvals or variances are legal requirements for major building renovations and additions, meaning they should be largely objective in the information they provide. Allocation of city resources (e.g., beautification efforts or economic development) or distribution of the city budgets by amount and location are also largely "bias free" in their measurement and now widely available electronically. The availability of such measures could provide new insight into processes such as gentrification and inequality in the delivery of city services (e.g., Hwang and Sampson 2014).

Furthermore, in certain cases, the raw contents of the data are exactly what a researcher wants, and their face validity is sufficient to offer concrete interpretation. In such situations, researchers do not actually want to adjust for any biases. For example, a recent paper used noise complaints from New York City's 311 hotline as a direct reflection of social conflict between neighbors (Legewie and Schaeffer 2015). Regardless of actual noise levels or norms of reactivity, each call in this analysis reflects an objective case of one neighbor asking the government to regulate the behavior of another. More generally, the electronic availability in many cities of citizen reporting systems offers a wide variety of domains (in our Boston data, 178 unique types of service calls) to test Black's (1976) theory of the behavior of law and citizen initiation of government control.

Of course, the fundamental issues of measurement error and validity bear down at some level on all methodologies: survey reports can be skewed by other perceptual factors, including implicit judgments of race and class (Sampson and Raudenbush 2004), and observational work is dependent on interrater reliability that is always less than unity. The dominant investigator-driven research method is to conduct surveys or interviews, but even here, there is continuing controversy over the idea that researcher control leads to validity. For example, a recent critique argues that interviews are a weak basis for studying culture or inferring the motives for an individual's behaviors (Jerolmack and Khan 2014, and responses). Although we would not go that far, our point is that assumptions must always be invoked in the analysis of social science data.

It remains significant, however, that administrative data are outside of a researcher's direct control and that assumptions may sometimes be required that are uncheckable because of unobserved processes related to reporting or administrative filtering. It follows that validation is imperfect and should be viewed as a continuing process, one that will need to be undertaken for new administrative data sets that become available. Some might argue that these caveats obviate the usefulness of administrative data and other forms of "naturally occurring" digital information. Our position is to recognize both strengths and weaknesses of the new data being made available, using the most rigorous methods possible to address limitations. In defense of our approach, we would also note the significant advantages of the CRM data we analyzed relative to big data more generally. The CRM data are characterized by their richness and geographic precision, and their longitudinal nature permits long-term tracking. In addition, some of the content that is most difficult to validate stems from the fact that it cannot be measured by direct means and was thus previously unavailable, making it novel. If used properly, such data can broaden the range of questions that we can examine and the manner in which we do so. Our hope is that future efforts will capitalize on the advantages of large-scale administrate records and to combine them in meaningful ways with survey and observational protocols.

In sum, instead of an either/or approach, the debate between those who believe that only data generated directly as part of the research process are valid and those who believe that administrative and other types of naturally occurring data can be of use pushes both sides to improve the quality of their research, which certainly can only lead to better science. Meanwhile, because of the increasing availability of big data at little or no cost and at unprecedented temporal and geographic scales, such data remain a resource to be tapped, and it is incumbent upon researchers to develop methodologies that do so in ways that fulfill the expectations of rigorous science.

7. METHODOLOGY, THEORY, AND THE FUTURE OF BIG DATA

Although this paper was tailored to the specifics of ecometrics, the rise of big data illustrates the challenges facing computational social science writ large. There is a clear need to demonstrate what these novel data sources can measure and how constructed metrics are theoretically relevant. Furthermore, they must be demonstrated to be both reliable and valid in their measurement before modeling can begin, which unfortunately seems to be the default in many current approaches that emphasize "econometrics" over "ecometrics" or simply the power to predict. However powerful predictive analytics may be, it does not answer the substantive questions about social processes and mechanisms that motivate most social scientists.

In this paper, therefore, we set out to accomplish a linked set of measurement goals that was rooted in substantive concerns. We grounded our study in a measure that is influential in urban research and theory, and we closely examined validity in a manner that goes beyond previous work. Though others have used supplementary data to give context to the patterns in Facebook or cell phone calls (Eagle, Pentland, and Lazer 2009; Kosinski, Stillwell, and Graepel 2013), ours is the only study that we know of that has gone a step further, using multiple internal measures to reduce measurement error and then validating this technique with external sources and substantive theory—an approach that was not simply data driven. Given the size and novelty of aptly termed "big" data, there is the temptation to allow such data to guide analysis and, in turn, dictate theory. Indeed, some have claimed that the era of big data will eliminate the need for theory, as it will be derived from the massive size of the data available. The former editor of *Wired* magazine was perhaps the most bold, claiming "the end of theory" and that "the data deluge makes the scientific method obsolete" (quoted in Pigliucci 2009). We strongly disagree. Purely data-driven approaches run the risk for producing models and algorithms that are overfit to the idiosyncrasies of a particular data set, leading to new theoretical models that are artifactual or just plain wrong—something that has been partially blamed for the failure to predict the crash of the housing bubble in 2008. Big data hubris is indeed a problem (Lazer et al. 2014). Accordingly, we have had theory take the lead throughout, determining the case types reflecting physical disorder and the measures of civic response rate.

A balance must nonetheless be maintained. As Lazer et al. (2009) rightfully pointed out, our current theories are not well suited to the complexity of information contained in these sorts of data and consequently are often unequipped to offer conjectures about them. In the current case, there was no model of disorder that was sufficiently articulated to predict a priori categories for the 28 indicators that we identified. Thus, there is something to be learned from these data about the causal dynamics that underpin disorder and its various manifestations, though such insights will of course be subject to the same rigorous evaluation required of any new theory. This "checks-and-balances" relationship between theory and empirics is instructive, and it will probably characterize the continued efforts of scientists to incorporate big data into their work, as well as to facilitate the emergence of a fully mature field of computational social science.

APPENDIX A

Table A1. Case Types That Reflect an Issue in the Public Space and Counts in 2011

Case Type	Count
Abandoned bicycle	71
Abandoned building	103
Abandoned vehicles	2,233
Bridge maintenance	29
Building inspection request	822
Catch basin	13
Construction debris	101
Empty litter basket	292
Exceeding terms of permit	68
Fire hydrant	8
General lighting request	460
Graffiti removal	3,893
Highway maintenance	3,297
Illegal auto body shop	46
Illegal dumping	831
Illegal occupancy	263
Illegal posting of signs	116
Illegal rooming house	177
Illegal use	62
Illegal vending	32
Improper storage of trash (barrels)	1,745
Install new lighting	25
Miscellaneous snow complaint	1,407
Missed trash/recycling/yard waste/bulk item	6,211
Missing sign	671
New sign, crosswalk or pavement marking	976
New tree requests	831
Overflowing or unkempt Dumpster	149
Park improvement requests	3
Park maintenance requests	87
Park safety notifications	2
Parking enforcement	685
Parking meter repairs	139
Parking on front/back yards (illegal parking)	132
Parks general request	106
Parks lighting issues	5
Pavement marking maintenance	272
Pick up dead animal	1,374
Pigeon infestation	29
PWD graffiti	160
Request for litter basket installation	80
Request for pothole repair	4,603
Request for snow plowing	7,270
Requests for street cleaning	953

(continued)

Table A1. (continued)

Case Type	Count
Requests for traffic signal studies or reviews	96
Roadway repair	306
Rodent activity	1,241
Sidewalk cover/manhole	3
Sidewalk repair	1,294
Sidewalk repair (make safe)	2,119
Sign repair	1,172
Snow removal	2,103
Streetlight knock-downs	476
Streetlight outages	8,127
Traffic signal repair	2,585
Trash on vacant lot	121
Tree emergencies	3,446
Tree maintenance requests	3,336
Upgrade existing lighting	15

Note: PWD = Public Works Department.

Acknowledgments

We thank the City of Boston's Office of New Urban Mechanics and Department of Innovation and Technology for supporting our examination of government data; Jeremy Levine for assistance with the data; and the editor and reviewers of *Sociological Methodology* for helpful comments on earlier drafts. A version of this paper was presented at the annual meeting of the American Association for the Advancement of Science in Chicago, February 15, 2014.

Funding

Funding assistance was provided by the National Science Foundation (grant SMA 1338446), the John D. and Catherine T. MacArthur Foundation (grant 13-105766-000-USP), and the Radcliffe Institute for Advanced Study.

Notes

1. We thank an anonymous reviewer for spurring our thoughts on this issue.
2. This is encouraged by the directors of the CRM system, who see following up with constituents as central to their goal of establishing open communication between citizens and the government.
3. Users who made one or more reports as department members at any time (including 2010 or 2012) were removed because city employees differ from other constituents in their motivation for making reports. This excluded five individuals, a number that is small because for many employee-specific case types, user IDs were stripped before data sharing.

4. Two CBGs were excluded from analysis because there were concerns that calls from there might not reflect use of the CRM system by actual residents: (1) the CBG that contains City Hall, because many reports without addresses are attributed to that location, and (2) the CBG that contains a large park, zoo, and golf course but includes the houses that ring the park.

5. The number of snowplow requests (log-transformed to adjust for a skewed distribution) was regressed on these three measures, accounting for 14 percent of the variation across CBGs.

6. The home location was estimated in two ways, depending on the geographic range of an individual's requests for service. If the individual reported cases over a range with diameter smaller than .5 miles (90 percent of users), location was defined as the centroid of all reports made, which was then attributed to the appropriate CBG. Because of the small range, this estimate can be assumed to be reasonably precise. For those whose range had a diameter greater than .5 miles, this precision was weaker. These individuals were attributed not to a centroid but to the CBG from which they made the most calls. This was done using the entire period of the database (March 2010 to June 2012) to make the greatest use of available information. This estimation technique was validated against a sample of 7,433 users for whom home locations were known. Of these, 78 percent were attributed to the correct CBG. More important, the counts generated by this process correlated with actual counts at $r = .93$. There is reason to believe that this correlation is underestimated. The sample used in the validation had an above-average number of calls per person, a subsample for which the estimates had greater error.

7. Note that this means that a streetlight might have been reported before the audit, as long as the city had not completed the job until afterward.

8. It was possible to distinguish whether a report was made by a constituent or a city employee. Thus, a continuous measure of the time before reporting would not necessarily reflect the strength of constituent response. Instead, the dichotomous measures were created so that employee-reported outages could be considered not reported until the date the employee report appeared. Thereafter, they were omitted from the data, as it is not possible to know whether a constituent would have reported up to that point. For example, a streetlight outage reported 16 days later by a city employee takes the value zero for the measure of being reported within two weeks but would take no value (omitted) for the measure one month.

9. The response rate was standardized and centered before the interaction was calculated. The physical disorder measures were left uncentered, with a minimum of zero, so that the response rate would adjust up or down proportional to the total number of actual reports.

10. The BNS was a telephone survey based on the methodology from Raudenbush and Sampson (1999) with 3,428 participants in two waves (2008: $n = 1,710$; 2010: $n = 1,718$) recruited by random-digit dialing. The two waves were combined to provide a reasonable number of respondents to create measurements at the scale of CBGs. Scales measuring physical disorder and collective efficacy were calculated first for each individual respondent. Neighborhood-level measures were then calculated by fitting multilevel models that nested individuals within their CBG and controlled for individual-level demographic characteristics (gender, age, ethnicity,

and parental status). The Bayes residuals for the neighborhood-level model were then extracted as neighborhood measures adjusted for measurement error.

11. For example, there were 28 one-month time windows between March 10 and June 12, generating that many counts for each CBG. The resultant data set then contained 15,176 counts (28 × 542), each attributed to a CBG and a time window.

12. A distinction created by the Boston Redevelopment Authority for administrative purposes but based on historically salient regions, many of which are once independent municipalities that were annexed. Using an analysis of variance, the planning districts account for about 50 percent of the variation in ethnic composition and median income across census tracts.

13. This number diminishes with some measures that allow greater time between identification of an outage and reporting, being that those reported by city employees in that time span were removed.

References

Black, Donald. 1976. *The Behavior of Law*. New York: Academic Press.

Brown, Barbara B., Douglas D. Perkins, and Graham Brown. 2004. "Incivilities, Place Attachment, and Crime: Block and Individual Effects." *Journal of Environmental Psychology* 24:359–71.

Burdette, A. M., and T. D. Hill. 2008. "An Examination of Processes Linking Perceived Neighborhood Disorder and Obesity." *Social Science and Medicine* 67:38–46.

Caughy, M. O., S. M. Nettles, and P. J. O'Campo. 2008. "The Effect of Residential Neighborhood on Child Behavior Problems in First Grade." *American Journal of Community Psychology* 42:39–50.

Caughy, Margaret O., Patricia J. O'Campo, and Jacqueline Patterson. 2001. "A Brief Observational Measure for Urban Neighborhoods." *Health and Place* 7:225–36.

Cohen, Deborah, Suzanne Spear, Richard Scribner, Patty Kissinger, Karen Mason, and John Widgen. 2000. "'Broken Windows' and the Risk of Gonorrhea." *American Journal of Public Health* 90:230–36.

Eagle, Nathan, Alex Pentland, and David Lazer. 2009. "Inferring Friendship Network Structure by Using Mobile Phone Data." *Proceedings of the National Academy of Sciences* 106:15274–78.

Fischel, William A. 2005. The *Homevoter Hypothesis: How Home Values Influence Local Government Taxation, School Finance, and Land-use Policies*. Cambridge, MA: Harvard University Press.

Franzini, Luisa, Margaret O'Brien Caughy, Saundra Murray Nettles, and Patricia O'Campo. 2008. "Perceptions of Disorder: Contributions of Neighborhood Characteristics to Subjective Perceptions of Disorder." *Journal of Environmental Psychology* 28:83–93.

Furr-Holden, C. D. M., M. J. Smart, J. L. Pokorni, N. S. Ialongo, P. J. Leaf, H. D. Holder, and J. C. Anthony. 2008. "The Nifety Method for Environmental Assessment of Neighborhood-level Indicators of Violence, Alcohol, and Other Drug Exposure." *Prevention Science* 9:245–55.

Furr-Holden, C. Debra M., Adam J. Milam, Elizabeth K. Reynolds, Laura MacPherson, and Carl W. Lejuez. 2012. "Disordered Neighborhood Environments and Risk-taking

Propensity in Late Childhood through Adolescence." *Journal of Adolescent Health* 50:100–102.

Hwang, Jackelyn, and Robert J. Sampson. 2014. "Divergent Pathways of Gentrification: Racial Inequality and the Social Order of Renewal in Chicago Neighborhoods." *American Sociological Review* 79:726–51.

Jacobs, Jane. 1961. *The Death and Life of Great American Cities.* New York: Random House.

Jerolmack, Colin, and Khan, Shamus. 2014. "Talk Is Cheap: Ethnography and Attitudinal Fallacy." *Sociological Methods and Research* 43:78–209.

Kosinski, Michal, David Stillwell, and Thore Graepel. 2013. "Private Traits and Attributes Are Predictable from Digital Records of Human Behavior." *Proceedings of the National Academy of Sciences* 110:5802–5805.

Lazer, David, Ryan Kennedy, Gary King, and Alessandro Vespignani. 2014. "The Parable of Google Flu: Traps in Big Data Analysis." *Science* 343:1203–1205.

Lazer, David, Alex Pentland, Lada Adamic, Siana Aral, Albert-Laszlo Barabasi, Devon Brewer, Nicholas A. Christakis, Noshir Contractor, James Fowler, Myron Gutmann, Tony Jebara, Gary King, Michael Macy, Deb Roy, and Marshall Van Alstyne. 2009. "Computational Social Science." *Science* 323:721–23.

Legewie, Joscha, and Schaeffer, Merlin. 2015. "Contested Boundaries: Explaining Where Ethno-Racial Diversity Provokes Neighborhood Conflict." Working paper, New York University.

Mujahid, M. S., A.V.D. Roux, M. W. Shen, D. Gowda, B. Sanchez, S. Shea, D. R. Jacobs, and S. A. Jackson. 2008. "Relation between Neighborhood Environments and Obesity in the Multi-Ethnic Study of Atherosclerosis." *American Journal of Epidemiology* 167:1349–57.

O'Brien, Daniel Tumminelli. 2012. "Managing the Urban Commons: The Relative Influence of Individual and Social Inventives on the Treatment of Public Space." *Human Nature* 23:467–89.

O'Brien, Daniel Tumminelli. 2015. "Custodians and Custodianship in Urban Neighborhoods: A Methodology Using Reports of Public Issues Received by a City's 311 Hotline." *Environment and Behavior* 47:304–27.

O'Brien, Daniel Tumminelli, and Richard A. Kauffman. 2013. "Broken Windows and Low Adolescent Prosociality: Not Cause and Consequence but Co-symptoms of Low Collective Efficacy." *American Journal of Community Psychology* 51:359–69.

O'Brien, Daniel Tumminelli, and David S. Wilson. 2011. "Community Perception: The Ability to Assess the Safety of Unfamiliar Neighborhoods and Respond Adaptively." *Journal of Personality and Social Psychology* 100:606–20.

Pigliucci, Massimo 2009. "The End of Theory in Science?" *European Molecular Biology Organization Reports* 10:534.

Putnam, Robert. 1993. *Making Democracy Work: Civic Traditions in Modern Italy.* Princeton, NJ: Princeton University Press.

Raudenbush, Stephen W., Anthony Bryk, Yuk Fai Cheong, Richard Congdon, and Mathilda du Toit. 2004. *Hlm 6: Hierarchical Linear and Nonlinear Modeling.* Lincolnwood, IL: Scientific Software International.

Raudenbush, Stephen W., and Robert J. Sampson. 1999. "Ecometrics: Toward a Science of Assessing Ecological Settings, with Application to the Systematic Social

Observation of Neighborhoods." Pp. 1–41 in *Sociological Methodology*, Vol. 29, edited by Michael E. Sobel and Mark P. Becker. Boston, MA: Blackwell.

Ross, Catherine E., and John Mirowsky. 1999. "Disorder and Decay: The Concept and Measurement of Perceived Neighborhood Disorder." *Urban Affairs Review* 34: 412–32.

Ross, Catherine E., J. Mirowsky, and S. Pribesh. 2001. "Powerlessness and the Amplification of Threat: Neighborhood Disadvantage, Disorder, and Mistrust." *American Sociological Review* 66:568–91.

Rundle, A. G., M.D.M. Bader, C. A. Richards, K. M. Neckerman, and J. O. Teitler. 2011. "Using Google Street View to Audit Neighborhood Environments." *American Journal of Preventive Medicine* 40:94–100.

Sampson, Robert J. 2012. *Great American City: Chicago and the Enduring Neighborhood Effect*. Chicago: University of Chicago Press.

Sampson, Robert J., and Stephen W. Raudenbush. 2004. "Seeing Disorder: Neighborhood Stigma and the Social Construction of 'Broken Windows.'" *Social Psychology Quarterly* 67:317–42.

Skogan, Wesley G. 1992. *Disorder and Decline*. Berkeley: University of California Press.

Tabachnick, Barbara G., and Linda S. Fidell. 2006. *Using Multivariate Statistics*. New York: Allyn & Bacon.

Taylor, Ralph B. 2001. *Breaking Away from Broken Windows: Baltimore Neighborhoods and the Nationwide Fight against Crime, Grime, Fear, and Decline*. Boulder, CO: Westview.

Verba, Sidney, Kay Lehman Schlozman, and Henry E. Brady. 1995. *Voice and Equality: Civic Volunteerism in American Politics*. Cambridge, MA: Harvard University Press.

Wen, Ming, Lousie C. Hawkley, and John T. Cacioppo. 2006. "Objective and Perceived Neighborhood Environment, Individual SES and Psychosocial Factors, and Self-rated Health: An Analysis of Older Adults in Cook County, Illinois." *Social Science and Medicine* 63:2575–90.

Wilson, James Q., and George L. Kelling. 1982. "The Police and Neighborhood Safety: Broken Windows." *Atlantic Monthly* 127:29–38.

Author Biographies

Daniel Tumminelli O'Brien is an assistant professor in the School of Public Policy and Urban Affairs and the School of Criminology and Criminal Justice at Northeastern University. He is also the research director for the Boston Area Research Initiative, an interuniversity program based at Harvard University's Radcliffe Institute for Advanced Study that pursues and fosters an urban research agenda for the digital age. His research examines the behavioral and social dynamics of urban neighborhoods, focusing on models of collective function and decline, including the "broken windows theory." His work uses large administrative data sets (i.e., "big data") in conjunction with traditional methodologies to study the city. He earned his PhD in evolutionary biology from Binghamton University.

Robert J. Sampson is the Henry Ford II Professor of the Social Sciences at Harvard University and Director of the Boston Area Research Initiative at the Radcliffe Institute for Advanced Study. Former president of the American Society of Criminology, he is a member of the National Academy of Sciences and fellow of the American Academy of Arts and Sciences and the American Philosophical Society. In 2011, he received the Stockholm Prize in Criminology. Professor Sampson's research focuses on urban inequality, crime, the life course, neighborhood effects, civic engagement, and the social structure of the contemporary city. His most recent book, *Great American City: Chicago and the Enduring Neighborhood Effect* (University of Chicago Press, 2013, paperback ed.), received the Distinguished Scholarly Book Award from the American Sociological Association in 2014.

Christopher Winship is the Diker-Tishman Professor of Sociology, a Harvard Kennedy School of Government faculty member, and faculty codirector of the Boston Area Research Initiative. He holds a BA in sociology and mathematics from Dartmouth College and a PhD in sociology from Harvard. He held postdoctoral fellowships at the Institute for Research on Poverty at the University of Wisconsin and the National Opinion Research Center at the University of Chicago. He was a professor of sociology, statistics, and economics (by courtesy) at Northwestern University and served as director of the Program in Mathematical Methods in the Social Sciences before he returned to Harvard in 1992. He has edited *Sociological Methods and Research* since 1995. He is affiliated with the Harvard Institute for Quantitative Social Science and the Harvard Hauser Center for Nonprofit Organizations. His research has focused on the Ten Point Coalition, a group of black ministers working with the Boston police to reduce youth violence; statistical models for causal analysis; the effects of education on mental ability; the causes of racial difference in performance at elite postsecondary institutions; and changes in the racial differential in imprisonment rates.

Sociological Methodology
2015, Vol. 45(1) 148–183
© American Sociological Association 2015
DOI: 10.1177/0081175015581378
http://sm.sagepub.com

⛬ 3 ⛬

$$SAGE

A PROGRESSIVE SUPERVISED-LEARNING APPROACH TO GENERATING RICH CIVIL STRIFE DATA

Peter F. Nardulli*
Scott L. Althaus*
Matthew Hayes†

Abstract

"Big data" in the form of unstructured text pose challenges and opportunities to social scientists committed to advancing research frontiers. Because machine-based and human-centric approaches to content analysis have different strengths for extracting information from unstructured text, the authors argue for a collaborative, hybrid approach that combines their comparative advantages. The notion of a progressive supervised-learning approach that combines data science techniques and human coders is developed and illustrated using the Social, Political and Economic Event Database (SPEED) project's Societal Stability Protocol. SPEED's rich event data on civil strife reveal that conventional machine-based approaches for generating event data miss a great deal of within-category variance, while conventional human-based efforts to categorize periods of civil war or political instability routinely misspecify periods of calm and unrest. To demonstrate the potential

*University of Illinois at Urbana-Champaign, Champaign, Illinois, USA
†Indiana University, Bloomington, Indiana, USA

Corresponding Author:
Peter F. Nardulli, University of Illinois at Urbana-Champaign, Cline Center for Democracy, 2001 S. First Street, Suite 207, Champaign, IL 61820-7461, USA
Email: nardulli@illinois.edu

of hybrid data collection methods, SPEED data on event intensities and origins are used to trace the changing role of political, socioeconomic, and sociocultural factors in generating global civil strife in the post–World War II era.

Keywords

civil strife, content analysis, event data, automated learning, unstructured data

1. THE CONTINUING CHALLENGE OF UNSTRUCTURED DATA

The "big data" revolution has enhanced the ability of scholars to create useful knowledge out of structured data such as ordered numbers and unstructured data such as text or images. This notwithstanding, fully automated processing of unstructured data still yields less sophisticated output than human analysis of texts and images. Yet because human analysis does not scale well, this traditional solution to unstructured data analysis cannot take full advantage of the proliferation of information generated by the data revolution. Because so much of the information of interest to social scientists is embedded in unstructured data (Franzosi 2004; Grimmer and Stewart 2013), social researchers must find a way to leverage developments in data science if they are to advance social science knowledge and keep pace with other disciplines.

Both the challenges and opportunities posed by big data can be seen in research on civil strife, which has become an increasingly important topic for conflict and development scholars. Data on civil strife events are traditionally harvested from news reports. Recent advances in information technologies have led to the proliferation of digitized news sources and prodigious amounts of digitized news content. Technological innovations have also enhanced the ability of researchers to access this diverse array of available content. These developments make it possible to mitigate what civil strife researchers have long known to be an important validity threat to media-based data: selection biases that may distort the true distribution of events (e.g., Althaus et al. 2011; Danzger 1975; Franzosi 1987; Jackman and Boyd 1979; Woolley 2000). Unfortunately, conventional approaches to content analysis require analysts to make a trade-off that limits the methodological benefits of diverse news sources: they must choose between the number of documents to be analyzed and the richness of the data to be extracted. Although human-based coding has long been the norm for content analysis, the advent of big data has made its limits increasingly apparent.

In this paper, we introduce a hybrid model that leverages the strengths of both machine-based and human-centric approaches to content analysis. Our basic thesis is that until fully automated approaches can match the flexibility and contextual richness of human coding, the best option for generating near-term advances in social science research lies in hybrid systems that rely on both machines and humans for extracting information from unstructured texts. The utility of hybrid approaches has been demonstrated in document clustering applications (Grimmer and King 2011), and it has been recognized by such technologically advanced companies as Google, IBM, and Apple (Lohr 2013). Hybrid systems are a key part of the international email-monitoring system developed by the National Security Agency (Savage 2013). This paper illustrates the value of such hybrid approaches for social research using data generated by the Social, Political and Economic Event Database (SPEED) project. SPEED's information base contains more than 100 million news reports drawn from every country in the world and spans the period from World War II to the present; its Societal Stability Protocol (SSP) generates civil strife data. The enormous volume of unstructured data embedded in these news reports are transformed into quantitative data by a structured set of work flows, developed in collaboration with a team of data scientists, that yield more nuanced codings than automated systems can provide at scales that were previously impossible for human coders.

Our discussion continues through the following sections. In Section 2, we introduce two conventional approaches to information extraction and illustrate how they have been used to study civil strife. In Section 3, we outline SPEED's hybrid approach; in Section 4, we examine its added value by contrasting SPEED data with existing civil strife data. In Section 5, we illustrate the potential for creating new frontiers in this field. Section 6 concludes the paper.

2. ALTERNATIVE APPROACHES TO INFORMATION EXTRACTION

The systematic analysis of textual content by human coders has been a standard method within social science research since at least World

War II (Krippendorff 2004; Neuendorf 2002). For almost as long, social scientists have experimented with using computers to emulate human-coded methods at larger scales and higher speeds and with more precision (e.g., Holsti 1964; Stone 1962). A half century later, social scientists continue to experiment with the computational analysis of textual data (e.g., Monroe and Schrodt 2008; Franzosi, De Fazio, and Vicari 2012). Yet for all the technological sophistication of today's machine-driven methods, the computational analysis of unstructured data is still far from matching the interpretive nuance and sophistication of human-based approaches.

2.1. *Machine-based and Human-centric Approaches*

The limitations of machine-based approaches can best be understood by distinguishing between "manifest" and "latent" content in textual data (Berelson 1952). Manifest content is observable and can be recognized without making a subjective judgment about its presence: it is there, and obviously so, or it is not. Examples of manifest content include the number of words in a newspaper story, whether it appears on the front page, and whether the word *protest* appears in the text. In contrast, latent content resides in symbolic patterns within a text that must be holistically interpreted by a qualified analyst (Potter and Levine-Donnerstein 1999). Examples of latent content include identifying the text's topical focus and deciding whether it depicts the government in a positive light and whether a quoted source is arguing against a course of action. These symbolic patterns sometimes reside in the manifest content of a text. But proper interpretation of latent content often requires the analyst to draw from contextual knowledge not contained within the text.

Human- and machine-based approaches can be compared along an array of dimensions (for recent discussions, see Quinn et al. 2010; Young and Soroka 2012), but two are particularly important: their efficiency in analyzing large amounts of text and their ability to capture latent content. Machines are unquestionably better than humans at analyzing manifest content more quickly, consistently, and accurately. Computers also trump humans at naive inference and straightforward forms of deductive reasoning. Thus, machine-based approaches are preferred when information extraction involves simple concepts and is context free or when the context required for identifying latent content can be derived entirely from the text's manifest content (e.g., Liu 2011;

Witten, Frank, and Hall 2011). Examples include translating keywords into numerical scores for sentiment analysis, implementing rule sets that make simple queries about a text, and deriving patterns solely from manifest content (e.g., What are the most common verbs in sentences containing the word *demonstration*?). Thus, machines outperform humans with respect to such tasks as named entity extraction, topically classifying documents on the basis of word co-occurrences, and determining whether different documents contain similar content.

Human-centric approaches can perform well in extracting latent content, particularly when coding judgments are context dependent or involve complex features of text or multiple dimensions of content. The comparative advantages of trained humans derive from their capacity to draw from contextual knowledge not embedded in the text, to deal with different patterns of language usage, and to use inductive reasoning to disambiguate textual references and meanings (Potter and Levine-Donnerstein 1999). Unlike computers, humans usually have little trouble determining which of several named persons any given *she* refers to, whether a date refers to the day of an attack or of a protest, and whether a quoted source is providing self-serving information. Moreover, humans can make complex judgments required to deal with ambiguity (e.g., understanding that a reference to "their concerns" elaborates upon a passage in the previous sentence) and to determine how to apply contextual information across multiple levels of analysis (e.g., whether a headline is useful for interpreting an ambiguous phrase). Humans remain superior to machines when the task requires inductive reasoning to spot a complex pattern or to decide how that complex pattern should be coded.

The extraordinary recent advances in computing capacity, machine learning, and natural language processing (NLP) have improved the ability of machines to emulate human processing of latent content. However, the efficiencies of machine-based approaches have most consistently been realized using the "bag of words" approach, which considers only patterns of word co-occurrence and proximity and ignores a text's narrative structure (e.g., Evans et al. 2007; Quinn et al. 2010). More complex forms of NLP use syntactical structure to derive meaning (e.g., Sudhahar et al. 2013; van Atteveldt et al. 2008). But because they are so computationally intensive and require texts that strictly adhere to formal grammatical rules, they are difficult to use at scale and on casually structured texts such as news reports. A more general concern with machine-based coding is that their results are rarely validated against human judgments. Sometimes computational methods deliver results similar to those of humans (e.g., King and Lowe 2003; Soroka 2012) and sometimes not (Conway 2006). In most cases the comparisons are never attempted, not only because they are time-consuming but also because many machine-based applications, such as document clustering, have no obvious human-coding counterpart.

One machine-based approach that permits testing of both the reliability and the validity of automated coding processes is a supervised-learning approach (for recent reviews, see Evans et al. 2007; Hillard, Purpura, and Wilkerson 2008; Witten et al. 2011). This approach uses two sets of human codings: (1) a "training set" of documents used to teach a machine system to optimally match human codings and (2) a "test set" of documents used to test the accuracy of the machine's outputs. The investment required to obtain these human-coded training and test sets can be substantial; they often consist of thousands, and ideally tens of thousands, of coded documents. Once a machine learning system demonstrates that it can reasonably reproduce human judgments, it is released to operate independently without further interaction with humans. However, applying the machine system to a different information source, or checking the system's accuracy over time, requires new sets of human-coded data. Conventional supervised learning systems therefore achieve optimal efficiencies over human coding only when the project parameters are invariant, the scale of the coding project is large, and the coding task is straightforward.

Supervised learning systems aside, the extent to which machines can reliably emulate human judgments remains an open question. One conclusion is clear: machine coding is no simple substitute for human coding. Earlier generations of researchers were warned against placing unwarranted faith in methodological shortcuts such as factor analysis (e.g., Armstrong 1967) and stepwise regression (e.g., Thompson 1995). The same cautions apply to automated processing of unstructured data, which presents no magic fix for the challenges in this field (Grimmer and Stewart 2013). Research on civil strife illustrates this point.

2.2. *Existing Approaches to Civil Strife Event Data*

The contemporary importance of civil strife was well articulated by Kahl (2006):

Civil strife in the developing world represents perhaps the greatest international security challenge of the early twenty-first century. Three-quarters of all wars since 1945 have been within countries rather than between them. . . . Wars and other violent conflicts have killed some 40 million people since 1945, and as many people have died as a result of civil strife since 1980 as were killed in the First World War. (p. 1)

In addition to the post–World War II shift from international to domestic conflict (e.g., Lacina and Gleditsch 2005; Themnér and Wallensteen 2011), scholars have noted that although civil wars have declined since 1992, other types of civil strife, such as state repression, one-sided violence, and nonviolent protests, have increased (Bernauer and Gleditsch 2012; Themnér and Wallensteen 2011; Urdal and Hoelscher 2012). These changes in the makeup of conflict have spurred renewed interest in generating civil strife event data. These efforts have included both human-centric and machine-based approaches.

The primary dependent variables in the study of civil strife derive from either *episodic* or *discrete* event data (Schrodt 2012). As illustrated in the first column of Table 1, episodic data such as that produced by the Uppsala Conflict Data Program/Peace Research Institute of Oslo (http://www.prio.org/Data/Armed-Conflict/UCDP-PRIO/) and the Correlates of War (COW) project (http://www.icpsr.umich.edu/icpsr web/RCMD/studies/9905) aim to capture a series of related happenings that unfold over a relatively long period of time (weeks, months, or years). Episodic data typically code a given country as being in a state of civil war (or not) during a given year; these judgments are made holistically by researchers drawing from a range of textual sources. For example, a minimum number of battlefield deaths in a country for a year might be used as a threshold for determining the existence of a civil war. Episodic data are normally operationalized as dummy variables.

In contrast to episodic data, discrete event data describe specific happenings—an attack, a boycott, an arrest—that unfold over a relatively short period of hours or days. Discrete event data are normally drawn from news reports and analyzed as event counts. Schrodt noted that discrete event data can be sparse or rich. Sparse event data (second column in Table 1) typically indicate whether a type of event occurred on a given date in a given country, without providing much additional detail. Most sparse event data are, therefore, temporally precise but geographically vague. The most important sparse event data sets are fully

Table 1. Types of Civil Unrest Event Data

	Episodic Data	Discrete Data	
		Sparse	Rich
Typical spatial resolution	Country	Country	City
Typical temporal resolution	Year	Day	Day
Level of detail	Whether a state of civil war or political instability exists	Whether a type of event occurred	Event intensity, origins, and outcome; number and identity of perpetrators and targets; linkage to previous events
Examples	UCDP/PRIO, COW	CAMEO, IDEA	ACLED, GTD
Largely automated	No	Yes	No
Advantage	Synthesizes discrete events into conflict periods even when event-specific data are lacking	Scale and speed of data collection using automated methods	Contextual data adds precision and depth to analyses
Disadvantage	Treats all conflicts as equivalent regardless of scale or intensity; subjective judgments used to identify and demarcate episodes	Treats all events of a given type as equivalent regardless of scale or intensity	Human involvement in data collection process limits scale and speed of data collection

Note. ACLED = Armed Conflict Location and Event Dataset; CAMEO = Conflict and Media Event Observations; COW = Correlates of War; GTD = Global Terrorism Database; IDEA = Integrated Data for Events Analysis; PRIO = Peace Research Institute of Oslo; UCDP = Uppsala Conflict Data Program.

automated efforts such as the Conflict and Media Event Observations project (Gerner et al. 2002) and the Integrated Data for Events Analysis project (Bond et al. 2003), which is a commercial enterprise that charges for access to its data.[1] Although each project required extensive upfront human investment, both are machine-based systems for extracting event data using news reports drawn principally from Reuters. Both also use an automated parser that analyzes the sematic structure of independent clauses within sentences for actions that fit their typologies.

Although these automated systems can quickly process huge amounts of text, the event data they generate capture little specific information on who did what to whom or when, where, and how it was done. Moreover, automated systems are limited to the information included in a particular independent clause. Thus, in addition to losing nuanced and context-specific meanings, they also cannot capture information that is expressed in more complex semantic structures (e.g., paragraphs or narratives).

Unlike sparse event data, rich event data—such as the Armed Conflict Location and Event Dataset (ACLED), Global Terrorism Database (GTD), the Social Conflict in Africa Database, and Worldwide Incidents Tracking System (citations and a more comprehensive listing and overview are provided in Schrodt 2012)—contain more extensive and precise information such as the event's actors, intensity, location, and date (column 3 of Table 1). This makes it possible to resolve these events to the city level, which means that rich event data tend to be both geographically and temporally precise. But this precision and contextual richness come at a cost: although sparse event data collection is usually highly automated, rich event data are normally collected using human-centric approaches. To illustrate the general approach taken by rich event data projects, we examine the ACLED project (Raleigh et al. 2010) and the GTD project (National Consortium for the Study of Terrorism and Responses to Terrorism 2012). Both are human-centered content analysis projects that do not use machine-learning techniques.

ACLED's greatest strengths are its rich diversity of sources[2] and the fact that it captures data on actors, dates, and locations. It has a "Notes" field containing various event-specific details. ACLED also has three important limitations: (1) restricted temporal and spatial coverage, focusing mostly on African countries and recording events occurring after 1996; (2) limited scope, considering only events that occurred within civil wars (as defined by the UCDP/PRIO data set); and (3) low levels of intercoder reliability (Eck 2012).

The strengths of the GTD project are its broad scope, its rich information base, and the amount of event-specific data it collects. GTD data begin in 1970 and have a global reach. GTD's historical archive was compiled by a commercial service; the 1998 to 2008 data were derived from more than 3.5 million news articles and 25,000 news sources. The event-specific data collected include information on actors as well as intensity indicators. GTD's most significant limitation is its event ontology, which includes only terrorist acts. By so limiting its event ontology, GTD ignores other important forms of civil unrest and state repression. This means that analysts using GTD data are limited in their ability to examine the contextual settings within which terrorism unfolds.

In sum, it is clear that conventional data collection strategies are highly limited in their ability to advance our understanding of civil strife. Automated approaches can efficiently document whether strife events occur across large spans of space and time, but they provide limited and inconsistent information about event-specific details. Human-centric approaches provide this rich contextual information, but only for applications with relatively narrow topical, geographical, and temporal horizons.

3. THE SPEED PROJECT: A PROGRESSIVE SUPERVISED-LEARNING SYSTEM

Dissatisfaction with the current research paradigm, together with the increasing importance and changing makeup of civil conflict, has generated calls for capturing rich event data involving a broader set of event types and actors (Chojnacki et al. 2012; Eck 2012; Raleigh 2012; Salehyan et al. 2012; Urdal and Hoelscher 2012). These calls are rooted in the need for greater flexibility and precision; the SPEED project was designed to address these needs. SPEED uses a hybrid work flow system that extracts rich event data at the city-day level from the full text of a diverse set of news sources. This hybrid system consists of both automated components and human-centric components. Together they form what we call a *progressive supervised-learning system*. In this system, human coders are presented with input data that have been automatically preprocessed and classified. Humans perform only the most difficult coding decisions, leaving the more mundane work to automated processes. Combining wide but shallow machine capabilities with deep but narrow human capabilities leverages the advantages of each while limiting their liabilities.

3.1. *Hybrid Work Flow Structure*

SPEED's hybrid approach integrates machine and human components in work flows that (1) assemble repositories of news documents, (2) classify and preprocess those documents, and (3) use technology-enhanced humans to extract structured data. Figure 1 provides a simplified view of SPEED's work flows. The circular components of the figure pertain to databases, the triangular components refer to human activity, and the square components denote automated processes. SPEED's work flows constitute a supervised-learning system because, although unsupervised applications and humans play key roles at various stages, its initial computational algorithms were derived from human-generated training data. SPEED's approach is progressive because the design of its work flows generates human feedback that updates the system's algorithms. This provides the means to enhance the role of automation as more training data and sophisticated machine learning techniques become available.

Central to SPEED's ability to advance social research is the information base from which it draws. An interdisciplinary team spent several years building a historical news repository that draws from tens of millions of news reports carried in the *New York Times* (*NYT*), the Foreign Broadcast Information Service, and the BBC's Summary of World Broadcasts (SWB) from World War II to the present. In addition to the millions of historical news reports from these sources, SPEED's contemporary news archive is continuously updated by a Heritrix Web-crawling system that draws daily from more than 800 global news Web sites.[3]

SPEED's work flow begins with several stages of machine-based processing that occur before humans access the news reports (see again Figure 1). The first wave of preprocessing involves document classification. News stories routinely provide information on many topics that form the core of scholarly interests across a variety of domains, which is why they are a potentially valuable source of structured data. Central to realizing this potential is identifying those with information relevant to a particular research focus. Fortunately, sophisticated supervised-

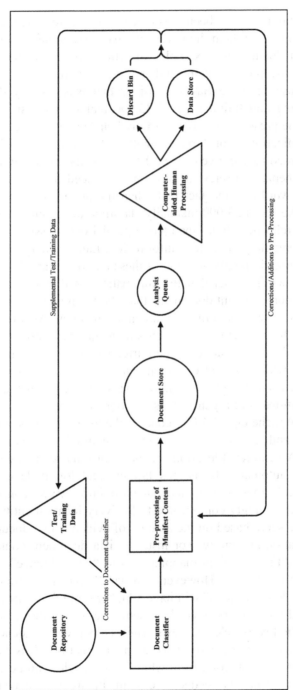

Figure 1. A progressive supervised-learning system.

learning techniques have been developed to automate textual classification.[4] Implementing them, however, involves assembling a set of training and test documents—examples of articles reflecting the semantic structure of documents that are, and are not, of interest.

SPEED uses a naive Bayes classifier that was initially developed from a testing and training set of 33,000 manually classified articles indicating the presence or absence of civil strife events.[5] Repeated tests of the classification algorithm eventually yielded a final model that correctly discarded four in five of the *NYT* documents and about half of the SWB documents as irrelevant, obviating the need for human review.[6] Just as noteworthy is the fact that when the automated classifier was applied to the set of 33,000 manually classified documents, it identified many more relevant articles than the original 1,600 classified by human coders as containing civil strife information. Later reanalysis by human coders confirmed that about 1,200 of these additional articles contained relevant events. The fact that the automatic classifier identified about 75 percent more relevant documents than did the human coders demonstrates that it enhances both accuracy and efficiency. As a result, it far outperforms human-centric approaches to document identification.

Once the documents are classified, irrelevant documents are sent to a discard bin, while relevant documents are subjected to a second wave of text analytics using NLP techniques. This wave extracts the names of people, locations, and organizations mentioned in the text. SPEED currently uses Apache OpenNLP to conduct the tokenization, sentence segmentation, and part-of-speech tagging required for named entity extraction. All extracted location names are then passed to a geolocation engine that automatically assigns latitude and longitude coordinates using the GeoNames geographical database (http://www.geonames.org), which is a deceivingly complicated task. Every location entity receives a confidence score based on the amount of evidence in a document that reduces location ambiguity. For instance, if a document contains both "Paris" and "France," then mapping this to "Paris, France" will get a higher score for "Paris." However, if it has "Paris" and "Illinois," then mapping to "Paris, Illinois" will have a higher score for "Paris."

Classified and preprocessed documents are placed into a Solr index that stores the text of relevant news articles along with associated metadata, extracted entities, and geolocation information. This Solr index serves as a document store, from which news articles can be channeled into analysis queues as needed (see again Figure 1). Analysis queues are subsets of the document store created to extract data for specific research projects using information extracted during the preprocessing stage (e.g., dates, places, names). To generate event data from these subsets of documents, analysis queues are paired with protocols—electronic documents that contain structured question sets that define the information to be humanly extracted. Human coders access protocols through a Web interface that integrates the protocol with a queued document.[7] Human coders are presented only those documents that have been machine-classified as relevant and make only those decisions that have not already been completed by machine-based modules.

Many human coding decisions (such as correctly associating names, places, and dates with separate events reported in a single article) are facilitated by embedded NLP tools that populate the drop-down menus in the Web interface used by coders to complete the event codings. For example, some drop-down menus are loaded with named entities from the article being analyzed so that the coder can identify which of those entities were targets or perpetrators of civil unrest. At the time a document is presented to coders, each sentence is further classified using NLP algorithms for relevance to civil unrest events. This sentence-level classifier, known as the Event Annotation Tool (EAT), color-codes relevant sentences containing information relevant to the SSP.[8] Because all machine-extracted NLP information from the preprocessing stage merely serves as input for coders, humans make all final judgments about the accuracy and relevance of machine-generated information. The coded events are stored in a data archive and are accessible for statistical analysis. Documents categorized by humans as irrelevant (i.e., false positives) are placed in a discard bin (see Figure 1).

What distinguishes SPEED's system as "progressive" is how its outputs are used for refining the machine-based modules. Within a progressive supervised learning system, the role of human coders is to reduce their menial work so that they can focus on more cognitively challenging tasks. This is achieved by generating feedback that teaches computers to better replicate human decisions. To illustrate this point, consider that a coder's first task in examining a screened document is to confirm the classifier's judgment, a task that requires about two minutes to complete. Our initial classifier was highly accurate at detecting irrelevant news stories but less accurate at identifying relevant stories. Although between 97 percent and 99 percent of the discarded documents were later confirmed by humans to contain no event-related information, only

33 percent of the documents sent to human coders contained relevant information. The other two thirds were "false positives." To improve the classification algorithm, approximately 60,000 documents that had been humanly processed were used as a second wave of testing and training data. The revised classifier increased the "true-positive" rate from 33 percent to 87 percent among articles classified as relevant, while maintaining a "true-negative" rate of 96 percent among articles classified as irrelevant, an improvement that generated enormous efficiencies.[9]

3.2. *SPEED's SSP*

The SSP[10] is designed to leverage SPEED's global news archive for the study of civil strife. It is organized around three categories of civil strife: (1) political expression (speeches, demonstrations, symbolic actions, etc.), (2) politically motivated attacks (riots, kidnappings, shootings, etc.), and (3) disruptive state acts (declarations of martial law, arrests of dissidents, censorship, etc.).[11] Data collection within the SSP is organized into six sections: (1) who (actor characteristics), (2) what (event type and consequences), (3) how (mode of expression, weapons used), (4) where (location and geophysical setting), (5) when (event date), and (6) why (event origins). The type of events covered by the SSP and the data it collects speak to the research agendas of a wide range of disciplines, from political science and sociology to psychology and anthropology. SSP data are of particular interest to sociologists concerned with such topics as the stated demands, motivating grievances, and political orientations of social movements (e.g., Walder 2009); the varieties and effects of state efforts to repress them (e.g., Earl 2011); the political consequences of civil unrest (e.g., Amenta et al. 2010; McAdam and Su 2002); and the temporal and spatial dimensions of social conflict (e.g., Owens, Su, and Snow 2013; Wagner-Pacifici and Hall 2012). All can be studied on a global scale using SPEED event data.

Because the SSP generates information on hundreds of variables, developing its analytic potential requires the construction of smaller subsets of composite variables. Two subsets are particularly important here. The first summarizes event origins by categorizing them as reflecting antigovernment sentiments, socioeconomic discontents, sociocultural animosities, political desires and beliefs, desire to retain power, ecoscarcities, and so on.[12] The second subset includes seven event intensity measures that have been calculated using SSP data.[13] Three deal with events initiated by nonstate actors: small-gauge expression, mass expression, and political violence. Three others pertain to events initiated by state actors: the abuse of ordinary state powers, the initiation of extraordinary state acts, and political violence. The last gauges the intensity of coups.[14]

3.3. *Quality Control*

Because SPEED uses humans working with a complex protocol, it is crucial to ensure that they are highly trained and that they operate proficiently. Thus, coders begin their tenure by participating in an extensive training and testing regimen that requires nearly 70 hr to complete. This regimen includes lectures, one-on-one training, and group training sessions. Training culminates in a series of tests that gauge the coder's ability to implement the protocol in accordance with established norms and understandings; the tests gauge their capacity to identify events and to code them properly. Trainees must pass these "gatekeeper tests" before they are allowed to generate production data. Reliability testing continues after coders begin production coding: they are blindly fed a set of precoded "test" articles at established intervals to detect slippages in reliability.[15]

4. LIMITS OF EXISTING CIVIL STRIFE DATA AND THE ADDED VALUE OF HYBRID DATA COLLECTION SYSTEMS

The added value of hybrid data collection efforts is illustrated in the next two sections by comparing SPEED's rich event data to sparse and episodic event data.

4.1. *Sparse Event Data*

Sparse event data mask meaningful, within-category variation in destabilizing events. Ignoring these differences is troubling, because the intensity of strife events varies considerably. Capturing those differences is important when gauging the threat posed to regimes as well as the scale of regime responses to those threats. Simply put, a nonviolent protest by 5 people poses different issues than one involving 15,000 people, even though sparse event data equate them. Events also vary in

Table 2. Within-category Variance in Expression Events

	Small-scale Expression Events	Mass Expression Events
Number of participants/initiators		
Mean	555	81,982
Median	2	2,450
Mode (proportion)	1 (.48)	1,250 (.17)
Mode of expression		
Verbal	.36	—
Written	.25	—
Symbolic action	.36	—
Demonstration	—	.69
Strike	—	.31
Intensity indicators		
Part of a sequence of events	.34	.42
Elicited a *post hoc* reaction	.10	.06
Lasted more than a single day	.12	.29
n	7,409	8,663

their origins, location, and timing, all of which are crucial to understanding such things as the reasons for civil strife, spatial diffusion patterns, and the pace at which the discontent unfolds. To illustrate the
importance of event-specific differences, in this section we focus on
event intensity; later sections demonstrate the importance of temporal
and spatial differences, as well as origins.

To examine within-category differences in destabilizing events, we
use SSP data from a global random sample of *NYT* stories that appeared
between 1946 and 2005[16]; the sample contains records for more than
70,000 codings.[17] Table 2 provides data on two types of political expression events: (1) small-gauge expressions (e.g., provocative speeches or
pamphlets, symbolic burnings) and (2) mass expression events (e.g.,
demonstrations, strikes). The first column in Table 2 examines small-
gauge expressions. An important intensity indicator for even small-
gauge expression events is the number of participants. The mode and
median for small-gauge events are 1 participant, but 10 percent involved
more than 100 participants. Also important is the mode of expression.
Verbal expressions and symbolic acts (e.g., sit-ins, self-immolations,
pickets) each constituted 36 percent; another 25 percent were written
expressions. More than 12 percent lasted more than a day, and one third
were integral parts of more complex sequences of actions; 10 percent

Table 3. Within-category Variance in Political Attacks

	Nonstate Attacks	State Attacks
Number of Initiators		
Mean	634	1,022
Median	4–5	4–5
Mode (proportion)	5 (.28)	5 (.56)
Relationship to other events		
Involved a linked event?	.41	.30
Elicited a *post hoc* reaction?	.04	.14
Weapon Type		
None	.30	.33
Crude	.11	.06
Small arms	.25	.20
Explosives	.31	.03
Military grade	.03	.38
Type of violence		
Attack against person	.81	.88
Personal injury	.51	.52
Egregious violence	.14	.08
Lethal injuries		
Proportion involving a death	.40	.49
Mean deaths (for lethal events)	1,859	1,780
Median deaths (for lethal events)	2	5
Modal deaths (for lethal events)	1 (.31)	1 (.25)
n	18,860	7,340

involved some type of *post hoc* reaction by a third party (counterdemonstrations, arrests, attacks, etc.). The second column in Table 2 reports variation within mass expression events; almost 70 percent were demonstrations or marches. Perhaps the most salient difference here is the number of participants. Although the median is 2,450 and the mode is 1,250, the mean is almost 82,000; 10 percent of these events involved more than 95,000 people. Almost 30 percent lasted more than a day, and more than two fifths were part of more complex sequences of actions.

Table 3 provides descriptive data on political attacks initiated by private actors and state actors. Most attacks involve just a handful of initiators, but state-initiated attacks generally involve more.[18] About a third of political attacks are linked to more complex sequences of actions. Much variance also exists in the weapons used. Nearly a third involve no weapon; moreover, nonstate actors are more likely to use small arms and explosives, while state actors are more likely to use military weapons. Personal attacks account for about 85 percent of the attacks, but injuries are reported in only about half. Egregious forms of violence, such as mutilation and brutality, occur in about 12 percent of attacks and are more likely to be perpetrated by nonstate actors. Deaths occur in just over 50 percent of personal attacks; the median number killed is three.

Most of the details reported in Tables 2 and 3 would be lost given the current state of fully automated systems. As the type of detail reported there is crucial to generating near-term advances in civil strife research, these data illustrate the need for more sophisticated information extraction and the potential of hybrid approaches in providing it.

4.2. Episodic Event Data

Conventional human-centric approaches to episodic event data share two limitations (see Table 1). First, they are constructed using holistic judgments that are often derived from poorly documented sources. In contrast, rich civil strife event data are systematically collected and aggregated from known populations. Second, the aggregation of discrete events into episodes often masks meaningful variation in conflict intensity over time and across space; rich event data can capture that variation. The next two sections illustrate the added value of rich event data by examining the two key episodic strife variables: civil wars and episodes of political instability.

4.2.1. *Civil Wars.* A number of prominent research projects have generated episodic data on the existence of a civil war, with the country-year as the unit of analysis: UCDP/PRIO (Gleditsch et al. 2002; http://www.prio.no), the COW project (http://www.correlatesofwar.org), and a project directed by Fearon and Laitin (2003; http://www.stanford.edu/group/ethnic/publicdata). The attention accorded civil wars is understandable: they are the most devastating form of civil strife. But there are three reasons why an exclusive civil war focus is unlikely to advance our understanding of civil strife. First, measurement efforts have been hampered by a paucity of data and a lack of consensus on what constitutes a civil war. This has led to high levels of disagreement across measures. For example, from 1945 through 1999, a total of 1,272 country-years of civil war are identified by at least one of these three projects. However, all three agree on only 28 percent (357 country-years), which undermines confidence about inferences drawn from these data sets.

Second, even if scholars generated a definitive body of data on civil war battles and reached a consensus on what constitutes a civil war at the country-year level, such an operationalization would have limited utility, as it would mask important patterns of temporal and spatial variation in strife. This can be illustrated with SSP data from a project using the SWB news archive to capture all relevant events from documents mentioning Guatemala, El Salvador, Nicaragua, Liberia, the Philippines, and Sierra Leone between 1979 and 2008 (see Rhodes et al. 2011). Figures 2a to 2d aggregate, by month, the number of conflict-related deaths for four of these countries; the lines at the top of each graph mark the periods defined by the three civil war projects. Figure 2 also suggests that much temporal variation exists in civil war conflicts. Some months show many casualties, but there are no reported deaths in about 60 percent of the months for which there is unanimous agreement among the projects on the existence of a conflict. Most violence appears to stop well before the war is judged to have ended. Although not shown in Figure 2, much spatial variance in the distribution of attacks also exists.[19]

Third, using more disaggregated death totals to gauge civil wars would be an improvement, but it would not address a another limitation: civil war variables capture only a small slice of civil strife perpetrated by a narrow set of actors—lethal violence caused by soldiers and insurgents. This can be illustrated by reexamining the SSP data used to produce Tables 1 and 2. Political attacks constitute about 52 percent of these events. However, only 5 percent of all destabilizing events reported involved violent attacks between soldiers and insurgents. Moreover, if we consider only soldier and insurgent attacks in which someone is killed (the core criterion for civil wars), the percentage drops to 2.6 percent of all destabilizing events.

4.2.2. Episodes of Political Instability. Research on political instability considers a broader range of event types than civil war research, and the Political Instability Task Force (PITF) has done important work in this area (http://globalpolicy.gmu.edu/political-instability-task-force-home/). Recently, it introduced a model that predicted the outbreak of major periods of instability with a two-year lead time (Goldstone et al. 2010). Although the authors have a powerful and parsimonious model, they are vague about how they created their dependent variable, noting only that "We identified 'instability

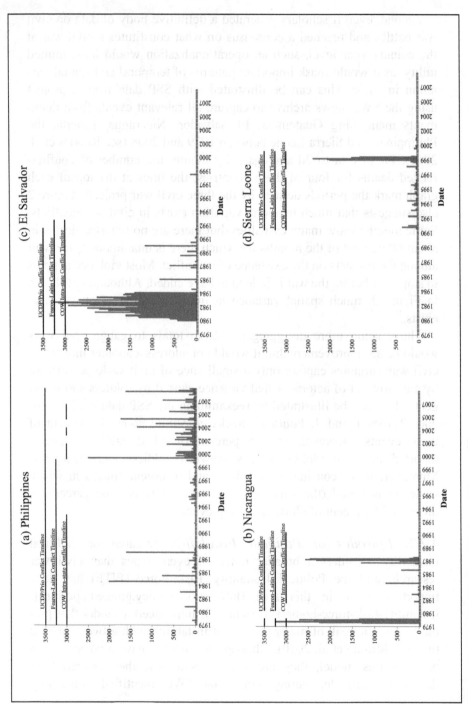

Figure 2. Monthly death totals for soldiers and insurgents.

episodes' in part by identifying conflicts from existing databases (such as the Correlates of War) and in part by consulting with area experts" (p. 191).[20] Delineating instability episodes using methods that are rigorous and replicable is essential to advancing civil strife research, and the opaqueness of PITF's holistic approach generates concerns about both.

PITF's definition of political instability includes civil wars, regime crises, and mass atrocities from 1955 to 2003. Thus, the 1946 to 2005 global random sample of strife events used in Tables 1 and 2 can be used to evaluate PITF's holistic approach. Our evaluative focus is on the specification of distinctive and cohesive episodes of instability; it includes PITF's ability to *identify* distinctive sequences of instability and to *demarcate* them precisely. If PITF has not identified distinctive and cohesive episodes of instability, then its dependent variable is poorly specified, which undermines confidence in its predictive model. Our concern with identification includes both false positives (PITF-specified periods that are not cohesive and markedly unstable) and false negatives (cohesive periods of marked instability that were not identified). With respect to demarcation, our concern is with PITF's ability to specify accurately episodic "bookends" (i.e., start points and endpoints). If they cannot, then their claim of predicting the outbreak of instability with a two-year lead time is unpersuasive.

To examine the PITF approach, we aggregated the seven intensity measures introduced earlier—which capture everything from the intensity of political expression and political violence to state repression and coups—to the country-month level and merged them with PITF data. We then reduced the seven measures to a weighted composite intensity variable. A score of zero on this intensity measure indicates a month with no reported unrest; increasing values reflect higher levels of instability.[21] Figure 3 graphs data for six countries that illustrate how our evaluation of PITF analysis was conducted. In these graphs, the *x*-axis plots country-months from 1955 through 2004, PITF episodes are shaded in gray, and our composite intensity measure is plotted on the *y*-axis.

Figure 3a, which reports data on Djibouti, illustrates an important type of false positive: episodes that do not appear to be distinctively unstable. Although the demarcated period for Djibouti is a PITF episode and is accorded the same value as all other episodes, its levels of instability are markedly lower than the others in Figure 3. Indeed, we find no recorded events during the PITF time frame, even though we

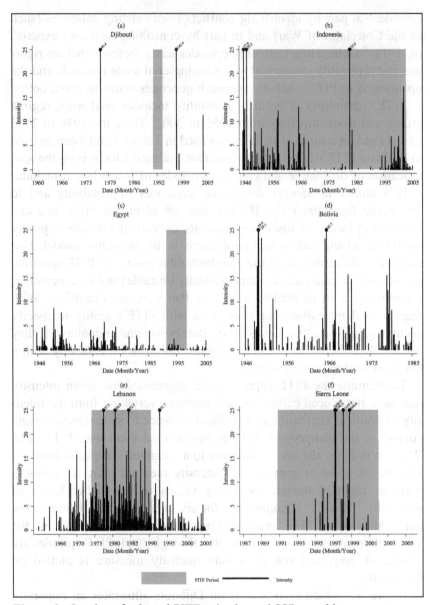

Figure 3. Overlay of selected PITF episodes and SSP monthly aggregates.
Note. PITF = Political Instability Task Force; SSP = Societal Stability Protocol.

find some major strife in Djibouti at other points in the postwar era. When the average intensity score of a PITF episode is less than the average intensity score for country-months falling outside PITF episodes, as is the case in Djibouti, we define the episode as a false positive. Fifty-five of the 145 PITF episodes (38 percent) fail to exceed this minimal intensity threshold and are excluded from the analyses that follow.[22] Figure 3b depicts intensity data for Indonesia and illustrates a second type of false positive. Although PITF data indicate that Indonesia was experiencing a good deal of instability during the PITF-defined time frame, SPEED data show intermittent instability with long interludes of calm. This suggests that several distinct episodes may be merged into one. We defined PITF episodes with interludes of calm that exceed two years—which is longer than 90 percent of the interludes in the PITF episodes—to be false positives. Thirty-two of the 145 episodes (22 percent) were affected by at least one interlude exceeding this interlude threshold; eight of these had more than one interlude.

Figures 3c and 3d provide illustrations of false negatives: cohesive sequences with average intensity levels that match those in PITF episodes yet are not captured in a PITF episode. Figure 3c shows that PITF captures only one of several important periods of instability in Egypt. Figure 3d shows that although Bolivia does not have a single PITF episode, it has several periods of strife that far exceed the average level for PITF episodes (mean = 2.45). Using criteria derived from the average value of SPEED's intensity variables within PITF episodes and applying them to country-months not included in a PITF episode, we found 979 additional episodes of civil strife.[23] Although PITF captured the most salient episodes of political instability in the postwar era, the additional episodes uncovered using SPEED data compare favorably with the PITF episodes in terms of intensity levels. Consider, for example, that the median intensity score for the 979 false negatives is slightly higher than that for comparable episodes derived from the PITF episodes: 3.3 (mean = 8.6) versus 3 (mean = 6.45). In contrast, the duration of validated PITF episodes is somewhat longer than for the false negatives: 11.5 months (mean = 32.5) for true-positive PITF episodes versus 1 month (mean = 8.7) for the false-negative episodes revealed in SPEED data. Finally, 4.8 percent of the country-months included in the false negatives involved some type of coup activity, which is somewhat higher than the 4.3 percent found in validated PITF episodes.

The last component of our analysis pertains to the accuracy with which the PITF approach demarcates episodic start points and end-points. Start points are particularly important because they affect PITF's ability to predict eruptions of instability. Figures 3e and 3f illustrate the demarcation analysis. Figure 3e shows that the SPEED data for Lebanon spill beyond PITF's temporal boundaries; Figure 3f shows that the instability in Sierra Leone begins well after the PITF episode starts and ends well before PITF's endpoint. To quantify the accuracy of PITF's bookends, we used a six-month criterion, which is 25 percent of the lead time that PITF uses in its analysis. We found that the start points were misspecified (i.e., off by at least six months) in 18 of the 90 validated PITF episodes; endpoints were misspecified in 40 validated episodes.

In sum, our analysis suggests that 55 of the 145 PITF episodes involve sequences of country-months that are not distinctively different from the country-months that fall outside PITF episodes. Of the remaining 90 PITF episodes, another 32 included interludes of calm of at least two years and did not constitute cohesive sequences of ongoing conflict. Fifty-eight episodes had misspecified bookends. After eliminating over-laps among the different types of error, SPEED data suggest that 107 of the 145 original PITF episodes had some type of serious measurement error. Even more troubling is what PITF failed to uncover: 979 episodes that had levels of strife comparable with the validated PITF episodes. No dependent variable in the social sciences is free of measurement error, but the level of noise in the PITF measure underscores the added value of rich event data in civil strife research.

5. NEW FRONTIERS IN CIVIL STRIFE RESEARCH

The value of SPEED's rich strife data goes beyond its methodological advantages. The strategic use of these data can advance the frontiers of civil strife research and yield fresh substantive insights. To illustrate this point, we join two sets of measures introduced earlier: our intensity and origins composites. Our efforts to glean the origins of individual events from news reports suggest that most destabilizing events are rooted in common grievances that vary in prominence across event type, space, and time. Comparing the intensity of events associated with different types of grievances enhances our understanding of the changing nature of contentious politics in the postwar era by generating more refined global insights into the type of grievances that are driving strife, how those drivers have changed over time, and the changes in how those discontents are manifested. This can be illustrated by examining the two most disruptive forms of citizen-initiated strife: mass expression and political violence.

To depict the relative importance of the different origins, and how they vary over time, Figure 4 displays a set of locally weighted scatterplot smoothing regression lines that track the global prominence of different grievances from 1946 to 2005. Because the range in the intensity of these two types of strife events is much different, we use different scales to depict them; moreover, for succinctness, we graph only the top four drivers of unrest: (1) antigovernment sentiments, (2) sociocultural animosities, (3) socioeconomic discontents, and (4) the desire for enhanced political rights. Figure 4a shows that the most important drivers of mass expression are antigovernment sentiments and socioeconomic discontents but that their relative prominence varies over time. In the late 1940s, socioeconomic concerns were the most important factor. But the role of socioeconomic discontents declines precipitously over time, and by the end of the period it is the weakest driver.[24] In contrast, antigovernment sentiments grow as a driver of mass expression and are the most important driver after the mid-1950s. Sociocultural animosities also play an increasingly important role in mass expressions from the mid-1950s through the late 1990s. The role of the desire for political rights is fairly stable throughout the time frame but it ebbs and flows.

Figure 4b shows that the use of violence to express discontent evidences a somewhat different pattern. The principal drivers of political violence are sociocultural animosities and antigovernment sentiments. Both evidence a relative decline until the early 1960s. But after that point, sociocultural animosities become much more potent until the mid-1980s, when they begin to recede. In contrast, antigovernment sentiments manifest a fairly stable pattern until the mid-1980s, when they evidence a decline. Both drivers demonstrate a slight upturn at the turn of the century. The desire for enhanced political rights is an important and largely stable factor throughout the period, but it too begins to decline in the mid-1980s until it upticks around 2000. In contrast socioeconomic discontents, which were comparable in potency with the desire for enhanced political rights at the start of the time frame, decline steadily over time.

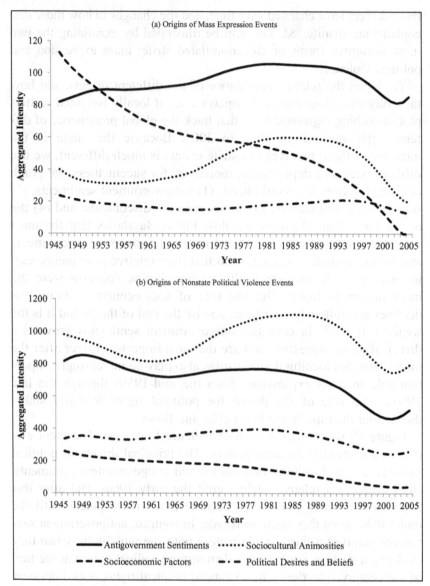

Figure 4. Origins of mass expressions and nonstate political violence.

6. SUMMARY

The revolution in information technologies—both by generating big data and by developing tools to transform such data into knowledge—

presents enormous opportunities for social scientists. The vast increases in computational capacities, combined with the adoption of data science techniques, can create exciting new research frontiers that will transform the social sciences in the same way that the molecular revolution transformed biology. Perhaps the only social science parallel to these contemporary developments is the widespread diffusion of telephones and the refinement of sampling techniques and survey methods after World War II. However, despite the enormous promise of the information revolution for social science, the trajectory forward is not likely to be linear or steep. The need to derive meaning from complex language patterns and the current state of data science techniques for analyzing unstructured data suggest that social scientists will continue to balance the relative advantages of machine-based and human-centric approaches into the foreseeable future. The central assertion of this article is that until machine-based approaches can more accurately emulate human-centric approaches, researchers should consider the use of hybrid approaches that strategically integrate the benefits of both.

The rationale for this assertion is that although wholly human-centric approaches will never realize the potential of the information revolution, the premature embrace of fully automated approaches when studying complex social phenomena will sacrifice validity and nuance to achieve scale. This article introduces one hybrid approach (the SPEED project) and demonstrates its added value in a complex domain (civil strife) that is of interest to an array of social scientists. Notwithstanding the results reported here, there are several reasons social scientists might justifiably continue employing human-centric analyses; three are particularly important.

First, the standard machine-based techniques for processing textual data work only when applied at scale to extremely large textual corpora. Many social scientists work with relatively small corpora (on the order of tens or hundreds of texts), and few computational approaches work with such small numbers. Second, computational approaches require data pipelines so complex and programming expertise so specialized that text-mining systems essentially function as black boxes to the nonexpert. Validating or bias-checking the process by which these work flows transform text into data is usually infeasible, even with publicly released code. In contrast, traditional content analysis methods involve the disclosure of codebooks and well-developed standards for assessing validity and reliability, making it straightforward for nonspecialists to evaluate data quality. Third, text-mining systems are so costly to build that even if the software components are open source and distributed without cost, they are hardly "free." Lexicoder (http://www.lexicoder.com), RapidMiner (http://www.rapidminer.com), and R (http://www.r-project.org) are three of many such components distributed free of charge, but the opportunity costs are steep for deploying them effectively.

The SPEED project illustrates the scale of these opportunity costs. The Cline Center began assembling its news archive and developing SPEED's work flow system in 2006, but it lacked an operational cyber-infrastructure until 2009. Seven years and well over a million dollars later, the Cline Center released its first SPEED data set. Opportunity costs and resource demands on this scale are formidable, but they need not deter serious scholars, as there is no need to duplicate the Cline Center's foundational efforts. Although agreements with commercial vendors and intellectual property rights prohibit the center from distributing its news archive, efforts are being made to provide nonconsumptive public access to the center's holdings. This access will allow researchers to evaluate the utility of the center's digital archive for their needs and to construct a research design to realize those needs. Using that design, researchers can access the center's various subcenters of expertise (document classification, training, coding, etc.) to implement it.

The benefits of extending the use of SPEED's hybrid system to a broader range of scholars, even at this early stage of data science, are substantial. In our view, the most immediate research benefits lie within three areas: (1) document classification, (2) text annotation, and (3) the clustering of documents about the same event from different sources. Classifying 5.9 million *NYT* articles on the basis of civil unrest content would have taken a single human analyst working 24 hr a day and 365 days a year more than two decades to complete. Once SPEED's classifier model was fine-tuned, this task was completed in a matter of hours. Using NLP solutions to preannotate relevant text so that humans can quickly scan for relevant content is vital to analyzing large numbers of classified documents efficiently. If SPEED's EAT module eventually reduces processing time by just two minutes an article, the time required to process all *NYT* civil strife articles would be reduced by almost 35,000 person-hours. Identifying articles on different news Web sites that describe the same event using different terms is the key to capitalizing upon the diversity of news Web sites and overcoming the biases introduced by relying on a small number of outlets. To use diverse sources without clustering reports of similar events will generate duplicate codings and undermine the validity of the data. SPEED has yet to finalize its approach to this problem, but finding a solution is at the top of its current development agenda.

As data science methods mature, their contributions will be even more profound and far reaching, further exacerbating the quandary faced by social scientists dealing with the opportunity costs of integrating automated components into content analysis projects. On the basis of our experience with SPEED, we believe that the most propitious path forward is to create collaborations between social scientists and data scientists. It is through such collaborations that social scientists will be able to capitalize on data science techniques while retaining the nuance needed for studying complex social phenomena. These collaborative efforts maximize a mutually beneficial division of labor across academic disciplines and are a highly efficient way of using automated techniques to generate important social science payoffs. Social scientists should be willing collaborators in these efforts as they have much to contribute to, and much to gain from, such joint enterprises.

Acknowledgments

The authors acknowledge the contributions of Loretta Auvil and Tom Redman, who provided technical expertise on the software and hardware aspects of SPEED, as well as Wendy Cho, Jake Bowers, and James Kuklinski for their useful advice. Ajay Singh and Gabriel Rodriguez trained and managed our software operators; Joseph Bajjalieh and Michael Martin made important contributions to data management and analysis.

Notes

1. Other automated efforts, such as the Defense Advanced Research Projects Agency's Integrated Crisis Early Warning System (O'Brien 2010), are based on technologies developed by these other projects.
2. A perusal of its data archive suggests that ACLED draws from hundreds of sources, including such diverse outlets as the *New York Times*, Reuters News, BBC Monitoring Service, Africa Research Notes, and African Contemporary Reports.
3. This Heretrix crawler (version 3.1.1) is an open-source platform that retrieves news articles published from a set of monitored RSS feeds. Before moving to the Heretrix platform, SPEED Web data were collected using a scratch-built RSS crawler. Data retrieved through the Heretrix system are sent through several cleanup steps before storage. We use Google's open-source language-detection software (http://code.google.com/p/language-detection) to exclude any crawled news stories in languages other than English. We also attempt to remove all

hypertext markup language tags as well as header, footer, and copyright data from the crawled content, so that only the raw text of the news article is stored. We then perform near duplicate detection (NDD) to eliminate duplicate copies of the same article that might have been retrieved from different RSS feeds. NDD is performed using a shingle approach that creates a hash for 50 characters created as a moving window across the text, saving 100 shingles for each document. The shingles for each document are saved for five days. Each incoming document is compared with every other document using the shingles that are currently saved and eliminated if the matching score is greater than 80 percent. Additional details on SPEED's global news archives can be found at http://www.clinecenter.illinois.edu/research/doc uments/SPEEDInformationBase.pdf.

4. Useful overviews of this field can be found in Murphy (2012); Hastie, Tibshirani, and Friedman (2009); and Abu-Mostafa, Magdon-Ismail, and Lin (2012).

5. Before settling on a naive Bayes algorithm, testing was also conducted using support vector machine, decision tree, and neural network classifiers. Naive Bayes using a term-frequency model outperformed the rest. More information on this classification system (labeled the BIN system) is provided at http://www.clinecen ter.illinois.edu/research/publications/SPEED-BIN.pdf. SPEED currently uses RapidMiner 5.3.008 open-source software to implement the classifier system.

6. Human reanalysis of the discarded news stories confirmed that nearly all of them were correctly classified: between 1 percent and 3 percent of the discards were found by human analysts to contain event-related information, which was considered an acceptable false-negative rate.

7. The protocols make extensive use of drop-down lists, response-activated questions, and branching commands that "hide" irrelevant questions. Moreover, NLP-based techniques automatically capture proper names, facilitate the identification of dates, and aid in the integration of geospatial data.

8. EAT was incorporated into SPEED's work flow in 2014 after a five-year collaboration with the Cognitive Computation Group (http://cogcomp.cs.illinois.edu) at the University of Illinois. The collaboration with the Cognitive Computation Group continues as efforts are currently being made to incorporate feedback loops to improve EAT's algorithms.

9. The revised classifier used a naive Bayes algorithm with a term-frequency model, as did the initial classifier. We used 10-fold cross-validation with the final model using all 10 models. The term-frequency model used a set of 5,673 words for the modeling. The average accuracy of the model was 84.03 percent. The false negatives and positives were 3.258 percent and 12.707 percent, respectively, which is a significant improvement, reducing both errors by about 50 percent over the initial models built.

10. We have worked on SPEED protocols for a variety of applications (security of property rights, integrity of elections, expressive freedoms). However, because of the increasing importance of civil strife, most of our developmental work has focused on the SSP. The architecture of the SSP is detailed in a white paper that can be found at http://www.clinecenter.illinois.edu/research/documents/AnOvervie woftheSSP.pdf.

11. The classifier used for the SSP generates statistical probabilities that a news report contains information on at least one event that falls within the SSP's event

ontology. A document detailing the operational definitions of each type of event in this ontology can be accessed at http://www.clinecenter.illinois.edu/research/publications/SPEED-Definitions_of_Destabilizing_Events.pdf.

12. The derivation of the origins composites is reported at http://www.clinecenter.illinois.edu/research/publications/SPEED-Origins_of_Destabilizing_Events.pdf.

13. A detailed discussion of how these intensity measures were derived can be found at http://www.clinecenter.illinois.edu/research/publications/SPEED-Gauging_the_Intensity_of_Civil_Unrest.pdf.

14. The data on coups come from the Coup d'état Project, found at http://www.clinecenter.illinois.edu/research/documents/Coup_Project.pdf, for reasons outlined in note 4 of the online supplemental material at http://www.clinecenter.illinois.edu/publications/SociologicalMethodsSupplement.pdf.

15. A fuller discussion of SPEED's training and testing procedures, including the results of the reliability tests, can be found at http://www.clinecenter.illinois.edu/research/publications/SPEED-Reliability.pdf.

16. This sample was generated by randomly sampling every *NYT* article that our automated classifier indicated had content relevant to a civil strife event.

17. Moving from unstructured media data to probabilistic estimates of various properties and relationships requires addressing a number of well-known challenges in a methodologically responsible manner. Advances in information technology have provided researchers with the potential to address some of these challenges, and the SPEED project has made a concerted effort to exploit this potential; its efforts are detailed at http://www.clinecenter.illinois.edu/research/publications/Media%20Data%20and%20Social%20Science%20Research.pdf. Particularly relevant for the cross-national analyses included in this section are SPEED's efforts to address the country biases embedded in the *NYT*. An examination of the random sample of events drawn from the *NYT* revealed a considerable bias in coverage toward rich, Western democracies and global competitors to the United States (Russia, China, etc.). The approach detailed in the aforementioned online document allowed us to minimize that bias.

18. Although not shown in Table 3, the vast majority of state attacks (87 percent) are initiated by soldiers or police officers, while only half of nonstate attacks are initiated by insurgent groups.

19. A Google Earth display showing the spatial distribution of SSP events in these countries can be found at http://www.clinecenter.illinois.edu.

20. Although the PITF Web site includes thumbnail descriptions of their episodes, they do not include concrete criteria for inclusion. The descriptions are available at https://webmail.illinois.edu/owa/redir.aspx?C=jWjTCOfh0E-YQVDbUlcQ8wS LZ4FkMNII9DDwn8-EgWKy-QnZwW4gaCFufQi6MikZETUEzJd1pso.&URL= https%3a%2f%2fwww.yumpu.com%2fen%2fdocument%2fview%2f27009908%2fpitf-consolidated-case-list2011pdf-center-for-systemic-peace.

21. For interested readers, a detailed explanation of the reformatting of the intensity measures and the derivation of the composite intensity measure is provided at http://www.clinecenter.illinois.edu/research/documents/SSP_Episodes_Demarcation.pdf.

22. The mean intensity score for the other PITF episodes is 2.68, and the median is .63. In contrast, the mean value for the 55 episodes identified here is just .03 (median = .01), a markedly lower level of unrest intensity compared with the other episodes.
23. Details on the procedures used to identify these episodes can be found at http://www.clinecenter.illinois.edu/research/documents/SSP_Episodes_Demarcation.pdf.
24. A different picture would likely emerge if the time line were extended to capture the effects of the 2008 global recession.

References

Abu-Mostafa, Yaser S., Malik Magdon-Ismail, and Hsuan-Tien Lin. 2012. *Learning from Data: A Short Course*. Retrieved April 11, 2015 (http://www.amlbook.com).

Althaus, Scott L., Nathaniel Swigger, Svitlana Chernykh, David Hendry, Sergio Wals, and Christopher Tiwald. 2011. "Assumed Transmission in Political Sscience: A Call for Bringing Description Back In." *Journal of Politics* 73(4):1065–80.

Amenta, Edwin, Neal Caren, Elizabeth Chiarello, and Yang Su. 2010. "The Political Consequences of Social Movements." *Annual Review of Sociology* 36(1):287–307.

Armstrong, J. Scott. 1967. "Derivation of Theory by Means of Factor Analysis or Tom Swift and His Electric Factor Analysis Machine." *American Statistician* 21(5):17–21.

Berelson, Bernard. 1952. *Content Analysis in Communication Research*. New York: Hafner.

Bernauer, Thomas, and Nils Petter Gleditsch. 2012. "New Event Data in Conflict Research." *International Interactions* 38(4):375–81.

Bond, Doug, Joe Bond, Churl Oh, J. C. Jenkins, and Charles Lewis Taylor. 2003. "Integrated Data for Events Analysis (IDEA): An Event Typology for Automated Events Data Development." *Journal of Peace Research* 40(6):733–45.

Chojnacki, Sven, Christian Ickler, Michael Spies, and John Wiesel. 2012. "Event Data on Armed Conflict and Security: New Perspectives, Old Challenges and Some Solutions." *International Interactions* 38(4):382–401.

Conway, Mike. 2006. "The Subjective Precision of Computers: A Methodological Comparison with Human Coding in Content Analysis." *Journalism and Mass Communication Quarterly* 83 (1):86–200.

Danzger, M. Herbert. 1975. "Validating Conflict Data." *American Sociological Review* 40(5):570–84.

Earl, Jennifer. 2011. "Political Repression: Iron Fists, Velvet Gloves, and Diffuse Control." *Annual Review of Sociology* 37(1):261–84.

Eck, Kristine. 2012. "In Data We Trust? A Comparison of UCDP GED and ACLED Conflict Events Datasets." *Cooperation and Conflict* 47(1):124–41.

Evans, Michael, Wayne McIntosh, Jimmy Lin, and Cynthia Cates. 2007. "Recounting the Courts? Applying Automated Content Analysis to Enhance Empirical Legal Research." *Journal of Empirical Legal Studies* 4(4):1007–39.

Fearon, James D., and David D. Laitin. 2003. "Ethnicity, Insurgency and Civil War." *American Political Science Review* 97:75–90.

Franzosi, Roberto. 1987. "The Press as a Source of Socio-historical Data: Issues in the Methodology of Data Collection from Newspapers." *Historical Methods* 20(1):5–16.

Franzosi, Roberto. 2004. *From Words to Numbers: Narrative, Data, and Social Science.* New York: Cambridge University Press.

Franzosi, Roberto, Gianluca De Fazio, and Stefania Vicari. 2012. "Ways of Measuring Agency: An Application of Quantitative Narrative Analysis to Lynchings in Georgia (1875–1930)." Pp. 1–42 in *Sociological Methodology*, vol. 42, edited by Tim Futing Liao. Thousand Oaks, CA: Sage Publications.

Gerner, Deborah J., Philip A. Schrodt, Rajaa Abu-Jabr, and Omur Yilmaz. 2002. "Conflict and Mediation Event Observations (CAMEO): A New Event Data Framework for the Analysis of Foreign Policy Intearctions." Presented at the 43rd Annual Convention of the International Studies Association. New Orleans, LA.

Gleditsch, Nils Petter, Peter Wallensteen, Mikael Eriksson, Margareta Sollenberg, and Havard Strand. 2002. "Armed Conflict 1946–2001: A New Dataset." *Journal of Peace Research* 39:615–37.

Goldstone, Jack A., Robert H. Bates, David L. Epstein, Ted Robert Gurr, Michael B. Lustick, Monty G. Marshall, Jay Ulfelder, and Mark Woodward. 2010. "A Global Model for Forecasting Political Instability." *American Journal of Political Science* 54 (1):190–208.

Grimmer, Justin, and Gary King. 2011. "General Purpose Computer-assisted Clustering and Conceptualization." *Proceedings of the National Academy of Sciences* 108(7): 2643–50.

Grimmer, Justin, and Brandon M. Stewart. 2013. "Text as Data: The Promise and Pitfalls of Automatic Content Analysis Methods for Political Texts." *Political Analysis* 21(3):267–97.

Hastie, Trevor, Robert Tibshirani, and Jerome Friedman. 2009. *The Elements of Statistical Learning: Data Mining, Inference, and Prediction.* 2nd ed. New York: Springer.

Hillard, Dustin, Stephen Purpura, and John Wilkerson. 2008. "Computer-assisted Topic Classification for Mixed-methods Social Science Research." *Journal of Information Technology and Politics* 4(4):31–46.

Holsti, R. 1964. "An Adaptation of the 'General Inquirer' for the Systematic Analysis of Political Documents." *Behavioral Science* 9(4):382–88.

Jackman, Robert W., and William A. Boyd. 1979. "Multiple Sources in the Collection of Data on Political Conflict." *American Journal of Political Science* 23(2):434–58.

Kahl, Colin H. 2006. *States, Scarcity and Civil Strife in the Developing World.* Princeton, NJ: Princeton University Press.

King, Gary, and Will Lowe. 2003. "An Automated Information Extraction Tool for International Conflict Data with Performance as Good as Human Coders: A Rare Events Evaluation Design." *International Organization* 57(3):617–42.

Krippendorff, Klaus. 2004. *Content Analysis: An Introduction to Its Methodology.* 2nd ed. Thousand Oaks, CA: Sage Publications.

Lacina, Bethany, and Nils P. Gleditsch. 2005. "Monitoring Trends in Global Combat: A New Dataset of Battle Deaths." *European Journal of Population* 21(2):145–66.

Liu, Bing. 2011. *Web Data Mining: Exploring Hyperlinks, Contents, and Usage Data.* 2nd ed. Berlin, Germany: Springer-Verlag.

Lohr, Steve. 2013. "Algorithms Get a Human Hand in Steering Web." *The New York Times*, March 11, p. A1.

McAdam, Doug, and Yang Su. 2002. "The War at Home: Antiwar Protests and Congressional Voting, 1965 to 1973." *American Sociological Review* 67(5): 696–721.

Monroe, Burt L., and Philip A. Schrodt. 2008. "Introduction to the Special Issue: The Statistical Analysis of Political Text." *Political Analysis* 16(4):351–55.

Murphy, Kevin P. 2012. *Machine Learning: A Probabilistic Perspective.* Cambridge, MA: MIT Press.

National Consortium for the Study of Terrorism and Responses to Terrorism. 2012. Global Terrorism Database [Data file] (http://www.start.umd.edu/gtd).

Neuendorf, Kimberly A. 2002. *The Content Analysis Guidebook.* Thousand Oaks, CA: Sage Publications.

O'Brien, Sean P. 2010. "Crisis Early Warning and Decision Support: Contemporary Approaches and Thoughts on Future Research." *International Studies Review* 12(1): 87–104.

Owens, Peter B., Yang Su, and David A. Snow. 2013. "Social Scientific Inquiry into Genocide and Mass Killing: From Unitary Outcome to Complex Processes." *Annual Review of Sociology* 39(1):69–84.

Potter, W. James, and Deborah Levine-Donnerstein. 1999. "Rethinking Validity and Reliability in Content Analysis." *Journal of Applied Communication Research* 27: 258–84.

Quinn, Kevin M., Burt L. Monroe, Michael Colaresi, Michael H. Crespin, and Dragomir R. Radev. 2010. "How to Analyze Political Attention with Minimal Assumptions and Costs." *American Journal of Political Science* 54(1):209–28.

Raleigh, Clionadh. 2012. "Violence against Citizens: A Disaggregated Analysis." *International Interactions* 38(4):462–81.

Raleigh, Clionadh, Andrew Linke, Håvard Hegre, and Joakim Karlsen. 2010. "Introducing ACLED: An Armed Conflict Location and Event Dataset." *Journal of Peace Research* 47(5):651–60.

Rhodes, A., A. Waleij, W. Goran, A. Singh, and P. Nardulli. 2011. "Proactive Peacebuilding with Natural Resource Assets." U.S. Army Corps of Engineers; Center for the Advancement of Sustainability Innovations. Unpublished manuscript.

Salehyan, Idean, Cullen S. Hendrix, Jesse Hamner, Christina Case, Christopher Linebarger, Emily Sull, and Jennifer Williams. 2012. "Social Conflict in Africa: A New Database." *International Interactions* 38(4):503–11.

Savage, Charlie. 2013. "N.S.A. Said to Search Content of Messages to and from U.S." *The New York Times,* August 8, p. A1.

Schrodt, Philip A. 2012. "Precedents, Progress, and Prospects in Political Event Data." *International Interactions* 38(4):546–69.

Soroka, Stuart N. 2012. "The Gatekeeping Function: Distributions of Information in Media and the Real World." *Journal of Politics* 74(2):514–28.

Stone, Philip J. 1962. "The General Inquirer: A Computer System for Content Analysis and Retrieval Based on the Sentence as a Unit of Information." *Behavioral Science* 7(4):484–98.

Sudhahar, Saatviga, Gianluca De Fazio, Roberto Franzosi, and Nello Cristianini. 2013. "Network Analysis of Narrative Content in Large Corpora." *Natural Language Engineering* 20:1–32.

Themnér, Lotta, and Peter Wallensteen. 2011. "Armed Conflict, 1946–2010." *Journal of Peace Research* 48(4):525–36.

Thompson, Bruce. 1995. "Stepwise Regression and Stepwise Discriminant Analysis Need Not Apply Here: A Guidelines Editorial." *Educational and Psychological Measurement* 55(4):525–34.

Urdal, Henrik, and Kristian Hoelscher. 2012. "Explaining Urban Social Disorder and Violence: An Empirical Study of Event Data from Asian and Sub-Saharan African Cities." *International Interactions* 38(4):512–28.

van Atteveldt, Wouter, Jan Kleinnijenhuis, Nel Ruigrok, and Stefan Schlobach. 2008. "Good News or Bad News? Conducting Sentiment Analysis on Dutch Text to Distinguish between Positive and Negative Relations." *Journal of Information Technology and Politics* 5(1):73–94.

Wagner-Pacifici, Robin, and Meredith Hall. 2012. "Resolution of Social Conflict." *Annual Review of Sociology* 38(1):181–99.

Walder, Andrew G. 2009. "Political Sociology and Social Movements." *Annual Review of Sociology* 35(1):393–412.

Witten, Ian H., Eibe Frank, and Mark A. Hall. 2011. *Data Mining: Practical Machine Learning Tools and Techniques*. 3rd ed. Amsterdam, the Netherlands: Morgan Kaufmann.

Woolley, John T. 2000. "Using Media-based Data in Studies of Politics." *American Journal of Political Science* 44(1):156–73.

Young, Lori, and Stuart Soroka. 2012. "Affective News: The Automated Coding of Sentiment in Political Texts." *Political Communication* 29(2):205–31.

Author Biographies

Peter F. Nardulli is a research professor of political science and law at the University of Illinois at Urbana-Champaign and was the founding director of the Cline Center for Democracy. He is the author of six books on various aspects of the legal process and empirical democratic theory, as well as numerous scholarly articles on a range of topics, including civil unrest.

Scott L. Althaus is the Merriam Professor of Political Science, a professor of communication, and the director of the Cline Center for Democracy at the University of Illinois at Urbana-Champaign. His research explores the communication processes that support political accountability in democratic societies and that empower political discontent in nondemocratic societies. He is author of a book and numerous scholarly articles on political communication, the uses of opinion surveys for political representation, popular support for war, the psychology of information processing, and communication concepts in democratic theory.

Matthew Hayes is an assistant professor of political science at Indiana University Bloomington. His research focuses on political behavior and racial and ethnic politics, with a particular interest in issues of representation and how institutions can shape individual political behavior. His research has appeared in the *Journal of Politics, Legislative Studies Quarterly*, and *Journal of Research in Personality*.

Sociological Methodology
2015, Vol. 45(1) 184–222
© American Sociological Association 2015
DOI: 10.1177/0081175015570095
http://sm.sagepub.com
⑤SAGE

❧ 4 ☙

A DESIGN AND A MODEL FOR INVESTIGATING THE HETEROGENEITY OF CONTEXT EFFECTS IN PUBLIC OPINION SURVEYS

Stephen L. Morgan*
Emily S. Taylor Poppe[†]

Abstract

Context effects on survey response, caused by the unobserved interaction between beliefs stored in personal memory and triggers generated by the structure of the survey instrument, are a pervasive challenge to survey research. The authors argue that randomized survey experiments on representative samples, when paired with facilitative primes, can enable researchers to model selection into variable context effects, revealing heterogeneity at the population level. The value of the design, and its associated modeling strategy, is demonstrated by its ability to deepen the interpretation of a treatment effect of international competitiveness framing on long-used items drawn from the Phi Delta Kappa/Gallup Poll and the General Social Survey about the quality of schooling in the United States, confidence in the leaders running public education, and support for spending to improve schools.

*Johns Hopkins University, Baltimore, MD, USA
[†]Cornell University, Ithaca, NY, USA

Corresponding Author:
Stephen L. Morgan, Johns Hopkins University, Department of Sociology, 3400 N. Charles Street, Baltimore, MD 21218, USA
Email: stephen.morgan@jhu.edu

Keywords

context effect, framing effect, heterogeneity, selection, public opinion, survey response

1. INTRODUCTION

The framing literature in public opinion research has grown dramatically in the past two decades (see Chong and Druckman 2007, 2011), following prior psychological research on priming effects in social judgment (see Wyer and Srull 1989) and methodological research on context effects in survey response (see Schuman and Presser 1981; Schwarz and Sudman 1992). Substantive studies of framing consider the extent to which public opinions, and possibly underlying attitudes, reflect the manner and method by which information is delivered to individuals. This literature is dominated by experiments on student populations, which Druckman and Kam (2011) argued have the dual benefits of control over subjects and the timing of frame exposure.

Methodological studies of context effects consider the extent to which the structure and content of survey instruments alter response patterns for particular survey items, such as when early questions trigger information retrieval that determines how respondents interpret and answer later questions (see Tourangeau, Rips, and Rasinski 2000). Like the substantive framing effects literature, the context effects literature has also taken advantage of convenience samples. However, an important goal of this research is to better understand how particular context effects may have structured survey responses to questions in long-running opinion polls and surveys. This goal has led to a preference for representative samples. Schuman (2008) wrote,

> Although much research on context effects can be done with convenience samples such as students, at some points it is important to work with probability samples of a well-defined and heterogeneous population. This is of course expensive and time-consuming, but needed nonetheless. (p. 109)

In this article, we draw together these two traditions of analysis and present a design for survey experiments and an associated model for estimation. Our approach enables modeling of treatment effects that result from frame exposure as well as the variability of response patterns across individuals that are attributable to pretreatment exposure to the same substantive frame. In the sections that follow, we first delineate the essential features of the design. We then offer a conventional treatment effects model, which we estimate for a national survey experiment on the effect of international competitiveness framing on public support for education (previously analyzed, in brief simplified form, in Morgan and Taylor Poppe 2012). We then introduce a model that exploits variation in response to the facilitative prime, which permits investigation of the individual-level heterogeneity that lies beneath the treatment effects estimated by the conventional model. We then show how weighting control group subjects after estimating propensity scores can strengthen interpretations of results by adjusting away the sources of heterogeneity that are not produced by information retrieval relevant to the frame. In conclusion, we discuss limitations of the design.

2. THE RESEARCH DESIGN

2.1. *Precursors*

The survey response literature has long appreciated the value of randomized ballot designs with representative samples for the study of response patterns (see Schuman 2008 for a history). The General Social Survey (GSS), for example, has used randomized ballots to consider the consequences of wording changes and question placement for two of the items we analyze below (see Rasinski 1988, 1989; Smith 1987, 1991, 2006). Randomized ballot designs have also been used to investigate how elicited attitudes vary when they are preceded by alternative priming questions that promote retrieval of subsets of stored information relevant to the attitude. Tourangeau et al. (1989), for example, assessed how respondents from a random sample of adults in Chicago answered a question on legalized abortion after first answering context-setting questions about either gender equity in the workplace or traditional values.

Substantive research on framing effects is now dominated by scholars of political science and communications who seek to determine how political preferences in the electorate are shaped by different issue motivation and persuasion strategies.[1] In these fields, the power of experiments to identify effects is widely acknowledged, a position that has been bolstered by the growing interest in experimental methods in political science in general (see Druckman et al. 2011). And here we also find particularly strong interest in population-level experiments with national samples, which Mutz (2011) argued "may be unmatched in their ability to advance social scientific knowledge" (p. 157).

2.2. The Design: A National Survey Experiment with a Facilitative Prime

Following from these precursors, we consider a design with the following essential components:

1. a random sample of subjects drawn from a target population,
2. outcomes from questions that have been used repeatedly in polls and surveys that use random samples from the same target population,
3. randomization of treatment and control conditions across subjects, where
   a. the control condition is a baseline condition that mimics the administration of the questions on extant polls and surveys, and
   b. the treatment condition is structured as a facilitative prime that encourages subjects to reveal if they have been drawn into the real-world frame that is the subject of investigation.

Although the specific components of this design are not novel on their own, their joint adoption allows for the analysis of effects that cannot be considered in most conventional framing experiments. Most important, we show that the pairing of a randomized and facilitative treatment prime with a random sample drawn from a diverse target population allows the analyst to (1) identify and estimate the population-level treatment effects and (2) model response heterogeneity that can reasonably be attributed to pretreatment exposure to the frame of interest in the target population. The latter is possible under the assumption that the facilitative treatment prime triggers retrieval of information among those who have been exposed to the frame prior to the study.

3. ANALYSIS AND DEMONSTRATION

Following and extending the analysis of Morgan and Taylor Poppe (2012), to demonstrate the proposed approach we use a four-part substantive question: Do international competitiveness frames that suggest that the education system in the United States is losing ground to its competitors alter (1) public opinion about the quality of local public schools in the United States, (2) public opinion about the quality of the public schools across the United States, (3) confidence in people running the education system in the United States, and (4) support for spending additional resources to improve the nation's education system?[2]

Data are drawn from the 2011 Cornell National Social Survey (CNSS), which is a random sample of 1,000 individuals ages 18 years or older resident in the continental United States, interviewed by telephone.[3] The Supplementary Appendix, which is available on the authors' personal Web sites as well as this journal's Web site, offers descriptive statistics that demonstrate that the CNSS generated a national sample with typical distributions across demographic characteristics. We analyze the survey data as a self-weighting national sample, but we use estimated weights to adjust for nonresponse for each of our four outcome measures. A small amount of item-specific missing data on covariates for our final set of models is imputed with best-subset linear and logistic regression.

The CNSS interviews began with questions from a split-ballot priming experiment. The two alternative experimental ballots are presented in Figure 1. A randomly selected 47.1 percent of respondents were allocated to the treatment group, and they began the interview with two questions that prime international competitiveness. They were then asked four questions that have been administered repeatedly over the past four decades in high-profile national surveys: the first two in the Phi Delta Kappa/Gallup Poll (PDK/GP) and the second two in the GSS.[4] The remaining respondents were allocated to the control group, and they proceeded immediately to the same four attitude questions that the treatment group answered only following the priming questions.[5]

Consider the structure of the two priming questions on the treatment ballot. Neither priming question gives respondents any information on international differences in economic competitiveness or educational performance. In fact, the second question allows respondents to disagree with the common framing of journalists and political elites that the United States is losing some of its international competitiveness because of a decline in the quality of its public K–12 education system. As such, these two questions constitute what we label in this article a "facilitative prime," rather than a standard manipulative prime. In particular, these two questions prompt respondents to reveal, on the basis of their own information and beliefs, whether they will approach the four subsequent attitude questions after first invoking the frame of reference that is the

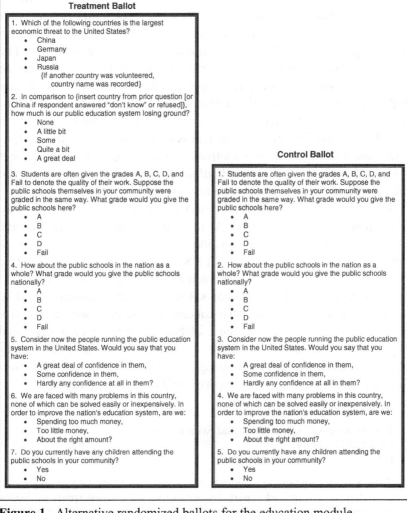

Treatment Ballot

1. Which of the following countries is the largest economic threat to the United States?
- China
- Germany
- Japan
- Russia
  {If another country was volunteered, country name was recorded}

2. In comparison to {insert country from prior question [or China if respondent answered "don't know" or refused]}, how much is our public education system losing ground?
- None
- A little bit
- Some
- Quite a bit
- A great deal

3. Students are often given the grades A, B, C, D, and Fail to denote the quality of their work. Suppose the public schools themselves in your community were graded in the same way. What grade would you give the public schools here?
- A
- B
- C
- D
- Fail

4. How about the public schools in the nation as a whole? What grade would you give the public schools nationally?
- A
- B
- C
- D
- Fail

5. Consider now the people running the public education system in the United States. Would you say that you have:
- A great deal of confidence in them,
- Some confidence in them,
- Hardly any confidence at all in them?

6. We are faced with many problems in this country, none of which can be solved easily or inexpensively. In order to improve the nation's education system, are we:
- Spending too much money,
- Too little money,
- About the right amount?

7. Do you currently have any children attending the public schools in your community?
- Yes
- No

Control Ballot

1. Students are often given the grades A, B, C, D, and Fail to denote the quality of their work. Suppose the public schools themselves in your community were graded in the same way. What grade would you give the public schools here?
- A
- B
- C
- D
- Fail

2. How about the public schools in the nation as a whole? What grade would you give the public schools nationally?
- A
- B
- C
- D
- Fail

3. Consider now the people running the public education system in the United States. Would you say that you have:
- A great deal of confidence in them,
- Some confidence in them,
- Hardly any confidence at all in them?

4. We are faced with many problems in this country, none of which can be solved easily or inexpensively. In order to improve the nation's education system, are we:
- Spending too much money,
- Too little money,
- About the right amount?

5. Do you currently have any children attending the public schools in your community?
- Yes
- No

Figure 1. Alternative randomized ballots for the education module.
Source: Data from Cornell National Social Survey, 2011.

subject of investigation. The label "facilitative" is due to Sniderman (2011), who wrote, "Manipulative designs aim to get people to do what they are not predisposed to do," whereas "facilitative designs involve a directional force in the form of a relevant reason to do what people are already predisposed to do" (p. 108).

This design feature is not common, in part we surmise because it gives less control to the investigator. A manipulative prime delivers precisely the information to respondents that the investigator wishes to deliver, generating a potential response among all respondents. The investigator can then examine the effects generated by the delivery of this information, without considering whether some subjects already had been exposed to the information in the past. In contrast, a facilitative prime triggers the retrieval of stored information and beliefs, which have been shaped before the treatment is delivered. As a result, manipulative and facilitative primes motivate the study of related but distinct effects: the effects of delivered information on responses versus the effects of retrieved information on responses.

To appreciate the difference, consider an alternative manipulative prime that we could have used. As investigators, we would first decide to deliver two pieces of information: (1) recent results from international testing competitions and (2) a statement by a prominent public figure reflecting on the current economic competitiveness of the United States in relation to these test scores. One standard procedure would be to select a newspaper article that contains this information and excerpt from it appropriately (or, in more elaborate form, develop structured vignettes from alternative newspaper articles). In this case, many articles are available, and the following paragraphs from a late 2010 *New York Times* article would have worked well for a 2011 study:

Top Test Scores From Shanghai Stun Educators
By SAM DILLON
Published: December 7, 2010

With China's debut in international standardized testing, students in Shanghai have surprised experts by outscoring their counterparts in dozens of other countries, in reading as well as in math and science, according to the results of a respected exam.
. . .

The test, the Program for International Student Assessment, known as PISA, was given to 15-year-old students. . . .

Shanghai students scored 556, ahead of second-place Korea with 539. The United States scored 500 and came in 17th, putting it on par with students in the Netherlands, Belgium, Norway, Germany, France, the United Kingdom and several other countries.

The article continues with authoritative quotations from opinion leaders:

"Wow, I'm kind of stunned, I'm thinking Sputnik," said Chester E. Finn Jr., who served in President Ronald Reagan's Department of Education, referring to the groundbreaking Soviet satellite launching.

. . .

"We have to see this as a wake-up call," Secretary of Education Arne Duncan said in an interview on Monday.

. . .

President Obama recalled how the Soviet Union's 1957 launching of Sputnik provoked the United States to increase investment in math and science education, helping America win the space race.

"Fifty years later, our generation's Sputnik moment is back," Mr. Obama said. With billions of people in India and China "suddenly plugged into the world economy," he said, nations with the most educated workers will prevail. "As it stands right now," he said, "America is in danger of falling behind."

For a manipulative prime, this article is ideal in some ways: It is detailed, authoritative, and unambiguous. Yet it would be hard to use for a national survey, including those such as the CNSS or the PDK/GP that use telephone interviews. Even for surveys that use face-to-face interviews, such as the GSS, this article would impose substantial cognitive burden on the respondent and absorb too much interview time.[6]

Instead, we use a facilitative prime that is short and easy to administer. With the first question, treatment group respondents are primed to be concerned about economic competitiveness. With the second question, they are asked to reflect on whether the U.S. education system is losing ground relative to the education system of its strongest current economic competitor. To answer this question, some respondents are likely to retrieve information from exposure to authoritative information from the past. Respondents who do not have information to retrieve, because they are not attuned to political discourse of this type, may approach the second question solely on the basis of personal experience and more general attitudes about social services. The question of first order is whether the prime, and the information that it is presumed to cause at least some respondent to retrieve, shifts response patterns for the treatment group relative to the control group. In our first set of analyses, presented in the next section, we offer an affirmative answer to this question.

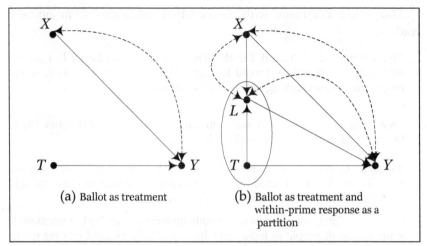

Figure 2. Directed graphs for the causal effect of the facilitative prime on attitudes.

3.1. *A Conventional Group-level Treatment Effect Analysis*

Figure 2a presents a directed graph that motivates the results of this section; see Pearl (2009, 2010) for a full treatment of causal graph methodology and Elwert (2013) for an introduction written for sociologists. The variable T is a dichotomous indicator variable for treatment group membership, equal to 1 for those randomly assigned to the treatment group and 0 otherwise. Note that the variable T encodes *only* exposure to the two questions that constitute the facilitative prime and does not encode any information on the responses that treatment group members provide in response to the questions. The variable Y represents the response distribution of any one of the four subsequent attitude questions (3–6 on the treatment ballot, which correspond to 1–4 on the control ballot). Finally, X represents a set of other observed variables measured for the CNSS, including baseline demographic characteristics of individuals, the response to the final question on each ballot that indicates whether the respondent currently has children attending a local public school, and other variables to be introduced later.

3.1.1. *Identification.* For this model, the treatment effect of T on Y is identified because the values of T are set by the ballot randomization. Because we consider below the more complex directed graph in Figure

2b, it is useful to state this claim more formally. In the causal graph tradition, this identification claim is written

$$P[Y|T] = P[Y|do(T)], \tag{1}$$

where $do(\cdot)$ is an abstract intervention operator (see Pearl 2009, 2010). In this case, the observed probability distribution of Y conditional on T can be given a causal interpretation in the values of T because T is set by an actual intervention. No confounding of the observed relationship between T and Y is present, because the distribution of T is completely random, except as would be produced by chance associations for the finite sample of respondents. Thus, the observed data represented by the left side of equation (1) identifies the causal effects defined by the right side of equation (1).

In the potential outcome tradition (see Morgan and Winship 2015 for an introduction written for sociologists, which also draws the connection to causal graphs), the same identification claim would be written on the basis of an independence assumption,

$$(Y^1, Y^0) \perp\!\!\!\perp T, \tag{2}$$

where Y^1 and Y^0 are potential outcome random variables that correspond to potential treatment exposures for values of T equal to 1 or 0 and where the symbol $\perp\!\!\!\perp$ denotes independence. When equation (2) is valid, which it is for this design because T is completely randomized, comparisons of analogous features of observed distributions of Y across values of T can be given warranted causal interpretations. Again, observed data are subject to sampling error, and the independence assumption in equation (2) applies to the design.

We assume for Figure 2a that the causal effects of the variables in X on Y are not identified, because of our assumption that common unmeasured causes of X and Y exist. In the causal graph literature, these common causes can be represented by a double-headed arrow, $\longleftrightarrow$, that connects X to Y. Finally, we do not assume that the effect of T on the distribution of Y is the same for all individuals in the sample. Rather, these effects may vary across individuals, even in interactive fashion with the characteristics measured by X. All such interactions are implicitly embedded in the causal graph. The causal arrows, $\rightarrow$, in Figure 2a signify only that both X and T are causes of Y, and they are mute on whether these assumed effects are interactive or separable.

3.1.2. *Results.* To estimate the effect of T on Y, a model for the response distribution of Y must be chosen. Although alternative models (such as ordinary least squares linear regression) would convey the same basic pattern of results that we report below, ordered logit models have become the standard for modeling forced-choice responses to survey items with categories that are ordered but cannot be assumed to be equidistant on a latent response scale. Accordingly, Table 1 presents estimated coefficients for the treatment for four separate ordered logit models with responses to the four attitude questions as the outcome Y.

Grades for schools are the dependent variables for the first two rows, and the estimated coefficients for the treatment group are −.28 and −.21. With the same associated standard error of .12, the first coefficient would be judged significant using a standard two-tailed test with a null hypothesis of zero and the second nearly so. Substantively, the coefficients indicate that respondents who were presented with the two-question facilitative prime gave lower grades to public schools in their communities and in the nation as a whole. Morgan and Taylor Poppe (2012) reported the coefficient for the question on community schools, presenting fitted values that indicated that the coefficient corresponded to 6.8 percent of respondents shifting their grades from A or B to C, D, or F. The second coefficient suggests a slightly smaller substantive shift for schools in the nation as a whole.

The third and fourth rows of Table 1 present analogous results for the two GSS items.[7] For confidence in the leaders of the public education system, the coefficient for the treatment is −.17. With a standard error of .13, the implied negative effect is not statistically significant by the usual standards. However, it is consistent with the direction of the effect for the overall ratings of schools by grades and is larger than its estimated standard error. For the attitudes toward spending to improve education, the estimated coefficient for the treatment is −.30. This is the same coefficient reported by Morgan and Taylor Poppe (2012), on the basis of which they concluded that the international competiveness prime leads respondents to decrease support for additional spending to improve schools. They report a predicted response difference of 7.2 percent for indicating that "too little" money is spent on improving the nation's education system, which they noted is "more than enough to alter the outcome of hypothetical elections for local school board seats and funding levies" (Morgan and Taylor Poppe 2012:265).[8]

Table 1. Treatment Group Coefficients from Ordered Logit Models for Each Outcome Question

Question	Treatment Group Coefficient (*SE*)	N	Chi-Square Test Statistic (*df*)
Grades for public schools "in your community"	−.28 (.12)	928	5.1 (1)
Grades for public schools "in the nation as a whole"	−.21 (.12)	926	2.8 (1)
Confidence in "people running the public education system"	−.17 (.13)	971	1.8 (1)
Support for spending "to improve the nation's education system"	−.30 (.13)	968	5.5 (1)

Source: Data from Cornell National Social Survey, 2011.
Note: For grades, the highest response category is A, and the lowest response category is fail. For the confidence question, the highest response category is "A great deal of confidence in them," and the lowest response category is "Hardly any confidence at all in them," with "Some confidence in them" as the middle category. For the spending question, the highest response category is "Too little money," and the lowest response category is "Too much money," with "About the right amount" as the middle category. All models are weighted by the inverse probability of providing a response to the outcome question, as estimated by a supplementary logit model.

3.1.3. Interpretation. The conclusions suggested by a conventional treatment effects analysis are straightforward. The facilitative international competitiveness prime causes respondents, on average and in a nationally representative sample, to lower their subjective assessments of the quality of schooling while decreasing support for additional spending to improve the nation's education system. This analysis, although entirely appropriate, does leave one important question on the table: Do the same types of individuals move in response to the treatment prime for all four of the outcome questions, such that those who lower their quality ratings are the same types of individuals who also do not wish to spend any more money on schools? As we show in the next two sections, the response to the second item of the facilitative prime allows us to address this question.

3.2. *A Simple Subgroup-level Response Heterogeneity Analysis*

Figure 2b presents a directed graph that motivates the extended results of this section and the next. The variables *T*, *X*, and *Y* are the same variables defined for Figure 2a. In addition to these variables, a variable L, denoting the attitude "losing substantial ground," is included within an ellipse along with T. The partition of the treatment group represented by L is the key to our analysis in this section and the next. Respondents who conclude their engagement with the facilitative prime by stating the opinion that schools in the United States are losing substantial ground to those of the nation's strongest economic competitor have, in our interpretation, entered into the frame of interest by retrieving stored beliefs based on prior exposure and responsiveness to the frame.

Consider, first, how L is coded for the observed data. L was set equal to 1 for treatment group respondents who answered the second priming question with "quite a bit" (23 percent) or "a great deal" (26 percent), and it was set equal to 0 for all other treatment group respondents— those who answered "none" (9 percent), "a little bit" (11 percent), "some" (23 percent), and "don't know" (3 percent) and those who refused (.6 percent). Accordingly, L is an indicator variable for the 49 percent of the treatment group that has a pronounced belief that the education system in the United States is losing substantial ground.

For subsequent data analysis, we use two distinct treatment subgroups: (1) the "losing ground" treatment subgroup for which $T = 1$ and $L = 1$ and (2) the "not losing ground" treatment subgroup for which $T = 1$ and $L = 0$. Both of these treatment subgroups are compared with the undifferentiated control group for which $T = 0$.

Figure 2b stipulates that L is caused by the observed variables X and unobserved common causes of X, L, and Y (collectively represented by the double-headed arrows in $X \longleftrightarrow L$ and in $L \longleftrightarrow Y$).[9] In the section that follows this one, we use the variables in X to develop our interpretations for the differences between the control group and the two treatment subgroups. For now, we consider only treatment effects defined in T and L.

3.2.1. *Identification.* The total causal of effect T on Y in Figure 2b remains identified for the same reasons stated in the last section. The effect defined only by the two values of T is still identified by the conditional distribution $P[Y|T]$, regardless of whether the treatment group can be or is partitioned using L. In causal graph terminology, no backdoor paths connect T to Y in Figure 2b, as in Figure 2a.

To begin to understand the complications that arise when we partition the treatment group using L, we need to explain (1) the missing data pattern for L and (2) the special nature of the partitioning variable

L. For the first explanation, note that the observed values for *L* are completely missing for control group respondents. Yet, because treatment and control group respondents are collectively exchangeable, we can assume that the unobserved distribution of *L* in the control group would be the same as the observed distribution in the treatment group, subject only to sampling error. In other words, had the control group respondents been exposed to the treatment conditions instead, they too would have responded to the second priming question and chosen values for *L* that would reproduce the same distribution observed in the treatment group, subject only to variation from finite sampling. Thus, we have a particular form of missing data. Data are missing on *L* as a deterministic function of *T*. And because *T* is set by randomization, whether the data are missing is completely random. However, because the particular values of *L* have nonrandom causes, which according to the assumptions embedded in Figure 2b include *X* as well as unobserved common causes of *L* and *X* and of *L* and *Y*, the individual-specific missing values on *L* are not missing at random.

For the second explanation, note that the causal effect that we have represented as $T \rightarrow L$ in Figure 2b is different than the other effects in the figure. We signify its special nature by embedding *L* within an ellipse that includes *T*.[10] On one hand, respondents who are in the treatment group are exposed to the first priming question, and as such the value that they then provide for *L* in response to the second question is a function of having been presented with the first priming question in the initial exposure to the treatment conditions. In this sense, being in the treatment group does entail exposure to a question that shapes the particular pattern of responses to the question that then generates *L*. On the other hand, only treatment group respondents receive the question that generates *L*. And, in fact, the content of the second priming question is set by the response to the first priming question—the country nominated as the largest economic threat. Thus, no observable data based on this design could ever identify a causal effect of *T* on *L* because, even in theory, we cannot intervene separately on *T* and *L* without changing the design that we have proposed and that has actually been implemented for this study.[11]

Because the treatment and control groups can be regarded as two independent samples from the same population, the randomization of *T* allows us to assert that $P[L|T=1] = P[L|T=0]$. Therefore, we can maintain that there is an effect of *T* on *Y* within strata of *L*. In other words, because we can conceive of an abstract scenario in which we could eliminate our missing data problem for L by repeatedly rerandomizing T until all individuals in the population have been exposed to the treatment at least once, we can maintain that causal effects defined within population strata enumerated by L exist in theory and are well defined. With this stochastic conceptualization in the background, the values of L are therefore unobserved latent classes within our observed control group, which we can assume exist because the treatment and control groups are exchangeable.

The causal effects of interest can then be defined with reference to the causal graph or by using potential outcome variables. With the first notation, we are interested in quantities defined by

$$P[Y|do(T), L = 1] \tag{3}$$

and

$$P[Y|do(T), L = 0]. \tag{4}$$

In Pearl's (2009, 2010) framework, equations (3) and (4) are intervention-induced distributions that result from exposure to the facilitative prime, defined separately for two subgroups that exist in the population: the losing ground group ($L = 1$) and the not losing ground group ($L = 0$). These effects exist in theory, but the observed data do not identify them because the design does not generate values for L when $do(T = 0)$.

Using potential outcome notation, equivalent causal contrasts are defined by the differences

$$P[Y^1|L = 1] \; v. \; P[Y^0|L = 1] \tag{5}$$

and

$$P[Y^1|L = 0] \; v. \; P[Y^0|L = 0], \tag{6}$$

where the "$v.$" operator is the general "versus" notation used, for example, by Rubin (2005) to allow the analyst to consider any contrasting feature of the two probability distributions for the potential outcome random variables. The potential outcome notation, along with the design, imply that the contrasts in equations (5) and (6) can instead be written

$$P[Y|T=1, L=1] \; v. \; P[Y^0|L=1] \tag{7}$$

and

$$P[Y|T=1, L=0] \; v. \; P[Y^0|L=0]. \tag{8}$$

This way of expressing the causal effects of interest might provide a more transparent explanation for the challenges that confront estimation with our observed data. We cannot form conditional probability distributions for the right-hand sides of these equations because L is not observed for the control group (and even though the sample analog distribution of $P[Y|T=0]$ is consistent for $P[Y^0]$).

3.2.2. Results. Although the negative identification results just presented may appear dire, much interpretable analysis is possible, as we demonstrate in this section and the next. Table 2 presents coefficients from four models analogous to those presented in Table 1. Rather than including a single variable T as the sole predictor, we include dummy variables for the two treatment subgroups differentiated by L, in effect representing T and L in the ellipse in Figure 2b as a single cross-classified factor whereby the two latent classes ($T=0, L=1$) and ($T=0, L=0$) are collapsed into an omitted reference group. As shown in the first two rows, the "losing ground" treatment subgroup is much more likely to offer lower grades to schools "in your community" and "in the nation as a whole" than is the control group, with ordered logit coefficients of $-.81$ and $-.83$ (and with the same standard error of .15). More surprising, perhaps, are the positive coefficients for the "not losing ground" treatment subgroup, which imply that these respondents offer higher grades in comparison with the control group.

Figures 3 and 4 present predicted response probabilities that correspond to the models for the first two questions.[12] These figures indicate that 37 percent of the control group offered grades of C, D, or fail to schools in their communities and that 72 percent of the control group offered grades of C, D, or fail to schools in the nation as a whole.[13] The two treatment subgroups, however, have very different predicted response patterns. Treatment group respondents who did not see schools losing substantial ground offered slightly more positive grades than the control group, with 5 percent and 9 percent fewer respondents offering grades of C, D, or fail, respectively. Treatment group respondents who saw schools losing substantial ground offered much worse grades than

Table 2. Treatment Group by Losing Ground Coefficients from Ordered Logit Models for Each Outcome Question

Question	Treatment Group by Not Losing Ground Coefficient (SE)	Treatment Group by Losing Ground Coefficient (SE)	N	Chi-square Test statistic (df)
Grades for public schools "in your community"	.23 (.14)	−.81 (.15)	928	45.8 (2)
Grades for public schools "in the nation as a whole"	.39 (.15)	−.83 (.15)	926	50.5.8 (2)
Confidence in "people running the public education system"	.31 (.17)	−.62 (.16)	971	25.9 (2)
Support for spending "to improve the nation's education system"	−.53 (.15)	−.03 (.16)	968	14.1 (2)

Source: Data from Cornell National Social Survey, 2011.

Note: For grades, the highest response category is A, and the lowest response category is fail. For the confidence question, the highest response category is "A great deal of confidence in them," and the lowest response category is "Hardly any confidence at all in them," with "Some confidence in them" as the middle category. For the spending question, the highest response category is "Too little money," and the lowest response category is "Too much money," with "About the right amount" as the middle category. All models are weighted by the inverse probability of providing a response to the outcome question, as estimated by a supplementary logit model.

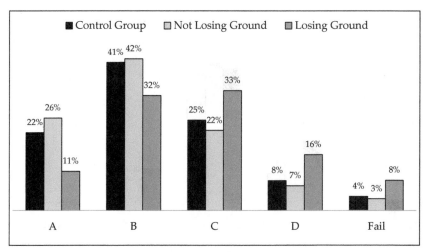

Figure 3. Predicted response probabilities for grades awarded to public schools "in your community," from the model reported in Table 2.

the control group, with 20 percent and 14 percent more respondents offering grades of C, D, or fail, respectively.

It is perhaps not surprising that individuals who express the belief that U.S. schools are losing ground to those of international competitors would then carry on to offer the lowest grades for schools. Yet the differences induced by the treatment are substantial and imbalanced across the two treatment subgroups defined by L, such that they combine to generate an overall decline in offered grades, as presented earlier in the first two rows of Table 1.

The third and fourth rows of Table 2 report analogous ordered logit coefficients for the two GSS questions. Treatment group respondents who indicated that schools in the United States were losing substantial ground expressed lower confidence in the people running the public education system, with an ordered logit coefficient of −.62 and a standard error of .16. Figure 5 shows that this difference is 14 percentage points in comparison with the control group, with 44 percent of this treatment subgroup having "hardly any confidence at all" in the people running the education system, in comparison with 30 percent of the control group. The other treatment subgroup again has the opposite pattern of responses, expressing more confidence in leaders than the control group. These results suggest substantial consistency across the PDK/GP

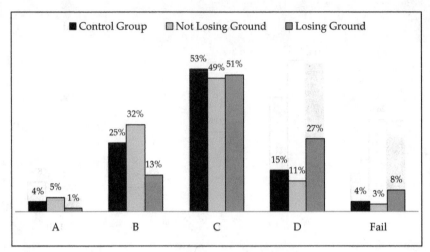

Figure 4. Predicted response probabilities for grades awarded to public schools "in the nation as a whole," from the model reported in Table 2.

and GSS items on rating the quality of schools and how they are run. In combination, the results suggest that leadership is one perceived weakness of current public schooling in the United States but also that overall grades for schools are based on additional perceived weaknesses about which the CNSS does not ask.

The final model in the fourth row of Table 2 assesses support for using additional money to improve the nation's education system. Here, the patterns are different, which reveals the utility of this design and the associated model for this application. For the "losing ground" treatment subgroup, there is no average response difference relative to the control group, given the coefficient of −.03. Instead, and unlike for the prior three questions, a negative coefficient of −.53, with a standard error of .15, applies instead to the "not losing ground" treatment subgroup. As shown in Figure 6, only 49 percent of this "not losing ground" treatment subgroup felt that "too little money" was being spent to improve the nation's education system, in comparison with 62 percent of respondents in the control group. In contrast, the "losing ground" treatment subgroup had a pattern of responses that is almost indistinguishable from that of the control group in Figure 6. In combination, these results imply that the negative treatment effect presented earlier in Table 1 for this question is produced entirely by the "not losing ground" members

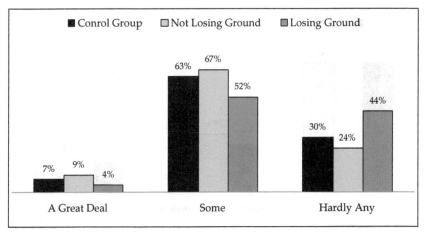

Figure 5. Predicted response probabilities for confidence in "people running the public education system," from the model reported in Table 2.

of the treatment group, which is the opposite of the pattern for the other three outcome variables.

3.2.3. Interpretation. Extending the warranted causal interpretation on the basis of the results reported in Table 1, there are two ways to interpret the additional insight offered by the elaborated models reported in Table 2. First, from an experimental design perspective, these elaborated models offer a consistency check, while deepening the account of why the effects presented in Table 1 were produced. The "losing ground" treatment subgroup is responsible for the overall negative treatment effect on the quality ratings and leadership of schools, but the "not losing ground" treatment subgroup is responsible for the overall negative treatment effect on support for spending to improve the nation's schools. Second, from a population polling perspective, these elaborated models suggest that the second priming question separates the treatment group into those who retrieve stored information that is in agreement with past exposure to the frame and those who do not.

What pattern of information retrieval could generate the results that differ between the first three questions and the fourth question? Before we offer an answer, we must first learn more about the pattern of responses among treatment group members that generates the distribution of L and then determine whether results similar to those presented in Table 2 persist after adjustment for X.

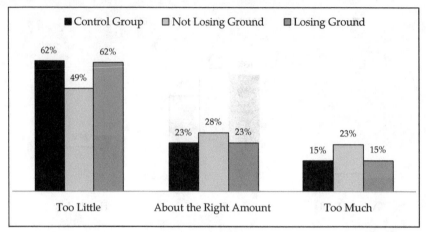

Figure 6. Predicted response probabilities for opinions on current spending "to improve the nation's education system," from the model reported in Table 2.

3.3. *A Response Heterogeneity Analysis with Conditioning on Observed Confounders*

Recall that for our discussion of Figure 2b, we noted that some of the determinants of L have been observed as X. Models that adjust for X may generate stronger interpretations. The key, as we show in this section, is to use the observed variables in X to weight the control group so that it can serve, sequentially, as a comparison group for each of the two treatment subgroups.[14]

3.3.1. *Identification.* The treatment subgroup coefficients reported in Table 2 are ordered logit–based summaries of differences:

$$P[Y|T=1,L=1] \ v. \ P[Y|T=0] \tag{9}$$

and

$$P[Y|T=1,L=0] \ v. \ P[Y|T=0]. \tag{10}$$

It would be incautious to claim that sample analogs to equations (9) and (10) identify the causal effects defined in equations (5) and (6) (or equations 3 and 4). There is no good reason to assume that $P[Y^0]=P[Y^0|L=1]=P[Y^0|L=0]$.[15] As a result, even though $P[Y|T=0]$ is consistent for $P[Y^0]$, this result provides no justification for regarding $P[Y|T=0]$ as consistent for either $P[Y^0|L=1]$ or $P[Y^0|L=0]$.

For the coefficients reported in Table 2, the primary threat to a causal interpretation on the basis of frame-specific information retrieval is the possibility that the "losing ground" partition is a proxy for underlying differences in unrelated characteristics and attitudes across members of the treatment group. Table 3 begins to assess this concern, presenting mean differences for individual characteristics measured in the CNSS for the two treatment subgroups. "Losing ground" treatment respondents were slightly more likely to have children currently attending public schools in their communities (27 percent vs. 24 percent) but were very similar on demographic characteristics, with the largest difference observed for the percentage African American (10 percent vs. 14 percent). Differences in home ownership, having taken the survey via cell phone, level of completed education, party identification, and self-labeled level of ideological conservatism were very small. Differences in family income were slightly larger (.07 on the log scale, which is commonly interpreted as a 7 percent difference in family income).

Table 3 also shows that other attitudes toward specific world affairs differed across the two treatment subgroups. In a later topical module in the CNSS, respondents were asked, "Do you agree or disagree with the statement 'The U.S. needs to play an active role in solving conflicts around the world'?" The "losing ground" treatment subgroup was considerably more likely to disagree (58 percent vs. 41 percent). In the same module, respondents were also asked,

> Some people believe that the war in Afghanistan will make America safer, while others believe that the war will not make America safer. To what extent do you agree with the following statement: "The war in Afghanistan will make America safer"?

Again, the "losing ground" treatment subgroup was more likely to disagree (70 percent vs. 60 percent).[16] Responses to these two items suggest that the "losing ground" treatment subgroup was less likely to favor active involvement of the United States in world affairs, even though the respondents in this subgroup were not more likely to self-identify with a particular political party or ideology.

Overall, then, because the only substantial measured difference between the two treatment subgroups is in attitudes toward world affairs, it is hard to make the case that these two subgroups are very different on the distribution of X. Still, the two subgroups are not identical with respect to the characteristics and attitudes reported in Table 3, and it is

Table 3. Mean Values for Additional Variables across the Two Subgroups within the Treatment Group

Variable	Treatment and Not Losing Much Ground	Treatment and Losing "Quite a Bit" or "a Great Deal" of Ground
Has children currently in public schools in the community	.24	.27
Demographic characteristics		
Female	.49	.52
Hispanic ethnicity	.06	.07
African American	.10	.14
Born in the United States	.93	.92
Age (years)	49.99	49.46
Residential characteristics		
Respondent owns home in which she or he lives	.75	.73
Question: "Do you own or rent the place where you live now?"		
Took interview on cell phone rather than land line	.31	.30
Socioeconomic status		
Family income from all sources (natural logarithm)	8.66	8.73
Education (in years completed)	14.90	14.82
Political affiliations and values		
Republican party identification	3.98	3.90
Seven-point scale with poles "strong Democrat" to "strong Republican" in response to the question "Generally speaking, when it comes to political parties in the United States, how would you best describe yourself?"		
Conservative ideology	4.15	4.12

(continued)

Table 3. (continued)

Variable	Treatment and Not Losing Much Ground	Treatment and Losing "Quite a Bit" or "a Great Deal" of Ground
Seven-point scale as responses to the question "When it comes to social issues, do you usually think of yourself as extremely liberal, liberal, slightly liberal, moderate or middle of the road, slightly conservative, conservative, or extremely conservative?"		
Attitudes toward engagement in world affairs		
Does not agree with interventions to solve conflicts around the world	.41	.58
Respondent expresses disagreement in response to the question "Do you agree or disagree with the statement 'The U.S. needs to play an active role in solving conflicts around the world'?"		
Does not feel the war in Afghanistan makes America safer	.60	.70
Respondent expresses disagreement when asked: "Some people believe that the war in Afghanistan will make America safer, while others believe that the war will not make America safer. To what extent do you agree with the following statement: 'The war in Afghanistan will make America safer'?"		

Source: Data from Cornell National Social Survey, 2011.

Note: The total Cornell National Social Survey sample size is 1,000 respondents, but this table presents results only for the 471 individuals in the treatment group. A small amount of missing data on these covariates was imputed with best-subset linear and logistic regression models.

possible that these small differences are nonetheless important for the pattern of responses to the attitude questions.

Modeling the consequences of these differences is possible because all of the variables in Table 3 are measured in the control group as well, even though the variable L is not observed for the control group. The first step is to model the propensity for members of the treatment group to indicate that public schools in the United States are losing ground, as predicted by X. The second step is to then use the estimated coefficients from the model estimated for the treatment group to generate weights that can be used for the control group, invoking a propensity score weighting rationale. These weights can then be used to weight all members of the control group in two ways: first to align the control group with the distribution of X that is observed for the "losing ground" treatment subgroup and then for the "not losing ground" treatment subgroup.

3.3.2. Results. As reported in Table A1 in the Appendix, we estimated a logit model in the treatment group with L as the outcome variable and all of the variables reported in the rows of Table 3 as the predictor variables. This model is not strongly predictive. Most coefficients are smaller in magnitude than their standard errors, but the "intervention to solve conflicts" variable has a coefficient that suggests a moderately strong association. And, net of other characteristics in the model, family income has a small positive coefficient that is statistically significant. The model chi-square value is only 24.3, with 14 degrees of freedom, which only narrowly exceeds the relevant .05 critical value of 23.7. These results are not surprising; we showed already in Table 3 that the two treatment subgroups are very similar with respect to the distribution of X.

Table 4 presents treatment subgroup coefficients analogous to those in Table 2 but which have been adjusted for differences in X, as reported in Table 3. For each of the four outcomes, the two treatment subgroup coefficients are estimated as doubly robust inverse probability weighted estimates for treatment subgroup–specific treatment effects. In particular, we take the specification from the logit model reported in Table A1 and use it to calculate estimated weights that can balance the distributions of the variables in Table 3 across the control group and each of the treatment subgroups (see Imbens 2004 and Morgan and Winship 2015, chap. 7, for details of the method). In essence, these two sets of weights, when applied to the control group, reweight control group members such that they represent each treatment subgroup with respect to X. We then reestimated the four models in Table 2, once for each set of weights, while including all of the variables in X as covariates to protect against misspecification of the logit model that estimated the weights. For Table 4, we then present the treatment subgroup coefficients from the models that use the relevant subgroup-specific weights, as well as model-specific chi-square values that correspond to the model from which the coefficient is drawn. Overall, the eight estimated coefficients reported in Table 4 are very similar to the corresponding coefficients reported in Table 2.

3.3.3. Interpretation. The results presented in Table 4 imply that differences in responses to the PDK/GP and GSS questions across the two treatment subgroups cannot be explained away by X. There is simply no basis for concluding that the response heterogeneity within the treatment group can be attributed to whether respondents have children in their local public schools, demographic characteristics, socioeconomic status, political party identification, self-rated conservatism, or even attitudes toward the appropriateness of foreign engagement by the government of the United States. These are the obvious sources of observable differences between these groups, and these results give us additional confidence that the response heterogeneity across the two treatment subgroups is specific to the substance of the frame.

3.4. Discussion of the Demonstration

To build the case for the value of the design and the modeling that it enables, we conclude the demonstration with a discussion of the deeper interpretation that has been generated. The two-question international competitiveness prime causes respondents, on average in a nationally representative survey, to lower their subjective assessments of the quality of local schooling while decreasing support for additional spending to improve the nation's education system. However, the analysis offered here suggests that it would be unwise to assume that the same individuals move in response to the treatment prime for all four of the outcome questions.

Our first set of results—for which we ignored the available partition in the treatment group—is not incorrect, but because it offers no information to the contrary, it implies that all members of the treatment group responded similarly to the two priming questions when

Table 4. Treatment Group by Losing Ground Coefficients from Ordered Logit Models for Each Outcome Question, with the Control Group Weighted Alternatively by Other Covariates

Question	Treatment Group by Not Losing Ground Coefficient (SE)	N	Chi-square Test Statistic (df)
Grades for public schools "in your community"	−.16 (.15)	928	75.0 (16)
Grades for public schools "in the nation as a whole"	.39 (.16)	926	77.2 (16)
Confidence in "people running the public education system"	.29 (.17)	971	69.2 (16)
Support for spending "to improve the nation's education system"	−.55 (.16)	968	148.6 (16)

	Treatment group by losing ground coefficient (SE)	N	Chi-square test statistic (df)
Grades for public schools "in your community"	−.88 (.16)	928	75.8 (16)
Grades for public schools "in the nation as a whole"	−.85 (.16)	926	100.0 (16)
Confidence in "people running the public education system"	−.60 (.16)	971	61.9 (16)
Support for spending "to improve the nation's education system"	−.09 (.18)	968	128.8 (16)

Source: Data from Cornell National Social Survey, 2011.

Note: For grades, the highest response category is A, and the lowest response category is fail. For the confidence question, the highest response category is "A great deal of confidence in them," and the lowest response category is "Hardly any confidence at all in them," with "Some confidence in them" as the middle category. For the spending question, the highest response category is "Too little money," and the lowest response category is "Too much money," with "About the right amount" as the middle category. All models are weighted by the inverse probability of providing a response to the outcome question, as estimated by a supplementary logit model.

formulating responses to the four outcome questions. In contrast, the results from our subgroup-level treatment effects analysis suggest that there are two subgroups within the treatment group whose average responses differed from each other. This suggests two complementary narratives for two distinct groups of individuals in the population. First, respondents who believe that public schools in the United States are losing substantial ground to those of international competitors offer lower grades for schools but continue to show interest in spending additional resources to improve them at the same level as the population as a whole. Second, respondents who believe that schools in the United States are not losing substantial ground to those of international competitors offer slightly higher grades but then express less support for increasing funding to improve them, again in comparison to response patterns in the population as a whole. This variation clarifies and extends the conclusions in Morgan and Taylor Poppe (2012), demonstrating the utility of a design that pairs a representative sample with a facilitative prime.

Our final set of models demonstrates how the control group can be weighted using estimated propensity scores to generate distinct comparison groups for the two alternative treatment subgroups. These models allow us to rule out response heterogeneity that could have been produced by other observed variables.

What produces these effects? One model for interpreting a context effect, and the one which we favor, is the belief-sampling model of Tourangeau et al. (2000). Here, the context effect is assumed to emerge because the context-setting treatment prime generates the retrieval of information, stored as personal beliefs, that is relevant to responses to the four outcome questions. The CNSS experiment, like nearly all other context effect experiments, does not reveal the specific stored beliefs that are retrieved and thereby made more salient as subsequent questions are interpreted and answered. However, the structure of the treatment prime offers a fairly straightforward set of conclusions nonetheless.

"Losing ground" treatment subgroup respondents are retrieving beliefs shaped by the statements of political elites (candidates for election, authoritative feature journalists, op-ed columnists, etc.) that public schools in the United States are performing below desired levels and falling behind the schools of our international competitors. As a consequence, they then offer lower grades for schools but continue to show interest in spending additional resources to improve them at the same level as the population as a whole.

"Not losing ground" treatment subgroup respondents are explicitly not retrieving this same set of beliefs. They either have not been exposed to these statements of political elites on the flagging performance of schools in the United States, or they have reasons to reject those statements. But why would these respondents offer slightly higher grades to schools than the control group? One answer is that the control group almost certainly includes some members of the population who are aware of the frame and retrieve the belief that schools are losing ground even when only presented with the first PDK/GP question that asks them to grade the schools in their communities, unlike the treatment subgroup that is composed only of individuals who explicitly reject the frame of interest.

The evidence also suggests that these respondents are retrieving beliefs that then prompt them to express less support for increasing funding to improve the nation's education system, again in comparison with response patterns in the population as a whole that are estimated by the control group. The most straightforward interpretation of this pattern is that these respondents are retrieving beliefs on the basis of the statements of political elites that the United States has robust economic competitors, perhaps more so than it did in prior decades. Because these respondents do not believe that shortfalls in the public education system of the United States are leaving the country vulnerable to competitors, some of these respondents may believe that money is better spent elsewhere shoring up whatever institutions they believe leave the country most vulnerable. Some respondents, for example, may believe that the existing federal deficit of the United States is the primary threat to the nation's competitiveness. These respondents, if primed to think about economic threats, may favor spending less money in general on all national priorities, regardless of the need for school reform or for addressing other social problems.

4. CONCLUSION

Context and framing effects in surveys are pervasive and variable across respondents. Because they are assumed to arise from unobserved interactions with beliefs stored in the memories of individuals with different prior experiences, the context-setting triggers embedded in survey instruments cannot be assumed to generate constant effects across respondents. In this article, we have demonstrated that a survey experiment, when paired with a facilitative prime, can enable models of variable context effects and genuine response heterogeneity at the population level.

As we noted above, none of the components of the design we have demonstrated is novel on its own, but their joint adoption allows for an analysis of conventional treatment effects as well as the patterns of response heterogeneity that underlie them. We have also shown how this heterogeneity can be modeled in pursuit of subgroup-level causal effect estimates, even though formal identification of these effects cannot be achieved.

It is a truism that all designs have limitations of some form; this design has three sets of weaknesses. First, it is impossible to conclude that the context effects revealed by the design would occur if similar facilitative primes were inserted into the national surveys from which the outcome questions are drawn. For example, it is impossible to exactly mimic the administration of the PDK/GP and the GSS at the same time, and in our demonstration, there are important differences between the CNSS and these surveys. The GSS is a face-to-face survey and offers an available Spanish-language questionnaire. The PDK/GP is a telephone survey, but it is based on the standing Gallup Panel. Thus, response and cooperation rates, as well as mode of administration, differ across these surveys. In addition, each survey has its own set of context effects, which could not be replicated for the CNSS. In particular, the spending question in the GSS is at the beginning of the survey and asked of everyone, but the confidence in leaders question has most recently been asked on two of the three different GSS ballots, and preceded by slightly different sets of questions based on the ballot. Thus, although it is a strength of our demonstration that it uses questions on which several decades of survey data are available, it is also the case that it is impossible to state definitively that the treatment prime analyzed here would produce analogous context effects if it were inserted into the questionnaires of these two long-running surveys. At most, we can conclude that there is a strong likelihood that such effects would emerge.

Second, the design itself has some inherent weaknesses, as judged relative to alternative designs in the substantive framing literature. In defending the value of student samples (and other convenience samples), Druckman and Kam (2011) privileged a broad criterion of external validity, stating "External validity refers to generalization not only of individuals, but also across settings/contexts, times, and operationalizations" (pp. 42–43). Although one might argue that such a broad definition is an attempt to paper over the very limited capacities of convenience samples to sustain narrower definitions of external validity, it is still the case that demonstrations such as the one offered here are based on a single operationalization, undertaken at a single point in time, and in an artificial interview context over which we, as investigators, have limited control. Carefully designed experimental studies, such as Druckman, Fein, and Leeper (2012), can generate results from repeated administrations that uncover the evolution of opinions in response to rich information sources. Such studies may still poorly mimic the true processes by which individuals form opinions in their nonexperimental lives, but it is without question that such artful and carefully controlled studies have some advantages that cannot be easily accommodated in this design.

Third, our favored interpretation is just that: an interpretation. One alternative interpretation, which is a plausible alternative, is that the facilitative prime only triggers an anchoring point for subsequent judgments. For this interpretation, respondents do not make any connection between economic competitiveness and school quality, regardless of the content of the statements that elites have offered in public and regardless of the content of the questions that explicitly prime economic competitiveness. Instead, respondents change only the reference point for their judgments and invoke an international standard as an anchoring point that, for whatever reason, causes them to lower the grades they offer to schools as well as their confidence in leaders. We believe that this alternative interpretation is less persuasive than our favored one, because we do not see how it generates the "losing ground" partition that then generates a particular pattern of variation across all four subsequent questions. In particular, it does not suggest as natural an interpretation for why the "not losing ground" treatment subgroup lowers its interest in spending money to improve the nation's schools. Even so, the larger point we wish to make here is that an interpretation must still be offered after results are generated using this design, and more than one interpretation will almost certainly be plausible. The design does not reveal which specific beliefs, if any, have been retrieved in response to the facilitative prime, even though it induces individual-level variation in response to the content of the prime that can help motivate alternative interpretations.

These limitations notwithstanding, the design demonstrated here does offer potential substantive insight into framing effects at the population level, demonstrating their relevance for responses to long-used items in important surveys. Moreover, the design's facilitative prime allows subjects to sort themselves in ways that the analyst can plausibly assume reflect real-world information storage and belief formation in response to frame exposure prior to the study. As such, even though the study does not come close to mimicking real-world frame exposure and issue motivation processes, it does offer the analyst leverage to determine which respondents are most likely to have observed and stored context-setting information in response to frame presentation by political elites and others. The analyst can then offer estimates of the proportion of the target population that has likely stored information in response to the frame prior to the study as well as the effect that this information, when retrieved, has on responses to relevant attitude items. When the items under study are long-used questions from important public opinion surveys and polls, such results offer more than just methodological insight into survey response artifacts. They offer substantive insight into how the preexisting beliefs of respondents shape their attitudes, in variable patterns within the target population. Results such as these can move models of context effects from studies that demonstrate their existence toward those that model their prevalence and magnitude. Such results have the potential to inform substantive research and also prompt the augmentation of survey instruments to directly measure any inferred heterogeneity.

APPENDIX

Table A1. Coefficients from a Logit Model That Predicts Whether Members of the Treatment Group Believe That the U.S. Education System Is Losing Substantial Ground

Variable	
Constant	−2.70
Has children currently in public schools in the community	.07 (.23)
Demographic characteristics	
Female	.09 (.20)
Hispanic ethnicity	.30 (.40)
African American	.51 (.33)
Born in the United States	.04 (.36)
Age	−.001 (.01)
Residential characteristics	
Respondent owns home in which she or he lives	−.34 (.26)
Took interview on cell phone rather than land line	−.15 (.22)
Socioeconomic status	
Family income from all sources (natural logarithm)	.28 (.14)
Education (in years completed)	−.02 (.05)
Political affiliations and values	
Republican party identification	.02 (.06)
Conservative ideology	−.001 (.07)
Attitudes toward engagement in world affairs	
Does not agree with interventions to solve conflicts around the world	.69 (.21)
Does not feel the war in Afghanistan makes America safer	.32 (.22)
N	471
Chi-square (df)	24.3 (14)

Source: Data from Cornell National Social Survey, 2011.

Acknowledgments

We thank the team at the Survey Research Institute at Cornell University for fielding the CNSS. We also thank the editor and anonymous reviewers for their helpful suggestions.

Notes

1. In this literature, the conceptual distinctions between the terms *framing* and *priming* have been a matter of discussion and debate; see Entman (1993) for an early review and Druckman, Kuklinski, and Sigelman (2009) for a later review. In this article, we do not make fine distinctions between frames and primes.
2. Morgan and Taylor Poppe (2012) considered parts 1 and 4 of this question, and they analyzed the same Cornell National Social Survey experiment but used only models for conventional treatment effects. In this article, we consider all four parts

of the question and extend the modeling strategy to fully reveal the pattern of results that generated their conclusions.

3. The sample was provided by Marketing Systems Group as a random-digit dialing list of telephone numbers drawn from telephone exchanges in the continental United States (including cell phones but excluding known nonhousehold numbers). Within contacted households, one respondent from each household was selected using a "most recent birthday" selection rule. Telephone data collection by the Survey Research Institute at Cornell University began on September 10, 2011, and was completed by December 10, 2011. All interviews were conducted in English, and the cooperation and response rates were 62.4 percent and 24.1 percent, respectively (calculated using definition 2 of the American Association for Public Opinion Research).

4. Although the PDK/GP questions are verbatim copies of their originals (see Bushaw and Lopez 2011, 2012), time constraints on the CNSS required changes to the two GSS questions. The first question asks only about confidence in leaders "running the public education system in the United States," rather than offering a menu of types of leaders associated with particular institutions in a battery of questions. The second question asks only about spending on education, not spending across the full menu of items on the GSS. These changes may generate context effects of their own, as we discuss in the final section of this article when detailing limitations of the design.

5. Both ballots conclude with the same question that asks respondents to indicate whether they currently have children attending public schools in their own communities. The PDK/GP asks a similar question as this last one, and reports based on these data suggest that respondents with children currently enrolled in school award higher grades to schools in their own communities, presumably based either on current information to which they have access or a more diffuse loyalty to the institutions that care for their children.

6. Other primes could also be used that are visual but not textual. The best example in this context would be a brief video of Mitt Romney's opening statement in the October 3, 2012, presidential debate, in which he offered a plan for economic growth: "My plan has five basic parts. One, get us energy independent, North American energy independent. That creates about 4 million jobs. Number two, open up more trade, particularly in Latin America, crack down on China, if and when they cheat. Number three, make sure our people have the skills they need to succeed and the best schools in the world. We're a far way from that now. Number four, get us to a balanced budget. Number five, champion small business. It's small business that creates the jobs in America." Note that Romney's remark on schools is sandwiched between statements that prime economic competitiveness with China and the debt-funded spending of the federal government. It was delivered to a television audience widely estimated to include at least 70 million viewers, during a performance that is regarded as the best two hours of his campaign. It is authoritative (although partisan), and it has the benefit of being real, short, and closer to a facilitative prime. Yet, like the *New York Times* article, it would be difficult to administer this prime to subjects selected as part of a national sample.

Respondent burden would be lower than for the *New York Times* article, but survey costs would remain high.

7. As noted earlier, the GSS has used split-ballot designs in the past to examine context effects, including for these questions. For the question that asks respondents to rate a series of national spending priorities ("I'd like you to tell me whether you think we're spending too much money on it, too little money, or about the right amount"), respondents were randomly assigned to one of two question wordings for the spending areas, generally in the pattern of "improving the nation's education system" (the original GSS wording used from 1973 through 2012) and "education" (a terse alternative introduced first in 1984 and used on a split ballot through 2012). Question wording effects for the education item (which is one of the questions analyzed in our experiment) were small. However, as the experiment has continued, additional power has accumulated to identify smaller effects, which are generally less than four percentage points (see Smith 1991, 2006).

8. Similar to this result, Simon and Davey (2010) offered a vignette-based framing study with an online national sample that evaluated a variety of framing strategies for generating support for higher education. Their results suggest that "a commonly advanced value in public discourse, Global Competitiveness, on the higher education level actually depresses support for progressive policy reform" (p. 3). Their vignette, however, stresses preparing the next generation of children for competition in a global economy, not the economic threat that other nations pose to the United States.

9. We could also use latent variables with hollow nodes (see, e.g., Morgan and Winship 2015) to allow the common causes represented by the double-headed arrows in $L \longleftrightarrow X$ and in $X \longleftrightarrow Y$ to be determined by distal common causes U. We do not offer such an elaborated graph, because the need for an explicit representation of U is vitiated by our inclusion of $L \longleftrightarrow Y$, which renders the effect of L on Y unidentified, regardless of whether conditioning on X would induce additional collider-stratification bias; see Pearl (2009) and Elwert (2013).

10. An alternative representation would be to join T to L by defining a new three-valued treatment variable as $Z = 0$ if $T = 0$ and $Z = 1 + L$ if $T = 1$. We chose the representation in Figure 2b because it remains consistent with Figure 2a by showing that the total effect of T on Y is still identified, while also revealing that the particular value of L is endogenous with respect to common causes that also determine both X and Y. An alternative graph that relied only on Z to represent both T and L would not reveal this consistency between Figures 2a and 2b. Relatedly, our position is that L is not a collider variable of the usual kind because it is missing entirely for the control group and is best regarded as inherent to the treatment conditions. By using L to partition the treatment group only, we are not generating induced nuisance associations between T and Y across the full population, as would be the case if we conditioned on L in the control group as well. Instead, we attach substantive interpretations to partition-defined treatment effects, even though some of the same reasoning for understanding collider-induced associations does obtain. As explained below, we give interpretations to the contrasts that we feel are substantively justified.

11. Alternative designs would allow for a genuine separation of T from L, but with associated costs that would not aid in identification. For example, the two priming questions could be asked of the control group after the four attitude questions, as in a question-order experiment. This design would generate values for L for the control group. However, we would then have a context effect whereby beliefs about the quality of schools may then exert their own effects on L. Any attempt to draw a full causal graph would then include cycles, such as $L \rightarrow Y \rightarrow L$. Without introducing further assumptions—such as assuming that the effect of Y on L is null—this alternative design would simply have twice as many unidentified effects.

12. See also Table S3 in the online Supplementary Appendix for the specific values depicted graphically in Figures 2 through 5.

13. This 35 percentage point difference between grades for schools in respondents' communities and in the nation as a whole is comparable with the differences reported in the PDK/GP (33 points in 2011 and 29 points in 2012; see Bushaw and Lopez 2011, 2012). The scale of these lower grades, however, is higher by about 10 percentage points in the PDK/GP, which may reflect a specific negative context effect in the PDK/GP. The questions on grades are the third through fifth questions on the PDK/GP poll (W. J. Bushaw, personal communication). The first question filters respondents on the basis of whether they have children in the local public schools. The second question, which may generate a negative context effect, asks respondents, "What do you think are the biggest problems that the public schools of your community must deal with?" It is unclear what the response categories to this question have been over the years, but Bushaw and Lopez (2012:10) reported that 43 percent of respondents indicated "lack of financial support," while another 16 percent listed "lack of discipline,'"overcrowded schools,'"fighting/gang violence," or "drugs."

14. In effect, we use the information in X to impute the nonrandom missing data in L for the control group, on the basis of the relationship between X and L in the treatment group. We do not actually impute any data. Instead, we reweight the control group so that its distribution of X matches, as closely as possible, the distribution of X for each treatment subgroup for each relevant model. When estimating subgroup-level casual effects, this is equivalent to imputing L in a way that would partition the control group according to X but is more efficient because it uses all control cases for each subsequent weighted model.

15. In other words, we can decompose $P[Y^1]$ using only observed quantities, such that $P[Y^1] = \lambda P[Y|T=1, L=1] + (1 - \lambda)P[Y|T=1, L=0]$, where λ is the proportion of the treatment group that sees schools as losing ground. However, we have no partition of the control group by L and therefore we cannot similarly decompose $P[Y^0]$ across L using observable quantities only. In particular, we have no way to estimate either $P[Y^0|L=1]$ or $P[Y^0|L=0]$ with the observed data, even though we can borrow the estimate of λ from the treatment group because both the treatment and control groups are representative samples from the same target population. We observe no data for sample analogs to either $P[Y|T=0, L=1]$ or $P[Y|T=0, L=0]$.

16. Although not impossible, it is unlikely that the treatment prime altered these responses. The education module was the first module in the CNSS interview

while the world affairs module was separated from it by 25 other questions on a variety of topics.

References

Bushaw, William J., and Shane J. Lopez. 2011. "Betting on Teachers: The 43rd Annual Phi Delta Kappa/Gallup Poll of the Public's Attitudes toward the Public Schools." *Phi Delta Kappan* 93:8–26.

Bushaw, William J., and Shane J. Lopez. 2012. "Public Education in the United States: A Nation Divided. The 44th Annual Phi Delta Kappa/Gallup Poll of the Public's Attitudes toward the Public Schools." *Phi Delta Kappan* 94:9–25.

Chong, Dennis, and James N. Druckman. 2007. "Framing Theory." *Annual Review of Political Science* 10:103–26.

Chong, Dennis, and James N. Druckman. 2011. "Public-elite Interactions: Puzzles in Search of Researchers." Pp. 170–88 in *The Oxford Handbook of American Public Opinion and the Media*, edited by R. Y. Shapiro and L. R. Jacobs. New York: Oxford University Press.

Druckman, James N., Jordan Fein, and Thomas J. Leeper. 2012. "A Source of Bias in Public Opinion Stability." *American Political Science Review* 106:430–54.

Druckman, James N., Green, Donald P., Kuklinski, James H., and Arthur Lupia, eds. 2011. *Cambridge Handbook of Experimental Political Science*. New York: Cambridge University Press.

Druckman, James N., and Cindy D. Kam. 2011. "Students as Experimental Participants: A Defense of the 'Narrow Data Base.'" Pp. 41–57 in *Cambridge Handbook of Experimental Political Science*, edited by J. N. Druckman, D. P. Green, J. H. Kuklinski, and A. Lupia. New York: Cambridge University Press.

Druckman, James N., James H. Kuklinski, and Lee Sigelman. 2009. "The Unmet Potential of Interdisciplinary Research: Political Psychological Approaches to Voting and Public Opinion." *Political Behavior* 31:485–510.

Elwert, Felix. 2013. "Graphical Causal Models." Pp. 245–73 in *Handbook of Causal Analysis for Social Research*, edited by S. L. Morgan. Dordrecht, the Netherlands: Springer.

Entman, Robert M. 1993. "Framing: Toward Clarification of a Fractured Paradigm." *Journal of Communication* 43:51–58.

Imbens, Guido W. 2004. "Nonparametric Estimation of Average Treatment Effects under Exogeneity: A Review." *Review of Economics and Statistics* 86:4–29.

Morgan, Stephen L., and Emily S. Taylor Poppe. 2012. "The Consequences of International Comparisons for Public Support of K–12 Education: Evidence from a National Survey Experiment." *Educational Researcher* 42:262–68.

Morgan, Stephen L., and Christopher Winship. 2015. *Counterfactuals and Causal Inference: Methods and Principles for Social Research*. 2nd ed. Cambridge, UK: Cambridge University Press.

Mutz, Diana C. 2011. *Population-based Survey Experiments*. Princeton, NJ: Princeton University Press.

Pearl, Judea. 2009. *Causality: Models, Reasoning, and Inference*. 2nd ed. Cambridge, UK: Cambridge University Press.

Pearl, Judea. 2010. "The Foundations of Causal Inference." Pp. 75–149 in *Sociological Methodology*, Vol. 40, edited by Tim Futing Liao. Boston, MA: Wiley-Blackwell.

Rasinski, Kenneth A. 1988. "The Effect of Question Wording on Public Support for Government Spending." GSS Methodological Report No. 54. Chicago, IL: National Opinion Research Center.

Rasinski, Kenneth A. 1989. "The Effect of Question Wording on Public Support for Government Spending." *Public Opinion Quarterly* 53:388–94.

Rubin, Donald B. 2005. "Causal Inference Using Potential Outcomes: Design, Modeling, Decisions." *Journal of the American Statistical Association* 100:322–31.

Schuman, Howard. 2008. *Method and Meaning in Polls and Surveys*. Cambridge, MA: Harvard University Press.

Schuman, Howard, and Stanley Presser. 1981. *Questions and Answers in Attitude Surveys: Experiments on Question Form, Wording, and Context*. New York: Academic Press.

Schwarz, Norbert, and Seymour Sudman, eds. 1992. *Context Effects in Social and Psychological Research*. New York: Springer-Verlag.

Simon, Adam F., and Lynn F. Davey. 2010. "College Bound: The Effects of Value Frames on Attitudes toward Higher Education Reform." A Frameworks Research Report. Washington, DC: The Frameworks Institute.

Smith, Tom W. 1987. "That Which We Call Welfare by Any Other Name Would Smell Sweeter: An Analysis of Question Wording on Response Patterns." *Public Opinion Quarterly* 51:75–83.

Smith, Tom W. 1991. "Context Effects in the General Social Survey." Pp. 57–72 in *Measurement Errors in Surveys*, edited by P. P. Biemer, R. M. Groves, L. E. Lyberg, N. A. Mathiowetz, and S. Sudman. New York: John Wiley.

Smith, Tom W. 2006. "Wording Effects on the National Spending Priority Items across Time, 1984–2004." GSS Methodological Report No. 107. Chicago, IL: National Opinion Research Center.

Sniderman, Paul M. 2011. "The Logic and Design of the Survey Experiment: An Autobiography of a Methodological Innovation." Pp. 102–14 in *Cambridge Handbook of Experimental Political Science*, edited by J. N. Druckman, D. P. Green, J. H. Kuklinski, and A. Lupia. New York: Cambridge University Press.

Tourangeau, Roger, Kenneth A. Rasinski, Norman Bradburn, and Roy D'Andrade. 1989. "Belief Accessibility and Context Effects in Attitude Measurement." *Journal of Experimental Social Psychology* 25:401–21.

Tourangeau, Roger, Lance J. Rips, and Kenneth A. Rasinski. 2000. *The Psychology of Survey Response*. New York: Cambridge University Press.

Wyer, Robert S., and Thomas K. Srull. 1989. *Memory and Cognition in Its Social Context*. Hillsdale, NJ: Lawrence Erlbaum.

Author Biographies

Stephen L. Morgan is the Bloomberg Distinguished Professor of Sociology and Education at Johns Hopkins University. His current areas of research include education, inequality, demography, and methodology. Along with Christopher Winship, he is the author of *Counterfactuals and Causal Inference: Methods and Principles for Social*

Research (Cambridge University Press, 2007; revised and enlarged second edition, 2015).

Emily S. Taylor Poppe is a doctoral candidate in sociology at Cornell University. Her research interests include inequality, sociology of law, and methodology. Her dissertation focuses on legal representation in residential foreclosure cases during the Great Recession.

Sociological Methodology
2015, Vol. 45(1) 223–271
© American Sociological Association 2015
DOI: 10.1177/0081175014562589
http://sm.sagepub.com

꿍 5 꿍

AN INTRODUCTION TO THE GENERAL MONOTONE MODEL WITH APPLICATION TO TWO PROBLEMATIC DATA SETS

*Michael R. Dougherty**

Rick P. Thomas[†]

Ryan P. Brown[‡]

*Jeffrey S. Chrabaszcz**

*Joe W. Tidwell**

Abstract

We argue that the mismatch between data and analytical methods, along with common practices for dealing with "messy" data, can lead to inaccurate conclusions. Specifically, using previously published data on racial bias and culture of honor, we show that manifest effects, and therefore theoretical conclusions, are highly dependent on how researchers decide to handle extreme scores and nonlinearities when data are analyzed with traditional approaches. Within LS approaches, statistical effects appeared or disappeared on the basis of the inclusion or exclusion of as little as 1.5% (3 of 198) of the data, and highly predictive variables were masked by nonlinearities. We then demonstrate a new statistical modeling technique called the

*University of Maryland, College Park, MD, USA
[†]Georgia Institute of Technology, Atlanta, GA, USA
[‡]University of Oklahoma, Norman, OK, USA

Corresponding Author:
Michael R. Dougherty, University of Maryland, Department of Psychology, College Park, MD 20742, USA
Email: mdougher@umd.edu

general monotone model (GeMM) and show that it has a number of desirable properties that may make it more appropriate for modeling messy data: It is more robust to extreme scores, less affected by outlier analyses, and more robust to violations of linearity on both the response and predictor variables compared with a variety of well-established statistical algorithms and frequently possesses greater statistical power. We argue that using procedures that make fewer assumptions about the data, such as GeMM, can lessen the need for researchers to use data-editing strategies (e.g., to apply transformations or to engage outlier analyses) on their data to satisfy often unrealistic statistical assumptions, leading to more consistent and accurate conclusions about data than traditional approaches of data analysis.

Keywords

data editing, monotone regression, maximum rank correlation estimator, culture of honor, racial bias

1. INTRODUCTION

Although recent high-profile cases of fraud have brought unwelcome attention to social sciences, these cases offer an opportunity to reflect on the state of our sciences as well as currently accepted practices (Crocker 2011; Fang, Steen, and Casadevall 2012). To be sure, sociologists have been somewhat ahead of the curve in addressing issues related to data quality, reproducibility (Freese 2007; Hauser 1987), replicability (King 1995), and publication bias (Gerber and Malhotra 2008; Leahey 2005). Of these, data quality arguably ranks as the foremost problem for social scientists because so much, including reproducibility and replication, depends on having good-quality data. Unfortunately, much of the data within the social sciences are messy, and they often require a good amount of editing (e.g., transformation, replacement of missing values, outlier removal) prior to analysis when used with traditional metric statistics. Data editing, however, enables the researcher to capitalize on chance, a problem that is compounded by the fact that there are not well-accepted (or followed) guidelines for how and when to use particular data-editing strategies (Leahey 2008; Leahey, Entwisle, and Einaudi 2003; Sana and Weinreb 2008). The plethora of available strategies, even for something as simple as outlier analysis, can promote flexibility in data analysis. Unfortunately, different approaches to data editing can yield different substantive conclusions, meaning that replications depend not only on the data but also on the specific choices one makes in data editing.

The use of data-editing strategies is just one end of the spectrum of the flexibility afforded to researchers. Modern computers and an ever expanding toolbox of available statistical algorithms permit researchers to easily explore their data in a variety of different ways under different modeling assumptions prior to settling on the subset of analyses that are to be reported (Ho et al. 2007). Coupled with methodological issues surrounding the use of data editing, flexibility in analysis techniques has been a major concern within the social sciences, leading some to call for open-source documentation of data analysis techniques (Freese 2007; Simonsohn 2013). Although there are many reasons to demand open-source documentation, it does not address the problem of flexibility of analysis; it only makes the use of flexible analysis methods public and open to scrutiny.

The work presented here has two related goals. The first is to illustrate the problem with implementing accepted practices on how to deal with messy data, showing just how sensitive substantive conclusions can be to different choices made in data analysis. The second goal is to provide an alternative approach to modeling messy data that reduces or eliminates the need for researchers to make such decisions. With regard to the first goal, using data on racial prejudice (Siegel, Dougherty, and Huber 2012) and culture of honor (Henry 2009), we show that the use of least squares (LS) regression techniques yields inconsistent conclusions across various accepted methods for dealing with messy data. These inconsistencies call into question the validity of statistical conclusions based on LS approaches and in general render the data less interpretable. We argue that the mismatch between the nature of one's data and standard statistical approaches can deceive researchers into drawing invalid conclusions, no matter how well intentioned or diligent the researchers are.

Turning to the second goal, we introduce a new statistical algorithm, the general monotone model (GeMM; Dougherty and Thomas 2012) that makes weaker assumptions than LS approaches about scale of measurement and the functional relationships among manifest variables. GeMM provides relatively more consistent statistical outcomes across several criteria for inclusion or exclusion of extreme scores and the presence of nonlinearities. We show that GeMM is more robust to extreme scores, it is unaffected by nonlinear monotone relationships, and it has superior predictive accuracy and better statistical power when compared with a variety of procedures based on LS. Our application of GeMM in this article goes beyond previous published applications. Specifically, our analyses evaluate the stability or robustness of GeMM relative to alternative modeling techniques under a variety of realistic conditions that might otherwise entice researchers to make tough decisions about how to handle nonlinear or nonnormal data or the presence of extreme scores. We argue that GeMM provides a promising solution to flexibility in data analysis by greatly reducing both the need for and the impact of data editing.

2. MESSY DATA AND TOUGH DECISIONS

Rarely do data neatly conform to the assumptions required for carrying out standard statistical procedures. For instance, it is well recognized that real data typically deviate, often nontrivially, from normality (Micceri 1989), which can result in violations of assumptions underlying standard statistical techniques. Real data are messy. As researchers, we are taught to be vigilant to aberrations in our data, and even to remove them through the use of transformations or "outlier" analyses. For example, Hays (1994) stated that

> the data should be inspected for unusually skewed or artificially restricted distributions, missing data, and the presence of unusually deviant cases or outliers. . . . Fortunately, even messy data can often be cleaned up enough to be used, but doing so requires many choices. (p. 721)

Many textbooks contain similar advice—advice that instructs researchers to clean their data through transformation and outlier deletion techniques. These techniques, which we refer to collectively as *data-editing strategies* (Leahey 2008; Leahey et al. 2003), allow researchers to clean and/or reexpress the data in a form that more closely conforms to the assumptions of the statistical model. However, the same textbooks that offer advice on how to handle nonnormalities and outliers also point out that standard LS estimation procedures and their robust implementations often perform reasonably well even when their assumptions are not met (see Howell 2002). This type of back-and-forth between prescribing data-editing strategies and touting robustness is typical.

The fact that many analysis techniques make strong assumptions about distributional (e.g., multivariate normality) and functional (e.g., linear) forms can present researchers with a potentially important dilemma: Should they engage in data editing to bring the data in line with the assumptions of the analytical procedure, recognizing that the statistical conclusions are conditional on the particular data-editing strategies used? Or should they analyze the data "as is," recognizing that the statistical conclusions are conditional on potential violations of assumptions? Obviously, the best-case scenario is that statistical conclusions are invariant across various data-editing strategies and methodologies. However, there may be cases in which researchers' statistical, and therefore theoretical, claims depend on *whether* or *how* they have transformed or trimmed the data. Indeed, in investigating Diederik Stapel's infamous body of work for instances of deceptive research practices, an investigatory panel specifically noted how the elimination or inclusion of extreme scores affected the statistical conclusions:

> On the one hand, "outliers" (extreme scores on usually the dependent variable) were removed from the analysis where no significant results were obtained. This elimination reduces the variance of the dependent variable and makes it more likely that "statistically significant" findings will emerge. . . . Conversely, the Committees also observed that extreme scores of one or two experimental subjects were kept in the analysis where their elimination would have changed significant differences into insignificant ones; there was no mention anywhere of the fact that the significance relied on just one or a few subjects. (Levelt Committee, Noort Committee, and Drenth Committee 2012:49)

Obviously, it strikes us as problematic when statistical and theoretical conclusions are dependent not on the data *per se* but on the creative use (or misuse) of statistical methods and data-editing strategies—what Simmons, Nelson, and Simonsohn (2011) have referred to as "experimenter degrees of freedom." Although Stapel may have been guilty of not disclosing his decisions to include or exclude participants (and outright fraud in other cases), the fact that he sometimes engaged in outlier elimination (and other times chose not to) is not inconsistent with standard practices. In fact, the authors of the Stapel report even seem conflicted about whether it was appropriate to eliminate extreme scores. The bottom line is that decisions about whether to engage in data editing that are based on whether the data meet the assumptions of the statistical model leave the researcher in a precarious position: damned if you do and damned if you don't.

Although there have been several documented cases of inappropriate data editing within the psychological literature (e.g., that of Diedrick Stapel), the issue of data editing is clearly of concern across all of the social sciences, including sociology (John, Loewenstein, and Prelec 2012; Leahey et al. 2003). The tension surrounding the appropriateness of eliminating outliers was illuminated by an exchange between Kahn and Udry (1986) and Jasso (1986) in the *American Sociological Review* regarding an analysis of intercourse frequency among married couples: Kahn and Udry criticized Jasso's original analysis by arguing that her inclusion of outliers was inappropriate and biased the statistical results; Jasso countered by arguing that the exclusion of outliers in Kahn and Udry's reanalysis produced "sample truncation bias." This divergence on the inclusion of outliers highlights a common predicament: There is not always a clear solution to the presence of outliers, and decisions to include or exclude them often come down to a judgment call.

The scope of the data-editing problem for statistical inference is difficult to assess from published work, in part because there is little oversight or consistency in regard to how data-editing procedures are carried out (Leahey 2008) and in part because few articles include serious discussion of how specific data-editing decisions affect statistical conclusions. Nevertheless, it is clear that data editing is a relatively common component of statistical analysis. Notable examples from the literature include the common use of logarithmic transformations for analyses that include estimates of income (e.g., Olsen and Dahl 2007; Semyonov and Lewin-Epstein 2011) and homicide rates (Lederman, Loayza, and Menéndez, 2002). Although decisions regarding whether to transform variables are presumably based on the need to bring the data in line with modeling assumptions, these decisions represent an important source of flexibility in data analysis—a flexibility that can be exploited either intentionally or unintentionally (Simmons et al. 2011).

The exploitation of flexible analysis techniques is a problem for science. However, the critical question concerns the precise nature of this problem: Is it that people fail to report faithfully the many decisions that ultimately exploit this flexibility? Or is it that there is too much flexibility with data analysis techniques to begin with? Depending on how we perceive the problem, it suggests different solutions. If the problem is that people do not faithfully report the many decisions that exploit the flexibility of available statistical algorithms, then the obvious solution is to require full disclosure of data analysis methods in an open-source forum, as suggested by Freese (2007). However, if the problem is that there is too much flexibility to begin with, then the solution would seem to lie in the development (or use of) procedures that reduce this flexibility (Ho et al. 2007). Thus, although full disclosure is important, we believe that the more fundamental problem lies with the use of standard statistical techniques, which permit, and in some cases demand, that researchers engage in data editing. Assuming this is the case, then one reasonable approach is to use analysis techniques that are robust to the types of decisions that researchers would otherwise be compelled to make in order to bring their data in line with the modeling assumptions (cf. Beck and Jackman 1998).

3. THE GENERAL MONOTONE MODEL

Fundamentally, the GeMM is an algorithm for detecting and modeling monotone statistical relationships in regression contexts. The primary difference between GeMM and standard LS approaches lies in the fitness function. In LS regression, the goal is to find the regression coefficients that minimize the sum of the squared differences between the observed and the predicted values. In contrast, in GeMM the goal is to find the regression coefficients that minimize the difference in the ordinal correspondence (i.e., that minimize the number of rank-order inversions) between the observed and predicted values, as defined by Kendall's (1938) τ. In this way, GeMM attempts to find the solution that provides the best *monotonic* (i.e., rank-order) fit to the data, as opposed to finding the best *linear* LS fit to the data. Thus, GeMM is a variant of the maximum rank correlation estimator (Cavanagh and Sherman, 1998; Han 1987). As demonstrated below, GeMM has superior statistical power relative to ordinary LS (OLS) to detect nonlinear but monotone statistical relationships, without requiring the researcher to model the nonlinearity directly or engage in data editing. The reason for this is that the rank-order correlation τ, on which GeMM is based, is invariant to monotone transformation on the criterion variable. It is also important to note that GeMM suffers little loss in statistical power compared with OLS when the statistical relationship is linear and the data satisfy standard OLS assumptions (Dougherty and Thomas 2012). Because GeMM is invariant to transformation on the criteria, unaffected by nonlinearities, and should be less sensitive to extreme scores (a property we demonstrate below), it provides a new tool for modeling messy data that would otherwise require editing or more specialized statistical algorithms.

In its simplest form, GeMM consists of a one-parameter model (i.e., one predictor), which is used to predict the criterion variable[1] of interest. In this context, GeMM is actually identical to Kendall's (1938) τ correlation coefficient, but it is expressed in a model form. Rather than expressing the relationship between X and Y directly, we substitute $\hat{Y}$ for X to show the model-form equivalence of τ for a single predictor:

$$\hat{Y} = \beta X. \tag{1}$$

In equation (1), we wish to find a value for β that minimizes the *incorrectly* predicted paired comparisons, as defined by equations (2) to (6):

$$\tau(\hat{Y}, Y) = (C - D)/\text{sqrt}\left[(\text{Pairs} - T_p) * (\text{Pairs} - T_c)\right], \tag{2}$$

$$C = Prop(Y_i > Y_j \cap \hat{Y}_i > \hat{Y}_j) + Prop(Y_i < Y_j \cap \hat{Y}_i < \hat{Y}_j), \tag{3}$$

$$D = Prop(Y_i > Y_j \cap \hat{Y}_i < \hat{Y}_j) + Prop(Y_i < Y_j \cap \hat{Y}_i > \hat{Y}_j), \tag{4}$$

$$T_p = Prop(Y_i \geq Y_j \cap \hat{Y}_i = \hat{Y}_j) + Prop(Y_i \leq Y_j \cap \hat{Y}_i = \hat{Y}_j), \tag{5}$$

and

$$T_c = Prop(Y_i = Y_j \cap \hat{Y}_i \leq \hat{Y}_j) + Prop(Y_i = Y_j \cap \hat{Y}_i \geq \hat{Y}_j), \tag{6}$$

where Pairs = $N(N-1)/2$, the number of unique paired comparisons; C is the number of concordant paired comparisons; D is the number of disconcordant pairs; T_p is the number of ties on the predictor; and T_c is the number of ties on the criterion. With only one predictor, only the sign of β matters, which provides the direction of the relationship between $\hat{Y}$ and Y. Thus, for the one-predictor case, the specific value of β is irrelevant, and the strength of the predictor is defined by the value of τ. Note that there is no intercept parameter in equation (1), because it is not necessary for predicting the ordered relationship.

Equation (1) can be generalized to the multiple predictor case:

$$\hat{Y} = \beta_1 X_1 + \beta_2 X_2 + \ldots + \beta_k X_k. \tag{7}$$

In equation (7), the different coefficients are estimated to maximize model fit and can therefore take on any real number, which allows the variables to differentially contribute to the overall fit between the data, Y, and the model estimates, $\hat{Y}$. In this context, the magnitudes of the β values are interpreted as the *relative* contribution of each predictor for predicting the ordinal values of Y. In contexts in which predictors are uncorrelated, the β weights can be viewed as the relative importance of each variable for characterizing the ordinal values of Y.

Parameter estimation is achieved computationally, rather than analytically, because there are no currently available methods for deriving optimal weights to maximize the rank-order correspondence between a model and the data. In the present analyses, we used a genetic algorithm to search the parameter space for the best-fit parameter estimates. Prior work (Dougherty and Thomas 2012) illustrated that genetic search works well for estimating the optimal weights for simulated data with known parameters.

In the analyses that follow, we fit data within the context of minimizing model complexity. This was achieved by using a variant of the Bayesian information criterion (BIC). Raftery (1995) showed that the BIC could be estimated from

$$BIC = N \log(1 - R^2) + k \log(N), \tag{8}$$

where N is the sample size, R^2 is the squared multiple correlation, and k is the number of parameters. One problem with applying equation (8) directly is that GeMM is designed to predict rank orders. However, Kendall and Gibbons (1990) showed that under bivariate normality,[2] Pearson's r could be estimated from τ using

$$r - tau = \sin(pi/2\tau). \tag{9}$$

Substituting equation (9) for the value of R^2 in (8) yields equation (10):

$$BIC_\tau = N \log(1 - (sin[pi/2\tau])^2) + k \log(N). \tag{10}$$

Equation (10) is the value of the BIC estimated from the τ-to-r transformation. However, because the value of r_τ shows greater variability than r (Rupinski and Dunlap 1996), we use an adjusted form of r_τ based on sample size and the number of predictors used in the regression. Specifically, we define r'_τ as

$$r'_\tau = sin[pi/2\tau\omega], \tag{11}$$

where

$$\omega = (N - P - 1)/N, \tag{12}$$

where ω is a weighting function based on the number predictors, P, used in the regression and sample size, N. Because ω serves to deweight the value of τ for smaller sample sizes, it reduces the variance of the τ-to-r transformation. Because ω goes to 1.0 as N increases, the asymptotic value of the τ-to-r transformation is preserved. Substituting r'_τ into equation (12) gives

$$\text{BIC}'_\tau = N \log(1 - r'^2_\tau) + k \log(N). \tag{13}$$

Model selection based on equation (13) (BIC'_τ) is assessed on the fit of the model to the data as given by the degree of monotonic relationship expressed by the τ-to-r transformation, adjusted for model complexity. Dougherty and Thomas (2012) showed that model fitting based on r'^2_τ is invariant to monotone transformation on y, whereas model fit based on the linear r^2 can suffer from considerable loss of power when statistical relations deviate from strict linearity. Furthermore, Dougherty and Thomas (2012) illustrated that GeMM's estimated parameters approximated the metric population values, and they were unaffected by nonlinearities. This later result occurs for the same reason that ordinal multidimensional scaling solutions approximate metric properties of the data: The number of constraints on the rank-order solution increases exponentially as sample size increases (Dougherty and Thomas 2012; see also Shepard 1962, 1966).

The base GeMM algorithm described above and in Dougherty and Thomas (2012) searches the parameter space to find coefficients that maximize the value of τ. However, a simple modification to this process involves maximizing the linear fit (R^2), conditional on the optimal ordinal fit. This can be achieved in GeMM by sorting all models with equivalent (maximal) ordinal fit by their corresponding values of R^2. This yields the vector of β values that optimize the *linear* fit, conditional on the set of coefficients that maximize ordinal fit. Note that the coefficients derived from this process are scale independent and are not directly comparable with coefficients derived from OLS, because there is an infinite number of parameter values that will yield an equivalent solution. This is because GeMM lacks an intercept term and because the fit statistic, τ, is invariant to monotone transformation. However, we may obtain a comparable LS model, one that is conditioned on maximizing τ, by regressing the criterion value Y on the predicted values of Y obtained from GeMM. In other words, we can use the OLS machinery to rescale the GeMM fitted weights to the LS solution that simultaneously maximizes the rank-order correspondence between the criterion and fitted values. We refer to this procedure as order-constrained least-squared optimization (OCLO; Tidwell et al. 2014). In principle, the OCLO solution is a special case of the base GeMM model in which weights are rescaled to minimize the sum of squared errors, conditional on the optimized ordinal fit. The end result of applying OCLO is a set of β coefficients that are directly comparable with those obtained via OLS regression.

4. REDUCING FLEXIBILITY IN ANALYSIS: AN ILLUSTRATION OF GEMM ON TWO DATA SETS

Flexibility in data analysis presents an appreciable challenge when different analysis techniques or data-editing decisions change the substantive conclusions. Here, we argue that GeMM offers a promising approach for reducing this flexibility. GeMM assumes that the predictors are interval scale, permitting the model to take the traditional additive form, but it treats the criterion variable as ordinal—allowing ordinal, interval, ratio, and even nominal (in some cases) scale variables to serve as the criterion. A key feature of GeMM is that it is designed to model the monotone relations of the data. This feature means that GeMM is invariant to transformation on Y and should be relatively robust to extreme scores, or outliers, compared with LS procedures. Consequently, GeMM's solution should be relatively stable across different methods for identifying and eliminating extreme scores. In contrast, because LS procedures seek to maximize linear fit, extreme scores can exert undue influence on LS solutions, even when only a small number of scores are extreme. Below, we demonstrate that a small number of extreme scores can sometimes drive manifest effects, and other times hide effects when data are analyzed using LS procedures. In addition, we illustrate that different methods for identifying and eliminating extreme scores and nonlinearities can lead to inconsistent statistical conclusions when analyzed with LS approaches. In contrast, GeMM provides more consistent statistical conclusions across multiple data-editing strategies in our demonstrations.

4.1. *When Extreme Scores Drive Effects: The Case of Racial Bias*

What is the relationship between explicit measures of racial bias, implicit measures of racial bias, and motivation to control prejudice? Prior work on this topic suggests that explicit measures of racial bias capture some element of a person's true underlying attitude but that they are subject to response biases on the part of the participant (e.g., Dunton and Fazio 1997; Fazio et al. 1995). For example, how people respond on the Attitudes Toward Blacks (ATB) scale appears to be moderated by people's motivation to control prejudice (Plant and Devine 1998). Plant and Devine (1998) identified two separate forms of such motivation: an internal motivational factor and an external motivational factor. The internal factor tests for motivations stemming from the belief that stereotypes are morally wrong or personally unacceptable. The external factor tests for motivations stemming from the desire to avoid social censure— in other words, the belief that *other people* believe that stereotypes are morally wrong or unacceptable. Either type of motivation could lead to similar self-censoring of socially unpopular attitudes, but that similarity belies the important differences between people who are driven by one versus the other motive type.

Partly to deal with this problem of self-censoring, considerable research has validated the use of implicit measures of racial bias. Perhaps the most well-known implicit measure is the implicit association test (IAT; Greenwald, McGhee, and Schwartz 1998), a measure that uses response times to assess the difficulty respondents have classifying white or black faces simultaneous to categorizing other stimuli as good or bad. More recently, other implicit measures have been developed that do not rely on response times. For example, Payne and colleagues (Payne et al. 2005; Payne, Burkley, and Stokes 2008) developed the affect misattribution procedure (AMP), which involves showing people a stimulus word or picture that they are told to ignore, followed by a Chinese pictograph. Participants are instructed to rate how pleasant the pictograph is, ignoring the stimulus that precedes it. However, the affect associated with the first stimulus is expected to "bleed over" to the pictograph, revealing how positively or negatively respondents *actually* feel about that *first* stimulus, which they are supposed to be ignoring. Payne and colleagues showed that scores on the AMP reflect subtle in-group preferences among both white and black respondents and that this in-group bias occurs whether or not participants are warned to avoid being biased on the measure (an external motivation to control prejudice). In contrast, participants who reported strong *internal* desires to avoid prejudice appeared to modify their *explicit* racial attitudes. Consequently, the self-reported attitudes of these participants hardly correlated at all with their scores on the AMP. Among participants who reported weaker internal desires to avoid prejudice, AMP scores were highly correlated with explicit prejudice.

An important question regarding the measurement of racial attitudes is the degree to which explicit measures of racial attitudes capture one's true attitude and the degree to which they are subject to people's motivation to control their expression of their attitude. This problem is reflected in the results found by Payne et al. (2005), as well as by many other researchers (e.g., Devine et al. 2002; Dunton and Fazio 1997; Plant and Devine 1998; Plant, Devine, and Brazy, 2003). Theoretically, a case can be made for both the inclusion and exclusion of external and internal motivation to control prejudice as predictors of racial attitudes. On one hand, it makes sense that participants would wish to avoid social censure (an external motivation) as a consequence of openly admitting that they are racially biased. For this reason, it is clear that explicit motivations should play an important role in how participants respond on the ATB scale and other such explicit attitude measures. On the other hand, the belief that racism is morally wrong (an internal motivation) might lead them to explicitly state more positive attitudes toward blacks than they actually hold. Either way, researchers who want to know people's *true* attitudes would seem to do well by accounting for these types of motivations in studies of prejudice or other socially sensitive topics.

4.1.1. *Data and Analyses.*

We reanalyzed data initially published by Siegel et al. (2012). The original sample included 213 University of Maryland undergraduate students (128 women). Of these, 15 participants were missing data on one or more measures and were therefore excluded from the analysis. Each participant was measured on 10 variables, including three measures of racial attitudes (the ATB scale, the Race AMP [Race-AMP], and the Racism IAT [Race-IAT]), the motivation to control prejudice subscales (the External Motivation Scale [EMS] and the Internal Motivation Scale [IMS]), two measures of cognitive control (the Stroop test and the Stop Signal Task), and three measures of political attitudes (explicit political attitudes [EPA], a Political

AMP [Pol-AMP], and a Political IAT [Pol-IAT]). Additional details of the study, including how the various tasks were constructed, administered, and scored, are provided in Siegel et al. (2012).[3]

Siegel et al. (2012) were concerned primarily with understanding the relationship between the IAT and the measures of cognitive control. Using factor analyses, they showed that both the Pol-IAT and the Race-IAT loaded on two factors: their respective attitude factor and a cognitive control factor. That is, performance on the IAT appeared to be predicted best by a model that assumed that the IAT measures both the target attitude and cognitive control. Although the Race-IAT was unrelated to the explicit ATB scale, it was highly related to the Race-AMP. Moreover, the ATB scale was correlated with the Race-AMP and both the EMS and IMS. This pattern of correlations suggests that scores on the ATB are dependent on an (implicit) attitude factor and both forms of motivation to control prejudice. However, Siegel et al. did not explore these relationships in depth. Thus, the substantive goal of our reanalysis was to identify the best predictors of scores on the ATB from the collection of variables included in the study by Siegel et al. There were two methodological goals: (1) to demonstrate that the substantive conclusions could change depending on how extreme scores were identified and treated and (2) to test whether GeMM was less sensitive to the treatment of outliers.

Using LS regression, we tested the hypothesis that both internal and external motivations to control prejudice were negatively related to participants' self-reported (explicit) racial biases, as measured by the ATB scale, independent of participants' implicit racial bias, as measured by the Race-AMP. Using the classical null hypothesis significance testing (NHST) approach with $\alpha = .05$, we found the predicted relationship: The ATB scale was significantly and positively related to the Race-AMP, and the ATB scale was negatively related to both the EMS and IMS. Summary statistics for this analysis are presented in Tables 1 and 2, in the top row, labeled "Full data." Overall, these three variables accounted for 13.2% of the variance in ATB scores, with the rank-order correlation between the predicted and the actual values of the ATB yielding a value of $\tau = .239$. Thus, on the basis of this analysis, it seems that we are justified in supporting the theory that self-reported (explicit) racial bias is a function of people's implicit racial bias, their internal motivations to control racial bias, and their external motivations to avoid being seen as racially biased. Or are we?

Table 1. Fit Indices from the Various Models

	BIC$'_\tau$	BIC	τ	R	k
OLS-NHST					
Full data (*N* = 198)	−9.905	−12.283	.239	.364	3
Univariate (*N* = 195)	−12.837	−6.282	.23	.288	2
DFFITS (*N* = 191)	−15.321	−10.142	.245	.321	2
Cook's *D* (*N* = 185)	−22.196	−24.986	.299	.444	3
Robust regression					
Huber	−15.651	−8.965	.241	.307	2
Bisquare	−15.005	−9.132	.238	.308	2
Hampel	−10.646	−11.886	.243	.362	3
OLS-BIC					
Full data (*N* = 198)	−9.242	−12.445	.236	.365	3
Univariate (*N* = 195)	−11.472	−6.551	.223	.29	2
DFFITS (*N* = 191)	−10.982	−11.093	.224	.328	2
Cook's *D* (*N* = 185)	−21.074	−25.253	.295	.445	3
Ordered logistic					
Full data (*N* = 198)	162.602	166.442	.277	.3	35
Univariate (*N* = 195)	153.567	157.535	.266	.285	33
DFFITS (*N* = 191)	147.438	150.248	.268	.298	32
Cook's *D* (*N* = 185)	132.55	131.86	.377	.443	33
GeMM					
Full data (*N* = 198)	−17.835	−5.878	.251	.282	2
Univariate (*N* = 195)	−15.389	−3.89	.242	.267	2
DFFITS (*N* = 191)	−17.348	−7.524	.254	.301	2
Cook's *D* (*N* = 185)	−23.914	−24.109	.306	.44	3

Note: k is the number of significant or retained parameters. For ordered logistic, *k* includes the number of significant threshold parameters. Thus, for *k* = 35, there are three significant predictors (External Motivation Scale, Race Attitude Misattribution Procedure, and Internal Motivation Scale) and 32 significant threshold parameters. BIC = Bayesian information criterion; GeMM = general monotone model; NHST = null hypothesis significance testing; OLS = ordinary least squares.

Figure 1 plots the histograms for the 10 variables in the study, and Figure 2 provides the bivariate scattergrams for each predictor (*x*-axis) plotted against the ATB scale. Three findings should be evident from inspection of the graphs. First, the relationships identified by linear regression are not easily discernible from the bivariate plots, although by itself, this fact might not be terribly concerning—subtle associations do not always yield their secrets to the naked eye. Second, many of the predictors are poorly distributed, which is somewhat more concerning, given the assumptions underlying LS regression. Third, there appears to be a small number of extreme scores (outliers?) in the distribution of the

Table 2. Standardized Regression Coefficients Revealed for Each Model

	P-EXP	Pol-IAT	Pol-AMP	Race-AMP	EMS	IMS	Race-IAT	Stroop	Stop Signal Task
OLS-NHST									
Full data ($N = 198$)	−.054	−.083	.016	**.17**	**−.217**	**−.172**	.016	.03	−.027
	(.074)	(.092)	(.081)	**(.073)**	**(.069)**	**(.074)**	(.082)	(.086)	(.074)
Univariate ($N = 195$)	−.059	−.076	.028	.152	−.194	−.11	.009	.035	−.034
	(.070)	(.088)	(.077)	(.070)	(.067)	(.070)	(.072)	(.081)	(.069)
DFFITS ($N = 191$)	−.103	−.017	.081	**.147**	**−.199**	−.127	.025	.014	−.02
	(.068)	(.083)	(.073)	**(.070)**	**(.063)**	(.069)	(.073)	(.079)	(.067)
Cook's D ($N = 185$)	−.04	−.054	.007	**.167**	**−.244**	**−.17**	.049	.045	−.039
	(.066)	(.079)	(.070)	**(.067)**	**(.064)**	**(.068)**	(.072)	(.077)	(.064)
Robust regression									
Huber ($N = 198$)	−.059	−.078	.018	**.19**	**−.229**	−.13	.034	.05	−.049
	(.071)	(.088)	(.078)	**(.070)**	**(.066)**	(.070)	(.078)	(.082)	(.070)
Bisquare ($N = 198$)	−.064	−.076	.02	**.201**	**−.222**	−.125	.025	.047	−.044
	(.074)	(.092)	(.081)	**(.081)**	**(.073)**	(.073)	(.081)	(.085)	(.073)
Hampel ($N = 198$)	−.063	−.078	.023	**.177**	**−.21**	**−.144**	.025	.034	−.036
	(.073)	(.090)	(.080)	**(.072)**	**(.068)**	**(.072)**	(.080)	(.084)	(.072)
OLS-BIC									
Full data ($N = 198$)	—	—	—	**.168**	**−.213**	**−.200**	—	—	—
				(.070)	**(.068)**	**(.069)**			
Univariate ($N = 195$)	—	—	—	**.181**	**−.172**	—	—	—	—
				(.066)	**(.065)**				
DFFITS ($N = 191$)	—	—	—	—	**−.233**	**−.196**	—	—	—
					(.061)	**(.063)**			
Cook's D ($N = 185$)	—	—	—	**.168**	**−.241**	**−.206**	—	—	—
				(.063)	**(.062)**	**(.063)**			

(continued)

Table 2. (continued)

	P-EXP	Pol-IAT	Pol-AMP	Race-AMP	EMS	IMS	Race-IAT	Stroop	Stop Signal Task
Ordered logistic									
Full data (N = 198)	-.098	-.15	.032	**.383**	**-.447**	**-.292**	.05	.071	-.061
	(.138)	(.161)	(.144)	**(.142)**	**(.141)**	**(.144)**	(.155)	(.158)	(.135)
Univariate (N = 195)	-.108	-.141	.048	**.375**	**-.431**	-.230	.043	.078	-.07
	(.139)	(.162)	(.145)	**(.144)**	**(.142)**	(.145)	(.156)	(.159)	(.137)
DFFITS (N = 191)	-.187	-.052	.147	**.338**	**-.466**	**-.326**	.058	.031	-.024
	(.144)	(.165)	(.148)	**(.148)**	**(.145)**	**(.151)**	(.160)	(.164)	(.141)
Cook's D (N = 185)	-.058	-.136	.005	**.436**	**-.573**	**-.409**	.067	.107	-.046
	(.144)	(.167)	(.150)	**(.150)**	**(.150)**	**(.155)**	(.164)	(.168)	(.142)
GeMM									
Full data (N = 198)	—	—	—	.133	**-.236**	—	—	—	—
				(.077)	**(.085)**				
Univariate (N = 195)	—	—	—	.113	**-.217**	—	—	—	—
				(.071)	**(.084)**				
DFFITS (N = 191)	—	—	—	.112	**-.224**	—	—	—	—
				(.067)	**(.074)**				
Cook's D (N = 185)	—	—	—	.146	**-.270**	**-.147**	—	—	—
				(.076)	**(.079)**	**(.098)**			

Note: Boldface indicates predictor retained by the model using BIC (OLS-BIC and GeMM) or predictor was significant at $p \leq .05$ (OLS-NHST, robust regression, ordered logit). Dashes indicate that the predictor variable was not included in the model. Coefficients and standard errors listed for GeMM were computed on the basis of 1,000 bootstrap runs. BIC = Bayesian information criterion; EMS = External Motivation Scale; GeMM = general monotone model; IMS = Internal Motivation Scale; NHST = null hypothesis significance testing; OLS = ordinary least squares; P-EXP = explicit political attitude; Pol-AMP = Political Affect Misattribution Procedure; Pol-IAT = Political Implicit Association Test; Race-AMP = Race Attitude Misattribution Procedure; Race-IAT = Racism Implicit Association Test.

239

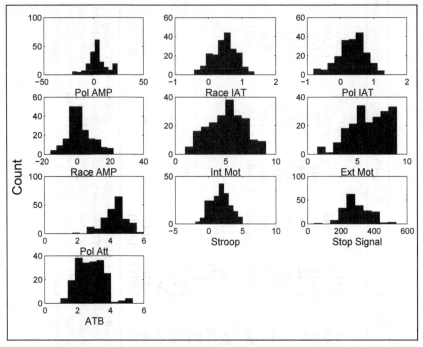

Figure 1. Histograms for the 10 variables reported in Siegel et al. (2012).
Note: AMP = affect misattribution procedure; Ext = external; IAT = implicit association test; Int = internal; Mot = motivation; Pol = political; Pol Att = explicit political attitude.

ATB scale, which could prove to be especially problematic for standard regression techniques and might even "require" data editing prior to analyzing the data with OLS. Given the presence of extreme scores and the nonnormality of the distributions, we conducted a series of follow-up analyses to determine the robustness of the conclusions to different methods for reducing the influence of violations of the assumptions of linear LS regression. The first approach was to conduct outlier analyses to identify and eliminate potentially problematic data points. There are a variety of outlier detection methods, but we confined ourselves to three techniques: (1) univariate outlier analysis, (2) Cook's *D*, and (3) DFFITS.[4] Application of these three approaches to the data set resulted in the identification of 3, 13, and 8 extreme scores, respectively. After trimming these data points out of the sample, we reanalyzed the data, again using OLS with an α value of .05.

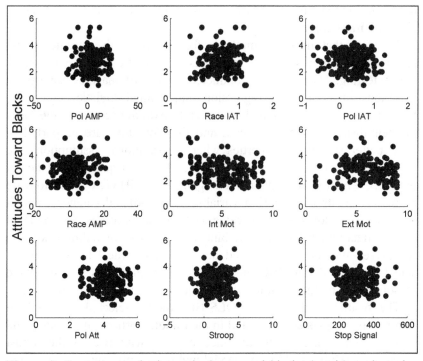

Figure 2. Scattergram plotting attitudes toward blacks (*y*-axis) against nine predictor variables.

Note: AMP = affect misattribution procedure; Ext Mot = external motivation to control prejudice; IAT = implicit association test; Int Mot = internal motivation to control prejudice; Pol = political; Pol Att = explicit political attitude.

The results of the analyses after eliminating these extreme data points are also presented in Tables 1 and 2. As can be seen, two approaches to eliminating extreme scores revealed that two predictors were significant, and one approach revealed three significant predictors. Surprisingly, the elimination of a mere 1.5% of the data (three data points) was sufficient to knock out internal motivation as a significant predictor. This was not just a matter of the *p* value's hovering around .05 and bouncing back and forth over the threshold, as the *p* value for IMS was .02 for the full data set, but it jumped to nearly .12 after eliminating only three data points. Thus, the decision to exclude IMS for the univariate trimmed data is not an inconvenient by-product of the conventional, yet arbitrary, value of α = .05. Combined with the analyses using the full data set, there appears to be no clear "winner" regarding which statistical conclusions are most appropriate.

The fact that different methods for dealing with extreme scores resulted in different statistical models is problematic for the purposes of theory testing. Therefore, we conducted a series of analyses using three variations on robust LS regression and ordinal logistic regression. Robust statistics are designed to deweight extreme scores on the basis of their distance from the mean, and therefore they are purported to have better statistical properties when distributional assumptions are violated. The methods used here are the Huber, bisquare, and Hampel methods, which were implemented again using NHST. Ordinal logistic regression treats the criterion variable as an ordered category, and it estimates thresholds for each category. For our purposes, we modeled the raw data rather than creating binned responses.[5] In addition, we also reanalyzed the full and trimmed data sets using the BIC as a model selection method. The BIC model selection method has the advantage of not relying on the arbitrary .05 threshold for statistical significance.

The results of the robust, OLS-BIC model selected, and ordinal regression analyses are presented in the middle portions of Tables 1 and 2. Once again, the results are inconclusive, with two of the robust approaches (Huber and bisquare) yielding two significant predictors and one approach (Hampel) yielding three significant predictors. Model selection using the BIC to select predictors was even more inconsistent, as it yielded *two different* two-predictor models, as well as a three-predictor model. The results of the ordinal logistic model are a bit more complicated. This model fits the ordinal properties of the data, but to do so, it estimates thresholds for each of the ordered categories using the full model with all predictors. As can be seen, this model fits the ordinal properties quite well, but at the expense of a considerable increase in model complexity due to the need to estimate the threshold parameters. Even so, this method also produced different models between the full data set and the univariate trimmed data set in which only three observations were eliminated: three predictors were significant on the full data set, but only two were significant on the reduced (univariate trimmed) data set.

The inconsistency across outlier and data analysis methods is undesirable for many reasons, but principally *because it allows the researcher the freedom to choose which theoretical conclusions to draw from the data*, rather than forcing theoretical conclusions to be constrained by the data—a principle at the heart of basic science. Given these inconsistencies, we reanalyzed the data using GeMM. In contrast to traditional LS approaches, GeMM models data at the level of paired comparisons, as we explained earlier. Because GeMM does not model data using a distance metric and makes less stringent assumptions of the data, it should be more robust to the presence of extreme scores and nonlinearities.

The results using GeMM are presented at the bottom of Tables 1 and 2.[6] As can be seen, GeMM resulted in a two-parameter solution when applied to the full data set, and this solution was consistent for both the univariate and DFFITS methods for eliminating outliers. Note that the two-predictor solutions include the same predictors (EMS and Race-AMP) identified as significant by the Huber and bisquare procedures. GeMM was not completely insensitive to outlier deletion methods, as it identified a three-predictor solution when the 13 observations were trimmed using Cook's *D*. However, the fact that it was stable for both the univariate and DFFITS methods (which required deleting only 3 and 8 observations) suggests that it is relatively more robust than OLS. In fact, further analyses on these data indicated that the OLS solution changed from a three- to a two-predictor model even after eliminating just one data point, the single most extreme value on the ATB scale. This pattern of analyses suggests that GeMM has a much greater tolerance for extreme scores than OLS. Coincidentally, the robust regression procedures also resulted in a three-predictor model when applied to the Cook's *D*–trimmed data.

If we consider the full data set, is the two-parameter GeMM solution preferable to the three-predictor LS solutions, and are we justified in accepting the two-parameter model over one that includes three predictors? There are two ways to address this question: (1) compare the fit indices for GeMM with those of OLS and (2) conduct cross-validation analyses. We consider both in turn.

4.1.2. *Comparing Fit and Cross-validation.*

Inspection of the fit indices indicates that the two-parameter GeMM solution actually provides a better fit to the data in terms of accurately capturing the ordinal properties of the data than all of the other approaches except ordinal regression, even the models that included three parameters, as shown by the values for BIC_τ' and τ. Although the LS solutions fit the data better when evaluated in terms of the multiple R and BIC, these indices are highly suspect because they require the assumption of linearity: Inasmuch as the linear (LS) solution is relatively poor at capturing the monotonic relations of the data (as given by τ and BIC_τ'), we must be wary of interpreting a solution that makes the stronger assumptions of normality and linearity. Although ordinal logistic regression had a higher value of τ, this came with considerable increase in model complexity. As we show below, this increase in model complexity can lead to overfitting.

One interesting aspect of these fit indices is that although the LS versions (ordinary and robust regression) provide better fit to the data in terms of R^2, this fit comes at a cost of accurately capturing the ordinal properties of the data. For instance, for the full sample, OLS accounts for 13.2% of the variance ($R^2 = .132$), but it has a rank-order correlation of only .239. In contrast, when GeMM is applied to the same data it accounts for only 8.0% of the variance ($R^2 = .080$), but it is better able to account for the ordinal properties of the data, with a rank-order correlation of .251. This pattern also holds for all three methods for trimming outliers.

We used split-half cross-validation to evaluate out-of-sample prediction: Which statistical algorithm provides the best predictive accuracy when the estimated parameters are used to predict new observations? This approach has the advantage that it directly addresses the problem of overfitting, in which statistical models tend to show poorer accuracy (i.e., shrinkage) at predicting new observations compared with the fit to the original estimation sample. The cross-validation approach has the added benefit, however, of allowing us to evaluate statistical power, or the probability that each of the predictor variables will be identified as a "significant" predictor (or included in the selected model). We conducted a split-half cross-validation using the full data set ($N = 198$), in which half of the data were randomly sampled and used to estimate model parameters. The remaining half of the data were used as the hold-out sample. For each "replication" of this procedure, we recorded for each algorithm which parameters were recovered, fit indices, and β weights. For methods using NHST, a parameter was classified as recovered if it was significant at the .05 level using a t test on the regression coefficient. Out-of-sample predictive accuracy was assessed by applying the recovered statistical model to the holdout sample (i.e., the β weights for nonsignificant predictors were set to zero). We computed the multiple R, τ, and the corresponding values of BIC and BIC_τ'. This procedure was repeated 500 times for each statistical model.

The results of the cross-validation analyses are presented in Tables 3 and 4. Table 3 shows the probability of recovering each predictor when each algorithm is provided half of the data. Recall that on the full sample, OLS recovered a three-predictor model consisting of the Race-AMP, the IMS, and the EMS, whereas GeMM recovered a two-predictor model consisting of the Race-AMP and the EMS. Overall, GeMM was more likely to recover both the AMP and the EMS than OLS, indicating that GeMM had more power to detect these effects. The remaining models are less straightforward, but on balance GeMM showed recovery rates that were either approximately equal to (Robust LS-Huber, ordinal logistic) or better than the other alternatives.

Perhaps more instructive are the fit statistics provided in Table 3, which illustrate the average fit (top half) and average cross-validation accuracy (bottom half). GeMM provided better out-of-sample predictive accuracy than all of the alternatives in terms of τ and even outperformed many of the alternatives in terms of the multiple R. Note that logistic regression showed the worst out-of-sample prediction in terms of R and second worst in terms of τ, despite the fact that it showed the best performance in terms of τ (and second best in terms of R) on the estimation sample.

To summarize, on the basis of the statistical fit and predictive accuracy of the various statistical models, it is clear that the best and most defensible conclusion to draw from the data is that responses on the ATB scale in Siegel et al.'s (2012) study are best accounted for by both implicit racial prejudices (as measured by the Race-AMP) and external motivations to control prejudice (EMS), but not internal motivation to control prejudice (IMS). However, the bigger point to be made from these analyses is that statistical conclusions based on LS approaches proved to be highly suspect, a situation often due to a very small number of observations. Removing merely three of the 198 data points was sufficient to change the statistical conclusions, and the use of robust procedures only muddled the picture. The main problem, as we see it, is that the labile nature of LS procedures and their sensitivity to the removal or deweighting of extreme scores *licenses the researcher to choose which theory to support via the selection of a data-analytic strategy.* Thus, rather than the data constraining the theory, the theory can constrain the data in the name of making sure the data adhere to statistical

Table 3. Probability of Recovering Each Model Coefficient Given Half (*N*/2) the Full Sample, for Each Algorithm

	P-EXP	Pol-IAT	Pol-AMP	Race-AMP	EMS	IMS	Race-IAT	Stroop	Stop Signal Task
GeMM	.062	.028	.014	**.336**	**.716**	.198	.02	.000	.008
OLS-NHST	.024	.016	.002	**.306**	**.596**	.368	.032	.006	.008
OLS-BIC	.068	.068	.008	**.402**	**.566**	.486	.036	.012	.004
RLS-bisquare	.028	.012	.002	**.458**	**.576**	.164	.014	.012	.010
RLS-Huber	.034	.016	.004	**.422**	**.642**	.214	.016	.012	.010
RLS-Hampel	.032	.012	.000	**.336**	**.572**	.268	.028	.010	.010
Ordinal logistic	.030	.020	.004	**.432**	**.636**	.266	.026	.012	.018

Note: Boldface values correspond to predictors that were recovered on the full sample as indicated in Table 2. BIC = Bayesian information criterion; EMS = External Motivation Scale; GeMM = general monotone model; IMS = Internal Motivation Scale; NHST = null hypothesis significance testing; OLS = ordinary least squares; P-EXP = explicit political attitude; Pol-AMP = Political Affect Misattribution Procedure; Pol-IAT = Political Implicit Association Test; Race-AMP = Race Attitude Misattribution Procedure; Race-IAT = Racism Implicit Association Test; RLS = recursive least squares.

Table 4. Cross-validation Results for Analyses Predicting Attitudes toward Blacks

Cross-validation Using Selected (Best Fit) Models

	BIC'_τ	BIC	τ	R	k
Estimation					
GeMM	−7.847	−4.881	.259	.314	1.397
OLS-BIC	−5.293	−7.321	.245	.363	1.647
Bisquare	−6.686	−5.787	.255	.337	1.542
Huber	−6.796	−6.041	.259	.344	1.604
Hampel	−6.864	−6.755	.255	.348	1.513
OLS	−6.209	−6.894	.251	.352	1.559
Ordered logit	120.919	114.465	.299	.354	28.042
Cross-validation					
GeMM			.155	.18	
OLS-BIC			.134	.178	
Bisquare			.145	.18	
Huber			.149	.183	
Hampel			.141	.169	
OLS			.147	.179	
Ordered logit			.137	.157	

Note: BIC = Bayesian information criterion; GeMM = general monotone model; OLS = ordinary least squares.

assumptions. GeMM appears to be more resistant to outliers, which means it will be less affected by decisions to eliminate them.

4.2. When Nonlinearities Mask Effects: The Case of Homicide Rates and the Culture of Honor

A recent topic of interest in social-psychological research concerns cultures of honor, which are societies in which defense of reputation is a central organizing theme (Nisbett 1993; Nisbett and Cohen 1996). Such societies are especially common, according to Nisbett and colleagues, where scarce resources are highly portable (hence, easily stolen) and where the rule of law is weak or altogether absent (see also Brown and Osterman 2012). Nisbett (1993) argued that this combination is quite common in societies whose economies are based on herding rather than agriculture or industry. Because herding societies tend to be resource poor, their resources are quite portable, and they tend to be poorly managed by law enforcement, the latter due in part to the fact that herders are, by necessity, spread out. Under such conditions, people are especially vulnerable to social predation, both from within (via internal competition for scarce resources) and from without (via attack from other groups). This vulnerability, over long periods of time, has a tendency to breed the beliefs, values, and social norms that characterize honor cultures, such as a hypervigilance to reputational threats and aggressive responses to perceived honor violations.

Honor cultures tend to stress strength and toughness as primary qualities of value for men, and loyalty and purity as primary qualities of value for women (Nisbett and Cohen 1996; Vandello and Cohen 2003). These qualities are pursued vigorously by men and women in such societies, as they help protect them from their key sources of vulnerability. For instance, men who are known to be strong and brave are not likely to be targeted for attack, as long as there are other targets available. Arguably, a man does not have to be *absolutely* strong and brave to protect himself or his family—he has to be known only as being *relatively* stronger and braver than other men, as someone who should not be disturbed or "messed with." As long as he maintains his reputation for pugnacity, he can reduce the odds of predation from his neighbors and from hostile out-groups. Because of this combination of an extreme emphasis on reputation management and the types of reputations that are idealized for men and women, honor cultures tend to exhibit higher than average rates of argument-based homicides (Nisbett and Cohen 1996). In addition, research has shown that U.S. states classified as "honor states" (in the South and West) display higher levels of school violence (Brown, Osterman, and Barnes 2009), higher rates of suicide (Osterman and Brown 2011), and excessive levels of risk taking that lead to higher rates of accidental deaths (Barnes, Brown, and Tamborski 2012), compared with "nonhonor states."

In a series of studies, Henry (2009) argued that one of the reasons that herding cultures tend to develop honor norms, as Nisbett and Cohen (1996) suggested they do, is that such cultures tend to be characterized by strong status disparities. When a society has a large status hierarchy, with relatively few people controlling a relatively large amount of that society's resources, people at the bottom of the status hierarchy may feel especially vulnerable to social devaluation and be prone to hypervigilance and hyperreactance to status threats (see also Daly and Wilson 2010). Aggression in the face of insults is one prime example of the type of reaction that might be especially prevalent in members of low-status groups in such unequal societies. Henry tested this notion in part by showing that homicide rates were higher in cultures whose economies tended to be based heavily on herding, where (theory suggests) honor-related beliefs and values will tend to proliferate. Important, Henry showed that elevated homicide rates in herding-oriented countries were statistically accounted for by levels of social *wealth disparity* within those countries, independent of a country's overall level of wealth. Henry also expected to replicate past findings that overall wealth would independently predict homicide rates, which he showed in study 1 (at the county level) but failed to show in study 2 (at the country level).

4.2.1. *Data and Analyses.* We reanalyzed the data used for study 2 of Henry (2009). Our use of this data set was a matter of convenience, and it was motivated by Henry's failure to replicate the association between overall wealth and homicide rates obtained in his study 1 and other prior work (Nisbett and Cohen 1996). Using OLS regression, we were able to reproduce his international results: Countries with larger proportions of their lands devoted to uncultivated pastures and meadows appropriate to herding (hereafter *pastureland*) tended to exhibit higher homicide rates, but this association was largely accounted for by within-country levels of wealth disparity (as indexed by the Gini coefficient of income inequality, hereafter *Gini*), independent of overall levels of wealth across those countries (as indexed by gross domestic product per capita, adjusted for purchasing power parity, hereafter *GDP*). Replicating Henry (2009), GDP was not a significant predictor ($p = .36$), which remains as surprising to us as it did to Henry. However, a key question is raised: are our statistical conclusions robust?

Figures 3a and 4 show the bivariate scattergrams and histograms for the four variables: homicide rates, percentage pastureland, Gini, and GDP. As is clear, the data are poorly distributed, yet there is obvious structure in the bivariate scattergrams. In particular, there appears to be a monotone but nonlinear relationship between GDP and homicide rates. Indeed, in terms of Kendall's τ, the strength of the relationship between Gini and homicide ($\tau = +.39$), is virtually identical to the strength of the relationship between GDP and homicide ($\tau = -.36$). In contrast, the pattern of correlations obtained using Pearson's r yields a much stronger relation between Gini and homicide ($r = +.50$) compared with GDP and homicide ($r = -.30$). There appears to be not only substantial

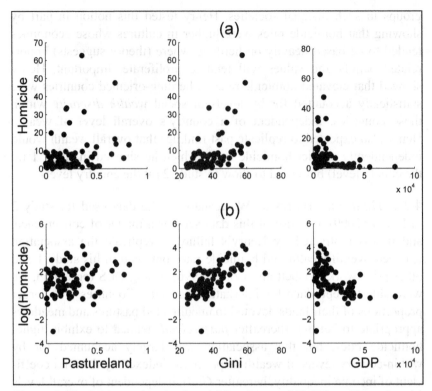

Figure 3. Scattergram showing homicide rates per 100,000 residents (*y*-axis) plotted against three predictor variables used by Henry (2009). (a) Untransformed data. (b) Data after applying the log transformation to the homicide rate (per 100,000 residents).

nonlinearity in the data but also a small number of extreme scores and substantial nonnormality.

Given the obvious violations of assumptions for the linear model, it is likely that OLS regression is ill equipped to model these data accurately.[7] But, how *should* the data be modeled? Henry (2009) modeled homicide rates in their raw form using OLS, but other researchers interested in understanding factors contributing to homicide rates have used different approaches. For example, in testing the social capital theory of cross-national homicide rates, Lederman et al. (2002) modeled the natural logarithm of homicide. In a replication of this study, Robbins and Pettinicchio (2012) used negative binomial regression, which they argued more accurately captures the modeled distribution. Because the

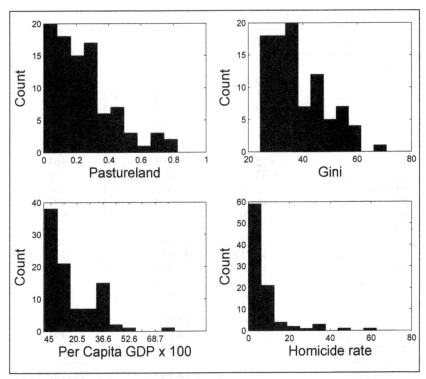

Figure 4. Histograms for three predictor variables and the criterion used by Henry (2009).

data are transformations on count data (homicides per 100,000), both Poisson and quasi-Poisson regression are logical alternatives as well. The fact that there are multiple potential analysis techniques raises two questions: (1) Which method is "most" appropriate? and (2) Do the different methods yield different substantive conclusions? The question of which method is most appropriate is debatable, though addressing the second question seems straightforward. To start, we reanalyzed the data using two reasonable and common transformations: the natural logarithm and the square root. We used these transformations in two ways: first where only the criterion variable (homicide rate) was transformed and second where all of the variables were transformed. As an illustrative example, Figure 3b plots the bivariate scattergram after applying the log transformation to homicide rate. As can be seen, the nonlinear

Table 5. Fit Indices for Models

Transformation	BIC$'_\tau$	BIC	τ	R	k
OLS-NHST					
None	−29.332	−22.289	.391	.503	1
sqrt(homicide)	−41.419	−30.888	.471	.593	2
sqrt(all)	−29.332	−30.682	.391	.564	1
Log(homicide)	−42.672	−32.096	.476	.6	2
Log(all)	−29.332	−28.687	.391	.55	1
OLS-BIC					
None	−32.709	−22.289	.391	.503	1
sqrt(homicide)	−32.709	−31.062	.391	.566	1
sqrt(all)	−32.709	−30.682	.391	.564	1
Log(homicide)	−46.769	−32.129	.471	.601	2
Log(all)	−32.709	−28.687	.391	.55	1
GeMM					
None	−45.712	−13.636	.488	.467	2
sqrt(homicide)	−45.712	−27.531	.488	.573	2
sqrt(all)	−42.328	−26.307	.475	.565	2
Log(homicide)	−45.712	−30.677	.488	.592	2
Log(all)	−38.647	−25.71	.459	.561	2
GLM					
Poisson	−35.999	−12.302	.467	.495	3
Quasi-Poisson	−40.521	−16.824	.467	.495	2
Negative binomial	−40.298	−16.267	.466	.49	2

Note: In all cases in which $k = 1$, the predictor included in the model (or identified as significant) was Gini. In all cases in which $k = 2$, the predictors included in the model or identified as significant were both Gini and GDP. BIC = Bayesian information criterion; GDP = gross domestic product per capita, adjusted for purchasing power parity; GeMM = general monotone model; GLM = generalized linear model; NHST = null hypothesis significance testing; OLS = ordinary least squares.

relationships in the raw data are mostly linearized after the transformation.

Table 5 provides the results of the analyses using LS regression and GeMM both on the original (raw) data and on the transformed data. As should be evident, only GeMM provided a consistent model form across the various transformations. In particular, both versions of LS regression (OLS-NHST and OLS-BIC) recovered a one-predictor model consisting of Gini when applied to the raw data but a two-predictor model consisting of Gini and GDP when the criterion variable was log-transformed (p values < .001 across methods for both Gini and GDP). When all of the variables were transformed, however, both OLS-NHST and OLS-BIC again recovered the single-predictor model consisting of Gini. The square-root transformation also yielded inconsistent findings across methods. GeMM recovered a two-parameter model (Gini and GDP), and this was consistent across all of the transformations. Also included in Table 5 are the results from using three variants from the generalized linear model (GLM) family. Poisson regression identified all three predictors as significant, whereas both quasi-Poisson and negative binomial regression identified both Gini and GDP as significant.

Arguably, given the distributions presented in Figure 4, the data could legitimately be transformed to remove the skew prior to using traditional LS regression. However, whether the transformation should apply only to the criterion variable (homicide rate) or to all variables is a matter of debate and an existing "researcher degree of freedom" under traditional analysis methods. Although explicit transformations are unnecessary for negative binomial and the two Poisson regressions, they are implicitly carried out via the link function within GLM, of which researchers have many options. In contrast, with GeMM there is no need to transform the criterion variable because the rank-order correlation, τ, is invariant to monotone transformation. Thus, whether the homicide rate is transformed by taking the logarithm, square root, or any other monotonic function or left untransformed is immaterial for GeMM's solution and therefore removes this potentially important researcher degree of freedom.

The analyses presented above indicate that LS regression procedures are sensitive to decisions about whether (and how) the data are transformed. This should not be too surprising, because LS procedures fit distance information and because the distance information changes under different transformations. But just how distorted can it get? To explore this sensitivity, we analyzed the data again, but this time after adding a constant before applying the logarithmic transformation. The need to add a constant to the data prior to taking the logarithm arises when responses take on the value of 0 or are negative. Negative values are likewise problematic for the square-root transformation, but so are positive values less than 1 (as a square-root transformation on values between 0 and 1 will *increase* these values, while *decreasing* all values greater than 1; adding a constant to raise all raw values to a number greater than 1 eliminates this transformation disequilibrium). If OLS-NHST is used, adding any constant between .2 and 1.4 leads to both Gini and GDP identified as significant. Adding any constant above 1.4 or below .2 results in only Gini as statistically significant. The LS models yield different models with different additive constants; GeMM does not. The use of the negative binomial and Poisson regression models from the GLM family does not really solve the underlying issue: For these models, whether the number of homicides in each country is conceptualized as a count or a rate problem can actually change the form of the statistical model. Furthermore, if homicides are interpreted as a rate (number of homicides per unit of population), the model form can also depend on the choice of scaling constant. For example, both Pearson's r and rank-order correlation (τ) between the fitted values and the data vary depending on whether the homicide variable is expressed per 1,000, per 100,000, or per 10,000,000. How likely is it that researchers are aware of these sources of variation when they choose to add or divide by a constant as part of their data transformation routines?

As mentioned above, GeMM provides a two-predictor model regardless of transformation. But how well does this solution succeed when evaluated in terms of fit indices and cross-validation?

4.2.2. _Comparing Fit and Cross-validation._ A comparison of the relative fit indices favors the solution identified by GeMM. First, consider the results of the OLS. The one-predictor solution on the raw data has the highest value for R among the various procedures. However, despite having the best _metric_ fit, this model is much poorer at capturing the ordinal properties of the data compared with GeMM and the GLMs. That is, to fit the ordinal properties of the data, it is necessary to give up a little accuracy in predicting the metric properties. Both the GeMM and the GLMs do just this. Comparing GeMM with the GLMs, however, also reveals that GeMM performs favorably in terms of τ and BIC_τ'. GeMM's fit to the metric properties is somewhat poorer than that of the GLMs.

Using the same split-half methodology described in the discussion of the racial bias data, we evaluated the predictive accuracy and statistical power of GeMM relative to the various LS procedures. Figure 5a plots the probability of recovering each predictor using $N/2$ for raw and transformed data for OLS-NHST, OLS-BIC, and GeMM. Table 6 provides the fit and out-of-sample predictive accuracy for all of the models. As is strikingly clear, GeMM recovers each of the two predictors (Gini and GDP) identified in the full sample on approximately 95% of runs, with statistical power remaining high across the various transformations. For comparison, for the full data set all three procedures recovered Gini and

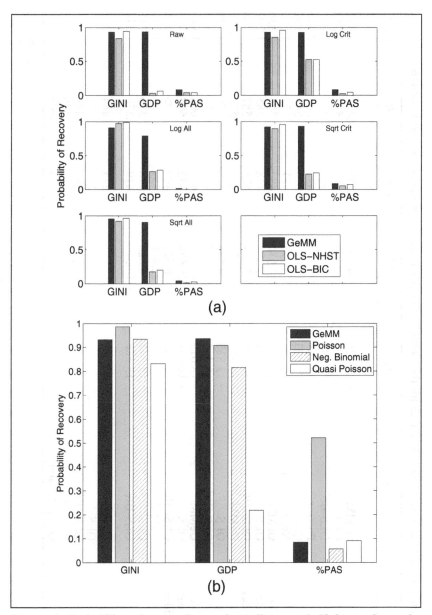

Figure 5. Probability of recovering each predictor on half the total sample. (a) Comparison with least squares procedures across various transformations. (b) Comparison with various forms of generalized linear modeling. GDP = gross domestic product per capita, adjusted for purchasing power parity; GINI = wealth disparity index (Gini coefficient of income inequality); %PAS = percentage pastureland.

Table 6. Estimation and Cross-validation Analyses for the Culture of Honor Data Using Various Transformations

Transform	Model	BIC'_τ	BIC	τ	R	Mean k
Estimation						
None	GeMM	−18.626	−4.903	.495	.48	1.952
None	OLS	−12.554	−11.398	.4	.527	1.051
None	OLS-BIC	−12.344	−10.501	.397	.512	1.05
None	Poisson	−14.289	−8	.473	.54	2.416
None	Quasi-Poisson	−19.113	−13.078	.474	.546	1.197
None	Negative binomial	−17.556	−8.458	.481	.513	1.806
Sqrt(homicide)	GeMM	−18.616	−11.686	.495	.578	1.936
Sqrt(homicide)	OLS	−13.771	−15.292	.418	.585	1.202
Sqrt(homicide)	OLS-BIC	−13.736	−15.184	.421	.587	1.268
Sqrt(all)	GeMM	−17.356	−11.472	.482	.573	1.9
Sqrt(all)	OLS	−13.533	−14.895	.413	.578	1.129
Sqrt(all)	OLS-BIC	−13.463	−14.732	.415	.579	1.186
Log(homicide)	GeMM	−18.619	−14.427	.495	.603	1.94
Log(homicide)	OLS	−16.088	−16.689	.452	.608	1.474
Log(homicide)	OLS-BIC	−15.702	−16.321	.449	.605	1.528
Log(all)	GeMM	−15.673	−12.401	.459	.568	1.712
Log(all)	OLS	−13.541	−14.623	.418	.576	1.248
Log(all)	OLS-BIC	−13.566	−14.547	.419	.576	1.278
Cross-validation						
None	GeMM			.453	.463	
None	OLS			.379	.48	
None	OLS-BIC			.382	.487	
None	Poisson			.442	.428	
None	Quasi-Poisson			.373	.405	

(continued)

Table 6. (continued)

Transform	Model	BIC'$_\tau$	BIC	τ	R	Mean k
None	Negative binomial			.438	.436	
Sqrt(homicide)	GeMM			.452	.554	
Sqrt(homicide)	OLS			.382	.532	
Sqrt(homicide)	OLS-BIC			.393	.545	
Sqrt(all)	GeMM			.44	.547	
Sqrt(all)	OLS			.385	.536	
Sqrt(all)	OLS-BIC			.391	.543	
Log(homicide)	GeMM			.453	.567	
Log(homicide)	OLS			.402	.526	
Log(homicide)	OLS-BIC			.416	.541	
Log(all)	GeMM			.406	.516	
Log(all)	OLS			.392	.529	
Log(all)	OLS-BIC			.395	.531	

Note: BIC = Bayesian information criterion; GeMM = general monotone model; OLS = ordinary least squares.

GDP when homicides were log transformed, but it is notable that GeMM substantially outperforms both versions of OLS in terms of recovering these predictors when provided half the data, in particular for GDP. Thus, not only does GeMM accurately recover GDP on the full data set, it does so with much higher power compared with OLS, even under conditions in which the data are transformed to make them more suitable for OLS.

Given the relatively poor showing of the LS procedures in recovering the predictors identified on the full data set, it should not be surprising that GeMM substantially outperformed its LS competitors in out-of-sample prediction. Indeed, even if we restrict our analyses to only the subset of nonnull models identified by the LS procedures, which we have done here in Table 6, it is clear that GeMM is the hands-down winner of the cross-validation contest. GeMM uniformly outperforms OLS and OLS-BIC in terms of predicting the rank order of homicide rates across nations, and in some cases even outpredicts OLS in terms of Pearson's R, for example, sqrt(homicides), and log(homicides).

A comparison of GeMM with the GLMs is a bit more complicated. GeMM clearly outperforms quasi-Poisson in probability of recovery (Figure 5b) and out-of-sample predictive accuracy (Table 6). Standard Poisson regression recovered both Gini and GDP at the approximate level of GeMM, but it also recovered percentage pastureland more than 50% of the time. The inclusion of percentage pastureland in the model is particular problematic here, because adding it to the model actually decreases ordinal predictive accuracy. Negative binomial regression performed nearly identical to GeMM across the board, with GeMM having a modest advantage in probability of recovery and a small (.015) advantage in terms of τ. Thus, overall GeMM performed better than all three of the models from the GLM family.

To summarize, we argue that homicide rates across the 92 countries analyzed in this data set are best accounted for by both wealth disparity and a country's overall wealth per capita. Although the finding was tangential to Henry's (2009) main theoretical conclusions, it nevertheless explains a failure to replicate a classic finding in one of his studies, that of the relationship between GDP and murder rates. This finding is consistent with Henry's original prediction, which presumably was masked by the substantial nonlinearity present in the data. GeMM was able to accurately capture both Gini and GDP as important predictors of homicide rates without transformation and without requiring specific assumptions about the form of the underlying distribution of homicides. In contrast, within OLS, the decision to include GDP in the statistical model was contingent on how the data were transformed, and within GLM, it was contingent on which distribution was assumed.

5. GENERAL DISCUSSION

The analyses presented in this article identified two important problems faced by behavioral and social scientists in their use of standard and robust LS procedures and a possible solution to these problems. First, LS regression procedures are highly sensitive to violations of assumptions and the presence of extreme scores. In our reanalysis of the racial bias data, we illustrated that a small number of extreme scores was sufficient to drive or mask statistical effects. Eliminating a mere 1.5% of the data was sufficient to render internal motivation to control prejudice as unnecessary to predict explicit attitudes toward blacks. In contrast, for the culture of honor data, violations of the linearity assumption and/ or the presence of extreme scores resulted in the failure of LS regression to identify expected patterns for which there was structure in the data. Taken together, these results suggest that nuances within one's data can either drive effects or mask them when using LS procedures. The fact that violations of assumptions and messy (which is to say, real) data can undermine statistical conclusions is not a new insight, of course. What is new, we believe, is that accepted procedures for dealing with messy data offer no real solutions to the problem, which leads to the second finding.

The second finding identified by our analyses is that accepted methods for dealing with messy data do not uniformly converge on a consistent statistical, and therefore theoretical, conclusion. This is especially problematic because the failure to find consistency across methods leaves too much decision-making power in the hands of the scientist. Unfortunately, scientists are not always unbiased observers of their data, and they are probably most likely to use the data-editing strategies that result in outcomes supportive of their theories, although they might not be aware that they are doing so. Thus, standard practices for dealing with messy data increase the number of researcher degrees of freedom (cf. Simmons et al. 2011), which we argue can undermine the search for valid scientific conclusions and hamper scientific progress.

Our solution to these two problems is to advocate for statistical procedures that reduce or eliminate the need for conducting outlier analyses and data transformations. As we showed throughout this article, GeMM provides a promising new approach that maximizes fit at the ordinal level. To illustrate the fundamental importance of modeling the ordinal level of data, imagine that a new scoring system were proposed for use at the Olympic Games. This scoring system, statisticians show, does a good job of accounting for variance in athletes' past scores (analogous to a high R^2), although it does not do particularly well at recovering ordinal outcomes, in other words, in postdicting who came in first, second, or third place. We cannot imagine that such a scoring system would ever see the light of day, and whoever proposed it would be laughed out of a career in statistics. Nonetheless, that is essentially what the present two studies suggest is happening with LS procedures when it comes to modeling ordinary, messy data in the behavioral sciences. As we have shown, GeMM's solution was relatively more robust across a variety of reasonable methods for identifying and eliminating extreme and influential scores. This is a major advantage of GeMM, as it removes some of the degrees of freedom that researchers have to make the results "turn out" in favor of their hypotheses (Simmons et al. 2011).

As a side note, it is interesting to comment on what constitutes an outlier in the traditional sense. Outliers are typically identified by their distance from the center point of a distribution of scores, or how much influence they have on the fit of a regression model. Measures of influence, such as Cook's D and DFFITS, are defined within a LS function and provide a metric for how influential a particular data point is on the overall LS fit of a model. Thus, the more extreme an observation is, the more influence it exerts on the LS solution. In contrast, within the GeMM framework, a score that is 3 standard deviations from the mean is treated as no different than a score that is 100 standard deviations from the mean. Indeed, the only influence an extreme score has on the overall fit of the model is gauged by how many inversions it creates in the predicted rank orders when included in the data set. This implies a need for influence statistics that operate in ordinal, rather than metric, space. Because GeMM models data on an ordinal level, it has a higher bar in terms of what constitutes an outlier.

Reconceptualizing data through the lens of ordinality redefines the meaning of outliers as those observations that have undue influence on the rank-order fit of the model. These observations may be true aberrations—data points that represent illegitimate responses given the measurement instruments (e.g., a response of 12, when the scale is bounded at 10)—or they may be real observations. For example, there are many cases in which extreme scores might be produced by data-entry errors, distracted subjects, or other processes external to an experiment. However, in the great majority of cases there is no ground truth by which researchers can determine whether an extreme score is a legitimate member of the population distribution or an aberration due to an external factor. The uncertainty surrounding the cause of an extreme score is problematic for justifying its exclusion. If the decision to exclude is based on the need to meet the assumptions of a statistical algorithm, this strikes us as a poor justification and is tantamount to forcing a round peg into a square hole.

Obviously, there are a number of alternative regression procedures not included in our modeling competition, and one might take issue with our focus on LS regression. However, we believe that this focus is warranted given the widespread use of the OLS (and its robust implementations) across the social sciences. Still it is quite possible that other models might perform better than GeMM, though the appropriate candidates for the two data sets presented here (ordinal logistic, negative binomial, Poisson and quasi-Poisson regressions) did not offer any performance advantages over GeMM, and in most cases underperformed relative to GeMM.

At the same time, one might argue that decisions regarding whether to transform one's data should be based on sound justification and the need to do so prior to engaging in data analysis. We agree, of course, but also argue that transformation for the purpose of analyzing a particular data set seems potentially opportunistic. Hence, we suggest that decisions to transform a data set in a particular way should be based on an understanding of the population distribution and driven by theory, not based merely on characteristics of the sample distribution. In the absence of theoretically justified reasons for transformation, we suggest that procedures such as GeMM are more appropriate for handling data where there are even slight departures from linearity, except where the form of the nonlinearity is of theoretical interest.[8]

Substantively, the findings based on GeMM for the racial bias and culture of honor data were at odds with what were found using traditional LS approaches. First, analysis of the race data suggests that responses on the ATB scale are a function of two variables: an unconscious racial attitude, as measured subtly by the AMP, and an external motivation to control prejudice. The AMP was positively predictive of people's responses on the ATB scale, whereas external motivation to control prejudice was negatively related to people's responses on the ATB. This pattern supports the idea that individuals are motivated to conceal their racial attitudes because they know that racial prejudice is socially unacceptable.

The fact that internal motivation to control prejudice was not included in the GeMM contradicts the conclusions drawn by Plant and Devine (1998) and more recent findings of Payne et al. (2005). There are many possible reasons that our findings are at odds with these prior studies, including the fact that racial attitudes likely differ across geographical regions (i.e., attitudes toward blacks may differ across different subject populations) and change over time (i.e., the data collected by Plant and Devine are at least 15 years old). We therefore do not question the validity of these prior findings. Rather, the critical point for the present purposes is that *the statistical, and therefore theoretical, conclusions drawn from our data were heavily dependent on decisions about how to deal with its messiness.*

Second, for the culture-of-honor data, we showed that homicide rates are predicted by both wealth disparity (Gini) and overall country wealth (GDP). Wealthier countries experience fewer homicides, whereas countries with greater *wealth disparity* experience *more* homicides. These variables are theoretically independent of one another, as a country could be poor but exhibit complete social equality in its distribution of its few resources (not likely, but theoretically possible), or a country could be wealthy and exhibit a similar degree of social equality. Indeed, developed nations with high GDPs per capita differ widely in terms of how their overall wealth is distributed across their people. This potential independence of GDP and Gini, however, is largely theoretical, as overall wealth and wealth disparity are, in fact, negatively correlated in analyses at the level of nations, states, and even counties within states (e.g., Henry 2009). In poorer countries, resources are more likely to be controlled by a few powerful people, compared with the more abundant resources of wealthier countries. Because of this typical association, researchers studying wealth or wealth disparities must consider both of these variables if they want to avoid confounding one with the other.

According to the analyses presented here, *how* a researcher decides to handle messy data can have an enormous impact on whether or to what extent variables (e.g., GDP, internal motivations to control prejudice) reveal their influences. Because of both nonlinear patterns and the influence of extreme scores, traditional LS analyses will sometimes overestimate a variable's influence, as in the case of internal motivations to control prejudice as a predictor of racial attitudes. Traditional LS analyses can also *underestimate* a variable's influence, as is the case in the association between a country's wealth and homicide rates, due to nonlinear relations and extreme scores in the data.

5.1. What Are the Practical Advantages of GeMM?

These substantive issues aside, what might compel one to use GeMM in lieu of traditional LS regression? As with other regression techniques, GeMM is a tool for prediction, inference, and data mining and exploration, though we believe that it offers some practical advantages over standard LS techniques. We articulate these next.

5.1.1. GeMM as a Tool for Prediction.
As demonstrated with the two data sets presented in this article, GeMM provides a computational algorithm for optimizing rank-order prediction that can outperform more complex algorithms on the basis of LS. The trade-off, of course, is that GeMM is not guaranteed and likely will not optimize prediction of metric values. However, we believe that this trade-off is warranted in many contexts. For example, consider any task that entails a selection decision on the criterion or outcome variable, such as selecting among job applications, choosing graduate applicants (if you are a faculty member), or choosing graduate programs (if you are a student). In all of these cases, the goal of the decision maker is to predict the relative ordering on the criterion, rather than to predict a specific quantitative value. As should be clear from the two example data sets presented here, GeMM generally showed greater accuracy for out-of-sample prediction when assessed in terms of predicting the ordinal values. Inasmuch as one of the principal goals of the social and health sciences is to predict real-world behaviors, having statistical models that can, first and foremost, accurately predict ordered relations is important: what good is a statistical model with a high R^2 value if it does poorly in predicting the relative ordering of the criterion variable?

5.1.2. GeMM as a Tool for Inference.
In an ideal world, inferences drawn from data should be invariant across data-editing strategies. The

problem, of course, is that there is theoretically an infinite number of ways in which data can be transformed, and numerous justified ways of identifying outliers. Although it is certainly possible to explore a variety of potential data-editing strategies to assess the robustness of the conclusions, it would be virtually impossible to explore all possible transformations and outlier deletion methods. In this respect, GeMM offers many practical advantages over standard techniques: It is (1) invariant to transformation on the criterion variable, (2) more robust to transformation on the predictors, and (3) more robust to outliers. These advantages follow from the use of tau as the fit metric, which, unlike Pearson's r, is invariant to monotone transformation. Because transformation on the predictors can affect the additive form of the predicted values, GeMM can still be affected by transforming the predictors, but only if the transformation results in changes in the ordinal properties of the additive model. In contrast, the use of transformation on the predictors is *guaranteed* to affect the LS fit. In other words, many of the decisions that could be exploited for analysis on the basis of LS approaches are unnecessary for analyses based on GeMM. Furthermore, unlike linear LS, GeMM does not lose statistical power under deviations from linearity.

As an example, consider our analysis of the culture-of-honor data. In this analysis, we illustrated that GeMM was relatively insensitive to transformation and had higher statistical power than linear LS. Thus, making fewer assumptions about one's data can pay off in an increased likelihood of detecting effects and more robust conclusions that are not conditional on having met specific model assumptions or on particular data-editing strategies. Importantly, the conditions in which researchers are most inclined to engage in data editing are precisely those conditions in which the data are unlikely to satisfy metric statistical assumptions.

On the flip side, GeMM's strength as a method for identifying monotone relationships limits the specificity of the inferences that can be drawn from the data. Although it can identify any nonlinear monotone relationship with equal probability without the need to transform the data, it cannot characterize the nature of those relationships. Thus, if researchers are interested in modeling the specific functional relationship between a set of variables, then GeMM would not be an appropriate tool. It should be noted though that the application of GeMM does not preclude them from further exploring these functional relationships with nonlinear LS methods, if they are comfortable drawing conclusions that go beyond the ordinal properties.

5.1.3. *GeMM as a Tool for Exploration.*

As with traditional LS methods, GeMM can also be used in the context of data exploration. Note, however, that in this context the fact that GeMM relaxes assumptions about functional form can be advantageous. Consider, for example, a data set in which a researcher has no *a priori* hypotheses about which variables should be related to the criterion. In these cases, it is even less likely that the researcher has any *a priori* guess about the form of the functional relationships that might exist therein. The problem with using traditional LS regression approaches in these contexts is that they require either that the researcher commit to modeling specific functional forms, engage in a great deal of data editing, or explore various alternative modeling approaches. With GeMM, identifying potentially interesting statistical relations can be accomplished with minimal data editing and without loss of power when those relations are nonlinear.

5.2. Interpreting the Output of Regression Coefficients within GeMM

The most straightforward interpretation of GeMM is in its model form, wherein the GeMM returns the model that best accounts for the rank-ordered properties of the criterion. The regression coefficients derived from GeMM have the exact same interpretation as those obtained from OLS once the OCLO solution is obtained, with one caveat. The OLS solution minimizes LS, whereas the rescaled OCLO-GeMM weights minimize LS conditional on maximizing ordinal fit.

Although in many cases the actual parameter values derived from GeMM may be close in magnitude to those obtained from other statistical procedures, there may be cases in which the relative magnitudes of the parameters differ in important ways. For example, for the homicide data set, the standardized regression coefficients derived from OLS yielded $|B_{Gini}| > |B_{GDP}|$ (.42 vs. −.09), but the GeMM solution yielded $|B_{Gini}| < |B_{GDP}|$ (.25 vs. −.29). This is informative because it tells us that the relative contributions of GDP and Gini are different if we are interested in using these variables to predict the rank order of homicide rates (GeMM) versus predicting the metric values of homicide rates (OLS). The implications of the GeMM solution compared with the OLS solution could be rather important. For example, a policymaker who wishes to reduce homicide rates would make different policy decisions if using OLS as the basis of that decision than if GeMM were used as the basis of that decision: the OLS solution implies that efforts at reducing homicide rates should focus primarily on decreasing wealth disparity (Gini), whereas the GeMM solution implies both that wealth disparity should be decreased and overall wealth (GDP) increased. This is not to suggest that GDP or wealth disparity cause homicides but rather to highlight the two very different policies that could result from using OLS versus GeMM.

5.3. *Availability and Extensions*

The bulk of this article has focused on the application of GeMM in contexts in which we must deal with messy data in one way or another. To facilitate the use of GeMM, we have developed versions in MATLAB, Mathematica, SAS, and R. MATLAB code and an accompanying user's guide are available at the first author's Web site (http://www.damlab .umd.edu/gemm.html); Mathematica and SAS code is available upon request. The development version of the GeMM package for R, and associated code and data used in this article, are available for free from the authors. The R package will be posted to Cran when completed. In its present form, the R package automatically produces the OCLO solution proposed in Tidwell et al. (2014).

We have a number of active lines of work aimed at extending the GeMM framework. A key limitation of GeMM thus far is that it is constrained to modeling monotonic relationships and therefore is not applicable to data sets that include nonmonotonic relationships. To address this, we have begun developing a version of GeMM that permits inflection points between the criterion and the modeled data, where an inflection point implies a change in the direction (sign) of the modeled relationship (Lawrence, Thomas, and Dougherty 2014).

A second area of work motivated by GeMM involves the development of leverage or influence statistics that identify outliers in ordinal space. Although GeMM should in principle be more robust to many different types of extreme scores, it will still be sensitive to extreme scores that create a large number of rank-order inversions. This is likely the reason that GeMM showed some sensitivity to the outlier deletion in racial bias data set. Although these types of extreme scores might be identifiable with traditional leverage statistics such as Cook's D, we imagine that alternative methods for identifying highly influential scores in ordinal space will be required.

6. SUMMARY

The existence of "uncooperative" and messy data poses a major challenge for behavioral and social science researchers. Unfortunately, within the standard approaches, traditional methods for handling nonlinearities, nonnormalities, and outliers provide the data analyst with a great deal of freedom for reconditioning the data to remove these properties, a freedom that can be exploited, intentionally or otherwise, to tell the preferred story. The more freedom allotted to the data analyst to make decisions that are not well justified, the more likely it is that the stories that get told are little more than myths. The goal of discovering fundamental facts about nature should not lead us to treat data and data analysis as if it were fine art requiring delicate hands. Rather, it should compel us to approach data analysis the way an engineer approaches the development of a new jetliner, which is to ensure that the plane flies even under nonideal conditions. As a public good that informs social and health policy, we argue that the same standard should operate for scientific claims. GeMM provides a new tool that we believe can help ensure that scientific claims are robust and invariant to data-editing strategies.

Notes

1. We use the term *criterion variable* to refer to the outcome or dependent variable.
2. The assumption of bivariate normality is not crucial for the operation of GeMM. One way to conceptualize the τ-to-r transformation is that it allows one to estimate the value of r under any order-preserving transformation of the data, without actually needing to transform the data. When assumptions of bivariate normality and linearity are met, then the τ-to-r transformation should closely approximate the value of r on the untransformed data.
3. Siegel et al. (2012) used structural equation modeling to examine the factor structure of the various measures of attitude and cognitive ability. For that analysis, the absolute (unsigned) scores were used.
4. The univariate outliers were identified by observations ± 3 standard deviations from the mean. Cook's D and DFFITS are standard leverage statistics that quantify the influence of each individual point on the regression solution. Observations were trimmed from the data set if the value of Cook's D exceeded $4/N$ and if the value of

DFFITS exceeded 2[sqrt(p/N)], where p is the number of predictors in the regression.

5. On the basis of the full sample, there are 37 distinct response categories, for which ordered logistic regression must fit 36 threshold parameters. For the full sample, only 32 of these thresholds were statistically significant at $p < .05$.

6. Model fitting for GeMM consisted of a two-step process in which we first fit GeMM to the full sample to find the subset of predictors that minimized BIC_τ'. We then ran 1,000 bootstrap samples to estimate the standard errors of the coefficients. The coefficients listed in Table 2 correspond to the mean coefficients (and corresponding standard errors) from the 1,000 bootstrap samples. Model fits listed in Table 1 are based on the analysis of the full sample.

7. Both the Henze-Zirkler and Mardia tests of multivariate normality revealed significant departures from multivariate normality, a finding that held for both the untransformed and transformed data.

8. However, we suggest that in most cases in the social sciences, theories are not specified in such detail and instead are expressed largely as ordinal predictions (see also Cliff 1996).

References

Barnes, Collin D., Ryan P. Brown, and Michael Tamborski. 2012. "Living Dangerously: Culture of Honor, Risk-Taking, and the Nonrandomness of 'Accidental' Deaths." *Social Psychological and Personality Science* 3(1):100–107.

Beck, Nathaniel, and Simon Jackman. 1998. "Beyond Linearity by Default: Generalized Additive Models." *American Journal of Political Science* 42(2):596–627.

Brown, Ryan P., Lindsey L. Osterman, and Collin D. Barnes. 2009. "School Violence and the Culture of Honor." *Psychological Science* 20(11):1400–405.

Brown, Ryan P., and Lindsey L. Osterman. 2012. "Culture of Honor, Violence, and Homicide." Pp. 218–32 in *Oxford Handbook of Evolutionary Perspectives on Violence, Homicide, and War*, edited by T. Shackelford and V. W. Shackelford. New York: Oxford University Press.

Cavanagh, Christopher, and Robert P. Sherman. 1998. "Rank Estimators for Monotonic Index Models." *Journal of Econometrics* 84(2):351–81.

Cliff, Norman. 1996. *Ordinal Methods for Behavioral Data Analysis*. New York: Psychology Press.

Crocker, Jennifer. 2011. "The Road to Fraud Starts with a Single Step." *Nature* 479(7372):151.

Daly, Martin, and Margo Wilson. 2010. "Cultural Inertia, Economic Incentives, and the Persistence of "Southern Violence."" Pp. 229–41 in *Evolution, Culture, and the Human Mind*, edited by Mark Schaller, Ara Norenzayan, Steven J. Heine, Toshio Yamagishi, and Tatsuya Kameda. New York: Taylor & Francis.

Devine, Patricia G., E. Ashby Plant, David M. Amodio, Eddie Harmon-Jones, and Stephanie L. Vance. 2002. "The Regulation of Explicit and Implicit Race Bias: The Role of Motivations to Respond without Prejudice." *Journal of Personality and Social Psychology* 82(5):835.

Dougherty, Michael R., and Rick P. Thomas. 2012. "Robust Decision Making in a Nonlinear World." *Psychological Review* 119(2):321.

Dunton, Bridget C., and Russell H. Fazio. 1997. "An Individual Difference Measure of Motivation to Control Prejudiced Reactions." *Personality and Social Psychology Bulletin* 23(3):316–26.

Fang, Ferric C., R. Grant Steen, and Arturo Casadevall. 2012. "Misconduct Accounts for the Majority of Retracted Scientific Publications." *Proceedings of the National Academy of Sciences of the United States of America* 109(42):17028–33.

Fazio, Russel H., Joni R. Jackson, Bridget C. Dunton, and Carol J. Williams. 1995. "Variability in Automatic Activation as an Unobtrusive Measure of Racial Attitudes: A Bona Fide Pipeline?" *Journal of Personality and Social Psychology* 69(6):1013–27.

Freese, Jeremy. 2007. "Reproducibility Standards in Quantitative Social Science: Why Not Sociology?" *Sociological Methods and Research* 36:153–72

Gerber, Alan S., and Neil Malhotra. 2008. "Publication Bias in Empirical Sociological Research: Do Arbitrary Significance Levels Distort Published Results?" *Sociological Methods and Research* 37(1):3–30.

Greenwald, Anthony G., Debbie E. McGhee, and Jordan L. K. Schwartz. 1998. "Measuring Individual Differences in Implicit Cognition: The Implicit Association Test." *Journal of Personality and Social Psychology* 74(6):1464–80.

Han, Aaron K. 1987. "Non-parametric Analysis of a Generalized Regression Model: The Maximum Rank Correlation Estimator." *Journal of Econometrics* 35(2–3): 303–16.

Hauser, Robert M. 1987. "Sharing Data: It's Time for ASA Journals to Follow the Folkways of a Scientific Sociology." *American Sociological Review* 52(6):vi–vii.

Hays, William. 1994. *Statistics*. 5th ed. Belmont, CA: Wadsworth.

Henry, P. J. 2009. "Low-status Compensation: A Theory for Understanding the Role of Status in Cultures of Honor." *Journal of Personality and Social Psychology* 97(3): 451–66.

Ho, Daniel E., Kosuke Imai, Gary King, and Elizabeth A. Stuart. 2007. "Matching as Nonparametric Preprocessing for Reducing Model Dependence in Parametric Causal Inference." *Political Analysis* 15(3):199–236.

Howell, David C. 2002. *Statistical Methods for Psychology*. 5th ed. Pacific Grove, CA: Duxbury/Thomson Learning.

Jasso, Guillermina. 1986. "Is It Outlier Deletion or Is It Sample Truncation? Notes on Science and Sexuality." *American Sociological Review* 51(5):738–42.

John, Leslie K., George Loewenstein, and Drazen Prelec. 2012. "Measuring the Prevalence of Questionable Research Practices with Incentives for Truth Telling." *Psychological Science* 23(5):524–32.

Kahn, Joan R., and J. Richard Udry. 1986. "Marital Coital Frequency: Unnoticed Outliers and Unspecified Interactions Lead to Erroneous Conclusions." *American Sociological Review* 51(5):734–37.

Kendall, Maurice. 1938. "A New Measure of Rank Correlation." *Biometrika* 30(1/2): 81–93.

Kendall, Maurice, and Jean D. Gibbons. 1990. *Rank Correlation Methods*. 5th ed. New York: Oxford University Press.

King, Gary. 1995. "Replication, Replication." *PS: Political Science and Politics* 28(3): 444–52.

Lawrence, Ashley, Rick P. Thomas, and Michael R. Dougherty. 2014. "A Non-monotonic Approach to Ordinal Prediction." Unpublished manuscript.

Leahey, Erin. 2005. "Alphas and Asterisks: The Development of Statistical Significance Testing Standards in Sociology." *Social Forces* 84(1):1–24.

Leahey, Erin. 2008. "Overseeing Research Practice: The Case of Data Editing." *Science, Technology, and Human Values* 33(5):605–30.

Leahey, Erin, Barbara Entwisle, and Peter Einaudi. 2003. "Diversity in Everyday Research Practice: The Case of Data Editing." *Sociological Methods and Research* 32(1):64–89.

Lederman, Daniel, Norman Loayza, and Ana Maria Menéndez. 2002. "Violent Crime: Does Social Capital Matter?" *Economic Development and Cultural Change* 50(3): 509–39.

Levelt Committee, Noort Committee, and Drenth Committee. 2012. *Flawed Science: The Fraudulent Research Practices of Social Psychologist Diederik Stapel.* Commissioned by the Tilburg University, University of Amsterdam, and the University of Groningen.

Micceri, Theodore. 1989. "The Unicorn, the Normal Curve, and Other Improbable Creatures." *Psychological Bulletin* 105(1):156.

Nisbett, Jon, and Dov Cohen. 1996. *Psychology of Violence in the South.* Boulder, CO: Westview.

Nisbett, Richard E. 1993. "Violence and U.S. Regional Culture." *American Psychologist* 48(4):441–49.

Olsen, Karen M., and Svenn-Age Dahl. 2007. "Health Differences between European Countries." *Social Science and Medicine* 64(8):1665–78.

Osterman, Lindsey L., and Ryan P. Brown. 2011. "Culture of Honor and Violence Against the Self." *Personality and Social Psychology Bulletin* 37(12):1611–23.

Payne, B. Keith, Melissa A. Burkley, and Mark B. Stokes. 2008. "Why Do Implicit and Explicit Attitude Tests Diverge? The Role of Structural Fit." *Journal of Personality and Social Psychology* 94(1):16.

Payne, B. Keith, Clara Michelle Cheng, Olesya Govorun, and Brandon D. Stewart. 2005. "An Inkblot for Attitudes: Affect Misattribution as Implicit Measurement." *Journal of Personality and Social Psychology* 89(3):277.

Plant, E. A., Patricia G. Devine, and Paige C. Brazy. 2003. "The Bogus Pipeline and Motivations to Respond without Prejudice: Revisiting the Fading and Faking of Racial Prejudice." *Group Processes and Intergroup Relations* 6(2):187–200.

Plant, E. Ashby, and Patricia G. Devine. 1998. "Internal and External Motivation to Respond without Prejudice." *Journal of Personality and Social Psychology* 75(3):811.

Raftery, Adrian E. 1995. "Bayesian Model Selection in Social Research." Pp. 111–63 in *Sociological Methodology*, Vol. 25, edited by Peter V. Marsden. Cambridge, MA: Blackwell.

Robbins, Blaine, and David Pettinicchio. 2012. "Social Capital, Economic Development, and Homicide: A Cross-national Investigation." *Social Indicators Research* 105(3):519–40.

Rupinski, Melvin T., and William P. Dunlap. 1996. "Approximating Pearson Product-moment Correlations from Kendall's Tau and Spearman's Rho." *Educational and Psychological Measurement* 56(3):419–29.

Sana, Mariono, and Alexander A. Weinreb. 2008. "Insiders, Outsiders, and the Editing of Inconsistent Survey Data." *Sociological Methods Research* 36(4):515–54.

Semyonov, Moshe, and Noah Lewin-Epstein. 2011. "Wealth Inequality: Ethnic Disparities in Israeli Society." *Social Forces* 89(3):935–59.

Shepard, Roger N. 1962. "The Analysis of Proximities: Multidimensional Scaling with an Unknown Distance Function. Part I." *Psychometrika* 27:125–40.

Shepard, Roger. 1966. "Metric Structures in Ordinal Data." *Journal of Mathematical Psychology* 3:287–315.

Siegel, Eric F., Michael R. Dougherty, and David E. Huber. 2012. "Manipulating the Role of Cognitive Control While Taking the Implicit Association Test." *Journal of Experimental Social Psychology* 48(5):1057–68.

Simmons, Joseph P., Leif D. Nelson, and Uri Simonsohn. 2011. "False-positive Psychology: Undisclosed Flexibility in Data Collection and Analysis Allows Presenting Anything as Significant." *Psychological Science* 22(11):1359–66.

Simonsohn, Uri. 2013. "Just Post It: The Lesson from Two Cases of Fabricated Data Detected by Statistics Alone." *Psychological Science* 24(10):1875–88.

Tidwell, Joe W., Michael R. Dougherty, Jeffery S. Chrabaszcz, and Rick P. Thomas. 2014. "Order Constrained Linear Optimization." Unpublished manuscript.

Vandello, Joseph A., and Dov Cohen. 2003. "Male Honor and Female Fidelity: Implicit Cultural Scripts that Perpetuate Domestic Violence." *Journal of Personality and Social Psychology* 84(5):997–1010.

Author Biographies

Michael R. Dougherty is a professor of psychology at the University of Maryland, College Park. His areas of interest include research methods, computational and mathematical modeling, cognitive decision theory, and memory theory.

Rick P. Thomas is an associate professor of psychology at the Georgia Institute of Technology. His areas of interest include computational and mathematical modeling, cognitive decision theory, and engineering psychology.

Ryan P. Brown is a professor of psychology at the University of Oklahoma. His area of research includes understanding factors contributing to honor cultures and the impact honor cultures have on outcomes ranging from school violence to terrorism.

Jeffrey S. Chrabaszcz is a PhD student at the University of Maryland. His interests include research methods, computational and mathematical modeling, judgment and decision making, and anxiety.

Joe W. Tidwell is a PhD student at the University of Maryland. His interests include research methods, computational and mathematical modeling, judgment and decision making, and forecasting.

Sociological Methodology
2015, Vol. 45(1) 272–319
© American Sociological Association 2015
DOI: 10.1177/0081175015578740
http://sm.sagepub.com
$SAGE

ॐ 6 ॐ

BEYOND TEXT: USING ARRAYS TO REPRESENT AND ANALYZE ETHNOGRAPHIC DATA

Corey M. Abramson*
Daniel Dohan†

Abstract

Recent methodological debates in sociology have focused on how data and analyses might be made more open and accessible, how the process of theorizing and knowledge production might be made more explicit, and how developing means of visualization can help address these issues. In ethnography, where scholars from various traditions do not necessarily share basic epistemological assumptions about the research enterprise with either their quantitative colleagues or one another, these issues are particularly complex. Nevertheless, ethnographers working within the field of sociology face a set of common pragmatic challenges related to managing, analyzing, and presenting the rich context-dependent data generated during fieldwork. Inspired by both ongoing discussions about how sociological research might be made more transparent, as well as innovations in other data-centered fields, the authors developed an interactive visual approach that provides tools for addressing these shared pragmatic challenges. They label the approach "ethnoarray" analysis. This article introduces this approach and explains how it can help scholars address widely shared logistical and technical

*University of Arizona, Tucson, AZ, USA
†University of California, San Francisco, San Francisco, CA, USA

Corresponding Author:
Corey M. Abramson, University of Arizona, The University of Arizona Social Sciences Building, 1145 E. South Campus Drive, Room 400, Tucson, AZ 85721, USA
Email: coreyabramson@email.arizona.edu

complexities, while remaining sensitive to both ethnography's epistemic diversity and its practitioners shared commitment to depth, context, and interpretation. The authors use data from an ethnographic study of serious illness to construct a model of an ethnoarray and explain how such an array might be linked to data repositories to facilitate new forms of analysis, interpretation, and sharing within scholarly and lay communities. They conclude by discussing some potential implications of the ethnoarray and related approaches for the scope, practice, and forms of ethnography.

Keywords

mixed methods, transparency, visualization, ethnography, representation, data analysis, computational methods, computational ethnography

1. INTRODUCTION

Recent methodological debates in sociology and related social science disciplines have focused on how data and analyses might be made more open and accessible (Duneier 2011; Freese 2007), how the process of theorizing and knowledge production might be made more explicit (Leahey 2008; Swedberg 2014), and the importance of developing means of data visualization in addressing these issues (Moody and Healy 2014). The presence of basic common understandings found in many quantitative approaches, such as concerns with replicability, reliability, generalization, inference, and validity, facilitates these discussions by providing a shared cultural basis for developing new tools (Durkheim [1893] 1984; Latour and Woolgar 1986). In ethnography,[1] where scholars from various traditions do not necessarily share basic epistemological assumptions about the research enterprise with either their quantitative colleagues or one another, these methodological debates are particularly complex.

Ethnographers wishing to work toward producing new tools for transparency, sharing, and visualization must first confront a lack of consensus about whether this form of scholarship can or should attempt to follow the traditional models of inquiry in the social sciences. Following the postmodern turn, a host of scholars have argued that ethnography should be seen as a field of humanistic inquiry rather than social science (Clifford and Marcus 1986). While recognizing the influence and importance of this critique (for a discussion, see also Reed 2010), in this article, we discuss shared challenges faced by those who argue that ethnography remains a viable social science method. Even among these empirically inclined ethnographers, however, the question of how to situate ethnography relative to other methods is hotly debated. Some argue that concerns about validity, reliable representation, and generalizability are universal to social science and that ethnographers must contend with them in fundamentally the same way as scholars using other methods (Goldthorpe 2000; King et al. 2001; Sánchez-Jankowski 2002). Others argue that ethnography's value lies in discovering the unexpected and hidden, as well as in developing theory, and in these roles it provides a necessary and critical alternative to "positivist" social science (Burawoy 1998; Duneier 2011; Tavory and Timmermans 2009). Another group holds that ethnography is commensurate with, but different from, mainstream social science and thus necessitates a specialized logic and language of inquiry (Brady and Collier 2004; Lofland 1995; Small 2009). These divisions are deeply ingrained and often manifest as contentious public exchanges (cf. Becker 2009; Duneier 2002, 2006; Klinenberg 2006; Wacquant 2002). Consequently, ethnographers wishing to develop new tools must do so without many of the points of common ground (i.e., shared ontological, axiological, and epistemic assumptions) that researchers using other methods might take for granted.

In this article, we bracket debates about which approach to ethnography is most legitimate or appropriate. Rather, we focus on a core set of shared practical challenges faced by empirical investigators who aspire to data sharing, openness, and visualization. We focus here on two such practical challenges. First, ethnographers who do fieldwork must develop strategies to manage and make sense of the large volumes of context-rich data they collect over the course of research. Typically they do so without fully relying on quantitative data reduction techniques, as quantitative reduction is believed to strip data of the depth that makes it valuable in the first place. Second, ethnographers need to present evidence and communicate insights so readers will be engaged and convinced by their findings—a particular challenge, as typical ethnographic warrants mean that readers are often unfamiliar or misinformed about the social settings and actors that ethnographers describe (Katz 1997).

Following recent calls for a move from "tribalism" to pragmatic pluralistic engagement among divergent "qualitative" perspectives (Lamont and Swidler 2014), we grapple here with and introduce new techniques for addressing these challenges by proposing an approach that can help researchers identify, construct,[2] and present rich ethnographic data in a way that allows analysts to make sense of patterns in their data, characterize them in a way that allows readers to appreciate their context and contingency, and open up possibilities for collaboration and data sharing. We do so with the full acknowledgment that although we have found the resulting methods to be a useful complement to traditional approaches, it is inconceivable that a single tool can serve as a common platform for all ethnographic analysis. However, we proceed under the belief that reconnecting to broader methodological debates about transparency, process, innovation, and visualization can enhance ethnography's contribution to social science.

In the pages that follow, we outline a new approach featuring an interactive graphical display for representing and sharing data that we call an "ethnoarray." The "ethnoarray" is loosely adapted from the microarray, a graphical "heatmap"-based approach that is used in the biological sciences to present large volumes of complex data.[3] Functioning as more than aesthetics, graphical displays potentially provide a flexible way for sharing information, seeing patterns, and blending narrative and explanation, characteristics recognized by quantitative analysts (Moody and Healy 2014; Tufte 1983, 1997). Like other visual display approaches currently being developed in qualitative social science and the humanities (Henderson and Segal 2013; Mohr and Bogdanov 2013; Tangherlini and Leonard 2013), the ethnoarray allows the display of data in ways that can facilitate the discovery of relationships and thus help researchers understand the contextual richness of their own data, whether those insights ultimately manifest as a richer interpretation of theoretical constructs or comparative analyses and causal explanation. In other words, the ethnoarray is a part of a growing class of visual-analytic tools that facilitate data exploration and can yield insights for both "confirmatory" and "exploratory" data analysis projects (Moody and Healy 2014; Tukey 1977).

Our goal in developing this approach goes beyond within-project discovery, however. The ethnoarray may also allow ethnographers to enjoy greater empirical and analytical transparency by providing new ways of sharing data with colleagues, readers, and the public (Freese 2007). That is, it may open new possibilities for the analysis, representation (Moody and Healy 2014), and sharing (Freese 2007) of ethnographic data, an arena in which there is still much room for innovation. In sum, we introduce the ethnoarray as a pragmatic tool for preserving and bolstering ethnography's traditional strength in sharing deep contextualized narratives while speaking to new possibilities for exploring ethnography's relationship to causal analysis and the production of generalizable findings enabled by technological advances.[4]

To illustrate the ethnoarray approach, this article proceeds as follows: In section 2, we examine several pragmatic challenges faced by ethnographers and some extant responses. In section 3, we describe the microarray that is used in the biological sciences and explain how and why ethnographers can fruitfully adapt it for certain social science projects. We also provide an illustration using data from a five-year comparative ethnographic project examining the social and technical management of terminal illness. In section 4, we address the potential implications of the ethnoarray for current and future ethnographic practice, as well as the limits of this approach. In section 5, we conclude with a summary of how the ethnoarray and related approaches can lead to new possibilities for ethnographic representation and scholarly engagement that can go beyond traditional text. Two appendixes provide additional illustrations of how the array approach might be used for different units of analysis and cases.

2. BACKGROUND: APPROACHING ETHNOGRAPHY'S DATA CHALLENGES

Analyzing data produced during fieldwork creates substantial logistical challenges. Even brief episodes of ethnographic research can produce hundreds of pages of field notes or interview transcripts, as well as audio and video recordings, drawings, maps, or objects (Emerson et al. 1995; Sanjek 1990). Many ethnographers spend years in the field and produce commensurately large volumes of data. Upon commencing analysis, researchers cannot easily sample or thin their data lest they lose the richness that motivated the ethnographic engagement in the first place. Moreover, those researchers sensitive to the issue of generalizability may undertake multisite or comparative ethnographic studies as they explore counterfactual possibilities, flesh out social mechanisms, or seek to develop explanatory models (cf. Abramson 2015; Dohan 2003; Sallaz 2009; Sánchez-Jankowski 2008). Even though notes written by these researchers may address a more narrowly defined question, format, and unit of analysis that impart structure, the data's breadth and volume can still be daunting (Sánchez-Jankowski 2002). In either situation, as the notes, transcripts, recordings, documents, and objects accumulate, analysts may struggle to focus on the experiences, themes, or patterns they care most about.

Ethnographers who successfully grapple with large volumes of data during analysis then confront a second pragmatic hurdle: how to share data and analyses in order to substantiate findings and conclusions. Social scientists typically illustrate how their findings were produced by sharing data, describing analytical procedures, or both. However, in ethnography, there is no widely shared standard regarding what constitutes appropriate analysis or representation. Whichever method is used may be criticized and rejected by those using alternative approaches. This is intensified by a growing "tribalism" found among camps of qualitative researchers (Lamont and Swidler 2014). This issue, combined with the unique role of the ethnographer as an instrument of data collection, has incited heated exchanges (Duneier 2002, 2006; Klinenberg 2006; Wacquant 2002). Even if ethnographers could agree on the value (perhaps even the morality) of pluralism, the volume, sensitivity, and context dependence of ethnographic data make sharing a nontrivial challenge. Despite repeated calls for making research processes transparent to peers, informants, communities, and the general public (Burawoy 2004; Duneier 2011), there is little consensus about how this can be accomplished.

Within the social science community, in which an expectation of open and shared data is widespread among quantitative researchers, the inability to share data easily has substantial implications for ethnographic claims-making (Becker 1958; Cicourel 1964; Sánchez-Jankowski 2002; Small 2009). The horns of this dilemma appear clear. Not sharing data raises concerns about validity, transparency, and even the veracity of fieldwork in a way that has the potential to delegitimize hard-won ethnographic findings. At the same time, sharing all of the ethnographic data generated by a research project is typically neither ethical nor feasible, nor is it necessarily useful; sharing small amounts of selected data diminishes interpretive richness and can impede understanding; and no singular protocol can describe the various interpretative processes through which analysts immersed in the field assess whether a behavior such as the contraction of an eyelid is a wink, a twitch, or a conspiratorial gesture (Geertz 2000).

Contemporary quantitative social science research is impossible to imagine without computers, but computing has had a relatively smaller impact in ethnography. The emergence of computer-assisted qualitative

data analysis software (CAQDAS) over the past two decades has provided some promising new ways to analyze and present data. In terms of
data logistics, a growing number of CAQDAS platforms help analysts
enter, structure, code, organize, and retrieve large qualitative data sets
including text and other evidence (Dohan and Sánchez-Jankowski 1998;
Miles and Huberman 1994). New methods based on quantifying and
conducting formal textual analyses have emerged as well (Franzosi, De
Fazio, and Vicari 2012; Mohr and Bogdanov 2013; Mohr et al. 2013).
However, even for those interpretivist and humanist analysts who are
opposed to quantitative reduction, or even the notion of "coding" text
(cf. Biernacki 2014), these platforms can potentially offer a way to
organize and quickly cycle through voluminous data (Dohan and
Sánchez-Jankowski 1998).

Although CAQDAS has provided new options for approaching ethnography's data challenges, widely available commercial packages have
limitations.[5] Although increasingly flexible, most commercial software
emphasizes coding and retrieving textual "chunks" and exploring patterns of codes. In many ways, this originates from and reflects (and perhaps reinforces) an attempt to implement the code-heavy approach often
associated with grounded theory (Reeves et al. 2008). In terms of sharing, CAQDAS can help investigators share data within a research team.
Recently, software has even allowed networked collaboration in shared
data clouds. Nevertheless, there has been less attention around how to
share data with readers or other researchers. Although some software
features the basic underpinnings of interoperability that can facilitate
data sharing (such as an extensible markup language [XML] output),
techniques for doing so are relatively nascent. Furthermore, CAQDAS
output capabilities have not been widely invoked as a way to share data
itself, that is, as a way to put data into the hands of readers and allow
them to explore and reproduce analyses. Likewise, although online
repositories for qualitative data are beginning to emerge as a location
for hosting data (cf. Perez-Hernandez 2014), shared approaches for
summarizing the data while protecting both context and confidentiality
remain elusive.

What could help advance ethnographic inquiry beyond coding? First,
although not all ethnographic approaches are concerned with mapping
associations in data in either an exploratory or an explanatory manner,
this is central to a number of qualitative approaches, ranging from
grounded theory to more positivistic techniques. Analysts from

divergent camps frequently need support discovering patterns in their data, yet they also acknowledge that such support cannot come at the cost of disconnecting data from context. Second, among those concerned with transparency and replication, analysts need support for sharing data so that readers can assess claims making. Many contemporary CAQDAS packages provide tools for tagging themes and for team analysis, which constitutes a form of data sharing. Still, disseminating data more broadly is not a core goal of most CAQDAS packages available today, and shared methods that would make this more plausible have yet to be developed.[6] Finally, new approaches must go beyond the specific proprietary software architectures of CAQDAS platforms by offering adaptable public approaches that researchers can implement in their attempts to advance these conversations. In sum, although CAQDAS provides important tools for analysis, substantial opportunities exist for new tools and techniques to advance more open and transparent forms of ethnography.

2.1. *The Microarray: A Potential Tool from an Unlikely Source*

What might potential tools and techniques related to the microarray look like? Although ethnographers use a unique set of methods in their studies of social life, sharing and analyzing large volumes of context-dependent data is not a challenge unique to the social sciences. In molecular biology, a technique known as microarray analysis has proved powerful because it uses an interpretable heatmap visualization to help analyze and depict complex multilevel biological systems and processes to varied audiences. The term *microarray* refers to both a process for analyzing biological samples—typically patterns of gene expression in tissues—and a graphical product displaying results (Belacel, Wang, and Cuperlovic-Culf 2006; Eisen et al. 1998; Schena et al. 1995). The introduction of microarrays and their exploratory use has led to important advances. For example, microarrays helped scientists identify genetic patterns (overexpression vs. underexpression) in breast cancer tumors by analyzing and displaying expression profiles for a large number of tumor samples simultaneously (see Figure 1), differences that can help explain the course of illness, distribution within populations, and responsiveness to different types of therapy (Prat and Perou 2011).

Using microarrays, biologists can display, aggregate, analyze, and share complex, multilevel data using exploratory statistical procedures,

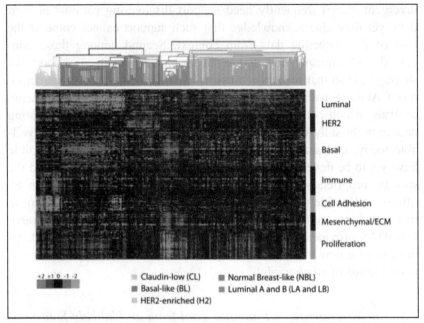

Figure 1. Microarray based on gene expression profiling data from 337 breast samples (in columns; 320 tumors, 17 normal tissues) and approximately 1,900 genes (rows).
Source: Prat and Perou (2011).

such as principal component analysis (PCA), that allow systemic inductive identification of group boundaries and pattern recognition (Stears, Martinskey, and Schena 2003). Figure 1 provides an existing example using gene expression data from breast tissue specimens.[7] At the same time, the microarray retains microlevel information about individual specimens so that analysts do not lose context. Analysts can "zoom in" to examine characteristics of an individual case in the array as readily as they can "zoom out" to see how that case fits within the array's overall pattern. Incorporating individual-level data within the microarray means that molecular biologists can use arrays not only to share findings but also to share the data and process by which those findings have been generated from voluminous underlying data.

Ethnographic field notes are quite different from the gene expression profiles found in microarrays. The former are typically more interpretative; the latter are expressed via quantitative reduction. Ethnography necessarily involves self-reflection; there is no directly comparable activity for biologists. But analyzing either kind of data requires scholars to shift their gaze between distinct analytical levels and to represent their interpretations to a wider audience. Biologists use the microarray to examine genes, markers, individuals, and populations. Ethnographers examine microlevel interactions, emergent themes, theoretical constructs, and social contexts, and in this way they engage their sociological imagination to explore connections among and between behavior and narrative, group and organization, institution and society (Mills 1959).

3. ETHNOARRAY: AN EXAMPLE

Just as a microarray facilitates the multilevel exploration of biological data, we suggest that an ethnoarray may similarly facilitate, document, and reveal the richness of ethnographic data in ways researchers and readers find useful. Bearing in mind the caveats mentioned above, we use data from a study of the technological and social management of serious illness to develop an ethnoarray mock-up.

Our data are drawn from the Cancer Patient Deliberation Study (PtDelib), which uses ethnography to explore, understand, and explain how patients move along different treatment pathways with a specific interest in which patients end up embarking on clinical trials compared with seeking out less aggressive palliative care as they approach the end of life. All of the patients in our study have metastatic cancer and typically are within one to three years of death. The study uses ethnography to examine not only interactions between providers and patients but also the physically and analytically distant social processes that structure those interactions, and how these are understood by actors, with an ultimate goal of tracing how happenings in the exam room reflect the institutional contexts of patients and clinicians.

Patients are recruited to the study as their disease progresses and as treatment options begin to dwindle. Recruitment occurs in person during a routine clinic visit, and patients are then followed longitudinally. The study uses a multifaceted approach. Data consist of semistructured interviews with patients conducted at multiple points in time, direct observation of clinical encounters (including the recruitment visit), a semistructured interview with a family member or caregiver, review of medical records, and surveys administered at each interview with patients and caregivers. The PtDelib cohort includes 82 patients as well as 31 caregivers and 63 providers. We have recorded approximately 4,000 pages of observational field notes and 8,000 pages of interview transcripts.

The research team includes four fieldworkers and three researchers who review and analyze transcripts and field notes. We use commercial qualitative data analysis software (ATLAS.ti) to organize the data, and we developed a coding scheme using both deductive and inductive techniques to facilitate retrieval of field notes, transcripts, and other data. This database must support multiple analytical goals and be accessible to multiple audiences. The study's research team and audience span diverse disciplines, including sociologists, bioethicists, linguists, health services researchers, and medical professionals. Consequently, PtDelib findings need to be interpretable and responsive to various viewpoints and questions along a continuum of analytical approaches. We began development of the ethnoarray approach as a way to address this core project need, but we found that its utility extends beyond this goal.

3.1. *Developing an Ethnoarray*

Using preliminary data from the PtDelib study, we developed a small-scale model of an ethnoarray. All of the data we use in this mock-up are drawn from field notes and interviews we had previously entered and coded via an iterative interpretive analysis using the ATLAS.ti software platform. An example of the coded database is presented in Figure 2, which shows a single paragraph from the transcript of a PtDelib patient interview. As this figure illustrates, passages of text typically include many codes. The software allows analysts to flexibly search the database to retrieve passages of interest using Boolean search procedures and even basic inductive tools such as co-occurrence tables. However, given that the ethnoarray involves a new approach, current software packages are not designed at this time to directly facilitate the production of ethnoarrays. In translating the data into an array, our first—and most analytically consequential—decision for this mock-up was to focus the ethnoarray on analyzing patients' trajectories into clinical trials. That is, we chose to organize this array to facilitate understanding differences and similarities between individuals.[8] After selecting the unit of analysis for the array, we chose five substantive domains that prior literature and our early iterative interpretive analyses suggested

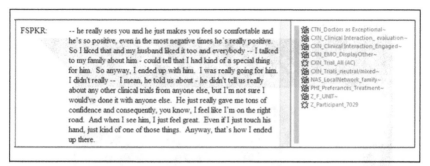

Figure 2. A single paragraph from the transcript of a Cancer Patient Deliberation Study patient interview, coded as an ATLAS.ti data set.

were relevant, discussed with team members how to properly represent those domains, ultimately selected three to four measures for each domain, and arranged the domains and measures as the array's 16 rows.[9]

For columns, we selected a sample of patients for whom we had sufficient data (i.e., for whom we had at least two interviews and field observations before they either died or left the study). We then debated how to represent time variation in their experiences. In Figure 3, we show an array in which all information has been aggregated into a single column (to create a 10-column array); Figures 4 to 6 show arrays in which patients' experiences and statuses at different times are shown in distinct columns (baseline [T1] and first follow-up [T2]), which creates a larger and perhaps less intuitively interpretable array that includes greater richness about patients' experiences and trajectories. The key to Figures 3 to 6 is provided below. Each cell reflects all interview and participant observation data associated with that individual, domain, and measure. The domains, measures, and rows are ordered with a temporal logic following our particular research questions, but future arrays need not follow this model. The rows of a grounded theory approach, for example, might include general emergent themes generated entirely inductively. Columns could represent organizations, events, interaction sequences, or other units depending on the analyst's goals. Appendix A shows a brief example of how ethnoarrays can use other units of analysis (such as neighborhood contexts) in a comparative participant observation study, but for the sake of clarity, we focus on individual trajectories from PtDelib data in the main text.

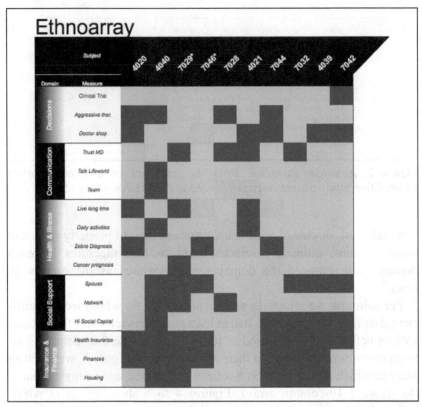

Figure 3. An ethnoarray based on data from 10 participants in the Cancer Patient Deliberation Study. The "Key to Figures 3–6" on p. 288 provides additional information regarding the domains, measures, and color assignment.

The sample array we present is organized by discrete units (characteristics and experiences of individuals at a given point in time evidenced by field notes and interviews). This corresponds with the analytical goals of the PtDelib project but raises important points about array construction. First, which type of data can be included in arrays? In any study, analysts must answer this question on the basis of the particular research question. For illustrative purposes here, we included only traditional ethnographic data derived from field observations and interviews, but the larger study also includes data from medical records, focus groups, and surveys, which could also be incorporated. A related question is which portions of data become part of the array. Again, analysts will make this decision on the basis of the nature of their study and

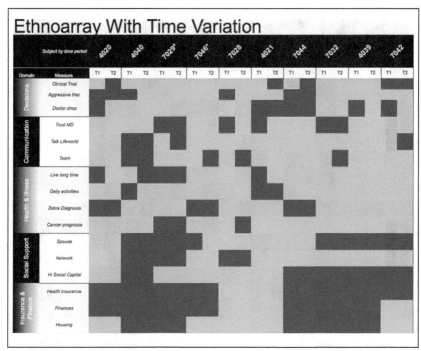

Figure 4. An ethnoarray based on data from 10 participants in the Cancer Patient Deliberation Study, with baseline (T1) and follow-up (T2) data. The "Key to Figures 3–6" on p. 288 provides additional information regarding the domains, measures, and color assignment.

question. Their decision will likely reflect the specific epistemic and intellectual tradition within which they situated their work.

For the sample array in this article, we used a broadly interpretive approach. We examined coded data in the ATLAS.ti database and narrative summaries of each patient's experience, and we held discussions among the team of researchers and fieldworkers who had firsthand knowledge of the patients, providers, and clinics represented in the array. Within this broad contextual framework, we interpreted specific interview passages and field notes according to whether and how they were related to array domains. We used all such passages in constructing the arrays in this article. The temporal structure of the array reflects the longitudinal design of the study, in which interviews and observations were conducted in a coordinated sequential fashion. Others who use ethnoarrays need not follow this model. Analysts might use only a

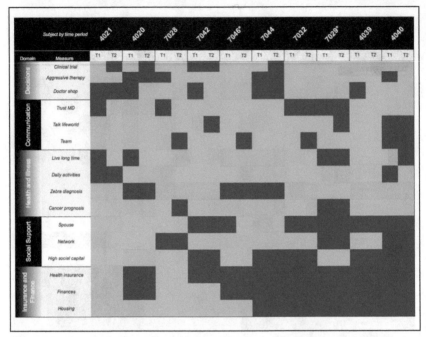

Figure 5. A sorted ethnoarray based on data from 10 participants in the Cancer Patient Deliberation Study. The "Key to Figures 3–6" on p. 288 provides additional information regarding the domains, measures, and color assignment.

single form of data (e.g., interviews or field notes). They might choose to deal with the question of inclusion differently as well. They might use formal linguistic tags to aid in categorization rather than relying on interpretive coding. "Uncoded" data (e.g., data that are not formally categorized according to substantive domains but are still associated with the columnar unit of analysis, such as individuals or neighborhoods) could be linked under a broad category labeled "other" (again, see Appendix A). Finally, researchers might decide that including all data for a person, site, and so on, is not feasible, ethical, or relevant. In this case, they would still be able to share summaries and still provide data beyond those in the traditional ethnographic report, but the array would not be inclusive. In short, like the quite varied notion of "coding," the array is a flexible tool whose use depends largely on researcher decisions and justifications (i.e., what to examine, how to measure it, and how to represent it) that parallel those found in other forms of social science (Cicourel 1964).

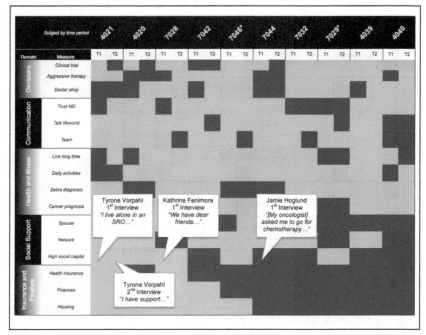

Figure 6. A sorted ethnoarray with selected quotations from linked data. The "Key to Figures 3–6" on p. 288 provides additional information regarding the domains, measures, and color assignment.

With a unit of analysis selected, inclusion criteria identified, and rows and columns defined and ordered, a final design decision concerns how to assign colors to the resultant cells in an analytically useful way. The goal of color coding in this array is not simply aesthetics; it is also to enable a visual summarization to facilitate examining data patterns. To this end, the model ethnoarray features a three-color matrix that indicates the degree to which a given characteristic is present (blue = less; gray = typical or unremarkable among study participants; red = more). These colors were based on the team's review, discussion, and interpretation of each patient's case and associated transcripts and field notes. That is to say, similar to the procedures used for deciding on data inclusion, color assignment in this particular example was based on the interpretations of fieldworkers who were deeply familiar with the site and individuals rather than formalistic procedures or automated approaches for text mining. Existing coding in our CAQDAS data set, which already tagged text according to themes of interest in the project, were used to

Domain	Measure	Color Assignment**
Decisions	Clinical trial	red = more aggressive therapy; blue = less aggressive
Decisions	Aggressive therapy	red = more doctor shopping or change in doctor; blue = relatively stable in doctor choice
Decisions	Doctor shop	red = more serious consideration of trial; blue = little consideration of a clinical trial
Communication	Trust MD	red = express/display trust in provider; blue = express/display mistrust in provider
Communication	Talk lifeworld	red = communication includes topics other than illness; blue = talk is only of cancer
Communication	Team	red = good provider-patient communication; blue = poor communication
Health and Illness	Live long time	red = live a long time; blue = end of life
Health and Illness	Daily activities	red = daily activities unaffected by illness; blue = daily activities are highly impacted
Health and Illness	Zebra diagnosis	red = unusual or rare condition; blue = unremarkable diagnosis
Health and Illness	Cancer prognosis	red = patient believes cancer is slow-growing; blue = patient believes cancer is fast-growing
Social Support	Spouse	red = highly involved spouse; blue = no spouse or spousal support available
Social Support	Network	red = large non-spouse network; blue = no non-spouse network
Social Support	High social capital	red = network w/high social capital; blue = lower capital in social network
Insurance and Finance	Health insurance	red = comprehensive medical insurance coverage; blue = poorer coverage
Insurance and Finance	Finances	red = finances are quite stable; blue = experiencing financial instability
Insurance and Finance	Housing	red = highly stable housing; blue = less housing stability including changes in housing

* Indicates participant is deceased
** Based on the interpretive procedures described in the text. Grey is typical for the sample of participants, red indicates higher or more intense than normal, blue indicates lower or less intense than typical.

Key to Figures 3–6. Overview of domains, measures, and color assignment.

help identify information about each cohort member and provide a level of confidence that we were not overlooking relevant data as we developed our interpretations of patients' experiences and understandings within the measures of each domain.

Embedding a traditional interpretation of rich ethnographic data within a structured tabular framework of domains and measures is, of course, only one approach to achieving a balance between more interpretive and formalistic approaches to analysis.[10] Other approaches may involve an explicit scoring procedure for determining cell color, for example, density or co-occurrence of codes from a CAQDAS database, linguistic algorithms, or word frequency counts. Color assignment schemes could be developed to indicate the absence of data for a particular theme of interest, for example, to capture different degrees of theoretical saturation or other types of unevenness in data collection that must be addressed in analysis. The tabular format may not be suitable for some projects, including those that do not have a clearly identified unit of analysis or take a more humanistic approach. Still, even within the broad spectrum of approaches falling under the umbrella of sociological participant-observation, many studies maintain a clear unit of analysis and examine variation within and across groups or contexts (cf. Abramson 2015; Cicourel 1968; Dohan 2003; Lareau 2011; Lutfey and Freese 2005; Sallaz 2009; Sánchez-Jankowski 2008).

Inset 1 outlines several different approaches to color assignment and illustrates how the ethnoarray can be used with a variety of analytical styles, from formal rules geared toward the quantification of observed behavior to flexible integration of interpretative insights. The ability to integrate and even combine these divergent approaches exemplifies the ethnoarray's ability to accommodate different analytical approaches, goals, and styles from diverse intellectual and epistemic traditions.

INSET 1: STRATEGIES FOR COLOR ASSIGNMENT

A fundamental task in constructing any ethnoarray is deciding upon a procedure for assigning cell color. A variety of techniques are possible, with different implications for different methodological approaches. Three common strategies drawn from existing forms of qualitative analyses include the following:

1. Analyst imputation and interpretation
2. Counting (frequency or co-occurrence)
3. Scale construction

It is important to note that just as these strategies represent different approaches for representing ethnographic data, color assignment does not necessarily privilege theory testing or deductive inference (although it may facilitate such an approach). As we illustrate below, color assignment can summarize valences of text without reducing it to quantitative information and can thus remain connected to the underlying narratives and subject-centered accounts. It can also be used as an exploratory as well as an explanatory tool. In either case, color assignment is a key part of making sense of observations, seeing how they are related, and communicating findings. Yet it does not devalue or replace the underlying qualitative data.[11]

In the interpretive strategy, an analyst (or a group of analysts) uses his or her own understanding of the social scene being analyzed, as well as judgment and experience based on immersion in the field, to constitute measures and domains and to assign colors to cells. This is the approach we followed in the mock-up ethnoarrays shown in Figures 3 to 6. Ethnographic data have often been analyzed using interpretive approaches that focus on meanings and the explanations that people give for their actions (e.g., Geertz 2000), which are reflected in this mode of color assignment. These analyses often do not rely on explicit rules but, rather, focus on creating a coherent understanding based on research subjects' actions and accounts. Interpretative strategies have also been formalized. In several strains of grounded theory, patterns within ethnographic data are identified inductively and leveraged to construct theories or explanations of social phenomenon (Glaser and Strauss 1967; Strauss and Corbin 1990). A grounded theory approach to color assignment might start by grounding emergent measures and domains. Although interpretative approaches typically rely on researchers' assessments rather than formal rules to assign colors, pattern analysis of the ethnoarray can still be done in a systematic or even rule-bound way (as in the PtDelib example below). A potential drawback of interpretive strategies is that some audiences may find their procedures opaque and, therefore, the findings unconvincing. Interpretative strategies, which necessarily involve substantial amounts of manual analysis, may also prove more burdensome for researchers than approaches that automate the color assignment processes.

The second strategy for color assignment relies on counting: calculations of the adjusted or unadjusted frequency of codes. Because the raw number of occurrences for the given outcome, factor, or phrase being measured is often less important than its likelihood to come up under particular circumstances in ethnographic research, analysts may find density or co-occurrence functions preferable to raw counts. An application of this approach is found in forms of conversation analysis that focus on the semiotics, words, and meanings of ethnographic data via procedures governed by formal rules about phrasing patterns, turns of speech, or thematic proximity. A conversation analysis approach to color assignment would use formal rules, for example, how frequently a phrase appears in a fixed segment of the database (a co-occurrence density function) or the proximity of key words. This approach could inform statistical techniques for automated color assignment so that arrays could be constructed without an analyst having read through all the data. This could also potentially facilitate approaches such as QNA (Franzosi et al. 2012) or topic modeling (Mohr and Bogdanov 2013; Mohr et al. 2013). The risk with frequency and co-occurrence functions is the increased possibility of generating erroneous associations based on statistical rather than substantive associations (i.e., false positives and the validity issues associated with automated imputation).

The third way of assigning colors is to construct scales using a series of measures. This approach comes closest to replicating strategies most commonly used in quantitative social science. Color assignment could reflect nominal, ordinal, or interval scales related to observable and measurable acts. In the PtDelib study, a scalar approach might assign colors on the basis of whether a cancer patient sees a doctor when she feels a lump in her breast (nominal), a person's highest academic degree (ordinal), or how many times clinical trials are mentioned to a potential enrollee (interval). In preliminary tests, with PtDelib data, we have found that when these measures are binary and comparatively objective (e.g., whether someone went to a doctor), the reliability of color assignment increases. Pattern analysis of the ethnoarrays produced from scalar color assignment can leverage the informational richness created through the use of nominal, ordinal, or interval measures. This increases the specificity with which results can be reported and may improve the credibility of reported findings for some audiences. On the other hand, this approach involves a substantial risk: the process of manipulating data into scales may make it harder to appreciate or interrogate the contextual richness that spurred ethnographic engagement in the first place. That is, it forces rigidity on the data that can impede connecting with the object of study (Cicourel 1964). Ethnoarrays may thus reasonably be seen as a complement to, rather than a replacement of, existing ethnographic approaches.

In practice, analysts likely will experiment with and combine approaches to color assignment. For instance, the PtDelib study primarily relies on an interpretative approach for color assignment, but we specified some domains and measures deductively, and when possible (e.g., when constructing measures of social standing), we developed simple scales to govern color assignment. If widely adopted, it would be important to investigate the advantages and drawbacks of developing arrays that shared common parameters and allowed cross-study comparisons.

3.2. Reading the Ethnoarray: The Experiences of Wayne Burley

Once constructed, the ethnoarray can be used in numerous ways to understand and represent large volumes of data. For analysts interested in examining and visually representing the experiences of specific patients to understand an outcome (e.g., whether they enter a clinical trial), data can be read along a single column or across the adjacent columns of a single patient's baseline and follow-up data. This can be useful to both contextualize interpretive insights and to provide information about the validity of inferences drawn using statistical methods that can group like trajectories such as sequence analysis (SA).

For example, the first columns of Figure 4 illustrate the experiences of Wayne Burley[12] (the array shows his study identifier number, 4020) derived from analysis of two in-depth interviews with him, an interview with his live-in girlfriend Heather Okeefe, and direct observation of two appointments around the time of the interviews with his oncologist, Antonio Akin, who was also interviewed (as well as observed in numerous other interactions with patients and colleagues). Wayne and Heather had been living on opposite coasts prior to his cancer diagnosis, and over the course of several months, he lived for short periods in three cities as he sought diagnosis and treatment for his cancer (a rare form of the disease; note the red cell under _Health and Illness>Zebra diagnosis_). He finally settled in northern California to make it easier for Heather to care for him, and the couple moved from a small one-bedroom apartment (where we conducted his baseline interview) to a larger two-bedroom apartment by the time of his follow-up interview (at which point we also interviewed Heather). Given this history, we characterized his _Insurance and Finance>Housing_ as relatively unstable with respect to the others in our cohort at the baseline interview (blue cell) and more typical by follow-up (gray cell). Wayne had a long career with a government employer, retired early, and had begun a second career teaching public school when his cancer was discovered. Although no longer working because of his illness, Wayne's employment history provided a stable pension and generous health benefits; we thus classified his _Insurance and Finance>Finances_ and _Insurance and_

Finance>Health insurance as higher than typical (red cells). Our interpretation of Wayne's situation in the domains of *Social Support, Health and Illness, Communication*, and *Decisions*, drawn in comparison with dozens of other study participants, can be read in a similar fashion by examining the color of each relevant cell.

Wayne and Heather's first visit with Dr. Akin was among the most contentious we have seen in the PtDelib study. Wayne relocated to northern California in part because Dr. Akin is acknowledged as an expert in his unusual cancer, but Wayne also received treatment from other oncologists. Before meeting Wayne and Heather for the first time, Dr. Akin reviewed Wayne's medical record in the clinic hub room (a physicians' work room out of earshot of patients) and commented to one of his colleagues that the other oncologists had been overly aggressive "cowboys" in their treatment approach. Although frank commentary is the norm in the hub room, we observed Dr. Akin repeat his "cowboy" comment to Wayne and Heather in the exam room. Their interactions became tense as a result, something Wayne and Heather commented on after the encounter. They both discussed this uncomfortable visit during their interviews but acknowledged that their relationship with Dr. Akin improved with time. They characterized him as a "straight talker" whose frank assessments of Wayne's progress and prospects were valuable, and they brushed aside his more insensitive remarks. In the ethnoarray, this trajectory in their relationship is reflected in the *Communication* domain, which we coded blue at baseline (indicating atypically poor communication) and gray (typical communication) at follow-up.

The ethnoarray also reflects other changes between baseline (T1) and follow-up (T2) observations. Initially Wayne's daily activities continued uninterrupted, and he believed that his life span would be unaffected by his illness (*Health and Illness>Daily activities* and *Health and Illness>Live long time*). At follow-up, he was experiencing substantial fatigue and was unable to do many of the things he had enjoyed just a few months previously (we characterized this as a blue cell for *Health and Illness>Daily activities*); like some of the patients in our study, at this point he acknowledged that his cancer would not be cured (*Health and Illness>Live long time* is now gray). Finally, examining the *Decisions* domain, we note that Wayne remained aggressive in his approach to his illness but that he seemed to be less interested in finding other doctors to manage his treatment; at his follow-up interview, he said he planned to stick with Dr. Akin. Although Wayne initially had said he was not interested in participating in a clinical trial during his baseline interview, a few months later he had begun to actively research trials to join (*Decisions>Clinical trial* is gray at T1 and red at T2). The resulting representation in the array summarizes key aspects of Wayne's trajectory and provides a useful visualization that helps contextualize his experience relative to other subjects. This also facilitates further pattern analysis and possibilities for data sharing that we now examine.[13]

3.3 *Relational Mapping*

The colored cells of the array can be used not only for reading narratives but also for mapping and understanding relationships among actors, institutions, and concepts, a fundamental goal for many ethnographic approaches. Take, for example, Wayne Burley's relationship with his physician. The array visualization summarizes that Wayne's trust in his physician changed over time, and on the basis of preliminary study data, it appears other patients have experienced similar shifts. Moreover, the array allows analysts to readily see that these relationships of trust occur not only between patients and their physicians but also in patients' experiences as members of the health care team that includes physicians, nurses, and other health care providers. Analytic memos provide one way of documenting and interpreting an individual patient's experiences of these relationships. The array provides a way to supplement those analyses by considering broader contextual elements that might also influence these experiences.[14]

Our preliminary analyses suggest that patients' experiences of trust and team membership reflect their estimations of physicians' competence and the congruence between clinicians' treatment preferences and their own, but these factors do not operate in a simple or mechanistic way. The array allows analysts to examine patients' experiences of trust and team membership within a much broader context, for example, whether their cancer is affecting their daily activities, how the progression of illness over time shapes these relationships, and how patients' own beliefs about whether their illnesses are life limiting color the trust and connection patients feel with their clinicians. For Wayne Burley, the progression of his illness, its impact on his daily activities, and the exhaustion of available treatments appeared to reshape his engagement with his oncologist and care team. Our preliminary data suggest that

Burley is not alone in this experience of illness progression—an element of physiology that can force patients of diverse values and expectations to rethink coping, engagement with family caregivers, and their relationship to the illness of cancer itself.

3.4. *Arranging and Sorting to Examine Patterns*

In addition to summarizing and representing ethnographic data and facilitating the interpretation of relationships, arrays can help bridge quantitative and qualitative analytical techniques by allowing researchers to combine statistical techniques for pattern recognition with interpretation of the underlying field notes and transcripts. It is important to recognize that although observations are tagged, they are not "reduced" to numbers or codes. That is to say, code patterns are meant to be orienting rather than reductive.[15] Depending on how they are sorted, ethnoarrays can also help facilitate either *explanatory* or *confirmatory* analysis. Examining cells within a column still facilitates interpretation of patient experiences or narratives, and sorting the ethnoarray can bolster interpretative insights through *exploratory* logics, for example, helping reveal or stimulate interpretations in the data that the analyst might have otherwise missed while reviewing or searching field notes and transcripts. That is, arrays can also be useful in examining whether a typology or pattern implied by a researcher or theory maps onto his or her data. Like the microarray on which it is based, the sorted ethnoarray would ideally allow analysts to identify patterns of similarity and difference in data and explore how these patterns resolve and translate into socially meaningful behaviors and theoretically meaningful categories and constructs.

Dating back to the popularization of exploratory data analysis (Tukey 1977), numerous quantitative techniques have been used to identify patterns in data that lack the strong sampling assumptions, claims to directionality, or assumptions about generalization that are typically associated with techniques like ordinary least squares regression. For instance, PCA, SA, latent structure analysis (LSA), multiple correspondence analysis (MCA), qualitative comparative analysis, and various applications of linguistic algorithms for mining large quantities of text data each provide useful ways of investigating patterns of colored cells that might be fruitfully integrated with the array approach. An in-depth discussion of the procedures involved in these techniques can be found elsewhere. However, it is worth noting that PCA, SA, LSA, and MCA are the most directly comparable with the simpler model of clustering we use in Figure 5. PCA is commonly used in biological microarrays to define groups on the basis of nominal, ordinal, or interval gene expression data. PCA requires only a shared and directional scale. LSA and MCA allow categorical data to be clustered without assuming directional scale. These techniques are more common in the social sciences. SA groups like sequences and trajectories of longitudinal data. Because any of these approaches can be applied to ethnoarray data, researchers must decide which approach to clustering (if any) is most useful for their projects, as well as whether the use of interval approaches provides more worthwhile insights than the categorical approaches. Depending on how domains are measured and organized within the ethnoarray, statistical patterns revealed via these techniques could address a range of research questions such as ascertainment of temporal sequence, explication of causal mechanisms, and discovery of new grounded-theoretical constructs.

In our mock-up, we used a simple scale and sorting procedure based on interpretive color assignment to show how inductive techniques for pattern recognition might be useful even in interpretive analyses. In Figure 4, patients are arranged arbitrarily. In Figure 5, the ethnoarray is based on patients' structural characteristics (the bottom two domains, *Social Support* and *Insurance and Finance*) to examine whether and how those characteristics might shape pathways and tendencies related to seeking aggressive care. Each cell in these domains was assigned an ordinal value on the basis of color (red = 1; grey = .5; blue = 0). For each patient, an index value was calculated as the sum of the 12 cells in the two domains at times 1 and 2; the index had a potential range of 0 to 12; the actual range in the 10-patient array in Figure 4 was 1 to 11.5. The ethnoarray was then sorted according to these scores. Patients with higher index scores had their columns of data moved to the right side of the array; those with lower scores had their columns placed toward the left. Thus, reading Figure 5 from left to right roughly corresponds to examining experiences of patients with fewer to greater social structural resources.[16]

In the case of the PtDelib project, prior research had suggested that more advantaged patients were more likely to be seen as "good study patients" whom clinician-investigators targeted for clinical trials recruitment (Joseph and Dohan 2009), and the ethnoarray provides an opportunity to examine this expectation in our preliminary PtDelib data. To examine the plausibility of this notion, we turned to the clustered array. The patients on the left side of Figure 5 tend to have less security in terms of *Insurance and Finance* and weaker *Social Support*. The distribution of the red cells in the *Decision* domain (at the top of the ethnoarray) may suggest that these patients are more aggressive in their pursuit of treatment and participation in clinical research. Given that we have arranged the domains in causal-temporal order, analysts and readers can then scan the array to try to identify patterns of color in the "intervening" domains—*Health and Illness* and *Communication*—that might suggest plausible social mechanisms. Analysts can then examine the underlying data (in this case interview transcripts and field notes) to see if these associations are likely real or spurious and to explain *how* the linking mechanisms operate in specific social contexts, a classic goal of ethnography.[17]

3.5 Representing Data

Ethnoarrays have the advantage of being able to summarize large amounts of data in a compact yet flexible form, a key feature of many forms of sociological analysis that has been underdeveloped in many ethnographic approaches. Figures 3 to 6 each summarize data from hundreds of pages of interview transcripts and participant-observation field notes from multiple sites. Just the data from Wayne Burley include dozens of pages of text—too much evidence to include in a journal article or even a monograph. As in the microarray, each color-coded cell reflects a rich storehouse of meaningful information. The color assignment both summarizes the data as an interpretable visual representation and enables new analytics, such as using clusters to identify new patterns in data or verify whether the typologies ethnographers create map onto the underlying data they represent. These visual summaries are meant to supplement, but do not replace, the narratives that form the standard for ethnographic representation.

Arrays also provide new possibilities for sharing information. Ideally, the data underlying cells could be bundled and shared along with the array, and interested readers could explore the underlying data for any array cell. We refer to this type of array as a "data-linked" ethnoarray, in contrast to the arrays shown in Figures 3 to 5, which we characterize as "flat" (i.e., a noninteractive summary representation). We do not yet have the technology to produce and publish a data-linked array, though tabular and XML output functions of current CAQDAS platforms could facilitate this production, as we discuss and illustrate below. Inset 2 presents segments of underlying data from interviews with three participants that informed our coding of the *High Social Capital* measure in the ethnoarray. Figure 6 illustrates how these excerpts are situated within the ethnoarray. In a fully data-linked array, each cell of the ethnoarray would be associated with one or more fragments of ethnographic data, perhaps a quotation from an interview, a document, or an extract from a field note. Here, we use quotations from patient interviews to illustrate the kind of data that would underlie each cell in a data-linked array.

INSET 2: EXCERPTS OF UNDERLYING DATA LINKED TO THE SAMPLE ARRAY

Kathrine Fenimore (ID 7028): GRAY—coded as typical social capital: We have dear friends at church and just dear life friends that pray with me, and then that has a ripple effect. I mean, they ask others to pray and I've got just so many people, and then people at work, you know, too, that pray and that are wonderful friends as well. And just good support that way.

  Tyrone Vorpahl (ID 4021): Change from BLUE (low for this study) at T1 to GRAY (typical for this study) at T2; Baseline/T1 (summer, 2011; BLUE): I live alone in an SRO and it's just a miserable environment. I want to relocate. I want to move someplace where I can live with family and friends. I have options right now . . . one of those options from the beginning were to go to [a city in this state] . . . and looking at—you know, my home is, where I'm from but [that State] is like, from my research, the most difficult state of all so I kind of ruled that out. And then the other option was [another state], 'cause I have close life-long friends there that I can go live with in a house outside of, you know, out of the city with like a bathroom and—I mean, just like I can live in a family home environment as opposed to in an SRO. So I'm trying to weigh—That's kind of a big part of my decision-making.

  Follow-up/T2 (fall, 2011, GRAY): [Fieldworker note: since baseline interview, 4021 has moved to the third state mentioned above.] I have support in terms of like, you know, they're just there every day.

> You know, just somebody to say good morning and goodnight and have dinner with every night. And they're very concerned and doing everything, basically, you know, and dealing with my insanity. You know, I've been going through, like I said, kind of a roller coaster and they've been very tolerant of my sort of roller coaster emotions and my depression and anxiety I've been dealing with and sort of tolerant of that and kind of very accommodating in terms of opening up their home to me and letting me live here with them.
>
> *Jamie Hoglund (ID 7044): RED — network with higher social capital:* [My oncologist] asked me to go for chemotherapy and I asked my neighbor, who is a kidney transplant surgeon . . . he consulted with I think four or five other doctors. Half of them told me to go for the chemotherapy and the other half, including the liver transplant surgeon—not the one who actually operated on me but one of them who is on the team—they told me don't even bother to go for chemotherapy 'cause I should just live out the last few months in comfort instead of suffering.

Data-linked arrays are dynamic and interactive and thus a poor fit for paper. However, modern computer interfaces are well suited to publishing and sharing such arrays, and we are working on developing the tools and techniques that will allow the construction and electronic publication of data-linked ethnoarrays. Using such an application, readers could explore particular cells or groups of cells within the ethnoarray by reading through the underlying data. Such an interface would also allow readers to sort or reorder the ethnoarray's rows (domains) and columns (cases) using various procedures to highlight or discover patterns. Computer applications and tablet "apps" would ideally allow the reader to navigate a data-linked ethnoarray as one currently navigates online maps: clicking or tapping on cells to reveal the underlying data, zooming in and out of the ethnoarray to focus on particular patterns of data, dragging domains and cases to explore alternative patterns in the data. However, before implementing a data-linked array, important questions of how qualitative data might be adequately deidentified for sharing must be addressed, an issue we discuss in the next section. These discussions are consistent with calls for more transparent "open-source" social sciences (e.g., Freese 2007) and the shift toward digital models of publication that can facilitate new connections between scholarship and underlying data.

4. IMPLICATIONS

The ethnoarray's visual approach to presenting and analyzing data may provide new opportunities for work at the boundary of ethnography and other forms of social scientific scholarship. In constructing an ethnoarray, researchers can decide between and perhaps even balance various analytical approaches when they define conceptual domains and measures, assign colors to array cells, and bundle (or not) data with the array. Analysts can use arrays to scan large amounts of ethnographic data and to explore the data in new ways—explorations that may reveal new narratives, elucidate patterns in the data reflective of social mechanisms, add broader context to individual experiences and events, or suggest contingencies or limitations related to study data. If data are appropriately anonymized, they can be bundled with the array and shared so readers can examine the ethnographic evidence more directly and probe cell-to-data links. Providing access to data and analysis in this way helps readers see patterns, understand the analyst's interpretations, evaluate reliability, and gain a sense of an argument's scope and grounding. The flexibility of the ethnoarray—in presenting and analyzing data as well as providing readers with additional options for exploring data—provides the beginnings of an approach that can help make the vast troves of ethnographic data more available to diverse audiences without resorting to reductionism.

We now examine some implications of arrays for ethnography, including the ethnoarray's potential to spur and cultivate a novel research infrastructure, opportunities for new avenues in claims-making and evaluation, the potential scope of ethnography in large studies and its impact on the traditional solo ethnographer, as well as some key limits of this approach.

4.1. *Research Infrastructure to Support Ethnographic Arrays*

A robust ethnoarray research infrastructure would include (1) computer, Web, or tablet applications to facilitate the creation, distribution, and examination of arrays; (2) policies and procedures for anonymizing ethnographic data; and (3) servers to store and share data. Software to support ethnoarrays would differ from—though ideally integrate with and extend the capabilities of—presently available analysis programs. Current software helps experts manipulate data using technical procedures. CAQDAS platforms help analysts code, sort, and explore data as well as tag or memo excerpts that will ultimately be presented to readers. Statistical analysis software allows researchers to fit models and produce tables or graphs. These packages all focus on manipulating data and producing output, and in most instances the output, not the underlying data, is all that is distributed to audiences. Array software would include similar tools to manipulate and analyze data (e.g., clustering and search functions) as well as provide a new form of output in "flat arrays." However, this software would also provide a mechanism for ethnographers to distribute findings. In short, ethnoarray software would help ethnographers not only *produce* output but also *be* part of their output and allow them to engage in communal research activities currently common to quantitative research such as archiving data and replicating analysis.[18]

As a data management tool, ethnoarray software would help analysts link data to array cells and to arrange and rearrange the cells to explore alternate definitions of domains or configurations of cases. Links between data and cells occur when assigning cell color (we describe multiple strategies for color assignment in Inset 1). Ideally, applications would remain agnostic about the process of color assignment to allow analysts flexibility in how they link cells to data. This would also allow analysts the freedom to arrange the data set on their own terms, albeit in a way that aids in making their work more transparent. Some analysts might rely on interpretation alone, while others might develop an automated formal process for coding, sorting, and linking data to cells. No matter how the data-cell link is created, however, array applications should help analysts rearrange data to examine patterns or explore new relationships.

The ethnoarray also allows the representation of ethnographic data in two key ways. First, analysts can publish arrays online or in printed articles or monographs. Used this way ethnoarrays, like any other visual representation of data such as graphs or charts, allow researchers a way to summarize a large volume of information. For some researchers, such a summary might represent a key finding of an ethnographic study. Other ethnographers might use the arrays color-coded tabular representation to supplement interpretative analyses of field notes, interview transcripts, and other data that are presented using more traditional narrative approaches. The second way is to share an entire array, including cells and linked data, with readers. Readers then have the ability to examine the array, to iteratively explore and arrange the cells, and to examine the links between cells and data.

Such dissemination strategies differ substantially from the dominant ethnographic practice of publishing monographs and research articles with solely narrative evidence, but it is not unprecedented. The Human Relations Area Files (HRAF), a nonprofit international consortium, aimed to provide a resource of ethnographic data focused on comparative societal analysis, and full text from early ethnographies exists online. However, to provide comparable data across societies, HRAF used rigid coding and analytical constructs, and the archive has been interpreted as a historical document illustrating the challenges—and perhaps folly—of a cumulative approach to knowledge production in cultural analyses (Clifford and Marcus 1986; Marcus 1998). The ethnoarray model shares HRAF's interest in making data available to a wide community of scholars, but scholars who use the ethnoarray need not format or categorize their data according to rigid preexisting conceptual schemata. They need not even agree about epistemic assumptions underlying ethnographic scholarship. They need only to specify what they do. In this sense only, data-linked ethnoarrays are more akin to publicly available quantitative data sets, such as the Integrated Public Use Microdata Series (IPUMS) or the General Social Survey, than the HRAF.

Researchers could produce array data sets as a part of their scholarly activities, but they need not adhere to a unified epistemic logic in doing so. They could then provide data sets to the sociological community with full documentation of how they were produced but without placing rigid boundaries on how the data are intellectually deployed. Similarly, data-linked ethnoarrays would not follow the rigid proscriptions of HRAF standardization but would instead exist as a series of independent data sets. Access could be provided via Web portals such as those seen at the Interuniversity Consortium for Political and Social Research (ICPSR). Researchers would ultimately have to decide if and how to reuse data sets and whether they were comparable with other data sets.[19]

This raises the question of how to handle data governance. Sharing IPUMS- or ICPSR-housed data relies on policies for depositing, storing, and distributing data that ensure the safety and rights of research participants. Sharing arrayed ethnographic data would require producing new policies or extending current policies. Although data warehouses that host qualitative data are beginning to emerge, such policies are in their nascent stages, and the lack of a shared format for summary representation and sharing of ethnographic data remains a major limitation. Providing a comprehensive solution is beyond the scope of this article, but the development of ethnoarray approaches could potentially advance work in this arena. Policies for protecting microlevel quantitative social science data or protected health information may offer some further guidance for ethnographic policies.

Ethnographers' own habits and practices regarding treatment of informants and other data, which have generally been passed along as craft rather than codified in policy, would need to be made more explicit. Sharing ethnographic data via arrays would also require a physical computing infrastructure, which could be provided via Internet-connected servers. Finally, even if the secure research infrastructure developed to accommodate arrays were never used to share data-linked ethnoarrays, it might prove to be a valuable resource for ethnographers to store, analyze, and reanalyze their own data, especially as the ethnoarray provides an analytical approach for linking data from multiple studies and points in time. In other words, although the array approach does not provide a universal solution to the challenges of sharing ethnographic data, it does provide a tool that can advance discussions about if and how this aim might eventually be reached.[20]

4.2. *Using Arrays to Support Ethnographic Claims-Making*

Evaluating ethnographic claims can be circuitous. Often, ethnographers collect and analyze data by themselves, and they can share only a fraction of their data with readers. Readers rely on self-reports of how field notes, interviews, and other data were collected; how these data were analyzed; and how insights were obtained and conclusions drawn. Ethnographers have long recognized that their authority derives in part from these reports of fieldwork and readers' trust in those reports (Rabinow 1997; Whyte 1993). Marked by interpretation and iteration, ethnographic data often gain legitimacy when the insights they produce appear plausible and comprehensible—when, in essence, the data take on the appearance of speaking for themselves. Thus, the quality of their presentation—including richly evoked empirical context and well-developed theoretical framing—helps establish the legitimacy of the data that produce those results.[21]

For many, a description of research procedures is a necessary first step, but an inadequate proxy, for a more direct examination of the links between data and claims. The limitations of this proxy become apparent when ethnographers debate whether the data support the claims made and even whether the data were collected. Such debates can flounder on irreconcilable divergences about the contextual or historical specificity of evidence and argument (Boelen 1992; Duneier 2002; Orlandella 1992; Sánchez-Jankowski 2002; Wacquant 2002). Sometimes a lack of standardization is associated with a lack of rigor. The combination of the requirement of trust without access to data to reconstruct analyses and the often charged nature of ethnography's research topics can lead to scholarly exchanges that generate as much heat as light. Given that the ethnographer is the data collection instrument, it is not entirely surprising that controversies over the validity of ethnographic claims can devolve into attacks on analysts' legitimacy or even morality (cf. Duneier 2002, 2006; Katz 2010; Wacquant 2002). Explicitly revealing how analysts link data and claims and encouraging readers to assess how the former sustains the latter could provide a more productive dialogue. We believe the ethnoarray represents a potentially useful tool to support ethnographic claims-making by facilitating such examinations. In Appendix B, we provide an example of how an array might be applied to examine the claims made in a well-known comparative ethnography.

Ethnoarrays can facilitate a more detailed examination of claims-making and, ideally, generate explicit discussion of how ethnographic data are invoked for causal or narrative purposes. This does not put the research community on an inexorable road toward an ethnographic equivalent of a $p < .05$ threshold for theoretical or substantive significance or even the conceptual standardization of HRAF, nor do ethnoarrays necessarily privilege causally or hypothesis-oriented research. Rather, we hope new tools can provide a way to examine how and why interpretations overlap or differ. Such discussions may provoke new ways of exploring fertile ethnographic questions.

4.3. *The Scope of Ethnography*

The ethnoarray may provide new capacities for analysis, but these capacities may come at the price of new burdens on those who choose to use the approach. A historical characteristic of ethnographic practice has been minimal barriers to entry; the lone ethnographer requires little more than time, a notebook, and access to enter the field and potentially contribute to the literature. In contrast, developing and contributing to ethnoarrays introduces new burdens for data collection and analysis. Consider the potential new burdens of an ethnoarray approach for ethnographers who conduct participant observation. When lone ethnographers collect notes in the field, they rely on their own judgment to decide what to observe and document.[22] Although many approaches encourage specifying a unit of analysis and identifying conceptual domains, this is not universally the case. Field notes may include everything from contextualized individual behaviors, to reflexive musings, to researcher descriptions of physical space (Emerson et al. 1995). In the midst of fieldwork, researchers decide what types of data to record and how to record it, but they rarely have the time, energy, or foresight to completely document how these decisions were made. Key background information in the form of schemata and headnotes may still remain unarticulated (Sánchez-Jankowski 2002). Even arrays thoughtfully constructed to include research questions, domains, and units of analysis may be incomplete when it comes to crucial details of how and why particular data were collected or recorded. Teams of ethnographic researchers may strive for more consistency in their procedures for conducting and documenting field sites, but the team's shared understandings of the site and the project may not be formally documented. In short, ethnographers currently write field notes for themselves or for small audiences of fellow fieldworkers. They consider broader audiences when designing a study, when deciding what data to collect, or when writing up results. But the ethnographers themselves are the usual audience for most study data that remains largely private.

In contrast, data bound for arrays must continually consider a broader audience. The broader audience may be unknown, but generally it does not know the field site. Data included in an ethnoarray must be clear to a naïve audience lacking the presumed *Verstehen* of the ethnographer. They must have a defined unit of analysis. Formal field notes may thus require greater attention to detail and context, be longer, and take more time to write. They may contain greater redundancies than field notes that are destined for more traditional ethnographic uses, and ethnographers may feel self-conscious about array-bound notes. In short, ethnographers producing arrays may collect data differently than ethnographers producing traditional monographs or articles.

Using arrays also requires analytical transformations after the field data have been collected. Developing and distributing a flat array means using computer software, while using a data-linked array requires a series of steps to anonymize and secure data. These steps have the potential to make ethnography more expensive and less nimble, and it seems certain that anonymizing data for use in data-linked arrays will lead to the development of new research tasks, infrastructure, and personnel that could change aspects of ethnographic production for those using the array method.[23]

5. CONCLUSIONS

In an influential article, Jeremy Freese (2007) described "the need to move beyond intermittent discussions of replication to standards of collective action" (p. 220) as a key step toward ushering in a more transparent sociology. The fact that Freese and colleagues are even able to engage in a coherent conversation around these issues points to a luxury that ethnographers do not necessarily possess—basic shared assumptions about the nature, language, and goals of the research enterprise. Although most quantitative researchers typically share concerns with replicability, reliability, generalization, inference, and validity, ethnographers differ remarkably in how they relate to these concepts and traditional social science frameworks more broadly. Consequently, those interested in issues of openness, process, and visualization must first confront not only the daunting methodological challenges this entails but also the lack of consensus and persistence of qualitative "tribalism" in the scholarly field (Lamont and Swidler 2014). Tensions among ethnographers with different epistemic approaches are intellectually legitimate, but ideally these tensions should not preclude attempts to address shared practical issues. Despite their differences, ethnographers from various social science traditions must each grapple with the complex logistical challenges of analyzing and presenting context-rich observations of meaningful human action. Most would like to speak to larger audiences, and some would even like a civil means of talking to one another. For ethnographers, developing tools for these ends is an important precursor to enhancing transparency.

In this article, we introduced the ethnoarray, an interactive visual approach for analyzing, representing, and sharing ethnographic data that we argue is consistent with enhanced transparency. We argued that the ethnoarray approach provides tools for addressing common challenges that face many sociological ethnographers as they seek to manage and analyze the rich, context-dependent data gathered through fieldwork.

We then discussed a number of technical considerations in developing an ethnoarray—how an analyst might define domains and measures, assign colors to cells, sort or reorder an array, interpret patterns within or across columns, link data to arrays, and so on—and how these techniques can potentially open new possibilities for sociological ethnography, particularly when used in conjunction with traditional narrative methods of presenting data. We provided a model to illustrate how an ethnoarray might be constructed.

It is important to reiterate a key limitation here: this tool requires further refinement. Our mock-up is small and noninteractive because of the need to outline its premises. It is also constrained by the limitations of the print medium. A functioning ethnoarray would include both finer levels of detail so patterns would be more striking and instructive as well as interactive links that would allow analysts to drill down to the data to which the patterns refer. It is also clear in the discussion of the mock-up that while the ethnoarray may provide a useful tool for managing or analyzing data, it cannot "solve" the more fundamental epistemic divides separating different types of ethnographic practice. Nor do we try to use it for these ends. Rather, we hope it will serve as a bridge that allows conversation across at least some subdisciplinary chasms.

Even as we bear these limitations in mind, we note that the fundamental goal of the ethnoarray reflects a core tenet of many ethnographic approaches: providing a way to bring readers close to the social phenomenon in question so they can appreciate its context, complexity, and contingency. "When assessing evidence," Tufte (1997) noted, "it is helpful to see the full data matrix, all observations for all variables, those private numbers from which the public displays are constructed. No telling what will turn up" (p. 45). Showing the "full data matrix" from an ethnographic study is likely impossible, but the principle that more data are preferable to fewer nevertheless applies. The ethnoarray provides a way of showing readers more information from the field. It allows them to discover and explore patterns in that information, adding context and breadth to specific observations. In this way, it is a tool that may help analysts and readers turn up new insights and one that may help them make sense of the richness and complexity of the social world using visual tools that are essential in other methods (Moody and Healy 2014), but which ethnographers have been slower to adopt. A fully developed ethnoarray may even help researchers and readers share ethnographic data sets to allow deeper engagement and understanding. To paraphrase Geertz (2000), the eth-noarray approach can potentially provide scholars and readers with an enhanced ability to converse, even if the end result is only the ability to vex one another with greater precision. In this capacity, it may pro-vide another tool in the pantheon of pluralistic techniques for social inquiry that enables communication and provides ethnographers with a platform to address shared challenges and may perhaps in the pro-cess even begin to challenge the growing tribalism found in qualita-tive methodology (Lamont and Swidler 2014).

APPENDIX A

How an Ethnoarray Can Employ Units of Analysis Other than the Individual

The sample arrays in the main text focus on examining differences and simila-rities in individual trajectories using both interviews and field observations. Columns in these examples represent individuals (see again Figure 3) or indi-viduals by time (Figures 4–6). However, as we noted earlier, this need not be the case. The array was designed to work with any form of data that assumes a basic structure (e.g., the structure has a unit of analysis and analytical domains or measures). This appendix provides a brief illustration using data from a recent comparative ethnographic work.

In *The End Game: How Inequality Shapes Our Final Years*, Abramson (2015) examined how persistent socioeconomic, racial, and gender divides in the United States create an unequal "end game" that structures the later years of the aging U.S. population. In doing so, the work provides a lens for examin-ing both the social stratification of later life and the lifelong consequences of inequality in the United States. The book is based primarily on two and a half years of comparative ethnographic research conducted in four urban neighbor-hoods and examines, among other issues, how disparate social contexts and resources shape the way people from different neighborhoods and backgrounds can respond to the shared challenges of "old age." One finding is that the abil-ity of older people to navigate the physical spaces of the real world (sidewalks, buildings, etc.) is an important form of inequality that stratifies how different groups can manage everyday life. This is conditioned in part by disparities in seniors' health (which reflect the stratified timing and severity of physical chal-lenges). However, it is also powerfully shaped by an unequal distribution of services and contextual material resources available to networks of people in

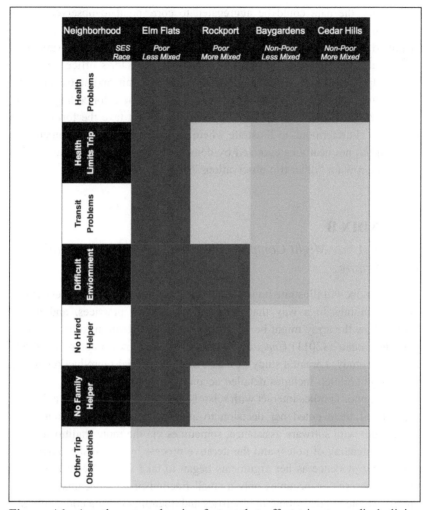

Figure A1. An ethnoarray showing factors that affect trips to medical clinics. Data from *The End Game: How Inequality Shapes Our Final Years* (Abramson 2015).

different neighborhoods—a finding generated using traditional field observations of neighborhood settings such as housing complexes.

An array approach could use this participant-observation data to support the claim of neighborhood-level contextual variation by examining how neighborhood context and other factors affect seniors' ability to navigate the physical environment and make visits to a medical clinic. Although this outcome affects individuals, the data could be aggregated to correspond to observed events nested in the four neighborhoods. In such a case, columns would represent neighborhoods rather than individuals. Paired with traditional observations of individuals' struggles and accounts of getting to a doctor's office, the array could help illustrate the similarities and differences within and across different communities. An array adapted to this task, following the color coding conventions introduced earlier in the PtDelib examples, might take the form seen in Figure A1. Furthermore, to illustrate where data related to the phenomenon in question but not neatly categorized by domains might be located, this version includes a row for "other trip observations."

APPENDIX B

How an Array Might Complement a Well-Known Comparative Ethnography

This appendix will illustrate how an ethnoarray might be used to present ethnographic findings in a way that complements current practices, and it will explain how the array might be used to explicate the claim making process in Annette Lareau's (2011) *Unequal Childhoods*, a well-known comparative ethnographic study. Lareau's study of class, race, and social reproduction among school-age children includes detailed accounts of how middle-class, working-class, and poor families interact with schools and other institutions. In a detailed appendix, Lareau noted her decision to analyze her data in different ways (sometimes with software assistance, sometimes via the more traditional reading and rereading of notes) and the iterative process by which she sought disconfirming evidence as her arguments began to take shape. Yet it is striking that this description occupies only a small fraction of her appendix, which is largely devoted to describing the logistics and dilemmas of data collection. She also noted that to make her findings more accessible, she presented her data narratively—focusing on one family at a time—rather than adopting a more analytical discursive approach.

This study presents an instance in which ethnoarrays might help achieve the author's ethnographic goals and explicate how conclusions are drawn. Ethnoarrays could maintain the work's accessibility to a wide audience, but at the same time, the use of array visualizations might provide a more explicit analytical schema that would be of interest to specialized sociologists and ethnographers examining claims. Given the multilayered comparisons in the study, a variety of different ways of developing and presenting ethnoarrays from the data suggest themselves. For example, domains (or rows) of an ethnoarray could be constructed from middle-class study participant Garrett Tallinger's (chapter 3) life: weekly events and activities, conversations with parents and siblings, exhaustion and elation brought on by events in his life, the absence of relatives, attention (or lack thereof) to money, his parents' Ivy League background, their job-related travel schedules, and the extent to which his schedule determines the routines of his siblings. If Garrett were the unit of analysis (column), such an array would paint a picture of how cultivation plays out in the routine activities of a middle-class family. Adding other children (and their activity domains) to the ethnoarray would provide insights into how patterns of cultivation versus natural growth play in the lives of the children Lareau studied, thus providing a more highly explicated analytical approach to her data that could supplement the book's chapter-based case studies.

Ethnoarrays could also enrich the analysis of *Unequal Childhoods* even without engaging Lareau's theoretical arguments about social reproduction. For example, a purely narrative approach might produce an ethnoarray that extends Lareau's Table 2, which currently conveys a sense of Garrett's busy cultivated life just by listing all the sporting and performing events on his calendar. If an individual day in the life of one child is the unit of analysis (column) and his activities during that day constitute the domains (rows), the resultant array would produce a rich, descriptive sense of which children are engaged in which activities when and how intensely. This ethnoarray need not carry the freight of an explanatory logic; it would simply provide a window into how the children Lareau studied spent their days and allow inductive exploration—through grounded or interpretative strategies—of the nature of childhood in contemporary America.

As this exegesis of *Unequal Childhoods* suggests, an ethnoarray can help summarize large amounts of data. As part of a traditional ethnographic article or monograph, an ethnoarray could include a broader sense of the study data and provide some context for analysts' specific claims that may help readers assess internal plausibility. However, data-linked arrays can go even farther and provide readers with the opportunity to examine directly the data that an analyst purports to justify a claim.

Acknowledgments

We would like to thank the anonymous reviewers and editor of *Sociological Methodology* for helpful comments, criticisms, and suggestions. We are also grateful to Martín Sánchez-Jankowski, Aaron Cicourel, Erin Leahey, James Wiley, Laura Dunn, Christopher Koenig, Laura Trupin, Susan Miller, Mario Small, Kathleen Cagney, and participants at the AJS/University of Chicago Conference on Causal Thinking and Ethnographic Research for comments on previous versions of this manuscript as well as to Susan Miller and Matthew Wenger for assistance with initial data analysis. We grate-fully acknowledge participants in the Cancer Patient Deliberation Study for their will-ingness to share their experiences with us.

Funding

The author(s) disclosed receipt of the following financial support for the research, authorship, and/or publication of this article: This project was supported by grant R01 CA152195 (Daniel Dohan, principal investigator) from the National Cancer Institute. The content presented here is solely the responsibility of the authors and does not neces-sarily represent the official views of the National Cancer Institute or the National Institutes of Health.

Notes

1. Emerson, Fretz, and Shaw (1995) provided a broad definition of the ethnographic craft, which they described as a research method that "involves the study of groups and people as they go about their everyday lives" (p. 1). In the case of sociological research, this normally involves participant observation with individuals, groups, or organizations, conducted over time. More broadly, ethnographers use a collec-tion of methods to understand individuals and the contexts in which they act, often (although not necessarily) spending time with people as they go about their lives, engaging with those individuals, and keeping some sort of notes or diary, then writ-ing findings on the basis of their observations (Becker 1958; Gans 1999).
2. We use the term *construct* because, as scholars have long pointed out, no piece of data simply "speaks for itself" (e.g., Berger 1963; Blumer 1969; Cicourel 1964).
3. Others have also turned to the natural sciences in developing social scientific ana-lytic approaches (e.g., Abbott and Hrycak 1990). Recently, those engaged in auto-mated analyses of text have turned to heatmap-centered approaches as a means of discovery and representation (cf. Mohr and Bogdanov 2013; Mohr et al. 2013).
4. It is important to recognize that the introduction of new techniques and modes of visualization can create new issues and debates as well as advances. One need only look to the discussions around geographic information systems in geography and related fields (e.g., see Pickles 1997). Although it is impossible to anticipate all such issues with the ethnoarray, we endeavor to discuss them throughout this article.
5. For a frequently updated review of the various CAQDAS progams on the market, see http://www.surrey.ac.uk/sociology/research/researchcentres/caqdas/.
6. There are, however, some promising basic tools for examining and representing co-occurrence and heatmaps of codes in off-the-shelf programs that might facili-tate the array approach with some adaptation.
7. The figure includes 337 columns, each containing data from a single specimen (320 tumorous and 17 normal tissues) and approximately 1,900 rows, each repre-senting a specific gene. The color of each cell in the table reflects the expression profile of one gene in one specimen. Genes that are overexpressed (i.e., that are

more active in metabolic processes) are shown in red; green indicates underexpression. In both cases, color intensity corresponds to the strength of overexpression or underexpression, and typical levels of gene expression are shown as black cells.

8. An alternative analysis using only field notes might examine differences and similarities in interactions across clinics. In that case, the ethnoarray's columns would each represent a clinic. The domains (or rows) of the array could also be redefined.

9. It is important to note a limitation of our mock-up. The 16-row demonstrative ethnoarray creates a relatively crude checkerboard that might mistakenly give the impression that this tool is simply a visual device for quantifying and decontextualizing rich qualitative data. To be useful for capturing the richness of ethnography, however, the ethnoarray would include many more domains and many more measures and submeasures within domains. Rather than constituting a crude checkerboard, a fine-grained visualization would reveal patterns of relationships among domains and facilitate interpretation of the rich data underlying the array. Furthermore, as we discuss in sections below, the cells of the array would be linked back to the underlying notes and transcripts.

10. Unlike critics who argue for the superiority of a given approach (e.g., Biernacki 2014), we believe these approaches can exist pluralistically.

11. The 2012 volume of *Sociological Methodology*, especially Franzosi et al.'s (2012) discussion of quantitative narrative analysis (QNA), explores some of these issues. In addition to introducing QNA, a tool for quantifying the structural properties of narrative, the volume includes useful discussions of the potentials and pitfalls of using computers to analyze qualitative data more generally (Junker 2012; White, Judd, and Poliandri 2012a, 2012b). Although the array differs from QNA in its focus on textual meaning rather than invariant structure, the broader discussions regarding the new avenues of qualitative inquiry and ways of representing and sharing data opened by computers is a useful analog to what we present here; see also Gorski (2004).

12. A pseudonym, as are all proper names in this paper, obtained from a random name generator.

13. Comprehensive array software would facilitate this process but is not yet available, a topic we address in section 4. To generate the representations above, we used data from the master data set for PtDelib, which is currently maintained in a secure data environment using CAQDA software. The field observations, interviews, and survey data were entered into the program, coded using an iterative process, and linked to "case summaries" that gave an overview of individual experiences, chronologies, and outcomes. These case summaries were sortable by various demographic and social characteristics and "hyperlinked" back to the observations on which they were based. The interpretive color coding is based on a reading of these summaries and their underlying data.

14. For a useful related discussion of how the co-occurrence tools of ATLAS.ti can be used to help identify context, see Contreras (2011).

15. A modified array approach might facilitate such a quantitative reduction, but this would involve a fundamentally different form of inquiry.

16. Analysts can decide how many and which domains or measures to use when sorting the array. However, in this article we deliberately provide this relatively

simplistic example to explicate the basic mechanics involved, without presupposing reader knowledge of advanced statistical techniques; see, for instance, the 2012 edition (volume 42) of *Sociological Methodology*.

17. The mock-up in Figure 5 is too basic to draw conclusions on the basis of an interpretation of patterns in the array, but we did arrange the domains to facilitate an explanatory-oriented interpretation of how particular factors, such as social capital, influence whether people enter into early phase trials to show how one might approach this analysis.

18. As our use of CAQDA software in the PtDelib study evidences, the array approach is not antithetical to the use of CAQDA software. ATLAS.ti and MAXQDA both have analytical tools for examining code associations in heatmap-like formats. Ideally array software could operate with, or independently of, commercial CAQA software packages to facilitate ethnoarray production and analysis. The Coding Analysis Toolkit (http://cat.ucsur.pitt.edu) provides a useful exemplar in its Web-based CAQDA suite, which can work either independently or import data from ATLAS.ti (Lu and Shulman 2008).

19. The ICPSR includes references to some ethnographic studies, including Hodson's (2004) data set that allows a comparative analysis of workplace ethnographies. These data sets often include survey data with an ethnographic component, or a representation of ethnographic monographs (as in Hodson's case), but the underlying ethnographic data are not generally available publicly, nor is there a standard mechanism for accessing these data. Recently, there have been moves to improve the repositories of qualitative data (cf. http://www.icpsr.umich.edu/icpsrweb/content/deposit/guide/chapter3qual.html).

20. This is a matter of great importance and likely contention. Although a full treatment is beyond the scope of this article, we hope the techniques and suggestions we outline in this text might further this discussion.

21. This intellectual process is not confined to ethnography, of course, but it is one of the fundamental social processes of scientific discovery and the production of authority in any knowledge-based field (Latour and Woolgar 1986; Timmermans and Berg 2003). In addition, applied ethnographers may be urged to establish bona fides by invoking theory or highlighting their use of CAQDA software, a different kind of procedural claims-making (Reeves et al. 2008).

22. Of course, a similar selection process is at play to a large degree in any research method, even when measures are more formalized (Cicourel 1964; see also Witzel and Mey 2004).

23. Once again, although we see this approach as a complement to rather than a replacement of traditional approaches, it is worth noting that arrays may also have unintended consequences for the traditional practice of ethnography. Many sociologists begin their ethnographic research careers as graduate students, entering and exploring a field site under the tutelage of an experienced faculty mentor and, in more than a few cases, producing studies with marked impact on their fields or the discipline (Anderson 1978; Bosk 1979; Burawoy 1979; Small 2004). A hallmark of this relationship is that the mentor need not provide the student with much in the way of material resources. This lack of resource dependence may allow forms of creativity that students training in other methodological

traditions—such as the graduate student researcher whose dissertation analyzes a faculty mentor's grant-funded survey—may experience less frequently. Although the traditional training model appears consistent with producing a flat ethnoarray, students who wish to participate in a community of ethnographic scholars who share their work via data-linked arrays may require further professional support to properly anonymize and contribute data to a central data resource. Obviously, this dynamic would apply to ethnographers at any stage of their career, but the implications on practices and structures of ethnographic training, which has long been the most common entry point to the ethnographic guild, may be worthy of careful consideration.

References

Abbott, Andrew, and Alexandra Hrycak. 1990. "Measuring Resemblance in Sequence Data: An Optimal Matching Analysis of Musicians' Careers." *American Journal of Sociology* 96(1):144–85.

Abramson, Corey M. 2015. *The End Game: How Inequality Shapes Our Final Years.* Cambridge, MA: Harvard University Press.

Anderson, Elijah. 1978. *A Place on the Corner.* Chicago: University of Chicago Press.

Becker, Howard. 1958. "Problems of Inference and Proof in Participant Observation." *American Sociological Review* 23(6):652–60.

Becker, Howard S. 2009. "How to Find Out How to Do Qualitative Research." *International Journal of Communication* 9:545–53.

Belacel, Nabil, Qian (Christa) Wang, and Miroslava Cuperlovic-Culf. 2006. "Clustering Methods for Microarray Gene Expression Data." *OMICS: A Journal of Integrative Biology* 10(4):507–32.

Berger, Peter L. 1963. *Invitation to Sociology: A Humanistic Perspective.* New York: Anchor.

Biernacki, Richard. 2014. "Humanist Interpretation versus Coding Text Samples." *Qualitative Sociology* 37(2):173–88.

Blumer, Herbert. 1969. *Symbolic Interactionism: Perspective and Method.* Englewood Cliffs, NJ: Prentice Hall.

Boelen, W. A. Marianne. 1992. "Street Corner Society: Cornerville Revisited." *Journal of Contemporary Ethnography* 21(1):11–51.

Bosk, Charles. 1979. *Forgive and Remember: Managing Medical Failure.* Chicago: University of Chicago Press.

Brady, Henry E., and David Collier. 2004. *Rethinking Social Inquiry: Diverse Tools, Shared Standards.* Berkeley, CA: Rowan & Littlefield.

Burawoy, Michael. 1979. *Manufacturing Consent: Changes in the Labor Process under Monopoly Capitalism.* Chicago: University of Chicago Press.

Burawoy, Michael. 1998. "The Extended Case Method." *Sociological Theory* 16(1): 4–33.

Burawoy, Michael. 2004. "Public Sociologies: Contradictions, Dilemmas, and Possibilities." *Social Forces* 82(4):1603–18.

Cicourel, Aaron V. 1964. *Method and Measurement in Sociology.* Glencoe, IL: Free Press.

Cicourel, Aaron V. 1968. *The Social Organization of Juvenile Justice.* New York: John Wiley.

Clifford, James, and George E. Marcus. 1986. *Writing Culture: The Poetics and Politics of Ethnography.* Berkeley: University of California Press.

Contreras, Ricardo B. 2011. "Examining the Context in Qualitative Analysis: The Role of the Co-Occurrence Tool in ATLAS.ti." *ATLAS.ti Newsletter*, August, pp. 5–6.

Dohan, Daniel. (2003). *The Price of Poverty: Money, Work, and Culture in the Mexican-American Barrios.* Berkeley: University of California Press.

Dohan, Daniel, and Martín Sánchez-Jankowski. 1998. "Using Computers to Analyze Ethnographic Field Data: Theoretical and Practical Considerations." *Annual Review of Sociology* 24:477–98.

Duneier, Mitchell. 2002. "What Kind of Combat Sport Is Sociology?" *American Journal of Sociology* 107(6):1551–76.

Duneier, Mitchell. 2006. "Ethnography, the Ecological Fallacy, and the 1995 Chicago Heat Wave." *American Sociological Review* 71(4):679–88.

Duneier, Mitchell. 2011. "How Not to Lie with Ethnography." Pp. 1–11 in *Sociological Methodology*, vol. 41, edited by Tim Futing Liao. Hoboken, NJ: Wiley-Blackwell.

Durkheim, Emile. [1893] 1984. *The Division of Labor in Society.* New York: Free Press.

Eisen, Michael B., Paul T. Spellman, Patrick O. Brown, and David Botstein. 1998. "Cluster Analysis and Display of Genome-Wide Expression Patterns." *Proceedings of the National Academy of Sciences* 95(25):14863–68.

Emerson, Robert M., Rachel I. Fretz, and Linda L. Shaw. 1995. *Writing Ethnographic Field Notes.* Chicago: University of Chicago Press.

Franzosi, Roberto, Gianluca De Fazio, and Stefania Vicari. 2012. "Ways of Measuring Agency: An Application of Quantitative Narrative Analysis to Lynchings in Georgia (1875–1930)." Pp. 1–42 in *Sociological Methodology*, vol. 42, edited by Tim Futing Liao. Thousand Oaks, CA: Sage.

Freese, Jeremy. 2007. "Overcoming Objections to Open-source Social Science." *Sociological Methods and Research* 36(2):220–26.

Gans, Herbert J. 1999. "Participant Observation in the Era of 'Ethnography.'" *Journal of Contemporary Ethnography* 28(5):540–48.

Geertz, Clifford. 2000. "Thick Description: Towards an Interpretive Theory of Culture." Pp. 3–30 in *The Interpretation of Cultures: Selected Essays.* New York: Basic Books.

Glaser, Barney G., and Anselm L. Strauss. 1967. *The Discovery of Grounded Theory: Strategies for Qualitative Research.* New York: Aldine Transaction.

Goldthorpe, John H. 2000. *On Sociology: Numbers, Narratives, and the Integration of Research and Theory.* Oxford, UK: Oxford University Press.

Gorski, Philip S. 2004. "The Poverty of Deductivism: A Constructive Realist Model of Sociological Explanation." Pp. 1–33 in *Sociological Methodology*, vol. 34, edited by Ross M. Stolzenberg. Boston: Blackwell.

Henderson, Stuart, and E. Segal. 2013 "Visualizing Qualitative Data in Evaluation Research." *New Directions for Evaluation* 139:53–71.

Hodson, Randy. 2004. "A Meta-ethnography of Employee Attitudes and Behaviors." *Journal of Contemporary Ethnography* 33(1):4–38.

Joseph, Galen, and Daniel Dohan. 2009. "Diversity of Participants in Clinical Trials in an Academic Medical Center: The Role of the 'Good Study Patient'?" *Cancer* 115(3):608–15.

Junker, Andrew. 2012. "Optimism and Caution Regarding New Tools for Analyzing Qualitative Data." Pp. 85–87 in *Sociological Methodology*, vol. 42, edited by Tim Futing Liao. Thousand Oaks, CA: Sage.

Katz, Jack. 1997. "Ethnography's Warrants." *Sociological Methods and Research* 25(4): 391.

Katz, Jack. 2010. "Review of Cracks in the Pavement." *American Journal of Sociology* 115(6):1950–52.

King, Gary, Robert O. Keohane, and Sidney Verba. 2001. *Designing Social Inquiry: Scientific Inference in Qualitative Research*. Princeton, NJ: Princeton University Press.

Klinenberg, Eric. 2006. "Blaming the Victims: Hearsay, Labeling, and the Hazards of Quick-hit Disaster Ethnography." *American Sociological Review* 71(4):689–98.

Lamont, Michèle, and Ann Swidler. 2014. "Methodological Pluralism and the Possibilities and Limits of Interviewing." *Qualitative Sociology* 37(2):153–71.

Lareau, Annette. 2011. *Unequal Childhoods: Class, Race, and Family Life*. Berkeley: University of California Press.

Latour, Bruno, and Steve Woolgar. 1986. *Laboratory Life: The Construction of Scientific Facts*. Princeton, NJ: Princeton University Press.

Leahey, Erin. 2008. "Overseeing Research Practice: The Case of Data Editing." *Science, Technology, and Human Values* 33(5):605–30.

Lofland, John. 1995. "Analytic Ethnography: Features, Failings and Futures." *Journal of Contemporary Ethnography* 24(1):30.

Lu, C.-J., and Shulman, S. W. 2008. "Rigor and Flexibility in Computer-based Qualitative Research: Introducing the Coding Analysis Toolkit." *International Journal of Multiple Research Approaches* 2(1):105–17.

Lutfey, Karen, and Jeremy Freese. 2005. "Toward Some Fundamentals of Fundamental Causality: Socioeconomic Status and Health in the Routine Clinic Visit for Diabetes." *American Journal of Sociology* 110(5):1326–72.

Marcus, George E. 1998. *Ethnography through Thick and Thin*. Princeton, NJ: Princeton University Press.

Miles, Matthew B., and A. Michael Huberman. 1994. *Qualitative Data Analysis: An Expanded Sourcebook*. 2nd ed. Thousand Oaks, CA: Sage.

Mills, C. Wright. 1959. *The Sociological Imagination*. New York: Oxford University Press.

Mohr, John W., and Petko Bogdanov. 2013. "Introduction—Topic Models: What They Are and Why They Matter." *Poetics* 41(6):545–69.

Mohr, John W., Robin Wagner-Pacifici, Ronald L. Breiger, and Petko Bogdanov. 2013. "Graphing the Grammar of Motives in National Security Strategies: Cultural Interpretation, Automated Text Analysis, and the Drama of Global Politics." *Poetics* 41(6):670–700.

Moody, James W., and Kieran Healy. 2014. "Data Visualization in Sociology." *Annual Review of Sociology* 40:105–28.

Orlandella, Angelo Ralph. 1992. "Boelen May Know Holland, Boelen May Know Barzini, but Boelen Doesn't Know Diddle about the North End!" *Journal of Contemporary Ethnography* 21(1):69–79.

Perez-Hernandez, Danya. 2014. "New Repository Offers a Home for Data That Aren't Numbers." *Chronicle of Higher Education*. Retrieved January 23, 2015 (http://chronicle.com/blogs/wiredcampus/new-repository-offers-a-home-for-data-that-arent-numbers/50865).

Pickles, J. 1997. "Arguments, Debates, and Dialogues: The GIS–Social Theory Debate and the Concern for Alternatives." Pp. 49–60 in *Geographical Information Systems: Principles, Techniques, Management, and Applications*, edited by D.R.P Longley, M. Goodchild, and D. Maguire. New York: John Wiley.

Prat, Aleix, and Charles M. Perou. 2011. "Deconstructing the Molecular Portraits of Breast Cancer." *Molecular Oncology* 5(1):5–23.

Rabinow, Paul. 1997. *Reflections on Fieldwork in Morocco*. Berkeley: University of California Press.

Reed, Isaac. 2010. "Epistemology Contextualized: Social-scientific Knowledge in a Postpositivist Era." *Sociological Theory* 28(1):20–39

Reeves, S., M. Albert, A. Kuper, and B. D. Hodges. 2008. "Why Use Theories in Qualitative Research?" *BMJ* 337:631–34.

Sallaz, Jeff. 2009. *The Labor of Luck: Casino Capitalism in the United States and South Africa*. Berkeley: University of California Press.

Sánchez-Jankowski, Martín. 2002. "Representation, Responsibility and Reliability in Participant Observation." Pp. 144–60 in *Qualitative Research in Action*, edited by Tim May. London: Sage Ltd.

Sánchez-Jankowski, Martín. 2008. *Cracks in the Pavement: Social Change and Resilience in Poor Neighborhoods*. Berkeley: University of California Press.

Sanjek, Roger, ed. 1990. *Field Notes: The Makings of Anthropology*. Ithaca, NY: Cornell University Press.

Schena, Mark, Dari Shalon, Ronald W. Davis, and Patrick O. Brown. 1995. "Quantitative Monitoring of Gene Expression Patterns with a Complementary DNA Microarray." *Science* 270(5235):467–70.

Small, Mario Luis. 2004. *Villa Victoria: The Transformation of Social Capital in a Boston Barrio*. Chicago: University of Chicago Press.

Small, Mario Luis. 2009. "'How Many Cases Do I Need?': On Science and the Logic of Case Selection in Field-based Research." *Ethnography* 10(1):5–38.

Stears, Robin L., Todd Martinskey, and Mark Schena. 2003. "Trends in Microarray Analysis." *Nature Medicine* 9(1):140–45.

Strauss, Anselm, and Juliet Corbin. 1990. *Basics of Qualitative Research: Grounded Theory Procedures and Techniques*. 2nd ed. Thousand Oaks, CA: Sage.

Swedberg Richard, ed. 2014. *Theorizing in Social Science: The Context of Discovery*. Stanford, CA: Stanford University Press.

Tangherlini, Timothy R., and Peter Leonard. 2013. "Trawling in the Sea of the Great Unread: Sub-corpus Topic Modeling and Humanities Research." *Poetics* 41(6):725–49.

Tavory, Iddo, and Stefan Timmermans. 2009. "Two Cases of Ethnography: Case, Narrative and Theory in Grounded Theory and the Extended Case Method." *Ethnography* 10(3):243–63.

Timmermans, Stefan, and Marc Berg. 2003. *The Gold Standard: The Challenge of Evidence-based Medicine and Standardization in Health Care*. Philadelphia: Temple University Press.

Tufte, Edward R. 1983. *The Visual Display of Quantitative Information*. 2nd ed. Cheshire, CT: Graphics Press.

Tufte, Edward. R. 1997. *Visual Explanations: Images and Quantities, Evidence and Narrative*. Cheshire, CT: Graphics Press.

Tukey, John. 1977. *Exploratory Data Analysis*. New York: Addison-Wesley.

Wacquant, Loïc. 2002. "Scrutinizing the Street: Poverty, Morality, and the Pitfalls of Urban Ethnography." *American Journal of Sociology* 107(6):1468–1532.

White, M. J., M. D. Judd, and S. Poliandri. 2012a. "Brightening the Bulb: Response to Comments." Pp. 94–99 in *Sociological Methodology*, vol. 42, edited by Tim Futing Liao. Thousand Oaks, CA: Sage.

White, M. J., M. D. Judd, and S. Poliandri. 2012b. "Illumination with a Dim Bulb? What Do Social Scientists Learn by Employing Qualitative Data Analysis Software in the Service of Multimethod Designs?" Pp. 43–76 in *Sociological Methodology*, vol. 42, edited by Tim Futing Liao. Thousand Oaks, CA: Sage.

Whyte, Willliam F. 1993. *Street Corner Society: The Social Structure of an Italian Slum*. 4th ed. Chicago: University of Chicago Press.

Witzel, Andreas,, and Günter Mey. 2004. "'I Am NOT Opposed to Quantification or Formalization or Modeling, but Do Not Want to Pursue Quantitative Methods That Are Not Commensurate with the Research Phenomena Addressed': Aaron Cicourel in Conversation with Andreas Witzel and Günter Mey." *Forum: Qualitative Social Research* 5(3):Art 41. Retrieved January 23, 2015 (http://www.qualitative-research .net/index.php/fqs/article/view/549/1186).

Author Biographies

Corey M. Abramson is an assistant professor of sociology at the University of Arizona and a research associate at the Center for Ethnographic Research at the University of California, Berkeley. Abramson's research uses both qualitative and quantitative methods to examine how persistent social inequalities structure everyday life and how they are reproduced over time. His recent book on this topic, *The End Game: How Inequality Shapes Our Final Years* (Harvard University Press, 2015), provides a comparative ethnographic analysis of how various facets of inequality profoundly shape life for older Americans and examines what this tells us about the mechanisms of social stratification more broadly. Abramson's current methodological work focuses on developing ways to improve rigor and transparency in the collection, analysis, and representation of qualitative data.

Daniel Dohan is a professor of health policy and social medicine at the Philip R. Lee Institute for Health Policy Studies at the University of California, San Francisco (UCSF). His research focuses on the culture of medicine: how it ameliorates and perpetuates societal inequalities, its relationship to science and discovery, and how training creates health professionals. In addition to his research, he is leading the development of a new master's degree in health policy and law, to be jointly offered by UCSF and the University of California Hastings College of Law.

Sociological Methodology
2015, Vol. 45(1) 320–356
© American Sociological Association 2015
DOI: 10.1177/0081175015570097
http://sm.sagepub.com

$$\mathfrak{S} \; 7 \; \mathfrak{E}$$

SHRINKAGE ESTIMATION OF LOG-ODDS RATIOS FOR COMPARING MOBILITY TABLES

Xiang Zhou*

Abstract

Statistical analysis of mobility tables has long played a pivotal role in comparative stratification research. This article proposes a shrinkage estimator of the log-odds ratio for comparing mobility tables. Building on an empirical Bayes framework, the shrinkage estimator improves estimation efficiency by "borrowing strength" across multiple tables while placing no restrictions on the pattern of association within tables. Numerical simulation shows that the shrinkage estimator outperforms the usual maximum likelihood estimator (MLE) in both the total squared error and the correlation with the true values. Moreover, the benefits of the shrinkage estimator relative to the MLE depend on both the variation in the true log-odds ratio and the variation in sample size among mobility regimes. To illustrate the effects of shrinkage, the author contrasts the shrinkage estimates with the usual estimates for the mobility data assembled by Hazelrigg and Garnier for 16 countries in the 1960s and 1970s. For mobility tables with more than two categories, the shrinkage estimates of log-odds ratios can also be used to calculate summary measures of association that are based on aggregations of log-odds ratios. Specifically, the author constructs an adjusted estimator of the Altham index and, with a set of calibrated simulations, demonstrates its usefulness in

*University of Michigan, Ann Arbor, USA

Corresponding Author:
Xiang Zhou, University of Michigan, Institute for Social Research, 426 Thompson Street, Ann Arbor, MI 48104, USA
Email: xiangzh@umich.edu

enhancing both the precision of individual estimates and the accuracy of cross-table comparisons. Finally, using two real data sets, the author shows that in gauging the overall degree of social fluidity, the adjusted estimator of the Altham index agrees more closely with results from the Unidiff model than does the direct estimator of the Altham index.

Keywords

shrinkage estimator, log-odds ratio, mobility tables, empirical Bayes methods, log-linear models

1. INTRODUCTION

Comparative mobility analysis has long been at the core of social stratification research. To investigate how patterns of intergenerational mobility differ across countries or vary over time, stratification researchers typically compare a collection of mobility tables that cross-classify fathers and sons by their occupations or classes. To draw such comparisons, researchers until the 1970s had relied on simple calculations of inflow and outflow rates (e.g., Lipset and Zetterberg 1956; Miller 1960) or the construct of "mobility ratios" (e.g., Glass and Berent 1954; Rogoff 1953), both of which turned out to be inadequate to separate changes in relative mobility (also known as exchange mobility, circulation mobility, or social fluidity) from changes in marginal distributions (i.e., structural mobility).[1] Beginning in the late 1960s, thanks to the pioneering work of Leo Goodman (1968, 1969), it has been recognized that all associations in an $I \times J$ contingency table can be captured by a sufficient set of $(I - 1)(J - 1)$ odds ratios.[2] This fundamental discovery paved the way for the subsequent development of log-linear and log-multiplicative models (e.g., Duncan 1979; Goodman 1979; Hauser 1980), in which the natural logarithms of odds ratios are expressed as regression coefficients or their linear combinations.

Given the centrality of odds ratios in depicting the structure of row-column association, a natural approach to comparing mobility tables, as suggested by Goodman (1969), is to directly compare their corresponding (log) odds ratios in search of similarities and differences. Although mobility studies in sociology have been dominated by log-linear modeling since the 1970s, this older model-free approach has its own appeal because it allows a panoramic view of the association between origin and destination without invoking parametric assumptions (see Hout and

Guest [2013] for an illustration). Meanwhile, using log-odds ratios as building blocks, Altham (1970) proposed a number of aggregate measures of association for comparing contingency tables. One of these measures (see section 3) has been recently used to examine long-term trends in occupational mobility in Great Britain and the United States (Ferrie 2005; Long and Ferrie 2007, 2013).

Unlike log-linear modeling, the model-free approach to comparing mobility tables imposes no parametric constraints on the pattern of association between origin and destination. Instead, it requires that every log-odds ratio be estimated separately from data. Estimation of single log-odds ratios, however, can be highly imprecise in practice. Indeed, the usual maximum likelihood estimator (MLE) of the log-odds ratio (i.e., $\log \frac{n_{11}n_{22}}{n_{12}n_{21}}$) will be accompanied by a large standard error unless all of the associated cells contain many cases,[3] a condition that often fails for real mobility tables. As a result, direct comparisons in sample log-odds ratios across tables are prone to conflate true variations in relative mobility with sampling fluctuations. On one hand, if relative mobility is constant and trendless in all complex societies, as implied by the hypothesis of constant social fluidity (CSF; Erikson and Goldthorpe 1992; Featherman, Jones, and Hauser 1975; Grusky and Hauser 1984), the observed differences will stem entirely from sampling and measurement errors. On the other hand, if social fluidity does differ across countries and change over time, sampling variability may also contaminate empirical comparisons between mobility regimes. In particular, when the mobility tables under investigation vary greatly in sample size, the relatively sparse tables are more likely to be estimated at the extremes of the mobility spectrum because they are subject to larger sampling errors. Because sample size is presumably unrelated to the true amount of social fluidity, this statistical artifact may distort the rank order of mobility regimes in the size of origin-destination association. Such a distortion can be substantively significant unless sampling errors are negligible relative to systematic variations among mobility regimes. The latter condition, unfortunately, seldom holds in comparative mobility research.

In log-linear modeling, estimation uncertainty is partly alleviated through parametric assumptions. For example, the CSF model assumes no cross-table variation in all log-odds ratios, and the Unidiff model (Erikson and Goldthorpe 1992; Xie 1992) stipulates that the relative magnitudes of different log-odds ratios are uniform in all tables. These assumptions, however, may accord poorly with real data. In this article, I propose a shrinkage method for estimating log-odds ratios that attempts to enhance estimation efficiency without explicitly constraining the patterns of row-column association. Building on an empirical Bayes model (Efron and Morris 1973; Fay and Herriot 1979), the shrinkage estimator "borrows strength" across multiple tables while placing no restrictions on the structure of association within tables. As I will show by simulation, the shrinkage method leads to lower total squared errors than does the usual MLE of the log-odds ratio. More important, when tables vary greatly in sample size—a situation that we often encounter in comparative mobility analysis—the shrinkage estimates exhibit markedly higher correlations with the true log-odds ratios than do the usual estimates. Therefore, the shrinkage method can enhance the accuracy of cross-table comparisons in the degree of row-column association. Moreover, the shrinkage estimates of log-odds ratios can be used to calculate summary measures of association that are based on aggregations of log-odds ratios. To illustrate this point, I construct an adjusted estimator of the Altham index (Altham 1970; Altham and Ferrie 2007), and, with a set of calibrated simulations, demonstrate its usefulness in enhancing both the precision of individual estimates and the accuracy of cross-table comparisons. Finally, using two sets of real mobility tables, I show that in gauging the overall degree of social fluidity, the adjusted estimates of the Altham index agree more closely with results from the Unidiff model than do direct estimates of the Altham index.

2. SHRINKAGE ESTIMATION OF LOG-ODDS RATIOS

2.1. *Usual Estimator of the Log-odds Ratio*

Let us consider K 2×2 contingency tables, which, say, cross-classify fathers and sons according to nonmanual and manual classes in K countries. Denoting by n_{ijk} the cell frequency pertaining to the ith row and the jth column in country k, the observed log-odds ratios for these tables can be expressed as

$$Y_k = \log \frac{n_{11k} n_{22k}}{n_{12k} n_{21k}}, k = 1, 2, \cdots K. \tag{1}$$

Assuming a multinomial sampling distribution for each country, these sample log-odds ratios are also the maximum likelihood estimates of population log-odds ratios.[4] They are therefore asymptotically normal, that is,

$$\sqrt{n_{++k}}(Y_k - \theta_k) \overset{d}{\to} N(0, V_k),$$

where n_{++k} and θ_k represent the sample size and the population log-odds ratio for country k. Using the delta method, it is not hard to show that the asymptotic variance of Y_k is

$$\sigma_k^2 = \frac{V_k}{n_{++k}} = \frac{1}{n_{++k}\pi_{11k}} + \frac{1}{n_{++k}\pi_{12k}} + \frac{1}{n_{++k}\pi_{21k}} + \frac{1}{n_{++k}\pi_{22k}},$$

where the π_{ijk}'s denote the unknown cell probabilities (Agresti 2002:75–76).

Substituting the observed proportions for the π_{ijk}'s, we obtain a sample estimate of σ_k^2:

$$\widehat{\sigma_k^2} = \frac{1}{n_{11k}} + \frac{1}{n_{12k}} + \frac{1}{n_{21k}} + \frac{1}{n_{22k}}. \tag{2}$$

Because there is a finite, however small, probability that any of the four cells are zero, the observed log-odds ratio (equation 1) may equal ∞ or $-\infty$. In such cases, a common practice is to add one half to all of the four cell frequencies, yielding a modified estimator (Agresti 2002:71):

$$\widetilde{Y}_k = \log \frac{(n_{11k} + 0.5)(n_{22k} + 0.5)}{(n_{12k} + 0.5)(n_{21k} + 0.5)}.$$

Haldane (1956) showed that this modification reduces the sampling bias from the order of $O(n^{-1})$ to the order of $O(n^{-2})$. Moreover, Gart and Zweifel (1967) noted that the corresponding variance estimator

$$\widetilde{\sigma_k^2} = \frac{1}{n_{11k} + 0.5} + \frac{1}{n_{12k} + 0.5} + \frac{1}{n_{21k} + 0.5} + \frac{1}{n_{22k} + 0.5}$$

is an unbiased estimator of $\mathrm{Var}(\widetilde{Y}_k)$ except for terms of $O(n^{-3})$. I therefore adopt these adjustments in the case of zero cells throughout the rest of the article.[5]

Since the observed log-odds ratio (equation 1) coincides with the MLE, it is consistent and asymptotically efficient. Nonetheless, the asymptotic variance estimator (equation 2) indicates that the MLE can be highly imprecise in small samples: Unless all of the four cells contain many cases, the standard error will be very large. As a result, if we directly compare the observed log-odds ratios from different tables, those from relatively sparse tables will be more likely to be ranked at the extremes. This is undesirable because sample size is presumably unrelated to the true degree of association. The shrinkage approach I present below aims to improve both the precision of estimates from sparse tables and the accuracy of ranking among different mobility regimes.

2.2. *Empirical Bayes Shrinkage*

To explicate the shrinkage approach, let us first accept the normal approximations of the observed log-odds ratios, that is,

$$Y_k | \theta_k \overset{indep}{\sim} N(\theta_k, \widehat{\sigma_k^2}). \tag{3}$$

Now consider a Bayes model in which the population log-odds ratios themselves follow a normal prior

$$\theta_k \overset{i.i.d.}{\sim} N(\mu, \tau^2), \tag{4}$$

where μ and τ^2 are hyperparameters representing the prior mean and the prior variance of the unknown θ_k's. It is easy to show that the posterior distribution of θ_k is also normal, and the Bayes estimator, that is, the posterior mean, can be written as

$$E(\theta_k | Y_k) = \mu + (1 - \frac{\widehat{\sigma_k^2}}{\tau^2 + \widehat{\sigma_k^2}})(Y_k - \mu). \tag{5}$$

Estimating the hyperparameters μ and τ^2 directly from the data, say, through maximizing the marginal likelihood, leads to an empirical Bayes estimator (Efron and Morris 1973, 1975)

$$\hat{\theta}_k^{EB} = \hat{\mu} + (1 - \frac{\widehat{\sigma_k^2}}{\widehat{\tau^2} + \widehat{\sigma_k^2}})(Y_k - \hat{\mu}). \tag{6}$$

In the statistics literature, $\hat{\theta}_k^{EB}$ has been described as a shrinkage estimator because it "shrinks" the observed outcome Y_k toward the estimated prior mean $\hat{\mu}$ with a shrinkage factor of $\frac{\widehat{\sigma_k^2}}{\tau^2 + \sigma_k^2}$. The shrinkage factor, clearly, depends on the precision of the observation Y_k: the larger is the sampling variance $\widehat{\sigma_k^2}$, the stronger is the degree of shrinkage. Indeed, the empirical Bayes estimator can be expressed as a precision-weighted average between Y_k and $\hat{\mu}$ (Raudenbush and Bryk 1985, 2002):

$$\hat{\theta}_k^{EB} = \frac{1/\widehat{\tau^2}}{1/\widehat{\tau^2} + 1/\widehat{\sigma_k^2}}\hat{\mu} + \frac{1/\widehat{\sigma_k^2}}{1/\widehat{\tau^2} + 1/\widehat{\sigma_k^2}}Y_k,$$

where the weight accorded to Y_k is proportional to its sampling precision $1/\widehat{\sigma_k^2}$ and the weight accorded to $\hat{\mu}$ is proportional to $1/\widehat{\tau^2}$, a measure of the concentration of the unknown θ_k's around the prior mean μ.

Because the shrinkage factor in the posterior mean (equation 5) is a convex function of the prior variance τ^2, a substitution of a nearly unbiased estimate $\widehat{\tau^2}$ for τ^2 would produce an upward bias for the shrinkage factor $\frac{\widehat{\sigma_k^2}}{\tau^2 + \sigma_k^2}$ (by Jensen's inequality). To alleviate this problem, Morris (1983) suggested that the estimator (equation 6) be replaced by

$$\hat{\theta}_k^{EB} = \hat{\mu} + [1 - \frac{(K-3)\widehat{\sigma_k^2}}{(K-1)\left(\widehat{\tau^2} + \widehat{\sigma_k^2}\right)}](Y_k - \hat{\mu}), \tag{7}$$

where the multiplying constant $\frac{K-3}{K-1}$ is used to offset the bias of $\frac{\widehat{\sigma_k^2}}{\tau^2 + \sigma_k^2}$ as an estimate of the shrinkage factor $\frac{\widehat{\sigma_k^2}}{\tau^2 + \sigma_k^2}$.

The empirical Bayes framework sketched above was initially proposed by Efron and Morris (1973, 1975) to interpret the James-Stein rule for estimating multivariate normal means. Indeed, Stein (1956) and James and Stein (1961) discovered that for simultaneous estimation of unrelated normal means, the usual MLE (i.e., Y_k's) can be inadmissible and dominated by a shrinkage estimator similar in form to the empirical

Bayes estimator (equation 7). On the other hand, the empirical Bayes method closely parallels the notion of best linear unbiased prediction (BLUP) in random-effects models (Robinson 1991). Specifically, when both the prior variance τ^2 and the sampling variances σ_k^2 are known, it can be shown that the following statistic minimizes the mean squared error between θ_k and any unbiased estimator of θ_k that is linear in the Y_k's (Harville 1976):

$$\hat{\theta}_k^{BLUP} = \hat{\mu} + (1 - \frac{\sigma_k^2}{\tau^2 + \sigma_k^2})(Y_k - \hat{\mu}). \tag{8}$$

Here $\hat{\mu} = \sum_{k=1}^{k} w_k Y_k / \sum_{k=1}^{k} w_k$ is the minimum variance unbiased estimator (MVUE) of μ, where $w_k = 1/(\tau^2 + \sigma_k^2)$. Replacing the variance components τ^2 and σ_k^2 with their estimates would yield the *empirical best linear unbiased predictor* (EBLUP) of θ_k, which coincides with the empirical Bayes estimator (equation 7), except for the lack of the multiplying constant $\frac{K-3}{K-1}$.

While the theoretical work by James and Stein (1961) demonstrates the advantage of shrinkage in a fixed-effects world, the concepts of BLUP and EBLUP justify the empirical Bayes estimator through a random-effects formulation. From either perspective, the key idea is to reduce the influence of sampling variability by "borrowing strength" from other observations (as reflected in $\hat{\mu}$). Because the shrinkage factor roughly equals the ratio of the sampling variance σ_k^2 to the overall variance of Y_k (i.e., $\tau^2 + \sigma_k^2$), the shrinkage rule may be interpreted as "purging" sampling errors from the estimation of true parameters. This procedure can be highly effective when sampling uncertainty is substantial relative to the true variation among the parameters of interest. As illustrated by Efron and Morris (1975), given data from the first 45 at-bats of 18 Major League Baseball players in the 1970 season, the shrinkage approach performs much better than the MLE in predicting their future batting averages. More recently, Savitz and Raudenbush (2009) showed that similar types of shrinkage estimators can improve the precision and predictive validity of ecometric measures in neighborhood studies. Considering that observed log-odds ratios frequently suffer from large sampling errors, we expect that the shrinkage approach can significantly enhance the estimation precision of log-odds ratios by pooling data from multiple mobility tables.

Meanwhile, we notice from equation (7) that the degree of shrinkage is higher for observations with larger sampling variances. This relationship is intuitive because the need for "borrowing strength" should be stronger for relatively imprecise estimates. Differences in the degree of shrinkage, moreover, can alter the rank order of the estimates; that is, the shrinkage estimates may rank the population log-odds ratios differently from the observed log-odds ratios. Efron and Morris (1975) noted that the empirical Bayes method typically outperforms MLE in ordering the true values. Therefore, besides improving the estimation precision of individual log-odds ratios, the shrinkage approach can also enhance the accuracy of cross-table comparisons.

2.3. *Estimation, Inference, and Implementation*

To empirically estimate μ and τ^2, a natural idea is to derive their MLE on the basis of the joint marginal distribution

$$Y_k \overset{indep}{\sim} N(\mu, \tau^2 + \widehat{\sigma_k^2}).$$

Unfortunately, the likelihood equation in this case defies an analytical solution. I now describe an alternative approach proposed by Carter and Rolph (1974), one that is closely related to the procedures used in Fay and Herriot (1979), Morris (1983), and Sidik and Jonkman (2005). As mentioned above, when τ^2 is known, the MVUE of μ is given by the weighted average of the Y_k's

$$\hat{\mu}\left(\tau^2\right) = \frac{\sum_{k=1}^{K} w_k(\tau^2) Y_k}{\sum_{k=1}^{K} w_k(\tau^2)},$$

where the weights are

$$w_k\left(\tau^2\right) = \frac{1}{\tau^2 + \widehat{\sigma_k^2}}.$$

Here $w_k(\tau^2)$ and $\hat{\mu}(\tau^2)$ highlight their dependence on τ^2. Meanwhile, we observe that the weighted sum of squared deviations of the Y_k's follows a chi-square distribution with $K - 1$ degrees of freedom, that is,

$$\sum_{k=1}^{K} w_k\left(\tau^2\right) \left(Y_k - \hat{\mu}\left(\tau^2\right)\right)^2 \sim \chi_{K-1}^2.$$

Thus we have

$$E\left[\sum_{k=1}^{K} w_k(\tau^2)(Y_k - \hat{\mu}(\tau^2))^2\right] = K - 1.$$

Carter and Rolph (1974) suggested that τ^2 be estimated as the unique positive solution that satisfies

$$\sum_{k=1}^{K} w_k\left(\widehat{\tau^2}\right)\left(Y_k - \hat{\mu}\left(\widehat{\tau^2}\right)\right)^2 = K - 1.$$

In the case in which no positive solution exists, $\widehat{\tau^2}$ is set to be zero. To solve the above equation, a simple Newton-Raphson procedure was described by Fay and Herriot (1979:276), which typically converges in fewer than ten iterations. With the converged value of $\widehat{\tau^2}$, the prior mean μ is estimated accordingly as $\hat{\mu}\left(\widehat{\tau^2}\right)$. By plugging $\hat{\mu}$ and $\widehat{\tau^2}$ into equation (7), we obtain the empirical Bayes estimates of the unknown θ_k's.

To fully assess the uncertainty of the empirical Bayes estimator (equation 7), we must take into account the estimation of μ, τ^2, and σ_k^2's. To avoid analytical challenges, I now consider a naive estimator of the standard error of $\hat{\theta}_k^{EB}$ that treats the variance estimates $\widehat{\tau^2}$ and $\widehat{\sigma_k^2}$'s as the true underlying parameters. Denoting by B_k the shrinkage factor $\dfrac{(K-3)\widehat{\sigma_k^2}}{(K-1)\left(\widehat{\tau^2 + \sigma_k^2}\right)}$ in equation (7), the mean squared error between $\hat{\theta}_k^{EB}$ and θ_k can be written as

$$
\begin{aligned}
E\left(\hat{\theta}_k^{EB} - \theta_k\right)^2 &= E[(1 - B_k)Y_k + B_k\hat{\mu} - \theta_k]^2 \\
&= E[(1 - B_k)(Y_k - \theta_k) + B_k(\hat{\mu} - \theta_k)]^2 \\
&= (1 - B_k)\widehat{\sigma_k^2} + 2(1 - B_k)B_k\left(\frac{w_k}{\sum w_k}\right)\widehat{\sigma_k^2} + B_k^2(\widehat{\tau^2} - \frac{2w_k\widehat{\tau^2}}{\sum w_k} + \frac{1}{\sum w_k}).
\end{aligned}
$$

Therefore, by taking the square root of the right-hand side, we obtain an estimator of the standard error of $\hat{\theta}_k^{EB}$. Alternatively, we can fit random-effects models using standard software for meta-analysis (such as the metafor package in R; see Viechtbauer 2010) and extract estimates of BLUPs and their standard errors, which should be very close to the empirical Bayes estimates.

The standard error derived above tends to underestimate the uncertainty of $\hat{\theta}_k^{EB}$'s because it ignores the estimation of τ^2 and σ_k^2's. A fully

Bayesian approach, as noted by Raudenbush and Bryk (2002), will take account of the estimation uncertainty of μ, τ^2, and θ_k's simultaneously. To build a full Bayes model, we may supply the hyperparameters μ and τ^2 with noninformative priors (e.g., by setting a normal prior with a variance of 10^6 for μ and a uniform prior from 0 to 10^4 for τ^2). Such a model can be easily implemented using standard Markov chain Monte Carlo software such as BUGS. In section 2.5, I illustrate both the empirical Bayes and the full Bayes methods using a set of 16 mobility tables.

2.4. *Usual Estimator versus Shrinkage Estimator in Simulation*

We now turn our attention back to the setting of K 2×2 mobility tables, each representing a country. As noted earlier, the shrinkage factor is decided by the sampling variance of the observed log-odds ratio relative to the true variation in log-odds ratio among the K countries. The influence of shrinkage, therefore, should be stronger when *the true variation in mobility* is relatively small compared with sampling errors. On the other hand, because sampling variance typically differs from country to country, the shrinkage estimates may exhibit a different rank order from that of the usual estimates. Clearly, the extent of this discrepancy should depend on *the extent of variation in sample size* among these countries. In this subsection, I use numerical simulation to examine how potential advantages of the shrinkage approach vary along these two dimensions. I compare the performance between the usual estimator (equation 1) and the shrinkage estimator (equation 7) in two aspects: (1) total squared error and (2) correlation with the true log-odds ratios.

Let us consider 100 2×2 mobility tables depicting, say, intergenerational mobility between white-collar and blue-collar occupations in 100 countries.[6] Following the convention in mobility table analysis, I represent father's occupation in rows and son's occupation in columns. In this simulation, I assume that these countries are at the same stage of industrial development such that 40% of the sample is from white-collar origin in all of the 100 mobility tables. In other words, the row marginal distribution is fixed to be (.4, .6). Despite the homogeneous origin distribution, I allow these countries to vary in the extent of relative mobility as measured by the log-odds ratio. In particular, I create three scenarios in which the true variation in log-odds ratio among these countries is small, medium, and large. Suppose that a son's occupation given a father's occupation follows a binomial distribution, and use $p_{1|1}^k$ and $p_{1|2}^k$

to denote the probabilities of working in a white-collar occupation respectively for a person from white-collar origin and for a person from blue-collar origin in country k. I assume that $p_{1|1}^k$ and $p_{1|2}^k$ are independently and uniformly distributed around .7 and .3, respectively, which means that the probability of being immobile (i.e., staying in the main diagonal of the table) is about .7 for both white-collar and blue-collar occupations. I then construct the three scenarios by letting the range of the two uniform distributions be .08, .16, and .24.[7] In other words, $p_{1|1}^k$ and $p_{1|2}^k$ are independently drawn from the following two distributions:

$$p_{1|1}^k \stackrel{i.i.d.}{\sim} \text{Uniform}(.7 - .04^*\alpha, .7 + .04^*\alpha), k = 1, 2, \cdots 100, \qquad (9)$$

$$p_{1|2}^k \stackrel{i.i.d.}{\sim} \text{Uniform}(.3 - .04^*\alpha, .3 + .04^*\alpha), k = 1, 2, \cdots 100, \qquad (10)$$

where the parameter α, which may take 1, 2, and 3, is used to generate settings in which the true variation in log-odds ratio is small, medium, and large.

The three scenarios above differ in the true variation of log-odds ratio and thus in the estimate of τ^2 in equation (7), which will affect the shrinkage factor uniformly for all countries. As mentioned earlier, the contrasts between the shrinkage estimator and the usual estimator may also depend on the amount of variation in sample size among the mobility tables, which shapes the variation among the $\widehat{\sigma_k^2}$'s. Therefore, I also compare the performance between the two estimators as variation in sample size changes from very small to very large. Specifically, I assume that the sample size follows a log-uniform distribution as below:

$$\log n_{++k} \stackrel{i.i.d.}{\sim} Uniform\left(\log 800^*2^\beta, \log 1250^*2^\beta\right), k = 1, 2, \cdots 100, \qquad (11)$$

where n_{++k} denotes the sample size for country k. I vary the parameter β from 0 to 4 with a step size of 1, thereby generating five scenarios with a gradual change in the variation of sample size while fixing the medium sample size among these countries to be about 1,000. For example, sample size will range between 800 and 1,250 when β takes 0 but range between 50 and 20,000 when β takes 4.

In this simulation, I exhaust all possible combinations of α and β, resulting in $3 \times 5 = 15$ scenarios. For each of these scenarios, I generated the 100 mobility tables in the following steps:

1. For each table k, generate the sample size using $n_{++k} = \lfloor \exp(M) \rceil$, where M is a random draw from the uniform distribution shown in equation 11 and $\lfloor \exp(M) \rceil$ means taking the integer closest to $\exp(M)$.

2. Calculate the row marginals (n_{1+k}, n_{2+k}) by assigning 40% of the sample size n_{++k} to the first category (i.e., white collar).

3. Generate the transition probabilities $p^k_{1|1}$ and $p^k_{1|2}$ using the uniform distributions shown in equations 9 and 10.

4. Create the mobility table $(n_{11k}, n_{12k}, n_{21k}, n_{22k})$ using binomial draws for each row, that is, binomial $(n_{1+k}, p^k_{1|1})$ for the first row and binomial $(n_{2+k}, p^k_{1|2})$ for the second row.

Given the simulated tables, I applied both the usual estimator (equation 1) and the empirical Bayes estimator (equation 7) to estimate the log-odds ratios. I then evaluated the performance of the two estimators using two criteria: (1) total squared error, i.e., $\sum_{k=1}^{100} \left(\hat{\theta}_k - \theta_k \right)^2$, and (2) Pearson's correlation coefficient (among the 100 countries), that is, $\text{Cor}(\hat{\theta}_k, \theta_k)$. To smooth random fluctuations, I averaged these two measures over 500 iterations of the above procedures (data generation, estimation, and evaluation) for each of the 15 scenarios.

Figure 1 presents the results, with panel A for total squared errors and panel B for the correlation coefficients. In both panels, I represent the usual estimator in squares and the shrinkage estimator in triangles. The three scenarios in which the true variation in log-odds ratio is small, medium, and large are represented respectively by solid, dashed, and dotted lines. First, we observe that in virtually all of the 15 scenarios, the shrinkage estimator exhibits lower total squared errors and higher correlations with the true values than does the usual estimator. This is consistent with theoretical results on joint estimation of normal means as discussed by Efron and Morris (1973, 1975). Second, as shown by both panels, the benefits of the shrinkage estimator are greater when the true variation in log-odds ratio is smaller. This relationship is intuitive because the shrinkage approach is essentially pooling information across cases, which should be more effective when these cases are more similar to each other. We also note that for both estimators, the correlation with the true values increases as the true variation in log-odds ratio increases. This is because when the true differences are larger, they are less likely to be confounded by sampling fluctuations and thus more likely to be detected from the data. Finally, reading along the x-axis, we find that the advantage of the shrinkage estimator becomes more pronounced as

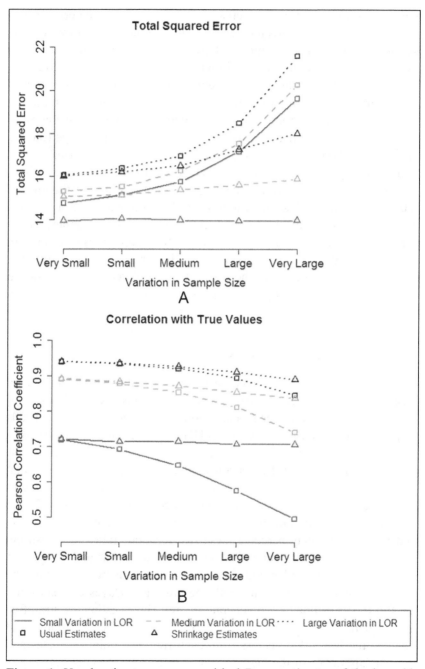

Figure 1. Usual estimator versus empirical Bayes estimator of the log-odds ratio (LOR) in total squared error (A) and Pearson's correlation with the true values (B) under different scenarios.

the variation in sample size increases. In fact, both estimators perform worse when there is greater variation in sample size. However, the shrinkage estimator is far more robust than the usual estimator in this aspect. For instance, in the case in which the true variation in log-odds ratio is small (solid lines), the correlation between the usual estimates and the true values declines from above .7 to below .5 as the variation in sample size changes from very small to very large, whereas the correlation between the shrinkage estimates and the true values stays roughly unchanged (about .71) regardless of the variation in sample size.

To sum up, this simulation study suggests that the shrinkage estimator almost always outperforms the usual estimator in joint estimation of multiple log-odds ratios, either in terms of total squared error or in terms of the correlation with the true values. Moreover, the advantage of the shrinkage estimator is more pronounced when there is less variation in the true log-odds ratio or more variation in sample size. In particular, the higher correlations with the true values exhibited by the shrinkage estimator reveal its great potential for enhancing the accuracy of cross-table comparisons.

2.5. Shrinkage at Work: An Example

I now apply the shrinkage method to the mobility data assembled by Hazelrigg and Garnier (1976), which provide 3×3 classifications of son's occupation by father's occupation for 16 countries in the 1960s and 1970s (henceforth referred to as HG-16). The data are displayed in Table 1. In each of the 16 tables, occupation is categorized as white collar, blue collar, or farm. Let us consider two sets of log-odds ratios that are of particular substantive interest: (1) the log-odds ratio pertaining to the 2×2 subtable of white-collar and blue-collar workers and (2) the log-odds ratio pertaining to the 2×2 subtable of blue-collar workers and farmers. We may perceive these two log-odds ratios as measuring the strengths of class boundaries between white collar and blue collar and between blue collar and farm. For each measure, I contrast the observed log-odds ratios with both the empirical Bayes estimates and the full Bayes estimates. To generate the full Bayes estimates, I ran five independent Markov chains, each containing 4,000 iterations, and retained the last 2,000 vectors from each run. The point estimates and the standard errors of the log-odds ratios were estimated respectively as the posterior means and the posterior standard deviations.

Table 1. Mobility Tables for 16 Countries, Father's Occupation by Son's Occupation

Australia			Belgium			France			Hungary		
292	170	29	497	100	12	2,085	1,047	74	479	190	14
290	608	37	300	434	7	936	2,367	57	1,029	2,615	347
81	171	175	102	101	129	592	1,255	1,587	516	3,110	3,751

Italy			Japan			Philippines			Spain		
233	75	10	465	122	21	239	110	76	7,622	2,124	379
104	291	23	159	258	20	91	292	111	3,495	9,072	597
71	212	320	285	307	333	317	527	3,098	4,597	8,173	14,833

United States			West Germany			West Malaysia			Yugoslavia		
1,650	641	34	3,634	850	270	406	235	144	61	24	7
1,618	2,692	70	1,021	1,694	306	176	369	183	37	92	13
694	1,648	644	1,068	1,310	1,927	315	578	2,311	77	148	223

Denmark			Finland			Norway			Sweden		
79	34	2	39	29	2	90	29	5	89	30	0
55	119	8	24	115	10	72	89	11	81	142	3
25	48	84	40	66	79	41	47	47	27	48	29

Note: The row and column categories are "white collar," "blue collar," and "farm" for all countries in the table.
Source: Grusky and Hauser (1983:56); see also Raftery (1995:115).

The results are shown in Table 2. On one hand, we observe that for countries with very large sample sizes, such as Spain, United States, and West Germany, both the point estimates and the standard errors are largely the same across different methods. Because within-sample precision is sufficiently high for these countries, the shrinkage factors assigned to the observed log-odds ratios are almost zero. The shrinkage estimates, therefore, closely resemble the MLE in both location and precision. On the other hand, for relatively sparse tables, such as Finland, Norway, and Sweden, both the point estimates and the standard errors are markedly changed under the shrinkage methods. However, the empirical Bayes approach and the full Bayes approach yield essentially identical point estimates, although the latter gives slightly larger standard errors as it incorporates the uncertainty of the prior variance τ^2.

Table 2. Point Estimates and Estimated Standard Errors for Two Sets of Log-odds Ratios in HG-16 under Different Estimation Methods

	LOR between White Collar and Blue Collar			LOR between Blue Collar and Farm		
	Observed	Empirical Bayes	Full Bayes	Observed	Empirical Bayes	Full Bayes
Australia	1.28	1.35	1.35	2.82	2.82	2.82
	(.12)	(.11)	(.12)	(.20)	(.19)	(.19)
Belgium	1.97	1.93	1.94	4.37	3.95	3.98
	(.13)	(.12)	(.13)	(.40)	(.34)	(.37)
France	1.62	1.62	1.62	3.96	3.91	3.90
	(.05)	(.05)	(.05)	(.14)	(.14)	(.14)
Hungary	1.86	1.85	1.85	2.21	2.21	2.21
	(.09)	(.09)	(.09)	(.06)	(.06)	(.06)
Italy	2.16	2.05	2.05	2.95	2.93	2.95
	(.18)	(.15)	(.16)	(.23)	(.22)	(.22)
Japan	1.82	1.81	1.81	2.64	2.66	2.66
	(.14)	(.13)	(.13)	(.25)	(.23)	(.23)
Philippines	1.94	1.89	1.90	2.74	2.74	2.74
	(.17)	(.14)	(.15)	(.12)	(.12)	(.12)
Spain	2.23	2.23	2.23	3.32	3.31	3.31
	(.03)	(.03)	(.03)	(.04)	(.04)	(.04)
United States	1.45	1.47	1.46	2.71	2.71	2.71
	(.06)	(.06)	(.06)	(.13)	(.13)	(.13)
West Germany	1.96	1.95	1.95	2.10	2.11	2.11
	(.05)	(.05)	(.05)	(.07)	(.07)	(.07)
West Malaysia	1.29	1.36	1.35	2.09	2.10	2.10
	(.12)	(.11)	(.12)	(.10)	(.10)	(.10)
Yugoslavia	1.84	1.80	1.80	2.37	2.45	2.43
	(.31)	(.21)	(.23)	(.31)	(.28)	(.30)
Denmark	1.61	1.67	1.67	3.26	3.14	3.13
	(.26)	(.19)	(.21)	(.41)	(.34)	(.37)
Finland	1.86	1.80	1.81	2.62	2.67	2.67
	(.33)	(.21)	(.23)	(.37)	(.32)	(.31)
Norway	1.34	1.52	1.52	2.09	2.27	2.26
	(.27)	(.19)	(.22)	(.38)	(.33)	(.33)
Sweden	1.65	1.69	1.69	3.35	3.11	3.09
	(.25)	(.19)	(.19)	(.63)	(.45)	(.49)

Note: Numbers in parentheses are estimated standard errors. HG-16 = the 16 3 × 3 mobility tables assembled by Hazelrigg and Garnier (1976); LOR = log-odds ratio.

Overall, shrinkage estimates based on either approach are more precise than the usual estimates.

To demonstrate the effects of shrinkage, I visualize the contrasts between the observed log-odds ratios and the empirical Bayes estimates in Figure 2, in which 9 of the 16 countries are marked for illustration: Belgium, France, Hungary, Italy, Spain, United States, West Malaysia, Norway, and Sweden. Panel A shows the log-odds ratio between white collar and blue collar. First, we find that most of the cross-country differences are consistent between the two sets of estimates: for example, according to either estimator, Spain and West Malaysia are respectively the least mobile (i.e., with the highest log-odds ratio) and the most mobile (i.e., with the lowest log-odds ratio) among the nine countries. However, because the observed log-odds ratios differ in sampling precision, the shrinkage estimator implies a slightly different rank order among these countries. In particular, Norway is more mobile than the United States according to the usual estimator (i.e., the observed odds ratio) but less mobile than the United States according to the shrinkage estimator. In other words, the empirical Bayes model suggests that the higher mobility of Norway exhibited by the raw data is due simply to its larger sampling variance, not because the barrier between white-collar and blue-collar jobs is more permeable in Norway than in the United States.[8]

Panel B demonstrates the effects of shrinkage for the log-odds ratio between blue collar and farm. Overall, these estimates are much higher than the estimates in panel A, indicating that the barrier between these two classes is much harder to cross than the barrier between white-collar and blue-collar jobs. Similar to panel A, the rankings among the nine countries are not much altered under the shrinkage approach, except that Norway is again "shrunk toward the mean." We also find that the influence of shrinkage is the most pronounced for Belgium, which is markedly less mobile than France according to the observed log-odds ratio but closely resembles France in their shrinkage estimates. This is clearly related to the sparse cell of (blue collar, farm) in the Belgian table (see again Table 1).

3. ADJUSTED ESTIMATION OF THE ALTHAM INDEX

For mobility tables with more than two categories, we can use the shrinkage estimator (equation 7) to calculate summary measures of association that are based on aggregations of log-odds ratios. In this section, I construct an adjusted estimator of the Altham index, an aggregate measure of association that has been recently used for studying intergenerational occupational mobility (Ferrie 2005; Long and Ferrie 2007,

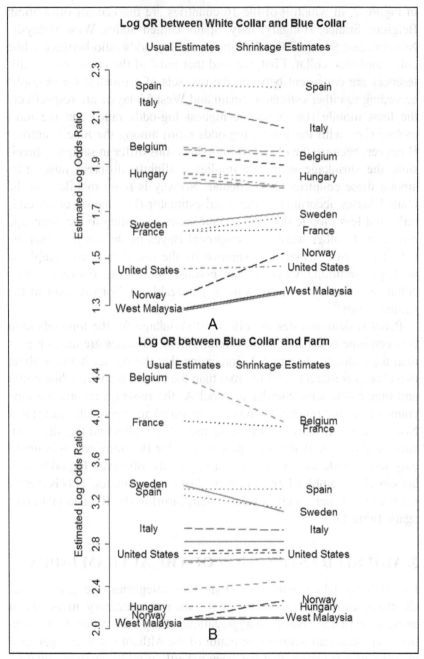

Figure 2. Usual estimates and shrinkage estimates for two sets of log-odds ratios in HG-16. HG-16 = the 16 3 × 3 mobility tables assembled by Hazelrigg and Garnier (1976); Log OR = log-odds ratio.

2013). Results from a set of calibrated simulations suggest that using shrinkage estimates of log-odds ratios can substantially improve the estimation precision of the Altham index.

3.1. *An Adjusted Estimator of the Altham Index*

To assess the total amount of association embodied in a two-way contingency table, Altham (1970) proposed a number of measures that are based on aggregations of log-odds ratios. One such measure is identical to the Euclidean distance between the full sets of log-odds ratios in two $I \times J$ tables P and Q, that is,

$$d(P,Q) = \left[\sum_{i=1}^{I} \sum_{j=1}^{J} \sum_{l=1}^{I} \sum_{m=1}^{J} \left| \log \frac{p_{ij}p_{lm}}{p_{im}p_{lj}} - \log \frac{q_{ij}q_{lm}}{q_{im}q_{lj}} \right|^2 \right]^{1/2},$$

where p_{ij} and q_{ij} denote the probabilities associated with the cell (i,j) in table P and table Q. Although the metric $d(P,Q)$ gauges the distance between the row-column associations in tables P and Q, it does not tell us in which table the rows and the columns are more closely associated. To answer this question, we can compare $d(P,J)$ with $d(Q,J)$, where J denotes a contingency table in which the rows and columns are completely independent. Because all of the log-odds ratios are zero in an independent table, we have

$$d(P,J) = \left[\sum_{i=1}^{I} \sum_{j=1}^{J} \sum_{l=1}^{I} \sum_{m=1}^{J} \left| \log \frac{p_{ij}p_{lm}}{p_{im}p_{lj}} \right|^2 \right]^{1/2}. \tag{12}$$

We can see that $d(P,J)$ is the square root of the sum of all squared log-odds ratios in table P. A larger value of $d(P,J)$ indicates a stronger association between the rows and columns. Hence, when P is a mobility table, a larger $d(P,J)$ corresponds to a more rigid class regime. Although this approach to comparing mobility tables is lesser known than log-linear models in comparative stratification research, it has been recently used by economic historians to study long-term trends in occupational mobility in Great Britain and the United States (Ferrie 2005; Long and Ferrie 2007, 2013). From here on, I use "the Altham index" to mean $d(P,J)$ for a contingency table P.

Now suppose we have a set of $I \times I$ mobility tables $M_1, M_2, \cdots M_k$ for K countries. For each country k, we can directly calculate the Altham index by substituting the observed log-odds ratios:

$$\hat{d}^{\text{Direct}}(M_k, J) = \left[\sum_{i=1}^{I} \sum_{j=1}^{J} \sum_{l=1}^{I} \sum_{m=1}^{J} \left| \log \frac{n_{ijk}n_{lmk}}{n_{imk}n_{ljk}} \right|^2 \right]^{1/2}, k = 1, 2, \cdots K,$$

(13)

where n_{ijk} denotes the observed frequency associated with the cell (i,j) in table k.[9] On the other hand, we can use the shrinkage estimator of the log-odds ratio for each row-column combination (i,j,l,m), yielding an adjusted estimator of the Altham index:

$$\hat{d}^{\text{Adjusted}}(M_k, J) = \left[\sum_{i=1}^{I} \sum_{j=1}^{J} \sum_{l=1}^{I} \sum_{m=1}^{J} \left| \hat{\theta}^{EB}_{(i,j,l,m),k} \right|^2 \right]^{1/2}, k = 1, 2, \cdots K,$$

(14)

where $\hat{\theta}^{EB}_{(i,j,l,m),k}$ denotes the shrinkage estimator (equation 7) of the log-odds ratio $\log \frac{p_{ij}p_{lm}}{p_{im}p_{lj}}$ in table k. Because the Altham index is not a linear function of the log-odds ratios, the adjusted estimator (equation 14) cannot be expressed as a weighted average between the direct estimator (equation 13) and a common mean as in equation (7). However, as we will see, the key effect of this adjustment is also "pulling" the direct estimates toward the middle, the extent of which depends on sample sizes of the corresponding tables.

3.2. Direct Estimator versus Adjusted Estimator in Simulation

Below, I use numerical simulation to evaluate the performance of the direct estimator (equation 13) and the adjusted estimator (equation 14) for the Altham index. As in the case of the log-odds ratio, I compare them in two aspects: (1) total squared error and (2) correlation with the true values. To mimic mobility regimes in the real world, I use HG-16 to motivate my simulation setup. First, I fitted the 16 3×3 mobility tables using four log-linear (or log-multiplicative) models: (1) quasi-perfect mobility, (2) uniform inheritance, (3) perfect blue-collar mobility, and (4) the Unidiff model with full row-column interaction. These models were proposed by Grusky and Hauser (1984) (a, b, c) and Xie

(1992) (d) to compare mobility regimes of the 16 countries.[10] I then treated the estimated parameters as the true parameters, yielding four data-generating models, that is, four simulation setups. For each of the four setups, I generated 1,000 independent samples of the 16 tables and, for each sample, obtained the direct and the adjusted estimates of the Altham index. With the "true" Altham indices readily available from the model parameters, I evaluated the two estimators using three criteria: (1) total squared error, (2) Pearson's correlation with the true values, and (3) Spearman's rank correlation with the true values. To smooth random fluctuations, each of the three measures was averaged over the 1,000 samples, thus producing the total mean squared error (total MSE) and the average correlation coefficients. The results are summarized in Table 3.

We first observe in this table that the adjusted estimator leads to a substantial reduction in total MSE in all of the four scenarios. For example, when data are generated from the Unidiff model, total MSE for the adjusted estimator is only about half of that for the direct estimator (38.8 / 77.0 = 50.4%). Moreover, the adjusted estimates compete well with the direct estimates in correlating with the true Altham indices. Specifically, the adjusted estimator (on average) brings an increase in Pearson's correlation in all of the four scenarios and an increase in Spearman's rank correlation in two of the four scenarios. Therefore, the shrinkage-based method for calculating the Altham index not only yields more precise individual estimates but may also enhance the accuracy of cross-table comparisons in the overall degree of association.

3.3. *An Illustration Using HG-16*

I now apply both estimators of the Altham index to the real data in HG-16. The results are shown in Figure 3A, in which the same nine countries as in section 2.5 are highlighted for illustration. Clearly, with the shrinkage estimates of log-odds ratios, the Altham index tends to be shrunk toward the middle, yet the degree of shrinkage varies considerably from country to country. For example, the adjusted estimate is very similar to the direct estimate for France, but the estimate for Sweden is heavily altered by the adjustment. According to the direct estimates, Sweden ranks as the least mobile (i.e., with the highest Altham index) among the 16 countries; but by the adjusted estimates, Sweden stands

Table 3. Direct Estimator versus Adjusted Estimator of the Altham Index in Simulation

Data-generating Model	Estimator	Total MSE	Average Correlation with $d(M_k, J)$	
			Pearson	Spearman's Rank
Quasi-perfect mobility	$\hat{d}^{\text{Direct}}(M_k, J)$	91.9	.916	.894
	$\hat{d}^{\text{Adjusted}}(M_k, J)$	73.5	.919	.886
Uniform inheritance	$\hat{d}^{\text{Direct}}(M_k, J)$	39.6	.904	.886
	$\hat{d}^{\text{Adjusted}}(M_k, J)$	22.3	.940	.918
Perfect blue-collar mobility	$\hat{d}^{\text{Direct}}(M_k, J)$	107.5	.894	.885
	$\hat{d}^{\text{Adjusted}}(M_k, J)$	74.0	.904	.873
Unidiff (full interaction)	$\hat{d}^{\text{Direct}}(M_k, J)$	77.0	.867	.855
	$\hat{d}^{\text{Adjusted}}(M_k, J)$	38.8	.906	.882

Note: MSE = mean squared error.

right in the middle, more mobile than Hungary, France, Belgium, Italy, and Spain. Such a sharp contrast suggests that the high (direct) estimate of the Altham index for Sweden is primarily a result of large sampling errors for some of the log-odds ratios in the Swedish data. As was shown in Table 1, the cell (white collar, farm) of the Swedish table contains no observation, which may have led to an incredibly high estimate of the Altham index.

We can also evaluate the Altham index for a subset of the mobility table. Figure 3B presents the results for the same set of tables with the farm-farm cells excluded. The uniqueness of the farm-farm cell has been emphasized by Xie and Killewald (2013), who argued that the extremely persistent degree of self-recruitment from farming among farmers (regardless of historical contexts) challenges the utility of odds ratio–based measures for comparing mobility regimes with very different levels of industrialization. Hence, calculating the Altham index without the farm-farm cell serves as a sensitivity check on the results in Figure 3A. Two findings emerge from this analysis. First, compared with panel A, we find that the exclusion of the farm-farm cell leads to significant changes in the positions of these countries along the mobility spectrum. For instance, when the full tables are analyzed, France and Hungary are fairly close to each other, both ranking among the least mobile regimes; when the farm-farm cells are excluded, France appears

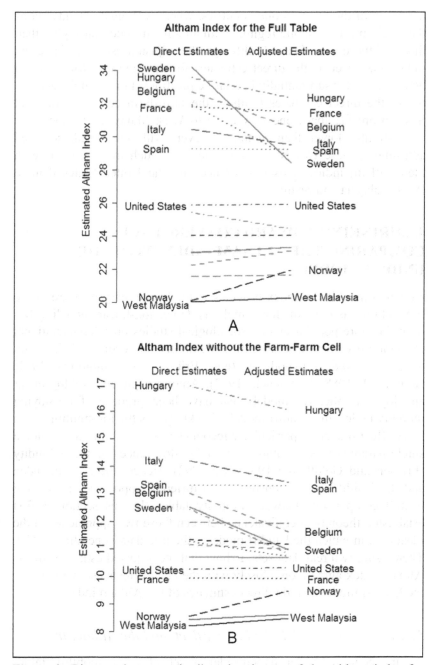

Figure 3. Direct estimates and adjusted estimates of the Altham index for HG-16 (A) and HG-16 without farm-farm cells (B). HG-16 = the 16 3 × 3 mobility tables assembled by Hazelrigg and Garnier (1976).

to be one of the most mobile countries, whereas Hungary stands out as the single most immobile regime, with an Altham index far higher than those of the others. Second, although the adjusted estimates have the same rank order as the direct estimates for the nine countries marked here, they differ substantially in relative positions. For example, according to the direct estimates (without the farm-farm cell), Norway and Sweden are far apart, one very close to West Malaysia and the other only slightly lower than Spain; however, with the shrinkage-based adjustment, these two Nordic countries are much more similar, with their Altham indices closer to France and the United States than to West Malaysia and Spain.

4. SHRINKING TOWARD CONVERGENCE: COMPARING THE ALTHAM INDEX WITH THE UNIDIFF MODEL

Although the Altham index provides a simple summary measure of the row-column association for a mobility table, log-linear modeling has been far more popular among sociological studies on intergenerational class mobility, in part because of its flexibility for accommodating fine-grained theoretical hypotheses (e.g., Erikson and Goldthorpe 1987; Hout 1984, 1988; Yamaguchi 1987). Among a plethora of log-linear and log-multiplicative models that have been proposed for studying mobility tables, the Unidiff model (also known as the log-multiplicative layer effect model) is particularly recognized for its ability to provide a single parameter that captures cross-table differences in social fluidity (Erikson and Goldthorpe 1992; Xie 1992). Hence, the Altham index and the Unidiff model constitute two different approaches to making overall comparisons between mobility tables. In this section, I first establish a theoretical equivalence between these two approaches in the ideal case in which the Unidiff model is the true data-generating model. Then, using two real data sets, I show that the adjusted estimates of the Altham index agree more closely with the layer effects estimated under the Unidiff model than do direct estimates of the Altham index.

4.1. *The Unidiff Model, the Layer Effect, and the Altham Index*

As in section 3.1, let us consider a set of $I \times I$ mobility tables $M_1, M_2, \ldots M_k$ for K countries. In a log-linear analysis, these tables are typically treated as a three-way table with I rows, I columns, and K layers. Denoting by F_{ijk} the expected frequency in the ith row, the jth column, and the kth layer (i.e., the kth country), the saturated log-linear model can be written as

$$\log F_{ijk} = \mu + \mu_i^R + \mu_j^C + \mu_k^L + \mu_{ik}^{RL} + \mu_{jk}^{CL} + \mu_{ij}^{RC} + \mu_{ijk}^{RCL}.$$

In this equation, the first six terms are used to saturate the marginal distributions of both the origin and the destination in each country, while the last two terms, μ_{ij}^{RC} and μ_{ijk}^{RCL}, capture variations in the origin-destination association across countries. However, because the saturated model exhausts all degrees of freedom, it would severely overfit the data. In practice, the researcher often wants to specify μ_{ij}^{RC} and μ_{ijk}^{RCL} in a parsimonious fashion. The Unidiff model, in particular, assumes that these countries share a common pattern of association between origin and destination while allowing the strength of association to vary across countries. As a result, the model can be written as

$$\log F_{ijk} = \mu + \mu_i^R + \mu_j^C + \mu_k^L + \mu_{ik}^{RL} + \mu_{jk}^{CL} + \psi_{ij}\phi_k. \tag{15}$$

Here, the parameter ψ_{ij} characterizes the common pattern of association, and the parameter ϕ_k, which is called the "layer effect," identifies the relative position of country k along the mobility spectrum.

According to equation (15), the expected log-odds ratio associated with the row-column combination (i, j, l, m) in table k can be calculated as

$$\theta_{(i,j,l,m),k} = \log F_{ijk} - \log F_{imk} - \log F_{ljk} + \log F_{lmk} = \theta_{i,j,l,m}^* \phi_k, \tag{16}$$

where $\theta_{i,j,l,m}^* = \psi_{ij} - \psi_{im} - \psi_{lj} + \psi_{lm}$. Therefore, under the Unidiff model, any log-odds ratio in a given table is the product of a common log-odds ratio $\theta_{i,j,l,m}^*$ and the layer effect ϕ_k. Clearly, a greater value of ϕ_k implies a lower degree of social fluidity. Substituting the above expression into equation (12), the Altham index becomes

$$d(M_k, J) = \left[\sum_{i,j,l,m} \left| \theta_{(i,j,l,m),k} \right|^2 \right]^{1/2} = \left[\sum_{i,j,l,m} \left| \theta_{i,j,l,m}^* \right|^2 \right]^{1/2} \phi_k. \tag{17}$$

Because the term $\left[\sum_{i,j,l,m} \left| \theta_{i,j,l,m}^* \right|^2 \right]^{1/2}$ does not depend on k, the Altham index $d(M_k, J)$ is directly proportional to the layer effect ϕ_k. In other words, these two measures of association are equivalent under the Unidiff model.

Real mobility data, however, may fail to support the assumptions of the Unidiff model. For example, according to the likelihood ratio test, the Unidiff model fits poorly for HG-16 (Xie 1992:390). In such cases, we may conclude that different mobility regimes exhibit different patterns of relative mobility, and proceed to develop more flexible models, such as the regression-type models proposed by Goodman and Hout (1998), to capture the nuances of cross-table differences. Nonetheless, tempted by such questions as "Overall, is country A more mobile than country B?" the researcher may still be interested in reducing subtle, multidimensional differences to simple, one-dimensional contrasts. In this regard, the Unidiff model and the Altham index constitute two reasonable yet distinct approaches. A natural question, then, is whether these two approaches would yield concordant results. Because the layer effect and the Altham index are equivalent when the Unidiff model is true, we would expect that they produce more similar results when data are more congruent with the Unidiff model. On the other hand, given the advantages of the adjusted estimator over the direct estimator for the Altham index, it is reasonable to conjecture that the adjusted estimator agrees more closely than the direct estimator with results from the Unidiff model. Below, I use two sets of real mobility tables to test these two hypotheses.

4.2. *Shrinking toward Convergence: Evidence from Two Data Sets*

I apply both estimators of the Altham index, along with the Unidiff model, to two data sets: (1) HG-16 (i.e., the 16 3×3 mobility tables assembled by Hazelrigg and Garnier [1976]) and (2) a collection of 149 6×6 mobility tables from 35 countries assembled by Ganzeboom, Luijkx, and Treiman (1989), henceforth GLT-149. Whereas occupation in HG-16 is crudely classified as white collar, blue collar, and farm, GLT-149 adopts the six-category version of the EGP class scheme (Erikson, Goldthorpe, and Portocarero 1979): the service class (I + II), routine nonmanual workers (III), petty bourgeoisie (IVa + IVb), farmers and agricultural laborers (IVc + VIIb), skilled manual workers (V + VI), and unskilled manual workers (VIIa).

Table 4. Correlations of Direct and Adjusted Estimates of the Altham Index with $\hat{\phi}_k^{\text{Unidiff}}$

Data Set	Estimator	Pearson's Correlation	Spearman's Rank Correlation
HG-16	$\hat{d}^{\text{Direct}}(M_k, J)$	.858	.832
	$\hat{d}^{\text{Adjusted}}(M_k, J)$	.852	.876
HG-15 (without Hungary)	$\hat{d}^{\text{Direct}}(M_k, J)$	.917	.846
	$\hat{d}^{\text{Adjusted}}(M_k, J)$	.939	.893
GLT-149	$\hat{d}^{\text{Direct}}(M_k, J)$	.817	.839
	$\hat{d}^{\text{Adjusted}}(M_k, J)$	.803	.899

To assess the extent to which different estimators of the Altham index accord with the layer effects estimated under the Unidiff model, I use Spearman's rank correlation as well as the Pearson correlation. Previous researchers analyzing HG-16 have pointed out that Hungary significantly deviates from the other 15 countries in patterns of inter-class mobility (Grusky and Hauser 1984; Xie 1992). For this reason, I analyzed both the full set of HG-16 and the 15 tables excluding the Hungarian case (henceforth referred to as HG-15). The results are shown in Table 4. We can see that for all three data sets, the fitted layer effects $\hat{\phi}_k^{\text{Unidiff}}$ tend to correlate more strongly with the adjusted esti-mates of the Altham index than with the direct estimates, especially by Spearman's rank correlation. For example, the rank correlation for GLT-149 is .839 between $\hat{d}^{\text{Direct}}(M_k, J)$ and $\hat{\phi}_k^{\text{Unidiff}}$ but .899 between $\hat{d}^{\text{Adjusted}}(M_k, J)$ and $\hat{\phi}_k^{\text{Unidiff}}$.

On the other hand, we notice that when Hungary is excluded from HG-16, both estimates of the Altham index become more aligned with the fitted layer effects. The Pearson correlation, for example, increases from .858 to .917 between $\hat{d}^{\text{Direct}}(M_k, J)$ and $\hat{\phi}_k^{\text{Unidiff}}$ and from .852 to .939 between $\hat{d}^{\text{Adjusted}}(M_k, J)$ and $\hat{\phi}_k^{\text{Unidiff}}$. These results accord well with our first hypothesis: because Hungary contributes the lion's share to the model deviance (i.e., G^2), its exclusion considerably improves the fit between the data and the Unidiff model, thereby producing greater con-sistency between model-free (i.e., the Altham index) and model-based (i.e., the Unidiff model) inferences. To explore this relationship further, I examine how the above correlations change as the most poorly fitted cases are progressively excluded from the data sets. Specifically, for

HG-16, I performed a stepwise elimination of Hungary, France, West Germany, the United States, and Spain—in order of decreasing G^2 under the Unidiff model—and recalculated the correlations for each subset of the 16 tables. For GLT-149, the same procedures were followed except that five tables, rather than one table, were removed at a time and the correlation coefficients were recalculated until 40 tables were deleted.

Figure 4 shows the results, with panel A for HG-16 and panel B for GLT-149. In both panels, I represent Pearson's correlation in solid lines and Spearman's rank correlation in dashed lines. Meanwhile, squares and triangles denote direct and adjusted estimates of the Altham index, respectively. From the four contrasts between squares and triangles, we notice that the adjusted estimates of the Altham index almost always correlate more strongly with the fitted layer effects than do the direct estimates. On the other hand, reading along the x-axis, we find that the correlation coefficients generally increase as the most poorly fitted cases are excluded from the data sets. The upward drift, however, is more noticeable for the adjusted estimator than for the direct estimator. As a result, the gap between $\hat{d}^{\text{Direct}}(M_k, J)$ and $\hat{d}^{\text{Adjusted}}(M_k, J)$ in their correlations with $\hat{\phi}_k^{\text{Unidiff}}$ grows larger as data align more closely with the Unidiff model. For example, when the full set of GLT-149 is analyzed, the Pearson correlation between $\hat{d}^{\text{Adjusted}}(M_k, J)$ and $\hat{\phi}_k^{\text{Unidiff}}$ is .803, slightly lower than that between $\hat{d}^{\text{Direct}}(M_k, J)$ and $\hat{\phi}_k^{\text{Unidiff}}$ (.817; see again Table 4); but when the 40 tables with the largest deviances are excluded, the adjusted estimates of Altham indices correlate much more strongly with the fitted layer effects than do the direct estimates.

In short, these results suggest that in assessing the overall degree of social fluidity, the adjusted estimator of the Altham index accords more closely with the Unidiff model than does the direct estimator. Moreover, the contrast becomes more pronounced when data are more congruent with the Unidiff model. How do we understand these findings? First, we note that the adjusted estimator of the Altham index differs from the direct estimator only in its reliance on shrinkage estimates of the log-odds ratios. As mentioned earlier, the underlying principle of the shrinkage method is to borrow information from other cases, particularly through an empirical Bayes model with a normal prior. The adjusted estimator of the Altham index, therefore, may be considered as a semi-parametric method because it uses a normal Bayes model to smooth data across multiple tables but imposes no parametric constraints on the pattern of association within tables. In contrast, the direct estimator of the

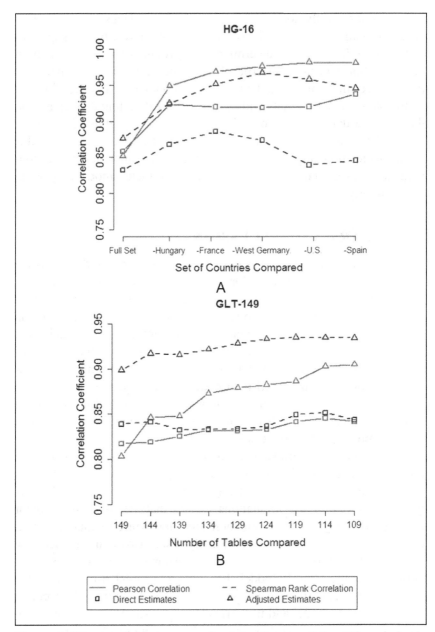

Figure 4. Direct estimates versus adjusted estimates of the Altham index in their correlations with $\hat{\phi}_k^{\text{Unidiff}}$ for varying subsets of HG-16 and GLT-149. HG-16 = the 16 3 × 3 mobility tables assembled by Hazelrigg and Garnier (1976); GLT-149 = a collection of 149 6 × 6 mobility tables from 35 countries assembled by Ganzeboom, Luijkx, and Treiman (1989).

Altham index is fully nonparametric, involving no data smoothing either across or within tables. On the other hand, the Unidiff model stipulates that all log-odds ratios are determined as a product of a common pattern of association and table-specific effects. This multiplicative specification requires the Unidiff model to pool data both across tables (for estimating ψ_{ij}) and across cells within tables (for estimating ϕ_k). Hence, in the way that data are pooled to draw inferences, the adjusted estimator of the Altham index stands closer than the direct estimator to the Unidiff model, which probably explains why the shrinkage approach boosts convergence between a descriptive index and a parametric model in gauging social fluidity.

5. SUMMARY AND DISCUSSION

Building on an empirical Bayes framework, I have proposed a shrinkage estimator of the log-odds ratio for comparing mobility tables. This estimator enhances estimation precision by borrowing information across multiple tables while placing no restrictions on the pattern of association within tables. This approach stands in stark contrast to the usual MLE of the log-odds ratio, which involves no data pooling either across or within tables. Numerical simulation suggests that the shrinkage estimator outperforms the usual MLE in both the total squared error and the correlation with the true values. Moreover, the benefits of the shrinkage method are greater when there is less variation among the true log-odds ratios or more variation in sampling precision.

Furthermore, the shrinkage estimator of the log-odds ratio can be used to calculate the Altham index, an aggregate measure of association that has been recently adopted in comparative mobility research. Results from a set of calibrated simulations suggest that the adjusted estimator can substantially improve estimation precision while maintaining high correlations with the true values. Finally, using two real data sets, we find that the adjusted estimator of the Altham index accords more closely with the Unidiff model than does the direct estimator of the Altham index. This finding, as I have discussed, stems from the fact that both the Unidiff model and the shrinkage approach enforce information sharing across tables, albeit via apparently different mechanisms.

The shrinkage estimator (equation 7) derives from a Bayes model in which a common prior, that is, equation (4), is assumed for all cases. This assumption can easily be relaxed to incorporate our prior knowledge about the similarities and differences between mobility regimes. In particular, we can extend the prior distribution (equation 4) to

$$\theta_k \stackrel{indep}{\sim} N(\alpha + \beta^T X_k, \tau^2),$$

where X_k denotes a group of exogenous variables posited to affect the true log-odds ratio. The empirical Bayes estimator (equation 7) then becomes

$$\hat{\theta}_k^{EB} = \hat{\alpha} + \hat{\beta}^T X_k + [1 - \frac{(K - R - 3)\widehat{\sigma_k^2}}{(K - R - 1)\left(\widehat{\tau^2} + \widehat{\sigma_k^2}\right)}](Y_k - \hat{\alpha} - \hat{\beta}^T X_k),$$

where $\hat{\alpha}$ and $\hat{\beta}$ denote estimates of α and β, and R represents the dimension of X_k.[11] In this formulation, the usual estimate Y_k is shrunk not toward a common mean but toward the conditional mean $\hat{\alpha} + \hat{\beta}^T X_k$. For example, if we assume that economic development promotes social mobility, as the "thesis of industrialism" suggests (Treiman 1970), X_k could be a measure of the level of industrialization in country k. In this case, the shrinkage estimator borrows information not uniformly from all countries but mainly from countries at similar levels of industrialization. Note that if the number of tables K far exceeds the number of predictors R, the adjustment factor $\frac{K-R-3}{K-R-1}$ will be close to one and the empirical Bayes estimates can be approximated by EBLUPs from mixed-effects meta-analysis of log-odds ratios (see Viechtbauer [2010] for a guide to implementation).

For evaluating the overall degree of social fluidity, the Unidiff model and the Altham index constitute two valid yet distinctive approaches. The Unidiff model stipulates that all log-odds ratios are determined multiplicatively by a common pattern of association and layer-specific effects. This is a flexible but nontrivial assumption. Not only does it require that different log-odds ratios within a table are of the same relative magnitudes in all mobility regimes, but it also means that the rank order among mobility regimes does not depend on which log-odds ratio is being examined. For example, a Unidiff model for HG-16 would imply that the two sets of log-odds ratios in Figure 2 exhibit the same relative positions in the two panels, which is obviously at odds with the data. The Unidiff model, therefore, may incur a model specification bias if the true mobility regimes being compared do not comport with the "common-pattern" assumption. In contrast, the Altham index is fully nonparametric, thus being exempt from any type of model specification bias. For the same reason, however, direct calculation of the Altham index is susceptible to large sampling errors, especially for sparse tables. The shrinkage approach presented in this paper—which exploits a parametric Bayes model to "borrow strength" across tables but remains model-free within tables—serves as an eclectic formula for comparing mobility regimes, striking a balance between sampling variance and model specification bias. Clearly, this approach is applicable not only to comparative mobility analysis but to any area of research that calls for comparisons of multiple two-way contingency tables.

Acknowledgments

I thank Harry Ganzeboom for making the GLT-149 data available. I am grateful to Yu Xie, Hongwei Xu, and two anonymous reviewers for their helpful comments. The ideas expressed herein are those of the author.

Notes

1. The inadequacy of mobility ratio as a measure of association has been discussed by Blau and Duncan (1967:93–97), Tyree (1973), Hauser (1980:426–30), and Hout (1983:17–18).
2. Typically, the same occupational classification is used for origin and destination, that is, fathers and sons. In this case, $I = J$.
3. This observation derives from the fact that an estimated variance of the sample log-odds ratio can be expressed as $1/n_{11} + 1/n_{12} + 1/n_{21} + 1/n_{22}$ (Agresti 2002:71). See also section 2.
4. The same conclusion holds when the sampling distribution is Poisson or product multinomial; see Powers and Xie (2008:79–80).
5. Clogg and Eliason (1987) noted that the practice of adding constants to all cells tends to shrink the data toward equiprobability. As we will see, this problem will be less relevant for the shrinkage estimator because the modified sample estimate Y_k is unlikely to receive much weight when there are zero cells.
6. For convenience, the agricultural sector is omitted in this simulation study.
7. The parameters for the row marginal distribution, the average transition probabilities, and the ranges of the transition probabilities are all chosen on the basis of the empirical mobility tables for 16 countries collected by Hazelrigg and Garnier (1976).
8. If we calculate the z score for the difference in observed log-odds ratio between Norway and the United States, we will find that it is not statistically significant.
9. As before, when any of the four cells are zero, one half is added to all of the four cells before calculation.

10. Models 1, 2, and 3 correspond respectively to models A2, A3, and A4 in Grusky and Hauser (1984:389); model 4 corresponds to model FI_x in Xie (1992:390).
11. The adjustment factor changes from $\frac{K-3}{K-1}$ to $\frac{K-R-3}{K-R-1}$ because R additional degrees of freedom are used to estimate the hyperparameters; see Morris (1983) for a more technical discussion.

References

Agresti, Alan. 2002. *Categorical Data Analysis*. Hoboken, NJ: John Wiley.

Altham, Patricia M. E.1970. "The Measurement of Association of Rows and Columns for an r×s Contingency Table."*Journal of the Royal Statistical Society, Series B* 32(1):63–73.

Altham, Patricia M. E., and Joseph P. Ferrie. 2007. "Comparing Contingency Tables Tools for Analyzing Data from Two Groups Cross-classified by Two Characteristics." *Historical Methods* 40(1):3–16.

Blau, Peter M., and Otis Dudley Duncan. 1967. *The American Occupational Structure*. New York: John Wiley.

Carter, Grace M., and John E. Rolph. 1974. "Empirical Bayes Methods Applied to Estimating Fire Alarm Probabilities." *Journal of the American Statistical Association* 69(348):880–85.

Clogg, Clifford C., and Scott R. Eliason. 1987. "Some Common Problems in Loglinear Analysis." *Sociological Methods and Research* 16(1):8–44.

Duncan, Otis Dudley. 1979. "How Destination Depends on Origin in the Occupational Mobility Table." *American Journal of Sociology* 84:793–803.

Efron, Bradley, and Carl Morris. 1973. "Stein's Estimation Rule and Its Competitors—An Empirical Bayes Approach." *Journal of the American Statistical Association* 68(341):117–30.

Efron, Bradley, and Carl Morris. 1975. "Data Analysis Using Stein's Estimator and Its Generalizations." *Journal of the American Statistical Association* 70(350):311–19.

Erikson, Robert, John H. Goldthorpe, and Lucienne Portocarero. 1979. "Intergenerational Class Mobility in Three Western European Societies: England, France and Sweden." *British journal of Sociology* 30(4): 415 -41.

Erikson, Robert, and John H. Goldthorpe. 1987. "Commonality and Variation in Social Fluidity in Industrial Nations. Part I: A Model for Evaluating the 'FJH Hypothesis.'" *European Sociological Review* 3(1):54–77.

Erikson, Robert, and John H. Goldthorpe. 1992. *The Constant Flux: A Study of Class Mobility in Industrial Societies*. New York: Oxford University Press.

Fay, Robert E., III, and Roger A. Herriot. 1979. "Estimates of Income for Small Places: An Application of James-Stein Procedures to Census Data." *Journal of the American Statistical Association* 74(366):269–77.

Featherman, David L., F. Lancaster Jones, and Robert M. Hauser. 1975. "Assumptions of Social Mobility Research in the US: The Case of Occupational Status." *Social Science Research* 4(4):329–60.

Ferrie, Joseph P. 2005. "History Lessons: The End of American Exceptionalism? Mobility in the United States since 1850." *Journal of Economic Perspectives* 19(3):199–215.

Ganzeboom, Harry B. G., Ruud Luijkx, and Donald J. Treiman. 1989. "Intergenerational Class Mobility in Comparative Perspective." *Research in Social Stratification and Mobility* 8:3–84.

Gart, John J., and James R. Zweifel. 1967. "On the Bias of Various Estimators of the Logit and Its Variance with Application to Quantal Bioassay." *Biometrika* 54(1–2): 181–87.

Glass, David Victor, and Jerzy Berent. 1954. *Social Mobility in Britain*. London: Routledge Kegan Paul.

Goodman, Leo A. 1968. "The Analysis of Cross-classified Data: Independence, Quasi-independence, and Interactions in Contingency Tables with or without Missing Entries." *Journal of the American Statistical Association* 63(324):1091–131.

Goodman, Leo A. 1969. "How to Ransack Social Mobility Tables and Other Kinds of Cross-classification Tables." *American Journal of Sociology* 75(1):1–40.

Goodman, Leo A. 1979. "Simple Models for the Analysis of Association in Cross-classifications Having Ordered Categories." *Journal of the American Statistical Association* 74(367):537–52.

Goodman, Leo A., and Michael Hout. 1998. "Statistical Methods and Graphical Displays for Analyzing How the Association between Two Qualitative Variables Differs among Countries, among Groups, or over Time: A Modified Regression-type Approach." Pp. 175–230 in *Sociological Methodology*, Vol. 28, edited by Adrian E. Raftery. Boston, MA: Blackwell.

Grusky, David B., and Robert M. Hauser. 1983. "Comparative Social Mobility Revisited: Models of Convergence and Divergence in Sixteen Countries." CDE Working Paper 83-6. Madison: Center for Demography and Ecology, University of Wisconsin.

Grusky, David B., and Robert M. Hauser. 1984. "Comparative Social Mobility Revisited: Models of Convergence and Divergence in 16 Countries." *American Sociological Review* 49(1):19–38.

Haldane, J.B.S. 1956. "The Estimation and Significance of the Logarithm of a Ratio of Frequencies." *Annals of Human Genetics* 20(4):309–11.

Harville, David. 1976. "Extension of the Gauss-Markov Theorem to Include the Estimation of Random Effects." *Annals of Statistics* 4(2):384–95.

Hauser, Robert M. 1980. "Some Exploratory Methods for Modeling Mobility Tables and Other Cross-classified Data." Pp. 413–58 in *Sociological Methodology*, Vol. 11, edited by Karl F. Schuessler. San Francisco, CA: Jossey-Bass.

Hazelrigg, Lawrence E., and Maurice A. Garnier. 1976. "Occupational Mobility in Industrial Societies: A Comparative Analysis of Differential Access to Occupational Ranks in Seventeen Countries." *American Sociological Review* 41:498–511.

Hout, Michael. 1983. *Mobility Tables*. Thousand Oaks, CA: Sage.

Hout, Michael. 1984. "Status, Autonomy, and Training in Occupational Mobility." *American Journal of Sociology* 89(6):1379–409.

Hout, Michael. 1988. "More Universalism, Less Structural Mobility: The American Occupational Structure in the 1980s." *American Journal of Sociology* 93(6): 1358–400.

Hout, Michael, and Avery M. Guest. 2013. "Intergenerational Occupational Mobility in Great Britain and the United States Since 1850: Comment." *American Economic Review* 103(5):2021–40.

James, William, and Charles Stein. 1961. "Estimation with Quadratic Loss." Pp. 361–79 in *Proceedings of the Fourth Berkeley Symposium on Mathematical Statistics and Probability*, Vol. 1. Berkeley, CA: University of California Press.

Lipset, Seymour Martin, and Hans L. Zetterberg. 1956. *A Theory of Social Mobility*. New York: Columbia University Press.

Long, Jason, and Joseph Ferrie. 2007. "The Path to Convergence: Intergenerational Occupational Mobility in Britain and the U.S. in Three Eras." *Economic Journal* 117(519):C61–C71.

Long, Jason, and Joseph Ferrie. 2013. "Intergenerational Occupational Mobility in Great Britain and the United States Since 1850." *American Economic Review* 103(5): 2041–49.

Miller, Seymour Michael. 1960. "Comparative Social Mobility." *Current Sociology* 9(1):1–61.

Morris, Carl N. 1983. "Parametric Empirical Bayes Inference: Theory and Applications." *Journal of the American Statistical Association* 78(381):47–55.

Powers, Daniel A., and Yu Xie. 2008. *Statistical Methods for Categorical Data Analysis*. Bingley, UK: Emerald Group.

Raftery, Adrian E. 1995. "Bayesian Model Selection in Social Research." Pp. 111–64 in *Sociological Methodology*, Vol. 25, edited by Peter V. Marsden. Cambridge, MA: Blackwell.

Raudenbush, Stephen W., and Anthony S. Bryk. 1985. "Empirical Bayes Meta-analysis." *Journal of Educational and Behavioral Statistics* 10(2):75–98.

Raudenbush, Stephen W., and Anthony S. Bryk. 2002. *Hierarchical Linear Models: Applications and Data Analysis Methods*. 2nd ed.Thousand Oaks, CA: Sage.

Robinson, George K. 1991. "That BLUP Is a Good Thing: The Estimation of Random Effects." *Statistical Science* 6(1):15–32.

Rogoff, Natalie. 1953. *Recent Trends in Occupational Mobility*. New York: Arno.

Savitz, Natalya Verbitsky, and Stephen W. Raudenbush. 2009. "Exploiting Spatial Dependence to Improve Measurement of Neighborhood Social Processes." Pp. 151–83 in *Sociological Methodology*, Vol. 39, edited by Yu Xie. Boston: Wiley-Blackwell.

Sidik, Kurex, and Jeffrey N. Jonkman. 2005. "Simple Heterogeneity Variance Estimation for Meta-analysis." *Journal of the Royal Statistical Society, Series C (Applied Statistics)* 54(2):367–84.

Stein, Charles. 1956. "Inadmissibility of the Usual Estimator for the Mean of a Multivariate Normal Distribution." Pp. 197–206 in *Proceedings of the Third Berkeley Symposium on Mathematical Statistics and Probability*, Vol. 1. Berkeley, CA: University of California Press.

Treiman, Donald J. 1970. "Industrialization and Social Stratification." *Sociological Inquiry* 40(2):207–34.

Tyree, Andrea. 1973. "Mobility Ratios and Association in Mobility Tables." *Population Studies* 27(3):577–88.

Viechtbauer, Wolfgang. 2010. "Conducting Meta-analyses in R with the Metaphor Package." *Journal of Statistical Software* 36(3):1–48.

Xie, Yu. 1992. "The Log-multiplicative Layer Effect Model for Comparing Mobility Tables." *American Sociological Review* 57(3):380–95.

Xie, Yu,, and Alexandra Killewald. 2013. "Intergenerational Occupational Mobility in Britain and the U.S. Since 1850: Comment." *American Economic Review* 103(5): 2003–20.

Yamaguchi, Kazuo. 1987. "Models for Comparing Mobility Tables: Toward Parsimony and Substance." *American Sociological Review* 52(4):482–94.

Author Biography

Xiang Zhou is a doctoral candidate in sociology and statistics at the University of Michigan. His research interests include social inequality in China and quantitative methods. His recent publications appear in *Social Forces, Sociological Methodology, Sociological Methods and Research*, and the *Proceedings of the National Academy of Sciences.*

Sociological Methodology
2015, Vol. 45(1) 357–387
© American Sociological Association 2015
DOI: 10.1177/0081175015570096
http://sm.sagepub.com

$\mathcal{E}$ 8 $\mathcal{E}$

CAN NON-FULL-PROBABILITY INTERNET SURVEYS YIELD USEFUL DATA? A COMPARISON WITH FULL-PROBABILITY FACE-TO-FACE SURVEYS IN THE DOMAIN OF RACE AND SOCIAL INEQUALITY ATTITUDES

*Alicia D. Simmons**
Lawrence D. Bobo[†]

Abstract

The authors investigate the potential utility of Web-based surveys of non-full-probabilistically sampled respondents for social science research. Specifically, they compare demographic, attitude response, and multivariate model results produced by two distinct survey modalities: the traditional full-probability sample face-to-face survey and the non-full-probability Web survey. Using data from the 2009 Race Cues, Attitudes, and Punitiveness Survey (RCAPS), the 2008 General Social Survey (GSS), and the 2008 American National Election Study (ANES), the authors find that (1) the unweighted demographic differences between surveys tend to be slight; (2)

*Colgate University, Hamilton, NY, USA
[†]Harvard University, Cambridge, MA, USA

Corresponding Author:
Alicia D. Simmons, Colgate University, Department of Sociology and Anthropology, 13 Oak Drive, Hamilton, NY 13346, USA
Email: asimmons@colgate.edu

in comparison with GSS and ANES respondents, RCAPS respondents are more interested in politics and ideologically polarized; (3) in comparison with ANES respondents, RCAPS respondents are more racially and socially conservative, often selecting the most extreme response option; (4) when the dependent variable is a more general and abstract measure of social attitudes, the multivariate models generated by the ANES and RCAPS show several differences that are trivial in magnitude, but when the dependent variable is a more specific and concrete measure, the models show remarkable similarity; and (5) RCAPS multivariate models consistently explain more variance than ANES models. Overall, these findings show both substantial similarities across the two survey modalities as well as a few clear, reasonably well-specified differences.

Keywords

methodology, survey, mode, sampling, attitudes, race

1. INTRODUCTION

Approaches to survey research have evolved in important ways over the years. To cite just two examples, a heavy reliance on open-ended questions and loosely structured guidelines yielded to closed-ended questions with tightly structured questionnaires, and quota sampling designs gave way to full-probability sample (FPS) designs (Converse 1987). The forces driving these changes, such as the desire for higher quality data and a push to collect data in more efficient and cost effective ways, continue to influence how researchers balance maintaining high-quality data standards against financial and temporal costs.

One current horizon for survey methodology concerns modes of survey administration; today, scholars are increasingly interested in using Web-based surveys for research purposes. In their examination of survey modes used in approximately 2,000 reports featured in issues of *Survey Research*[1] from 1995 to 2009, Brown and Johnson (2011) found that 70.5 percent were by telephone, 21.7 percent were face to face, 17.4 percent were by mail, and 5.6 percent were Web based. Although telephone surveys were dominant in the overall sample, trends revealed that the prevalence of telephone surveys declined over the 14-year span, while the prevalence of Web surveys increased. In 2009, Web surveys were the primary or secondary mode of administration in 33.3 percent of studies. Not only are Web surveys frequently used, they are used to conduct high-caliber research, appearing in leading journals such as the

American Sociological Review (e.g., Rosenfeld and Thomas 2012; Schwartz and Schuman 2005), the *American Journal of Political Science* (e.g., Ansolabehere and Jones 2010; Brooks and Geer 2007; Jerit 2009; Prior 2005), and the *Journal of Personality and Social Psychology* (e.g., Seery, Holman, and Silver 2010; Skitka et al. 2002).

In addition to investigating new survey modes, the field has also been exploring sampling techniques that differ from the consensual gold standard of full-probability designs. In the context of Web surveys, these non-full-probability designs rely on cultivating opt-in pools of respondents, and then applying sampling algorithms to the pool to construct representative samples for individual surveys (e.g., Rivers 2007).

In this article, we examine the potential utility of Web surveys of non-full-probabilistically sampled respondents for social science research. Specifically, we compare demographic, attitude response, and multivariate model results produced by two distinct survey modalities: a non-full-probability Web survey and two of the most highly regarded face-to-face social science surveys using FPSs, the General Social Survey (GSS) and the American National Election Study (ANES). Given its design, the present study cannot fully untangle the unique effects of mode and sampling strategy; however, it can compare and contrast their intersection, highlighting the important similarities and differences in the resulting data.

Although the bulk of contemporary research in this vein has focused on surveys of broad political attitudes (e.g., Chang and Krosnick 2009; Malhotra and Krosnick 2007; Stephenson and Crête 2011), this project advances the literature by focusing on social attitudes that underlie support for public policies: egalitarianism and racial resentment (Hutchings and Valentino 2004; Krysan 2000).[2] This focus is an important extension for two primary reasons. First, it creates an opportunity to explore how respondents' expressions of social attitudes vary with the presence of human interviewers (Krysan and Couper 2003). Krysan (1998) linked whites' expressions of racial attitudes to survey mode, finding a positive relationship between expressions of racial conservatism and the level of privacy provided by the survey context. Web surveys provide an ideal setting for respondent privacy, greatly benefiting researchers who are concerned about interviewers' effects on respondents' expressed opinions. Second, our work addresses researchers' critiques that experimental investigations of prejudice are overly reliant on convenience samples of college students (e.g., Henry 2008; Sears 1986). If data about social attitudes collected from non-full-probability sample (NPS) Web surveys are substantially similar to data collected from FPS face-to-face surveys, this strategy may provide a cost-effective and more efficient way to reach meaningful samples of respondents, while providing greater external validity.

To foreshadow a bit, our results point to five broad conclusions. First, the demographic representativeness of the NPS Web survey mode is roughly equivalent to the FPS face-to-face survey mode. Second, the NPS Web survey respondents are more interested in politics and tend to be stronger political ideologues than the FPS face-to-face survey respondents. Third, the NPS Web survey respondents tend to express more socially conservative opinions than the FPS face-to-face survey respondents, particularly when it comes to voicing the most extreme opinions. Fourth, the similarity of multivariate models produced by the surveys appears to be contingent on how general and abstract versus specific and concrete respondents perceive the attitude domain to be. When examining more general and abstract attitude constructs, the models show several differences that are substantively trivial in magnitude; in contrast, when the dependent variable is more specific and concrete, we see greater similarity across models. Fifth, the NPS Web survey consistently explains more variance in the dependent variables than the FPS face-to-face surveys. Given these findings, and in light of the potential cost savings and speed of data collection advantages NPS Web surveys provide, there are a variety of circumstances when this methodology may be used to study the empirical and theoretical relationships between variables, while remaining mindful of when and to what extent mode and sampling choices may affect results and the scope of legitimate inferences.

2. BACKGROUND

An exhaustive comparison of the full constellation of survey modes and sampling strategies is beyond the scope of our capabilities given the available resources; thus, this article illuminates one important set of comparisons, namely, how full-probability face-to-face surveys compare with non-full-probability Web surveys (henceforth we use "survey modalities" to denote this particular set of survey modes and sampling strategies). To do so, we begin with a brief review of the differences across survey modes and how these characteristics influence data quality. Next, we discuss the promises and pitfalls of full-probability and non-full-probability sampling designs. Finally, we discuss how the intersection of survey modes and sampling strategies can influence data quality.

2.1. *Characteristics of Survey Modes*

Our first concern is with how differences in the face-to-face and Web survey modes influence data quality. As outlined by de Leeuw (1992), survey modes can be differentiated along three broad dimensions: (1) media factors, (2) information transmission, and (3) interviewer impact.

The most important media factor distinguishing the face-to-face and Web modes is familiarity with the media. Although the majority of respondents likely have extensive experience with face-to-face interactions, familiarity with Web site environments may be more variable. Thus, those respondents who are less familiar with Web environments potentially face an added cognitive burden that could reduce data quality.[3]

An information transmission factor differentiating the face-to-face and Web modes is the presentation of stimuli, such that the modes differ with regard to their temporal ordering. Face-to-face modes are predominantly sequential, with little (perceived or actual) opportunity for backtracking. In contrast, temporal ordering is more variable in the Web mode. At one end of the continuum, there might be a great deal of respondent-driven choice, with several different questions appearing on one page, or an explicit option may be available for revising previous answers (e.g., a "back" button). Alternatively, there might be no opportunity for respondent-driven choice, such that respondents are provided with one question at a time and not given the option to revise previous responses. The ability of respondents to alter the order in which they answer questions or to revise previous answers may influence the resulting data via consistency or contrast effects occurring among questions involving identical or closely related issues (Schuman and Presser 1981).[4]

Finally, face-to-face and Web modes have differing opportunities for interviewer impact on respondents; although a human interviewer has a great potential to influence a respondent in the face-to-face mode, interviewer effects are largely absent in the Web mode.[5] The presence of a human interviewer may positively influence a respondent by providing motivation, clarifying the nature of questions, and clarifying the nature of respondents' answers. However, an interviewer may have negative impacts; most important, interviewers may reduce respondents' feelings of privacy, thus compromising the data they provide because of social desirability concerns. For example, Krysan (1998) argued that respondents holding racially conservative opinions view the basis of their beliefs as nonracial. In a public survey mode, respondents "cannot be certain that the interviewer will appreciate their 'nonracist' but 'conservative' response. Respondents . . . may feel pressure in the face-to-face conditions to give a 'safe' and 'liberal-sounding' response, lest their motives be misinterpreted by the interviewer" (p. 532).[6] Respondents can freely express racially conservative opinions in a private survey mode because in this mode, their nonracist self-image is not jeopardized.

2.2. Sampling Strategies in the Web Mode

Our second concern centers on how sampling strategy influences data quality. Here, the critical issue is how accurately the sample represents the target population. Couper (2000) argued that one of the primary concerns facing researchers using Web surveys is *coverage error*, a type of error that arises when members of the target population under study are excluded from the *sampling frame*, or the enumerable and bounded group from which a sample will ultimately be drawn. For example, researchers interested in studying the target population of American adults might use a sampling frame of residential telephone numbers; in this instance, coverage error arises because American adults without residential telephone numbers are excluded.

In the case of Web surveys, one factor influencing coverage error is the *coverage rate:* the proportion of the target population that can be accessed via the Internet (Couper 2000). This may be affected in two ways. First, the online sampling universe is limited to those who have Internet access.[7] Although the number of American adults online has grown dramatically from 46 percent in 2000 to 85 percent in 2013, a nontrivial segment of the population remains uncovered; in addition, 9 percent of those who do use the Internet do not do so at home, where respondents may be more likely to participate in Web-based surveys (Zickuhr 2013). Second, Zickuhr's (2013) work indicates that Internet access is not randomly distributed throughout the U.S. population. Although adult men and women are equally represented online, Internet use is lower among Hispanics compared with blacks and whites. Furthermore, Internet use is negatively correlated with age and positively correlated with education and income.

The second factor influencing coverage error in Web surveys concerns constructing a sampling frame that accurately represents the general population. Web surveys using FPSs use techniques such as recruiting individuals into the respondent pool through random-digit dialing (RDD) and providing computers and Internet access to those who do not already possess them free of charge. Survey firms then randomly select individuals from their pools for specific surveys. Although this method is quite costly, it creates a sampling frame of respondents that is representative of the general population, not merely the population that uses the Internet on its own accord.

In contrast, Web surveys using NPSs use recruiting techniques such as solicitations sent out to e-mail lists purchased from Internet marketing firms, banner advertisements appearing on popular Web sites, registration processes for sweepstakes, and RDD. Individuals are then sampled from these pools using an algorithm to obtain a sample that is representative of the target population.[8]

Constructing an NPS is less costly than creating a pool by exclusively using probability methods. However, because the sampling frame is assembled in a non-full-probability fashion, the distribution of demographic variables and attitudes in the pool are more likely to systematically differ from the general population. Poststratification weights can be used to more closely align the demographic characteristics of the sample and the overall population; however, if the variables of interest are weakly correlated with demographic variables, then weighting will not lead to alignment in the substantive answers of the two groups. Previous research by Chang and Krosnick (2009) and Malhotra and Krosnick (2007) indicates that before weighting, the demographic distribution of NPS Web surveys differs from their FPS counterparts; however, these differences are significantly reduced once the appropriate weights are applied.

2.3. *Response Quality Concerns in the Web Mode*

Ultimately, we are interested in how the intersection of survey mode and sampling strategy influences response quality. One aspect of response quality is the degree of similarity in response distributions produced by various survey modalities. Smith's (2003) comparison of 32 items tapping attitudes about government spending in the GSS and an FPS Web survey found that the distribution of responses produced by the two data sets was typically within five percentage points. Despite the similarities, two important differences were noteworthy. First, the Web survey produced more extreme responses on Likert-type scale items. Second, discrepant response distributions were particularly notable on questions dealing with spending on problems largely associated with the lower class.

Smith (2003) attributed both of these divergences to the lack of interviewer effects in the Web mode, which allows respondents the privacy and comfort to report more socially conservative responses. Supporting this interpretation, Chang and Krosnick's (2009) study about support for government aid to blacks found that data generated by Web surveys show less evidence of social desirability bias than telephone data. In addition, Kreuter, Presser, and Tourangeau (2008) surveyed university alumni via the Web, telephone, or interactive voice recognition about desirable (e.g., grade point average > 3.5; received honors) and undesirable characteristics (e.g., grade point average < 2.5; received a D or an F). When comparing respondents' self-reports with their university transcripts, they found that although the reporting of desirable information did not vary by mode, respondents were significantly more likely to report undesirable information in the Web mode than in telephone mode. Furthermore, Web respondents were significantly less likely than telephone respondents to misreport their information in a socially desirable way.

Beyond interviewer effects, response quality may be influenced by respondents' engagement with the survey's topic. Chang and Krosnick (2009) found that NPS Web respondents were more interested in and knowledgeable about the survey topic than FPS respondents, a finding they attributed to the former respondents' selectively completing surveys that they were highly interested in. Furthermore, Heerwegh (2009) found that Web respondents were no more likely than face-to-face respondents to engage in satisficing, a form of nonengagement with the survey instrument.

A second aspect of response quality is the degree to which the multivariate models produced by distinct survey modalities show similarities in the direction, magnitude, and significance of predictor variables. In their comparison of FPS telephone, FPS Web, and NPS Web surveys,

Berrens et al. (2003) found that although differences in the distributions of response options and relational inferences did arise, the multivariate results produced by the three survey types were overall quite similar.

2.4. *Hypotheses*

In light of the results of previous research, we offer four hypotheses. The first focuses on the extent to which the two survey modalities accurately reflect the demography of the United States.

> *Hypothesis 1:* Because of differences in coverage error, we expect that the demographic characteristics of the FPS face-to-face surveys will be more accurate than those of the NPS Web survey. However, we further expect that the divergences across surveys will not be overwhelming (e.g., Malhotra and Krosnick 2007), primarily because of the efforts of the proprietary algorithms the NPS Web survey uses to draw a representative sample from its pool.

We further expect to see some differences in the distribution of responses across the survey modalities.

> *Hypothesis 2:* We expect that Web respondents will report more extreme opinions than their face-to-face counterparts (Smith 2003). We expect that this is partially a sampling issue, as members of a survey pool exercise selectivity in choosing surveys in which to participate (Chang and Krosnick 2009), and partially a mode issue, as respondents may be more comfortable expressing extreme opinions when a human interviewer is absent.
>
> *Hypothesis 3:* Web respondents will report less socially desirable opinions than their face-to-face counterparts (Chang and Krosnick 2009; Kreuter et al. 2008). We expect this to occur because of the lack of a human interviewer in the Web survey mode (Krysan 1998).

Finally, we consider the degree of similarity across multivariate models produced by the two survey modalities.

> *Hypothesis 4:* Despite the slight differences in response distributions (occurring because of sampling and mode effects), we expect the multivariate models of the FPS face-to-face surveys and the NPS Web

survey to exhibit substantial similarity in the direction, magnitude, and significance of the coefficients of the predictor variables (Berrens et al. 2003).

3. DATA AND MEASURES

3.1. *Data*

Our analyses use three data sets: (1) the 2008 GSS, (2) the 2008 ANES, and (3) the 2009 Race Cues, Attitudes, and Punitiveness Survey (RCAPS). Although an ideal research design would examine surveys administered in the same year, we find a one-year discrepancy to be acceptable, given previous research indicating that the marginal distributions of the patterns of relationships between racial attitudes and other variables rarely undergo substantial shifts in short one-year time spans (e.g., Bobo et al. 2012; Schuman et al. 1997).

3.1.1. *GSS.* The 2008 GSS was conducted via face-to-face interviews. The sampling universe contained English- or Spanish-speaking U.S. household residents who were 18 years of age or older. Sampling occurred across multiple stages, each focusing on a geographic area of decreasing size. From February through April 2008, 2,044 interviews were completed, with an American Association for Public Opinion Research (AAPOR) response rate 5 of 70.4 percent.

3.1.2. *ANES.* The 2008 ANES was conducted via face-to-face interviews. The sampling universe contained English- or Spanish-speaking U.S. citizens living in the 48 coterminous states or the District of Columbia who were 18 years of age or older by October 31, 2008. Because rates of citizenship vary across race/ethnicity, the ANES included oversamples of Latinos and African Americans. Sampling occurred across multiple stages focusing on areas of decreasing geographic size, and it was stratified by metropolitan statistical area and race/ethnicity. Between September 2 and November 3, 2008, the preelection survey interviewed 2,323 respondents, with an AAPOR response rate 1 of 59.5 percent. The postelection survey interviewed 2,102 respondents between November 5 and December 30, 2008, a reinterview rate of 90.5 percent.

3.1.3. *RCAPS.* The 2009 RCAPS was conducted via the Internet,[9] achieving an AAPOR response rate 1 of 27.3 percent.[10] The sampling universe contained members of an opt-in survey pool, consisting of more than 1 million U.S. residents recruited through Internet advertising, email, postal mail, and RDD. Respondents were sampled from the pool using the *sample matching process*. First, the sampling frame was created by drawing a sample from the 2006 U.S. Census American Community Survey, stratified by age, race, gender, and education, with random sampling within the strata. The resulting data included information on respondents' age, race, gender, education, marital status, number of children under age 18, family income, employment status, citizenship, and state and metropolitan area of residence. Data on interest in politics and party identification were imputed into this sampling frame from the 2004 National Annenberg Election Study on the basis of age, race, gender, and education. The second step of sample matching was to create a profile of the target sample, known as a *target matrix*. This was accomplished by using a stratification scheme developed by cross-classifying gender, age (i.e., 18–24, 25–34, 35–54, and ≥ 55 years), race (i.e., black, Latino, and white plus all other nonblack/non-Latino), and education (i.e., high school graduate or less, some college, college graduate, and postgraduate education). In the final step of sample matching, individuals were selected from the opt-in pool such that each individual selected from the pool was as similar as possible on the range of characteristics to a specific member of the target sample. The resulting sample included 1,500 respondents who were representative of the U.S. population, and an oversample of 600 African American respondents.

3.2. Measures

The variables used in this study fall into three categories: demographic characteristics, political orientations, and social attitudes about egalitarianism and African Americans.[11] The demographic variables include sex, race/ethnicity, region of residence, age, education, and household income. The political orientation variables include interest in politics and political ideology. The latter variable is scored such that higher values indicate stronger affiliation with conservative ideology. The social attitudes variables include affect toward whites and blacks (calculated as a difference score between a respondent's ratings of the two groups), stereotypes about the industriousness and intelligence of whites and blacks (summed into an index and then calculated as a difference score between a respondent's ratings of the two groups), a six-item egalitarianism index, and a four-item racial resentment index. The affect and stereotypes measures are scored such that higher values indicate rating whites more positively than blacks. The egalitarianism index is scored such that higher values indicate greater social liberalism. The racial resentment index is scored such that higher values indicate greater racial conservatism.

4. ANALYSIS AND RESULTS

4.1. *Analytic Approach*

We begin by assessing the extent to which the two survey modalities accurately represent the demography of the U.S. population. To do so, we compare the distributions shown by each survey to estimates provided by the 2008 U.S. Census Current Population Survey March Supplement (CPS). We then assess data quality across survey modalities in two ways. First, we investigate the extent to which the modalities produce similar descriptions of the empirical world by comparing their distributions of political and social attitudes. Second, we assess the extent to which the modalities produce similar models of social processes by modeling the egalitarianism and racial resentment indexes. Our approach unfolds in two steps: We examine the models independently generated by each survey and then we pool the surveys, including a dummy variable for survey type.

All analyses are conducted on unweighted data, allowing us to assess their raw capabilities as opposed to the survey firms' success at constructing sampling weights. In addition, the analyses are constrained to white respondents only. We adopt this strategy because the ANES oversamples blacks and Latinos, and the RCAPS oversamples blacks. Given that variables such as education, income, and political ideology systematically vary with race/ethnicity, the unweighted data including varying oversamples are necessarily discrepant and would thus cloud the results.

4.2. *Demographic Representativeness*

Table 1 presents the unweighted[12] distribution of demographic variables from the CPS, GSS, ANES, and RCAPS, and the average percentage-point error of each survey when compared with the CPS benchmark. We used *t* tests to compare the means for each response option in the GSS, ANES, and RCAPS to the CPS benchmark.

Table 1. Comparison of Unweighted Demographic Variable Distributions with the CPS Benchmark

	CPS	GSS	ANES	RCAPS
Sex				
Male	47.9	−2.1	−3.8**	−.3
Female	52.1	2.1	3.8**	.3
Average error		2.1	3.8	.3
Region				
Northeast	22.8	−4.6***	−10.6***	−3.4**
Midwest	26.9	−1.9	−5.7***	−1.7
South	28.5	4.5***	11.3***	5.5***
West	21.8	2.0	5.1***	−.4
Average error		3.3	8.2	2.2
Age (years)				
18–29	18.5	−4.2***	−3.0**	−4.3***
30–39	18.3	−2.7**	−1.5	−4.0***
40–49	22.7	−4.6***	−3.5**	−5.0***
50–64	24.7	4.7***	3.3*	11.1***
≥ 65	15.9	7.9***	4.6***	2.0
Average error		4.8	3.2	5.3
Education				
Less than a high school diploma	9.0	2.9***	.6	−4.7***
High school graduate	30.7	−.5	−.5	13.4***
Some college	29.7	−5.1***	.2	−1.9
Bachelor's degree	20.1	−2.4*	−3.6***	−5.6***
Graduate school	10.5	5.1***	3.3***	−1.0
Average error		3.2	1.6	5.3
Household income				
≤ $24,999	17.7	5.8***	−3.2*	1.5
$25,000–$49,999	21.5	.9	1.2	5.0***
$50,000–$74,999	18.6	2.9*	4.4**	6.7***
$75,000–$99,999	14.5	−6.0***	1.1	−5.4***
≥ $100,000	27.6	−3.6**	−3.4*	−10.8***
Average error		3.8	2.7	5.9
Total average error		3.4	3.9	3.8

Note: The analysis contains white respondents only. CPS figures represent the percentage of the response option's distribution in the population. Other values indicate the magnitude of the target survey's divergence from the CPS benchmark. Negative values indicate estimates that are lower than the benchmark, while positive values indicate estimates that are higher. Significance is determined by *t* tests comparing each response option with the benchmark. ANES = American National Election Study; CPS = 2008 U.S. Census Current Population Survey March Supplement; GSS = General Social Survey; RCAPS = Race Cues, Attitudes, and Punitiveness Survey.
*$p \leq$ .05. **$p \leq$ .01. ***$p \leq$ .001.

Each survey shows notable similarities and differences to the CPS benchmark. The GSS is the most accurate in emulating the benchmark distributions, with an overall average error of 3.4 percentage points. Its estimates are statistically equivalent to the benchmark with regard to sex. Its divergences from the benchmark occur in its estimates of region (underrepresenting those in the Northeast and overrepresenting those in the South), age (underrepresenting younger Americans and overrepresenting older Americans), education (overrepresenting those at the tail ends of the distribution, and underrepresenting those with some college or bachelor's degrees), and income (overrepresenting those with the lowest income and underrepresenting those with the highest income).

The ANES has an overall average error of 3.9 percentage points from the CPS benchmark, a .5-point increase from the GSS. Its divergences occur in its estimates of sex (underrepresenting men), region (underrepresenting those in the Northeast and Midwest and overrepresenting those in the South and West), age (underrepresenting younger Americans and overrepresenting older Americans), education (underrepresenting those with bachelor's degrees and overrepresenting those with graduate education), and income (underrepresenting those at the tail ends of the distribution, and overrepresenting those in the middle).

Finally, the RCAPS has an overall average error of 3.8 percentage points, a .4-point increase from the GSS and a .1-point decrease from the ANES. Its estimates are statistically equivalent to the benchmark with regard to sex. Its divergences occur on measures of region (underrepresenting those in the Northeast and overrepresenting those in the South), age (underrepresenting the youngest Americans and overrepresenting those aged 50–64 years), education (underrepresenting those with less than high school and those with bachelor's degrees, while overrepresenting those with high school degrees), and income (overrepresenting those earning $25,000 to $74,999 and underrepresenting those with the highest incomes).

4.3. Response Quality I: Distributions

Table 2 presents the unweighted distribution of the interest in politics and political ideology variables. We used *t* tests to compare means of different survey sources with the benchmark.

First, there is a statistically significant difference in the degree of interest in politics in the ANES and RCAPS, such that RCAPS respondents report far more interest than ANES respondents.[13] Second, there are a variety of significant differences in political ideology across the surveys, with a broad pattern of the GSS and ANES being more similar

Table 2. Comparison of Unweighted Political Variable Distributions across Surveys

	GSS	ANES	RCAPS
Interest in politics			
Hardly at all	—	14.3^a	4.0^b
Only now and then	—	22.9^a	11.0^b
Some of the time	—	32.2^a	24.1^b
Most of the time	—	30.7^a	60.9^b
Political ideology			
Very liberal	3.1^a	3.2^a	6.1^b
Liberal	21.3^a	24.6^a	15.7^b
Moderate	36.3^a	26.5^b	29.9^a
Conservative	35.7^a	41.0^b	28.5^c
Very conservative	3.6^a	4.6^a	19.7^b

Note: The analysis contains white respondents only. Values represent the percentages of the response option's distribution in the population. Significance is determined by *t* tests. Superscripts denote differences that are significant at least at the $p \leq .05$ level. Items that share common superscripts do not differ significantly. ANES = American National Election Study; GSS = General Social Survey; RCAPS = Race Cues, Attitudes, and Punitiveness Survey.

to each other than to the RCAPS (although notably, the ANES reports the smallest number of moderates). In comparison with the other surveys, the RCAPS features heavier tail ends of the distribution.

Table 3 presents the unweighted distribution of the social attitude variables: affect toward whites and blacks, stereotypes about whites and blacks, egalitarianism, and racial resentment toward blacks. We used *t* tests to compare the means for each response option across surveys. Recall that the affect, stereotyping, and racial resentment variables are scored such that higher values indicate greater racial conservatism, while the egalitarianism variable is scored such that higher values indicate greater social liberalism.

First, there was a significantly larger gap in affect toward whites and blacks in the RCAP than in the ANES. Second, there was a significant difference in the gap in stereotyping of whites and blacks across all three surveys, with the ANES showing the largest gap and the GSS showing the smallest. Third, scores on the egalitarianism and racial resentment indexes significantly differ between the ANES and RCAPS,[14] such that RCAPS respondents reported less egalitarianism and greater resentment than ANES respondents.[15] In additional analyses not shown here, we

Table 3. Unweighted Distribution of Intergroup Social Attitude Variables across Surveys

	GSS	ANES	RCAPS
Affect score difference	—	.07ᵃ	.10ᵇ
Stereotyping difference	.07ᵃ	.11ᵇ	.09ᶜ
Egalitarianism index	—	.60ᵃ	.50ᵇ
Racial resentment index	—	.65ᵃ	.68ᵇ

Note: The analysis contains white respondents only. Values represent the mean response. The affect score and stereotype indexes represent the gap between ratings of white and black targets, with higher values indicating a greater distance between evaluations. Significance is determined by *t* tests. Superscripts denote differences that are significant at least at the $p \leq .05$ level. Items that share common superscripts do not differ significantly. ANES = American National Election Study; GSS = General Social Survey; RCAPS = Race Cues, Attitudes, and Punitiveness Survey.

find that these differences are attributable to RCAPS respondents disproportionately selecting the most conservative response option.

4.4. *Response Quality II: Multivariate Models*

The next portion of our analysis assesses the similarity of multivariate models produced by the two survey modalities. To do this, we use the unweighted data from white respondents to regress egalitarianism and racial resentment on the demographic, political orientation, and social attitude variables. The models proceed in several steps, first entering demographic variables, then political and social attitudes, and finally interest in politics, as this latter variable is a notable point of distinction between surveys, with the RCAPS respondents being particularly interested in politics.

Table 4 presents separate models from the ANES and RCAPS predicting egalitarianism.[16] Overall, these models reveal similarities and differences between the surveys. With regard to similarities, both surveys consistently show that income and increasingly conservative ideology are negatively related to egalitarianism and that interest in politics exhibits no significant relationship. After political ideology is entered in model 2, the ANES and RCAPS both reveal that southern residence has no significant relationship with egalitarianism. There are three points to note with regard to differences: First, whereas the ANES shows a negative relationship between age and egalitarianism, the RCAPS shows a

Table 4. Regression of Egalitarianism across Surveys

	ANES			RCAPS		
	Model 1	Model 2	Model 3	Model 1	Model 2	Model 3
Constant	.49***	.68***	.67***	.43***	.76***	.77***
	(.06)	(.06)	(.06)	(.07)	(.05)	(.06)
Age	−.12**	−.07	−.08*	−.07	.08*	.09*
	(.04)	(.04)	(.04)	(.04)	(.03)	(.03)
Education	.26***	.18**	.17**	.15	.05	.06
	(.07)	(.07)	(.06)	(.08)	(.07)	(.07)
Income	−.14***	−.08**	−.09**	−.13***	−.08**	−.08**
	(.04)	(.04)	(.03)	(.04)	(.03)	(.03)
Southern	−.06***	−.03	−.03	−.02	.004	.01
	(.02)	(.02)	(.02)	(.02)	(.02)	(.02)
Female	.05**	.03*	.04*	.07***	.03	.02
	(.02)	(.02)	(.02)	(.02)	(.01)	(.01)
Political ideology		−.32***	−.32***		−.55***	−.54***
		(.03)	(.03)		(.03)	(.03)
Interest in politics			.03			−.02
			(.03)			(.03)
R^2	.10	.23	.24	.04	.37	.37
N		537			867	

Note: The analysis contains white respondents only. ANES = American National Election Study; RCAPS = Race Cues, Attitudes, and Punitiveness Survey.
*$p \leq$ .05. **$p \leq$ .01. ***$p \leq$ .001.

positive relationship, a finding that runs counter to theoretical expectations. Predicted probabilities indicate that the magnitude of the age effect is trivial; a one-unit increase in age is associated with a −.001 change in egalitarianism in the ANES and a .002 change in the RCAPS. Thus, the egalitarianism scores of a 20-year-old and a 40-year-old would differ by .02 points in the ANES and by .04 points in the RCAPS.

Second, although the ANES reveals that education and being female have a positive relationship with egalitarianism, education never attains significance in the RCAPS models, and sex is rendered insignificant when political ideology is added to the RCAPS model. Predicted probabilities indicate that the magnitude of the education effect is trivial; a one-unit increase in education is associated with a .02 change in egalitarianism in the ANES and a .01 change in the RCAPS. Thus, the egalitarianism scores of a high school graduate and a college graduate would differ by .08 in the ANES and by .04 in the RCAPS. Likewise, the effect

Table 5. Regression of Egalitarianism across Pooled Surveys

	Model 1	Model 2	Model 3	Model 4	Model 5
Constant	.40***	.59***	.62***	.69***	.65***
	(.05)	(.04)	(.04)	(.04)	(.06)
Age	−.09**	.01	.03	.02	−.02
	(.03)	(.03)	(.03)	(.03)	(.04)
Education	.25***	.16***	.18***	.12*	.17*
	(.06)	(.05)	(.05)	(.05)	(.07)
Income	−.12***	−.06**	−.06*	−.08***	−.05
	(.03)	(.02)	(.02)	(.02)	(.04)
Southern	−.03*	.000	−.001	−.01	−.01
	(.01)	(.01)	(.01)	(.01)	(.01)
Female	.06***	.04***	.03**	.03**	.03**
	(.01)	(.01)	(.01)	(.01)	(.01)
Political ideology		−.30***	−.30***	−.30***	−.30***
		(.01)	(.01)	(.01)	(.01)
Interest in politics			−.06**	−.01	−.01
			(.02)	(.02)	(.02)
RCAPS				−.09***	−.02
				(.01)	(.08)
Age × RCAPS					.06
					(.05)
Education × RCAPS					−.10
					(.10)
Income × RCAPS					−.05
					(.05)
R^2	.05	.29	.29	.32	.32
N			1,404		

Note: The analysis contains white respondents only. RCAPS = Race Cues, Attitudes, and Punitiveness Survey.
*$p \leq$ .05. **$p \leq$ .01. ***$p \leq$ .001.

of sex is small; the shift from male to female is associated with a .05 change in the ANES and a .07 change in the RCAPS.

Third, it is noteworthy that models 2 and 3 of the RCAPS consistently explain a larger share of the variance than the ANES models.

Table 5 presents models from the pooled ANES and RCAPS data predicting egalitarianism. Here, we find that education and being female are positively related to egalitarianism, whereas income and increasingly conservative political ideology are negatively related. Importantly, we also find that the survey modality variable is significant, such that being an RCAPS respondent is negatively associated with egalitarianism. However, the substantive impact is small; shifting from the ANES to the RCAPS is associated with a −.03 change in egalitarianism. Finally, the interactions of survey with age, education, and income are not significant predictors of egalitarianism.[17] These latter findings bolster our confidence that the substantive importance of the divergences illustrated in Table 4 is trivial.

Table 6 presents separate models of the ANES and RCAPS predicting racial resentment.[18] Here, we find greater similarity across the two surveys. In the final model, both surveys show that education and egalitarianism have negative relationships with racial resentment. Furthermore, they reveal that racial resentment is positively related to southern residence, increasingly conservative political ideology, and increasingly large gaps in affective feelings and stereotyping of blacks and whites (such that whites are favored). The only difference between the models is that in model 1 the RCAPS shows a positive relationship between age and resentment, but this relationship becomes insignificant when the political and intergroup attitudes are added in model 2. Finally, as was the case in the egalitarianism models, the RCAPS explains a larger amount of variance than the ANES.

Table 7 presents models from the pooled ANES and RCAPS data predicting racial resentment. Here, we find that education and egalitarianism are negatively associated with racial resentment, whereas resentment is positively associated with southern residence, increasingly conservative political ideology, and increasingly large gaps in affective feelings and stereotyping of blacks and whites (such that whites are favored). Important, we find that the survey modality variable is not a significant predictor of racial resentment.[19] Finally, although the interaction of survey with age is not a significant predictor of racial resentment, the interaction of survey and education is.[20] Here, we find that the liberalizing effect of education is about 60 percent stronger among the RCAPS respondents than among the ANES respondents. Substantively, however, this is a small effect; predicted probabilities indicate that a one-unit increase in education is associated with a .027 change in racial resentment in the ANES and a .042 change in the RCAPS. Thus, the resentment scores of a high school graduate and a college graduate would differ by .11 in the ANES and .17 in the RCAPS.

5. DISCUSSION AND CONCLUSION

In support of hypothesis 1, we find that although an FPS face-to-face survey is the most accurate in emulating the CPS benchmark regarding

Table 6. Regression of Racial Resentment across Surveys

	ANES				RCAPS			
	Model 1	Model 2	Model 3	Model 4	Model 1	Model 2	Model 3	Model 4
Constant	.93***	.66***	.98***	.98***	1.04***	.69***	1.06***	1.07***
	(.06)	(.05)	(.06)	(.06)	(.06)	(.05)	(.05)	(.05)
Age	.04	−.04	−.06	−.06	.12**	−.05	−.01	−.002
	(.04)	(.03)	(.03)	(.03)	(.04)	(.03)	(.03)	(.03)
Education	−.42***	−.29***	−.26***	−.27***	−.55***	−.40***	−.41***	−.39***
	(.06)	(.06)	(.05)	(.05)	(.07)	(.06)	(.05)	(.05)
Southern	.10***	.05***	.05***	.05***	.06**	.03*	.03*	.03*
	(.02)	(.02)	(.01)	(.01)	(.02)	(.01)	(.01)	(.01)
Political ideology		.31***	.18***	.18***		.45***	.21***	.22***
		(.03)	(.03)	(.03)		(.02)	(.03)	(.03)
Affect difference		.12**	.09*	.09*		.20***	.13**	.13**
		(.05)	(.04)	(.04)		(.05)	(.04)	(.04)
Stereotype difference		.34***	.27***	.27***		.27***	.25***	.50***
		(.05)	(.05)	(.05)		(.05)	(.04)	(.04)
Egalitarianism			−.42***	−.42***			−.44***	−.44***
			(.04)	(.04)			(.03)	(.03)
Interest in politics				.002				−.04
				(.03)				(.03)
R^2	.09	.28	.37	.37	.08	.43	.54	.54
N			790				942	

Note: The analysis contains white respondents only. ANES = American National Election Study; RCAPS = Race Cues, Attitudes, and Punitiveness Survey.
*$p \leq .05$. **$p \leq .01$. ***$p \leq .001$.

Table 7. Regression of Racial Resentment across Pooled Surveys

	Model 1	Model 2	Model 3	Model 4	Model 5	Model 6
Constant	1.00***	.67***	1.00***	1.01***	1.03***	.98***
	(.04)	(.04)	(.04)	(.04)	(.04)	(.05)
Age	.07**	−.05*	−.04	−.03	−.03	−.06*
	(.03)	(.02)	(.02)	(.02)	(.02)	(.03)
Education	−.50***	−.34***	−.32***	−.31***	−.32***	−.25***
	(.05)	(.04)	(.04)	(.04)	(.04)	(.05)
Southern	.07***	.04***	.04***	.04***	.04***	.04***
	(.01)	(.01)	(.01)	(.01)	(.01)	(.01)
Political ideology		.40***	.20***	.21***	.20***	.20***
		(.02)	(.02)	(.02)	(.02)	(.02)
Affect difference		.17***	.10***	.11***	.11***	.11***
		(.03)	(.03)	(.03)	(.03)	(.03)
Stereotype difference		.30***	.27***	.27***	.26***	.26***
		(.03)	(.03)	(.03)	(.03)	(.03)
Egalitarianism			−.42***	−.43***	−.43***	−.44***
			(.02)	(.02)	(.02)	(.02)
Interest in politics				−.03	−.02	−.02
				(.02)	(.02)	(.02)
RCAPS					−.02	.08
					(.01)	(.06)
Age × RCAPS						.06
						(.04)
Education × RCAPS						−.16*
						(.07)
R^2	.09	.37	.47	.47	.47	.47
N			1,732			

Note: The analysis contains white respondents only. RCAPS = Race Cues, Attitudes, and Punitiveness Survey.
*$p \leq$ .05. **$p \leq$ .01. ***$p \leq$ .001.

social demographics, the average errors are comparable across the three surveys: the average error of the GSS is 3.4 percentage points, that of the RCAPS is 3.8 percentage points, and that of the ANES is 3.9 percentage points. Of the three surveys, the RCAPS is the most accurate at representing sex and region, and it is the least accurate at representing age, education, and income. The RCAPS significantly underrepresents respondents under age 49, while overrepresenting those aged 50 to 64. With regard to education, the RCAPS significantly underrepresents those with less than a high school diploma and those with bachelor's degrees, while significantly overrepresenting those who are high school graduates. Finally, the RCAPS significantly overrepresents those earning $25,000 to $74,999, while significantly underrepresenting those earning $75,000 or more.

Given that previous research indicates that Internet adoption is negatively correlated with age and positively correlated with education and income (Zickuhr 2013), our findings concerning demographic representativeness are surprising. Thus, it appears that access to the Internet is not the only important factor in determining who opts into NPS Web surveys. This finding resonates with research indicating that various demographic groups have divergent patterns in their use of the Internet once they are online. For example, social class has important implications for online activities; there are positive correlations between a user's income bracket and his or her engagement in activities such as researching products, getting news online, visiting government Web sites, and researching medical issues (Jansen 2010). In addition, research finds positive correlations between educational attainment and online activities such as email use and product purchasing, while finding negative correlations between age and activities such as social networking use and online banking (Zickuhr and Smith 2012).

The second set of analyses concerned the quality of the more substantive data provided by each survey. First, we compared the distribution of the political orientation and social attitudes across the three samples. In support of hypothesis 2, we find that NPS Web respondents report more extreme opinions than FPS face-to-face respondents. For example, in comparison with the GSS and ANES respondents, RCAPS respondents report far more interest in politics and are more likely to adopt "very liberal" and "very conservative" political ideologies. This finding may be based in respondent selectivity that occurs during the sampling process (e.g., Chang and Krosnick 2009). Selectivity might operate at the beginning of the process, whereby people who have strongly held views may be more likely to join opt-in pools than those with weaker views. Alternatively, it might operate later in the process; because Web respondents have a broad sense of the types of surveys that are available (because of their membership in a sample pool), they can exercise discretion about which surveys to complete, choosing to participate only in surveys that closely align with their interests. Although individuals are more likely to cooperate with surveys on topics they are personally interested in, this tendency does not necessarily influence data quality (Groves, Presser, and Dipko 2004).

In support of hypothesis 3, we find that NPS Web respondents report more socially undesirable attitudes than FPS face-to-face respondents. In comparison with ANES respondents, RCAPS respondents report less egalitarianism and more racial resentment. On one hand, these findings may occur because of NPS Web respondents' differential selectivity during the sampling process, such that respondents with strongly held views are more likely to agree to participate in this survey. On the other hand, these findings may have roots in survey mode; without a human interviewer present, Web respondents may feel more comfortable expressing socially undesirable opinions than face-to-face respondents (e.g., Krysan 1998).

As a second test of data quality, we compared multivariate models predicting egalitarianism and racial resentment. Here, we find mixed support for hypothesis 4, which asserts that the multivariate models would exhibit substantial similarity in the direction, magnitude, and significance of the coefficients of the predictor variables. Considering egalitarianism, we find several instances in which the survey modalities differ. Although the ANES shows that education and sex are significant predictors of egalitarianism, the RCAPS shows no such relationships. In addition, whereas the ANES reveals that age has a negative relationship with egalitarianism, the RCAPS reveals a positive relationship. Overall, we find the differences between the models to be substantively minor. First, the substantive importance of these differences is trivial. Each one-unit increase in age is related to a .001 to .002 shift in egalitarianism, while one-unit increases in education are associated with a .01 shift, and a transition from male to female is associated with a .05 to .07 shift. Second, the interactions of survey with age, education, and income are not significant predictors of egalitarianism. Furthermore, although in the pooled model we find that survey mode is a significant predictor of egalitarianism, such that RCAPS respondents are less egalitarian than ANES respondents, we find this to be a substantively small effect; shifting from the ANES to the RCAPS is associated with a −.03 change in egalitarianism.

Considering racial resentment, we find stronger support for hypothesis 4 in the form of remarkable similarity across survey modalities. In the separate regression models, we find only one instance of difference: When the demographic variables are entered in model 1, the RCAPS indicates age to be a significant predictor of resentment, while the ANES does not. In all of the subsequent models, the surveys reveal identical estimates of which predictor variables are significant, their directions, and their relative magnitudes. In the pooled models, the survey mode variable is insignificant, indicating that ANES and RCAPS respondents are similarly resentful. Further analyses reveal that there is a significant interaction between survey and education, such that RCAPS respondents experience a stronger liberalizing effect of education. This is, however, a small effect; predicted probabilities indicate that a one-unit increase in education is associated with a .027 change in racial resentment in the ANES and a .042 change in the RCAPS.

To understand why the survey modalities produce similar multivariate models of racial resentment but appear more dissimilar in the multivariate models of egalitarianism, we suggest that one likely explanation involves differences in the concreteness of the underlying measures. Research on question order and context effects has shown that abstract and general attitude items may be more susceptible to context effects than specific and concrete items (Schuman 2008; Schuman and Presser 1981). Specifically, how respondents understand the meaning of the former is more open to influence by preceding items in a questionnaire than is the latter. The measure of egalitarianism we use is aimed at tapping a highly general orientation toward inequality between a great variety of social groups, across many situations (e.g., "If people were treated more equally in this country we would have many fewer problems"). As such, the egalitarianism scale aims at the abstract ideas of equality of opportunity, legal equality, and equality of rewards (Feldman 1999; Sidanius and Pratto 1999). Almost of necessity, therefore, respondents are prompted to draw upon a very broad range of considerations when forming judgments, and a variety of differences in questionnaire content across the two survey modalities may, therefore, come to influence how individuals react. In contrast, the racial resentment items, relatively speaking, constitute a much more common and ordinary aspect of routine social discourse on black-white relations in the United States (Bobo et al. 2012; Edsall and Edsall 1991; Kinder and Sanders 1996; Lamont 2000). As such, these items are less sensitive than the egalitarianism measures to context effects.

Overall, our results point to five key findings. First, the ability to estimate the distribution of demographic characteristics in the general population is roughly equivalent across survey modalities. However, researchers must be aware that there are some instances in which predictable demographic divergences, such as in the distribution of age, education, or income may have implications for their results. Second,

NPS Web respondents tend to be more politically interested and ideologically extreme than FPS face-to-face respondents. Third, NPS Web respondents tend to produce more racially and socially conservative responses than respondents from traditional surveys, often choosing the most extreme response. Fourth, the extent to which FPS face-to-face and NPS Web surveys produce similar multivariate models appears to be contingent upon the nature of the dependent variable. When the dependent variable is a more general and abstract measure of attitudes, the survey modalities show several differences, yet these tend to be minor in magnitude. In contrast, when the dependent variable is a more specific and concrete measure, the survey modalities show greater similarity. Fifth, the NPS Web models explain noticeably more variance than traditional surveys. This is likely linked to the sampling process; because these respondents are more interested and politically engaged, there is more constraint and coherence in their opinions and thus more variance is explained. In addition, this may be an artifact of the disproportionate number of the NPS Web respondents selecting the most extreme response option.

To conclude, this project has illuminated how full-probability face-to-face surveys compare with non-full-probability Web surveys. Given its design, this study cannot determine when differences found between surveys are the result of mode (i.e., face-to-face vs. Web), sampling strategy (i.e., non-full-probability vs. full-probability), or a combination of the two; however, it can determine the degree to which the data collected from FPS face-to-face surveys are similar to data collected from NPS Web surveys. This is one important set of comparisons; a full research program that investigates the other intersections of survey modes and sampling strategies is a worthy next step.

With this limitation in mind, we do not wish to lose sight of the forest for having delved carefully into looking at each and every tree. A holistic reading of the results leads us to conclude that the data generated by NPS Web surveys are in many ways comparable to data from FPS face-to-face surveys, and they thus have a place in the social science toolkit. Researchers must be mindful, however, of the instances in which NPS Web surveys are unique: They contain notable error in the unweighted estimates of some demographic groups, their respondents are more politically interested and ideologically extreme, their respondents are more likely to select extreme response options, and their higher variance may be more of an artifact of sample composition than a true instance of enhanced explanatory power. Although weighting may correct for distortions in social demographic variables, it cannot smooth out all of the observed divergences in attitudes. Thus, given these differences, and the secretive nature of Internet survey houses' proprietary sampling algorithms, we agree with AAPOR's recommendation that this type of data should not be used to generate precise estimates of population values (Baker et al. 2010). This is one task in which the gold standard of face-to-face surveys using FPSs excel. Furthermore, these types of surveys are invaluable because there are many instances in which respondents can benefit from the presence of a human interviewer.

We also believe, however, that it is in the best interest of science for there to be an abundance of data available to researchers; this allows us to answer new questions and to replicate the findings of previous scholars. To meet these goals, it is not in the best interest of the scholarly community to hold everyone to the financially costly and time-consuming gold standard of FPS face-to-face surveys; as the work of Keeter et al. (2000) indicates, there are instances in which the empirical quality of data is unrelated to the amount of time and financial resources dedicated to collecting the data itself. Here, we have shown that the similarities of NPS Web surveys and FPS face-to-face surveys often outweigh their differences. Furthermore, we have specified the conditions under which these differences arise. With these specified limitations in mind, researchers should move forward in using NPS Web surveys for the types of projects they are well-suited for, exploring the relationships between variables and testing theories, while avoiding attempts to make precise population estimates.

Acknowledgments

We thank Adam Berinsky, Howard Schuman, Nicholas Valentino, and our anonymous reviewers for helpful comments on earlier drafts of this article.

Notes

1. The newsletter was produced by the Survey Research Laboratory at the University of Illinois at Chicago.
2. Despite popular narratives about a "postracial" America during the Obama era, many racial attitudes have not undergone a substantial transformation in the past 20 years, and these attitudes continue to have important implications for public policy preferences (Hutchings 2009; Bobo et al. 2012).

3. We do not anticipate this factor seriously affecting the present study, as our sample contains respondents who use the Internet of their own accord and have actively opted in to an Internet survey pool. However, this issue should be seriously considered in contexts where respondents are provided computers and Internet access to participate in a given study.

4. Although we do not explicitly engage this issue in the present study, it is a ripe area for future research.

5. The Web site mode may generate interviewer effects if it is used as a medium for teleconferencing or videoconferencing between a respondent and a human interviewer; otherwise, it acts as a self-administered questionnaire.

6. See McDermott (2006) for examples of how this censoring process occurs in everyday encounters.

7. This is comparable with telephone interviews, in which the sampling universe is limited to households with telephone connections.

8. Given that there is no universal set of best practices, survey firms vary in their methods of building and sampling from their panels; some firms treat their methods as proprietary and do not disclose their strategies to clients (Baker et al. 2010). This secrecy results in circumstances in which researchers are not fully informed about the conditions under which their data were generated. Although ideally researchers should have perfect knowledge of these conditions, in practice they are often faced with uncertainties. For example, researchers working with archival data have no control over which data are selected for inclusion in the archive, and the rationale behind these decisions may remain a mystery. Likewise, in most face-to-face interview settings, researchers are not provided with data that provide important insight into the interview context. For example, we generally lack data indicating if a respondent was distracted by others present or was obviously bored with the interview.

9. The RCAPS was conducted by the survey firm YouGovPolimetrix.

10. For this survey, 9,856 active panelists received the survey invitation, 3,414 respondents began the questionnaire, and 2,692 completed it.

11. An Appendix containing specific question wording can be found at www .colgate.edu/facultysearch/FacultyDirectory/alicia-simmons.

12. Unsurprisingly, the decision to apply weights greatly affects the representativeness of each survey's sample. Before weighting, the GSS significantly differed from the CPS in 15 of 21 instances (average error = 3.4 percentage points), the ANES differed in 15 instances (average error = 3.9 percentage points), and the RCAPS differed in 13 instances (average error = 3.8 percentage points). After weighting, the number of category estimates for which each survey significantly differed from the CPS was reduced. The GSS differed in 11 of 21 instances, an improvement of 4 (average error = 2.5 percentage-points, an improvement of .9). The ANES differed in 11 instances, an improvement of 4 (average error = 2.6 percentage points, an improvement of 1.3). The RCAPS differed in 11 instances, an improvement of 2 (average error = 2.9 percentage points, an improvement of .9).

13. The GSS did not ask about interest in politics in 2008; it is thus omitted from the analysis.

14. The GSS includes neither the full racial resentment battery nor any items of the egalitarianism battery; it is thus omitted from the analysis.
15. Although the α reliability of egalitarianism and racial resentment indexes was high in both surveys, reliability in the RCAPS was higher (α = .85 and .85, respectively) than in the ANES (α = .70 and .77, respectively).
16. These models are based on the work of Bobo (1991) and Kluegel and Smith (1986), who indicate that egalitarianism is a function of age, education, income, occupational prestige, race, region, and gender. Occupational prestige is omitted from these models as it is not available in the RCAPS data.
17. In analyses not shown here, we generated a series of models to test each interaction term individually; these coefficients were insignificant, and the inclusion of each interaction term failed to significantly improve the predictive power of the models.
18. These models are based on the work of Kinder and Sanders (1996), who indicated that racial resentment is a function of age, education, region, political ideology, antiblack affect, antiblack stereotypes, and egalitarianism.
19. Additional analyses not shown here indicate that the interest in politics does not serve as a proxy for the dummy variable indicating survey type. When interest in politics is removed from the regression, the survey dummy remains insignificant, and the overall r^2 value remains virtually the same.
20. In analyses not shown here, we generated a series of models to test each interaction term individually. The interaction of survey and age was insignificant and failed to significantly improve the predictive power of the model. The interaction of survey and education was significant and notably improved the model's r^2 value.

References

Ansolabehere, Stephen, and Philip E. Jones. 2010. "Constituents' Responses to Congressional Roll-call Voting." *American Journal of Political Science* 54(3): 583–97.

Baker, Reg, Stephen Blumberg, J. Michael Brick, Mick P. Couper, Melanie Courtright, Mike Dennis, Don Dillman, Martin R. Frankel, Philip Garland, Robert M. Groves, Courtney Kennedy, Jon Krosnick, Sunghee Lee, Paul J. Lavrakas, Michael Link, Linda Piekarski, Kumar Rao, Douglas Rivers, Randall K. Thomas, and Dan Zahs. 2010. "AAPOR Report on Online Panels." Retrieved January 3, 2013 (http://www.aapor.org/AM/Template.cfm?Section=AAPOR_Committee_and_Task_Force_Reports&Template=/CM/ContentDisplay.cfm&ContentID=2223).

Berrens, Robert P., Alok K. Bohara, Hank Jenkins-Smith, Carol Silva, and David Weiman. 2003. "The Advent of Internet Surveys for Political Research: A Comparison of Telephone and Internet Samples." *Political Analysis* 11(1):1–22.

Bobo, Lawrence D. 1991. "Social Responsibility, Individualism, and Redistributive Policies." *Sociological Forum* 12(1):147–76.

Bobo, Lawrence D., Camille Z. Charles, Maria Krysan, and Alicia D. Simmons. 2012. "The Real Record on Racial Attitudes." Pp. 38–83 in *Social Trends in American Life: Findings from the General Social Survey since 1972*, edited by P. V. Marsden. Princeton, NJ: Princeton University Press.

Brooks, Deborah Jordan, and John G. Geer. 2007. "Beyond Negativity: The Effects of Incivility on the Electorate." *American Journal of Political Science* 51(1):1–16.

Brown, Ethan, and Timothy P. Johnson. 2011. "Diffusion of Web Survey Methodology, 1995–2009." *Survey Research* 42(1):1–3.

Chang, LinChiat, and Jon A. Krosnick. 2009. "National Surveys via RDD Telephone Interviewing versus the Internet: Comparing Sample Representativeness and Response Quality." *Public Opinion Quarterly* 73(4):641–78.

Converse, Philip E. 1987. "Changing Conceptions of Public Opinion in the Political Process." *Public Opinion Quarterly* 51(50th Anniversary Issue):S21–S24.

Couper, Mick P. 2000. "Web Surveys: A Review of Issues and Approaches." *Public Opinion Quarterly* 64(4):464–94.

de Leeuw, Edith Desiree. 1992. *Data Quality in Mail, Telephone, and Face to Face Surveys*. Amsterdam, the Netherlands: TT-Publikaties.

Edsall, Thomas B., and Mary D. Edsall. 1991. *Chain Reaction: The Impact of Race, Rights, and Taxes on American Politics*. New York: Norton.

Feldman, Stanley. 1999. "Economic Values and Inequality." Pp. 167–69 in *Measures of Political Attitudes*, edited by J. P. Robinson, P. R. Shaver, and L. S. Wrightsman. San Diego, CA: Academic Press.

Groves, Robert M., Stanley Presser, and Sarah Dipko. 2004. "The Role of Topic Interest in Survey Participation Decisions." *Public Opinion Quarterly* 68(1):2–31.

Heerwegh, Dirk. 2009. "Mode Differences between Face-to-Face and Web Surveys: An Experimental Investigation of Data Quality and Social Desirability Effects." *International Journal of Public Opinion Research* 21(1):111–21.

Henry, P. J. 2008. "College Sophomores in the Laboratory Redux: Influences of a Narrow Data Base on Social Psychology's View of the Nature of Prejudice." *Psychological Inquiry* 19(2):49–71.

Hutchings, Vincent L. 2009. "Change or More of the Same? Evaluating Racial Attitudes in the Obama Era." *Public Opinion Quarterly* 73(5):917–42.

Hutchings, Vincent L., and Nicholas A. Valentino. 2004. "The Centrality of Race in American Politics." *Annual Review of Political Science* 7:383–408.

Jansen, Jim. 2010. "Use of the Internet in Higher-Income Households." Washington, DC: Pew Research Center's Internet and American Life Project. Retrieved September 15, 2014 (http://www.pewinternet.org/files/old-media/Files/Reports/2010/PIP-Better-off-households-final.pdf).

Jerit, Jennifer. 2009. "How Predictive Appeals Affect Policy Opinions." *American Journal of Political Science* 53(2):411–26.

Keeter, Scott, Carolyn Miller, Andrew Kohut, Robert M. Groves, and Stanley Presser. 2000. "Consequences of Reducing Nonresponse in a National Telephone Survey." *Public Opinion Quarterly* 64(2):125–48.

Kinder, Donald R., and Lynn M. Sanders. 1996. *Divided by Color: Racial Politics and Democratic Ideals*. Chicago, IL: University of Chicago Press.

Kluegel, James R., and Eliot R. Smith. 1986. *Beliefs about Inequality: Americans' Views of What Is and What Ought to Be*. Piscataway, NJ: Transaction.

Kreuter, Frauke, Stanley Presser, and Roger Tourangeau. 2008. "Social Desirability Bias in CATI, IVR, and Web Surveys." *Public Opinion Quarterly* 72(5):847–65.

Krysan, Maria. 1998. "Privacy and the Expression of White Racial Attitudes: A Comparison across Three Contexts." *Public Opinion Quarterly* 62(4):506–44.

Krysan, Maria. 2000. "Prejudice, Politics, and Public Opinion: Understanding the Sources of Racial Policy Attitudes." *Annual Review of Sociology* 26(1):135–68.

Krysan, Maria, and Mick P. Couper. 2003. "Race in the Live and Virtual Interview: Racial Difference, Social Desirability, and Activation Effects in Attitude Surveys." *Social Psychology Quarterly* 66(4):364–83.

Lamont, Michele. 2000. *The Dignity of Working Men: Morality and the Boundaries of Race, Class, and Immigration*. New York: Russell Sage.

Malhotra, Neil, and Jon A. Krosnick. 2007. "The Effect of Survey Mode and Sampling on Inferences about Political Attitudes and Behavior: Comparing the 2000 and 2004 ANES to Internet Surveys with Nonprobability Samples." *Political Analysis* 15: 286–323.

McDermott, Monica. 2006. *Working Class White: The Making and Unmaking of Race Relations*. Berkeley: University of California Press.

Prior, Markus. 2005. "News vs. Entertainment: How Increasing Media Choice Widens Gaps in Political Knowledge and Turnout." *American Journal of Political Science* 49(3):577–92.

Rivers, Douglas. 2007. "Sampling for Web Surveys." Presented at the Joint Statistical Meetings, Salt Lake City, UT.

Rosenfeld, Michael J., and Ruben J. Thomas. 2012. "Searching for a Mate: The Rise of the Internet as a Social Intermediary." *American Sociological Review* 77(4):523–47.

Schuman, Howard. 2008. *Method and Meaning in Polls and Surveys*. Cambridge, MA: Harvard University Press.

Schuman, Howard, Charlotte Steeh, Lawrence D. Bobo, and Maria Krysan. 1997. *Racial Attitudes in America: Trends and Interpretations*. Cambridge, MA: Harvard University Press.

Schuman, Howard, and Stanley Presser. 1981. *Questions and Answers in Attitude Surveys: Experiments on Question Form, Wording, and Context*. New York: Academic Press.

Schwartz, Barry, and Howard Schuman. 2005. "History, Commemoration, and Belief: Abraham Lincoln in American Memory, 1945–2001." *American Sociological Review* 70(2):183–203.

Sears, David O. 1986. "College Sophomores in the Laboratory: Influences of a Narrow Data Base on Social Psychology's View of Human Nature." *Journal of Personality and Social Psychology* 51(3):515–30.

Seery, Mark D., E. Alison Holman, and Roxane Cohen Silver. 2010. "Whatever Does Not Kill Us: Cumulative Lifetime Adversity, Vulnerability, and Resilience." *Journal of Personality and Social Psychology* 99(6):1025–41.

Sidanius, Jim, and Felicia Pratto. 1999. *Social Dominance: An Intergroup Theory of Social Hierarchy and Oppression*. New York: Cambridge University Press.

Skitka, Linda J., Elizabeth Mullen, Thomas Griffin, Susan Hutchinson, and Brian Chamberlin. 2002. "Dispositions, Scripts, or Motivated Correction? Understanding Ideological Differences in Explanations for Social Problems." *Journal of Personality and Social Psychology* 83(2):470–87.

Smith, Tom W. 2003. "An Experimental Comparison of Knowledge Networks and the GSS." *International Journal of Public Opinion Research* 15(2):167–79.

Stephenson, Laura B., and Jean Crête. 2011. "Studying Political Behavior: A Comparison of Internet and Telephone Surveys." *International Journal of Public Opinion Research* 23(1):24–55.

Zickuhr, Kathryn. 2013. "Who's Not Online and Why." Washington, DC: Pew Research Center's Internet and American Life Project. Retrieved January 8, 2014 (http://www.pewinternet.org/~/media//Files/Reports/2013/ PIP_Offline%20adults_092513_PDF.pdf).

Zickuhr, Kathryn, and Aaron Smith. 2012. "Digital Differences." Washington, DC: Pew Research Center's Internet and American Life Project. Retrieved September 15, 2014 (http://www.pewinternet.org/files/oldmedia//Files/Reports/2012/PIP_Digital_ differences_041312.pdf).

Author Biographies

Alicia D. Simmons is an assistant professor of sociology in the Department of Sociology and Anthropology at Colgate University. Her research focuses on media, race, and the politics of criminal justice.

Lawrence D. Bobo is the W. E. B. Du Bois Professor of the Social Sciences at Harvard University. His research focuses on the intersection of social inequality, politics, and race. He is coauthor of *Racial Attitudes in America: Trends and Interpretations* and senior editor of *Prismatic Metropolis: Inequality in Los Angeles*. His most recent book is *Prejudice in Politics: Group Position, Public Opinion, and the Wisconsin Treaty Rights Dispute*.

Sociological Methodology
2015, Vol. 45(1) 388–428
© American Sociological Association 2015
DOI: 10.1177/0081175015583985
http://sm.sagepub.com

⊗SAGE

က 9 ಕಾ

DECOMPOSITION OF GENDER OR RACIAL INEQUALITY WITH ENDOGENOUS INTERVENING COVARIATES: AN EXTENSION OF THE DINARDO-FORTIN-LEMIEUX METHOD

Kazuo Yamaguchi*

Abstract

This paper begins by clarifying that propensity-score weighting in the DiNardo-Fortin-Lemieux (DFL) decomposition analysis—unlike propensity-score weighting in Rubin's causal model, in which confounding covariates can be endogenous—may generate biased estimates for the decomposition of inequality into "direct" and "indirect" components when intervening variables are endogenous. The paper also clarifies that the Blinder-Oaxaca method confounds the modeling of two distinct counterfactual situations: one in which the covariate effects of the first group become equal to those of the second group and the other in which the covariate distribution of the second group becomes equal to that of the first group. The paper shows that the DFL method requires a distinct condition to provide an unbiased decomposition of inequality that remains under each counterfactual situation. The paper then introduces a combination of the DFL method with Heckman's two-step method as a way of testing and eliminating bias in the DFL estimate

*University of Chicago, Chicago, IL, USA

Corresponding Author:
Kazuo Yamaguchi, NORC/University of Chicago, 1155 East 60th Street, Chicago, IL 60637, USA
Email: kyamagu@uchicago.edu

when some intervening covariates are endogenous. The paper also intends to bring gender and race back to the center of statistical causal analysis. An application focuses on the decomposition of gender inequality in earned income among white-collar regular employees in Japan.

Keywords

decomposition analysis, causal analysis, gender inequality, endogeneity, propensity score

1. INTRODUCTION

The aim of this paper is to reconceptualize, and reformulate, from the point of view of Rubin's causal model (RCM) (Rosenbaum and Rubin 1983, 1984; Rubin 1985), the DiNardo-Fortin-Lemieux (DFL) method (DiNardo, Fortin, and Lemieux 1996) for the decomposition of inequality on the basis of propensity-score weighting and to extend the method for handling cases when covariates include intervening variables that are endogenous. Decomposition analysis is typically concerned with dividing the effects of a dichotomous group variable X, such as the distinction between men and women, on the outcome into two components, a component explained by the difference in covariates $\mathbf{V}$ between the groups, and a component not explained. (See Fortin, Lemieux, and Firpo 2011 for a comprehensive review of decomposition analysis.)

The decomposition method of analyzing inequality that has been most frequently used is the Blinder-Oaxaca (BO) method (Blinder 1973; Oaxaca 1973). Further extensions or modifications of this method to solve its "identification issue" have also been discussed (e.g., Jones and Kelley 1984; Kim 2013; Oaxaca and Ransom 1999; Yun 2008). Extending it to decomposition for hazard rate has also been proposed (Powers and Yun 2009). For decomposition analysis based on the BO method, the two counterfactual situations described below are always treated as identical. The method assumes a pair of regression equations, such as $y^M = \beta'^M \mathbf{V}^M + \varepsilon$ for men and $y^W = \beta'^W \mathbf{V}^W + \varepsilon$ for women. Then, under the assumed independence of the error terms from covariates, we obtain

$$\bar{y}^W - \bar{y}^M = \left[\beta^{W'}(\bar{\mathbf{V}}^W - \bar{\mathbf{V}}^M) \right] + \left[(\beta^{W'} - \beta^{M'})\bar{\mathbf{V}}^M \right]. \quad (1)$$

Because $\beta^{W'}\bar{\mathbf{V}}^M$ represents the mean of Y for a counterfactual situation in which the covariate distribution is that of men while the covariate effects are those of women, the first component of the equation can be interpreted as the sex difference in the mean of Y, which would be eliminated *if women had men's covariate distribution*, and the second component can be interpreted as the sex difference in the mean of Y that would be eliminated *if men had women's covariate effects*. Considering either of those two counterfactual situations leads to the same decomposition result in the BO method. The first portion is also called the "explained component" of the inequality because it is attributable to sex differences in covariate values. The second component, called the "unexplained component," reflects inequality in society that results from different "treatments" of men and women with the same covariates. In their review of decomposition analysis, Fortin et al. (2011) discussed the fact that the latter component of the BO method can be interpreted as the *average treatment effect for the treated* (Morgan and Winship 2007) when the group variable can be regarded as a treatment variable. As explained later in this section, this component becomes equivalent with the *average treatment effect for the untreated* for the case in which the group variable, such as the sex dummy variable, is time constant. Generally, the two counterfactual situations described above differ when covariates are endogenous, as explained below. This point has not been mentioned in the previous literature.

The DFL method makes a weaker assumption for the outcome than the BO method. In the original formulation, the pair of equations assumed for men and women are expressed as $y^M = \phi(\mathbf{V}^M, \boldsymbol{\theta}^M) + \varepsilon$ for men and $y^W = \phi(\mathbf{V}^W, \boldsymbol{\theta}^W) + \varepsilon$ for women, where ϕ is an unspecified function and $\boldsymbol{\theta}^M$ and $\boldsymbol{\theta}^W$ are parameters that indicate the covariate effects on the outcome for men and women, respectively. Under the assumed independence of the error term from the covariates (i.e., if the covariates are exogenous) we obtain the following decomposition:

$$\bar{y}^W - \bar{y}^M = \left[\overline{\phi}(\mathbf{V}^W, \boldsymbol{\theta}^W) - \overline{\phi}(\mathbf{V}^M, \boldsymbol{\theta}^W))\right] + \left[\overline{\phi}(\mathbf{V}^M, \boldsymbol{\theta}^W) - \overline{\phi}(\mathbf{V}^M, \boldsymbol{\theta}^M))\right]. \quad (2)$$

Similar to equation (1) of the BO method, the first component of equation (2) reflects inequality that would be eliminated if women had men's covariate distribution, and the second component reflects inequality that would be eliminated if men were treated like women. Because the estimates of $\overline{\phi}(\mathbf{V}^M, \boldsymbol{\theta}^M)$ and $\overline{\phi}(\mathbf{V}^W, \boldsymbol{\theta}^W)$ are simply sample means, we need an estimate of only $\overline{\phi}(\mathbf{V}^M, \boldsymbol{\theta}^W)$ obtainable from the following equation for a dichotomous variable X that takes a value of 0 for men and 1 for women:

$$\bar{\phi}(\mathbf{V}^M, \mathbf{\theta}^W) \equiv \int_{\mathbf{v}} \phi(\mathbf{v}, \mathbf{\theta}^W) f(\mathbf{v}|X=0) d\mathbf{v} = \int_{\mathbf{v}} E(Y^W|\mathbf{v}) f(\mathbf{v}|X=0) d\mathbf{v}$$
$$= \int_{\mathbf{v}} \omega(\mathbf{v}) E(Y^W|\mathbf{v}) f(\mathbf{v}|X=1) d\mathbf{v} = E_{\omega}(Y^W) \tag{3}$$

where $f(\mathbf{v}|X)$ indicates the conditional probability density of $\mathbf{V}$, and E_{ω} indicates the weighted mean with weights:

$$\omega(\mathbf{v}) \equiv \frac{f(\mathbf{v}|X=0)}{f(\mathbf{v}|X=1)} = \frac{p(X=0|\mathbf{v})f(\mathbf{v})/p(X=0)}{p(X=1|\mathbf{v})f(\mathbf{v})/p(X=1)} = \frac{p(X=1)p(X=0|\mathbf{v})}{p(X=0)p(X=1|\mathbf{v})}. \tag{4}$$

A consistent estimate of the weight can be obtained by a consistent estimate of $p(X|\mathbf{v})$ via logit or probit regression.

Hence, the DFL method generalizes the BO method by weakening the assumption for the outcome equation by semiparametric modeling. As Barsky et al. (2002) pointed out, a major limitation of the BO method is that it requires a linear relationship between the dependent variable and its covariates. In contrast, the DFL method does not assume such a relationship. In particular, the DFL method can be applied to the decomposition of difference in proportion, as in the decomposition analysis of gender difference in the proportion of managers, while the BO method may not be applied to such an analysis. This is because linear probability models for regression analysis usually fail to yield consistent parameter estimates, with the exception of saturated models with categorical covariates where estimates of outcome probabilities always lie between 0 and 1.

The BO and DFL methods also differ where some covariates are endogenous. For the BO method, a typical method of handling an endogenous covariate is the instrumental variable (IV) method for linear regression. The application of the BO method using least-squares or maximum likelihood estimation is invalid when covariates are endogenous because the regression coefficient estimates become inconsistent.

The situation differs for the DFL method, as described in this paper. Note that when the covariates are endogenous, $E(\varepsilon|\mathbf{v}) \neq 0$ holds, and therefore a change in the combination of the covariate distribution and the error distribution affects the mean outcome. In particular, two counterfactual situations become different. For the set of parameters, covariates, and the error term $\{\theta, V, \epsilon\}$ that affect the outcome, the counterfactual situation in which women have men's covariate distribution implies a combination of women's $\{\theta, \epsilon\}$ and men's V. On the other hand, the counterfactual situation in which men have women's covariate effects implies a combination of men's $\{V, \epsilon\}$ and women's θ. Hence, the error distribution differs for these two counterfactual situations. This paper shows that the DFL method can reflect each of these counterfactual situations under different conditions. In particular, as explained later, the direct effect of X on Y not through V will be equated with the counterfactual effect that would be eliminated when people in one group with covariates V were treated the same in the society as members of the other group with the same V. That is, the direct effect will be equated with the counterfactual effect that would be eliminated if men had women's covariate effects and not equated with the other counterfactual effect that would be eliminated if women had men's covariate distributions.

It is also necessary to discuss the misconception of some researchers that time-constant variables such as gender or race cannot be the "treatment variables" in causal analysis. The argument is based on the fact that if we use the person-specific fixed effects model, or the difference-in-difference (DID) estimation, with panel survey data, the effect of race or gender is wiped out because it is completely collinear with, or is explained by, unobserved population heterogeneity.

In fact, the argument has two conceptual confusions. One is a confusion regarding whether gender or race can be conceived as a variable for treatment or can be conceived as a variable for treatment assignment. Causal analysis based on the use of propensity scores (Rosenbaum and Rubin 1983, 1984; Robins, Hernan, and Brumback 2000; Rubin 1985), called the RCM, distinguishes between treatment and treatment assignment. In the standard conception, the treatment assignment distinguishes between the treatment group and the control group. Subjects are assigned to one of those two groups, and only subjects in the treatment group get treated. The causal analysis, however, conceives for each subject both the outcome under treatment and the outcome under no treatment, one of which is unobserved and counterfactual, and therefore the difference between the two is always unobservable. The observed variable that distinguishes between two sexual or racial groups is not a variable that indicates a treatment but can be considered a variable that indicates a treatment assignment. Unlike a distinction in the standard conception, however, it is not a distinction between the treatment group and the control group but a distinction between two different control groups. The treatment itself is a hypothetical change in sex or race that nobody in the sample experienced. Hence, no sample subjects are in the treatment group, and as a result, the average treatment effect for the treated (Morgan and Winship 2007) cannot be estimated. Although there can be such cases as transgender persons, we are concerned here with the effect of a hypothetical change in the value of a time-constant variable. We can conceive, however, the average treatment effect for the untreated, the effect of treatment in the outcome obtained by comparing the observed outcome under each control state of the variable with the counterfactual outcome under treatment among those whose observation is made for just one of the control states. We can estimate such average treatment effect under certain assumptions described later.

The other confusion is between the question of whether the treatment effect of change in sex or race can be conceived and that of whether the treatment effect of such a change is estimable. The argument about the fixed effects model or the DID estimation indicates only that if we assume unconstrained time-constant unobserved population heterogeneity in determining the outcome, we cannot estimate the treatment effect of a time-constant variable. On the other hand, if we make some different assumptions, the effect of a hypothetical change in sex or race becomes estimable. A major problem, however, is that the standard ignorability assumption that the RCM makes is not likely to hold when intervening variables that the decomposition analysis uses as covariates are endogenous, as explained below.

Another argument against the conception of causal analysis about the effect of sex or race is substantive. According to this argument, if women are discriminated against (e.g., in employment), the cause of discrimination is employer's attitude, and the effect of gender would disappear if such employers' discrimination against women became absent, which would therefore indicate that gender is not a true cause. Although it is true that gender is not a cause of discrimination, gender discrimination has been concerned with whether men and women with the same set of attributes other than sex are treated unequally in society. The analysis of racial or gender discrimination based on an experimental audit study (Correll, Benard, and Source 2007; Pager 2003) is concerned with an estimation of the effect of race or gender on the outcome through a differential treatment of people on the basis of gender or race in a society.

We are interested in such a "treatment effect" of gender, and although it is methodologically different from the experimental audit study, what we refer to as *causal analysis* in this paper is a method of estimating the average treatment effect as defined initially by Rosenbaum and Rubin (1983) on the basis of the counterfactual conception of treatment.

An important issue for a causal modeling of the decomposition analysis is the endogeneity of covariates. As shown below, the ignorability assumption that the method makes may not hold when some intervening covariates are endogenous or if the population is defined by a state of an endogenous intervening variable. Such a situation will occur when an intervening covariate includes, for example, educational attainment, and uncontrolled selectivity into higher education affects the outcome. It may also occur when the analysis is applied only to the population of employees, and uncontrolled selectivity into and exit from employment affects the outcome. In other words, both selection bias in the state of an intervening variable and sample selection that results from using a population that corresponds to a particular state of an intervening variable may generate bias in the DFL decomposition as a causal analysis.

Because the DFL method relies on propensity-score weighting (Robins, Hernan, and Brumback 2000; Rubin 1985) and implicitly makes an ignorability assumption that appears to be similar to that of the RCM for the analysis of cross-sectional survey data, one may consider that the method can handle endogenous covariates because in the standard use of propensity-score weighting, the endogeneity of confounding variables is allowed, and that is one of the major merits of the RCM. The situation, however, differs between the use of propensity-score weighting for the RCM and its use in the DFL method for decomposition analysis. Figure 1 clarifies this point with two simplified causal diagrams.

In the two diagrams, observed endogenous covariates V are endogenous because an unobserved confounder U that affects both V and Y exists. In case 1, covariates V are confounders of treatment variable X and outcome variable Y, and conditional independence of X and U, $X \perp U | V$, holds. In case 2, however, covariates V are intervening variables, and even though X is assumed to be independent of U, the control for covariates V, which are common causal descendants of X and U, induces nonindependence between U and X (Elwert and Winship 2014;

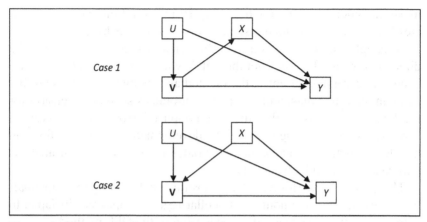

Figure 1. Two causal diagrams with endogenous covariates.

Morgan and Winship 2007; Pearl 2009). As an illustration, assume that latent ability U is independent of gender X, and both ability and gender affect education V such that people with higher ability are more likely to attend college, and because of gender inequality in educational opportunity, men are more likely than women to attend college. Assume further for simplicity of discussion that the top 50 percent of men in ability and the top 25 percent of women in ability go to college. Then, among college attendants, average ability is higher for women (because it is the average of the top 25 percent for women and the average of the top 50 percent for men). Similarly, among people who do not go to college, average ability is also higher for women than for men (because it is the average of the bottom 75 percent for women and the average of the bottom 50 percent for men). Hence, correlation between latent ability and gender emerges when education is held constant.

Generally, $X \perp U | V$ does not hold in case 2. Case 1 is the situation that the RCM assumes for causal analysis with cross-sectional data, and the condition $X \perp U | V$ is equivalent to the ignorability assumption described later. On the other hand, case 2 is the typical situation we have for decomposition analysis with endogenous covariates. Even though the independence of X and U may exist without controlling for **V**, by which the total treatment effect of X on Y becomes estimable, we are interested in the direct treatment effect of X on Y not through **V** in decomposition analysis. With the control for **V**, however, we cannot make the ignorability assumption $X \perp U | V$ unless all intervening covariates V are exogenous and not subject to selection bias by U.

Although the DFL method may thus yield a biased estimate for the direct treatment effect of X not through V when covariates include endogenous intervening variables, the method also enables an extension that can eliminate this bias, and this paper introduces such an extension for the DFL method. Note that the assumption of exogenous intervening variables is a very strong one, and the development of a method that can handle the issue of endogenous covariates for decomposition analysis will be a very useful advancement.

This paper also performs a decomposition analysis of gender inequality in earned income among white-collar regular employees in Japan to demonstrate the usefulness of the extension of the DFL method.

2. METHOD

2.1. The Causal Conception of Sex or Race and Conditions and Results for the Case in Which the Ignorability Assumption Holds

Three tasks are accomplished below: (1) I describe the standard set of assumptions for the RCM model, (2) I modify the assumptions for analysis of the decomposition of inequality between sexual or racial groups, and (3) I clarify the condition in which the ignorability assumption holds and the DFL estimate for the decomposition is unbiased as a causal analysis. A formal expression of bias in the DFL method that exists when the ignorability assumption does not hold and a method that eliminates this bias are introduced in the sections that follow.

The RCM for cross-sectional data analysis makes the following set of assumptions (Morgan and Winship 2007; Rosenbaum and Rubin 1983, 1984).

- A-1: The stable unit treatment value assumption (SUTVA) holds. This assumption justifies conceiving the treatment effect at the individual level to be independent of the results of treatment assignment. The SUTVA posits that the counterfactual treatment effect, defined as $Y_{1i} - Y_{0i}$ (where Y_{1i} indicates either the observed outcome or the potential outcome under the treatment, and Y_{0i} indicates either the observed outcome or the potential outcome under no treatment for subject i) does not depend on who else in the population is assigned to the treatment group.

- A-2: The treatment effects are heterogeneous and vary with persons. This leads to the dependence of the average treatment effect in the RCM on the specification of the population, such as the total population, the population of the treated, or the population of the untreated.
- A-3: The ignorability assumption, $(Y_1, Y_0) \perp X|\mathbf{V}$, applies, such that if observed confounding variables $\mathbf{V}$ that affect both the outcome and the treatment assignment X are controlled, the potential outcomes and the treatment assignment are conditionally independent. This assumption implies that no unobserved confounding variables exist.
- A-4: The confounding covariates can be endogenous; that is, they may not be independent of the unobserved determinant of the outcome.

Note that only A-1 and A-3 are constraining assumptions. Assumptions A-2 and A-4 imply the absence of the constraints imposed by many other methods, such as regression-based methods.

In the case of the treatment effect of sex or race, we retain assumption A-2 on the heterogeneity of treatment effects. Assumption A-1, the SUTVA in the original form, becomes irrelevant because no one in the sample has been treated, and the "treatment"—a change in gender or race—is only imaginary. However, we still need to make a modified SUTVA with which $Y_{1i} - Y_{0i}$ can be conceived at the individual level, such that individual potential outcomes do not depend on a change in the association of group variable X and covariates $\mathbf{V}$ that will occur in the population under a counterfactual situation.

We also need a notational change for Y_0 and Y_1, because the distinction of two sexual groups or two racial groups is a distinction between two control groups, not a distinction between the treatment group and the control group. Unlike the standard notation, in which Y_1 and Y_0 refer to the outcome under treatment and under no treatment, respectively, we use notations Y_1 and Y_0, in conceiving the treatment effect of gender or race, to indicate the observed or potential outcome that is generated when the subject is treated as a member of group 1 and group 0, respectively. Therefore, for example, for men for whom $X = 0$, Y_0 is the observed outcome, and Y_1 is the counterfactual potential outcome with a change of sex; for women for whom $X = 1$, Y_0 is the counterfactual potential outcome with a change of sex, and Y_1 is the observed outcome. Y_1-Y_0 indicates the effect of being treated as a woman versus being treated as a man and is the treatment effect for the untreated for

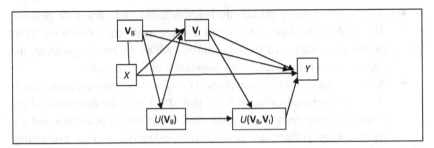

Figure 2. A general causal structure.

both men and women. The observed outcome can be expressed as $Y_{obs} = XY_1 + (1 - X)Y_0$, as in the case of the standard RCM.

The modification of assumptions A-3 and A-4 need to be discussed together. I will illustrate, though it is simplified because of the omission of various interaction effects and heterogeneity in the effects of variables on their causal descendants, with the causal diagram of Figure 2.

Variable X in Figure 2 is a time-constant treatment variable, such as gender or race. Note first that because variable X is by assumption not affected by any other variables, no confounders that affect both X and Y exist for the total population. However, an analysis based on a sample of a particular population, such as an analysis of gender inequality in wages among employees, may make unobserved as well as observed covariates of Y correlated with X because men and women may become employed and remain employed according to gender-specific selection processes. In Figure 2, such a sample selection bias is equated with a control for an intervening variable V_I that indicates the presence versus the absence of employment.

Even if there are no confounders that affect both X and Y, there can be exogenous causes of Y that are neither causal antecedents nor causal descendants of X but are correlated with X. We call such variables *exogenous correlated causes*. Various family-background characteristics as correlates of race, such as parents' education, occupation, and income, and family intactness at subject's birth, are examples. In Figure 2, variables V_B indicate exogenous correlated causes, and the line without arrowheads that connects X and V_B indicates a correlation without causation. Variable $U(V_B)$ is the unobserved determinant of Y that remains when we control for V_B. We assume that although correlated causes V_B affect $U(V_B)$, as family background affects a subject's latent trait

$U(\mathbf{V_B})$, and the affected $U(\mathbf{V_B})$ in turn affects the outcome, $U(\mathbf{V_B})$ is conditionally independent of X, controlling for $\mathbf{V_B}$, that is, $X \perp U(\mathbf{V}_B)|\mathbf{V}_B$. This is the ignorability assumption we will make in this section. However, we will also later introduce a method for the case in which this ignorability assumption does not hold.

The variables $\mathbf{V_I}$ indicate the intervening variables that can be subject to selection bias by an unobserved variable and can affect the unobserved variable, as in the case of selection bias in higher education by latent ability and the effect of educational attainment on latent ability. In Figure 2, the path from $U(\mathbf{V_B})$ to $\mathbf{V_I}$ and the path from $\mathbf{V_I}$ to $U(\mathbf{V_B},\mathbf{V_I})$ indicate those effects, where variable $U(\mathbf{V_B},\mathbf{V_I})$ indicates the unobserved determinant of Y that remains when we control for both $\mathbf{V_B}$ and $\mathbf{V_I}$. In accordance with the discussion of case 2 in Figure 1 in the previous section, even when $X \perp U(\mathbf{V}_B)|\mathbf{V}_B$ holds, $X \perp U(\mathbf{V}_B, \mathbf{V}_I)|\mathbf{V}_B, \mathbf{V}_I$ may not hold unless all intervening variables are exogenous and are not subject to selection bias by $U(\mathbf{V_B})$. In summary, in replacing assumption A-3, we make another assumption in this section:

- Modified A-3: $X \perp U(\mathbf{V}_B)|\mathbf{V}_B$ for exogenous correlated causes $\mathbf{V}_B$ of Y.

It follows that

- Corollary from modified A-3: $X \perp U(\mathbf{V}_B, \mathbf{V}_I)|\mathbf{V}_B, \mathbf{V}_I$ does not hold generally unless intervening variables $\mathbf{V}_I$ are all exogenous, and, therefore, independent of $U(\mathbf{V}_B)$.

We do not make assumption A-4. Instead, we distinguish below between the case in which all intervening variables are exogenous and, therefore, $X \perp U(\mathbf{V}_B, \mathbf{V}_I)|\mathbf{V}_B, \mathbf{V}_I$ holds and the case in which some intervening variables are endogenous and, therefore, $X \perp U(\mathbf{V}_B, \mathbf{V}_I)|\mathbf{V}_B, \mathbf{V}_I$ may not hold.

For the rest of this section, I will show that when $X \perp U(\mathbf{V})|\mathbf{V}$ holds, where $\mathbf{V}$ denotes covariates taken into account in the decomposition analysis, the DFL estimate of the decomposition provides an unbiased estimate of the direct treatment effect of X on Y not through $\mathbf{V}$. I derive this result by using both the standard RCM expression and an alternative expression that is more useful in identifying bias in the DFL estimate. In Section 2.2, I will formally express the bias in the DFL estimate when

$X \perp U(\mathbf{V})|\mathbf{V}$ does not hold, and in Section 2.3, I introduce a method that tests and eliminates this bias.

Generally, the average direct treatment effect of X on Y not through $\mathbf{V}$ is concerned with the estimation of $E(Y_1 - Y_0|\mathbf{V})$ and its average in the total population $E(Y_1 - Y_0) \equiv \int_\mathbf{v} E(Y_1 - Y_0|\mathbf{v})f(\mathbf{v})d\mathbf{v}$, where $f(\mathbf{v})$ is the probability density function of $\mathbf{V}$ in the total population, its average among the population of group 0, $E(Y_1 - Y_0|X=0) \equiv \int_\mathbf{v} E(Y_1 - Y_0|\mathbf{v})f(\mathbf{v}|X=0)d\mathbf{v}$, or its average among the population of group 1, $E(Y_1 - Y_0|X=1) \equiv \int_\mathbf{v} E(Y_1 - Y_0|\mathbf{v})f(\mathbf{v}|X=1)d\mathbf{v}$.

Suppose that we are interested in estimating $E(Y_1 - Y_0|X=0)$. Because the estimate of $E(Y_0|X=0)$ is simply the sample mean of Y for subjects in group $X = 0$, we need only an estimate of the counterfactual mean $E(Y_1|X=0)$. Suppose that an ignorability assumption, $(Y_1, Y_0) \perp X|\mathbf{V}$, holds. Then $E(Y_1|X=0)$ can be expressed as follows.

$$
\begin{aligned}
E(Y_1|X=0) &= \int_\mathbf{v} E(Y_1|X=0, \mathbf{v})f(\mathbf{v}|X=0)d\mathbf{v} \\
&= \int_\mathbf{v} E(Y_1|X=1, \mathbf{v})f(\mathbf{v}|X=0)d\mathbf{v} \quad \text{(by the ignorability assumption)} \\
&= \int_\mathbf{v} E(Y_{obs}|X=1, \mathbf{v})f(\mathbf{v}|X=0)d\mathbf{v} \\
&= \int_\mathbf{v} \omega(\mathbf{v})E(Y_{obs}|X=1, \mathbf{v})f(\mathbf{v}|X=1)d\mathbf{v} \\
&= E_\omega(Y_{obs}|X=1),
\end{aligned}
\tag{5}
$$

where $\omega(\mathbf{v})$ is a weight that is the same as that defined in equation (4), that is, $\omega(\mathbf{v}) = [p(X = 1)p(X = 0|\mathbf{v})]/[p(X = 0)p(X = 1|\mathbf{v})]$ and E_ω denotes the weighted mean with the weight $\omega(\mathbf{v})$. Note, however, that unlike the derivation of equations (3) and (4) for the original DFL method described in the introduction, this derivation relies on the ignorability assumption. Hence, a consistent estimator of the counterfactual mean $E(Y_1|X=0)$ is given as the weighted mean of observed Y among subjects in group $X = 1$ with weights that can be calculated using the consistent estimate of $p(X = 1|\mathbf{v})$ by logit or probit regression. However, weight estimates $\hat{\omega}_{1i}$ may not have the average of 1 for sample subjects in group $X = 1$, and therefore, it is better to use the following adjusted weight for the ratio estimator because it is known to be more efficient than the unadjusted estimate:

$$\hat{\omega}_i^* \equiv N_1 \hat{\omega}_i \Big/ \Big(\sum\nolimits_{i|x_i=1} \hat{\omega}_i \Big), \tag{6}$$

where N_1 is the number of sample subjects in group 1. Then we obtain the following decomposition of difference in the mean of Y between the two groups, and this is the same as the DFL decomposition:

$$\begin{aligned} E(Y|X=1) - E(Y|X=0) &= E(Y_1|X=1) - E(Y_0|X=0) \\ &= E(Y_1 - Y_0|X=0) + \{E(Y_1|X=1) - E(Y_1|X=0)\}. \end{aligned} \tag{7}$$

If X indicates the distinction between women ($X = 1$) and men ($X = 0$), then $E(Y_1 - Y_0|X=0)$ indicates the average direct treatment effect of gender on the outcome among men, that is, the average effect on men of being treated as a woman. The second component, $E(Y_1|X=1) - E(Y_1|X=0)$, represents the difference in the mean of Y that would be eliminated if women had men's covariate distribution, because

$$\begin{aligned} &E(Y_1|X=1) - E(Y_1|X=0) \\ &= \int_v \{E(Y_1|X=1, \mathbf{v})p(\mathbf{v}|X=1) - E(Y_1|X=0, \mathbf{v})p(\mathbf{v}|X=0)\} d\mathbf{v} \\ &= \int_v \{E(Y_1|X=1, \mathbf{v})(p(\mathbf{v}|X=1) - p(\mathbf{v}|X=0))\} d\mathbf{v} \end{aligned} \tag{8}$$

holds. Note that $E(Y_1|X=1) - E(Y_1|X=0)$ becomes equal to the amount explained by the difference in the covariate distribution, because $E(Y_1|X=0, \mathbf{v}) = E(Y_1|X=1, \mathbf{v})$ holds from the ignorability assumption, and without this assumption such an interpretation cannot be made for $E(Y_1|X=1) - E(Y_1|X=0)$.

We now consider a slightly different derivation of the average direct treatment effect. This alternative derivation becomes the basis of the extension of the DFL method for causal analysis described in the sections that follow. We keep the assumptions made above for the modification of the RCM model and, in addition, we make an additional assumption A-5, which may appear to make the model slightly more specific than the typical RCM model, though generality is actually not lost. The assumption is as follows:

- A-5: The unobserved determinant of outcome Y, including its possible interaction effects with $\mathbf{V}$, is functionally linear in affecting the outcomes.

With this additional assumption, we can express the observed and potential outcomes by excluding the random error term whose mean for each individual is zero without loss of generality as

$$Y_{0i} = \phi(\theta_0, \mathbf{v}_i) + \theta_{0u}(\mathbf{v}_i)u_i,$$

and

$$Y_{1i} = \phi(\theta_1, \mathbf{v}_i) + \theta_{1u}(\mathbf{v}_i)u_i. \tag{9}$$

Here, ϕ is an unknown function, θ_0 and θ_1 are parameters that characterize the effects of covariates $\mathbf{V}$ on Y_0 and Y_1, respectively, U is the unobserved determinant of the outcome, and $\theta_{0u}(\mathbf{v})$ and $\theta_{1u}(\mathbf{v})$, respectively, characterize the effect of U on Y_0 and Y_1 and its possible dependence on $\mathbf{V}$ due to interaction effects of $\mathbf{V}$ and U on Y_0 and Y_1. The RCM model, without assumption A-5, corresponds to a more general expression such that $Y_{0i} = \phi(\theta_0, \mathbf{v}_i, u_i)$ and $Y_{1i} = \phi(\theta_1, \mathbf{v}_i, u_i)$. However, because U is an unobserved variable that is not constrained in form, and because equation (9) can reflect the unconstrained interaction effects of U and $\mathbf{V}$ on the outcome, the expression of equation (9) does not lose the generality of the RCM.

The ignorability assumption can now be expressed as $X \perp U | \mathbf{V}$, because as assumed in equation (9), Y_0 and Y_1 are functions of variables $\mathbf{V}$ and U. Then, $E(Y_1 | X = 0)$ is given as follows:

$$
\begin{aligned}
E(Y_1 | X = 0) &= \int_{\mathbf{v}} \int_u (\phi(\theta_1, \mathbf{v}) + \theta_{1u}(\mathbf{v})u)f(\mathbf{v}, u | X = 0)du d\mathbf{v} \\
&= \int_{\mathbf{v}} f(\mathbf{v} | X = 0) \left[\int_u (\phi(\theta_1, \mathbf{v}) + \theta_{1u}(\mathbf{v})u)f(u | \mathbf{v}, X = 0)du \right] d\mathbf{v} \\
&= \int_{\mathbf{v}} f(\mathbf{v} | X = 0) \left[\int_u (\phi(\theta_1, \mathbf{v}) + \theta_{1u}(\mathbf{v})u)f(u | \mathbf{v}, X = 1)du \right] d\mathbf{v} \quad (\text{because } U \perp X | \mathbf{V}) \\
&= \int_{\mathbf{v}} E(Y_{obs} | \mathbf{v}, X = 1)f(\mathbf{v} | X = 0)d\mathbf{v} \\
&= \int_{\mathbf{v}} \omega(\mathbf{v})E(Y_{obs} | \mathbf{v}, X = 1)f(\mathbf{v} | X = 1)d\mathbf{v} \\
&= E_\omega(Y_{obs} | X = 1), \tag{10}
\end{aligned}
$$

where $\omega(\mathbf{v})$ is the same as that defined by equation (4). Naturally, we obtain the same results for $E(Y_1 | X = 0)$ as equation (5).

2.2. The Case in Which Endogenous Intervening Variables Exist

In this section, I assume that the ignorability assumption $X \perp U | V$ may not hold for the pair of equations (9) given in the previous section, either because (1) the covariates of the decomposition analysis include some endogenous intervening variables or (2) the ignorability assumption $X \perp U(V_B) | V_B$ does not hold even before the control for the intervening variables.

When X indicates a gender distinction as before, the mean of the counterfactual outcome where men had women's covariate effects is now given as

$$
\begin{aligned}
E(Y_1 | X = 0) &= \int_{\mathbf{v}} \int_{u} (\phi(\boldsymbol{\theta}_1, \mathbf{v}) + \theta_{1u}(\mathbf{v})u) f(\mathbf{v}, u | X = 0) du d\mathbf{v} \\
&= \int_{\mathbf{v}} \phi(\boldsymbol{\theta}_1, \mathbf{v}) f(\mathbf{v} | X = 0) d\mathbf{v} + E(\theta_{1u}(\mathbf{v})u | X = 0).
\end{aligned}
\tag{11}
$$

On the other hand, the weighted mean of observed outcomes among women with weights

$$
\omega(\mathbf{v}) \equiv \frac{f(\mathbf{v} | X = 0)}{f(\mathbf{v} | X = 1)} = \frac{p(X = 1)p(X = 0 | \mathbf{v})}{p(X = 0)p(X = 1 | \mathbf{v})}
$$

defined before in equation (4) is given as

$$
\begin{aligned}
E_\omega(Y_{obs} | X = 1) &= \int_{\mathbf{v}} \omega(\mathbf{v}) \left[\int_{u} (\phi(\boldsymbol{\theta}_1, \mathbf{v}) + \theta_{1u}(\mathbf{v})u) f(\mathbf{v}, u | X = 1) du \right] d\mathbf{v} \\
&= \int_{\mathbf{v}} \frac{f(\mathbf{v} | X = 0)}{f(\mathbf{v} | X = 1)} \left[\int_{u} (\phi(\boldsymbol{\theta}_1, \mathbf{v}) f(\mathbf{v} | X = 1) f(u | \mathbf{v}, X = 1) du \right] d\mathbf{v} + E_\omega(\theta_{1u}(\mathbf{v})u | X = 1)) \\
&= \int_{\mathbf{v}} \phi(\boldsymbol{\theta}_1, \mathbf{v}) f(\mathbf{v} | X = 0) d\mathbf{v} + E_\omega(\theta_{1u}(\mathbf{v})u | X = 1)).
\end{aligned}
\tag{12}
$$

Then from equations (11) and (12), we obtain

$$
E(Y_1 | X = 0) = E_\omega(Y_{obs} | X = 1) + \{ E(\theta_{1u}(\mathbf{v})u | X = 0) - E_\omega(\theta_{1u}(\mathbf{v})u | X = 1) \}. \tag{13}
$$

The DFL estimator of the "unexplained" inequality with covariates $\mathbf{V}$ is given as $E_\omega(Y_{obs} | X = 1) - E(Y_{obs} | X = 0)$, and, therefore

$$
\begin{aligned}
E(Y_1 - Y_0 | X = 0) = &[\text{DFL estimator for unexplained inequality}] \\
&+ \{ E(\theta_{1u}(\mathbf{v})u | X = 0) - E_\omega(\theta_{1u}(\mathbf{v})u | X = 1) \}.
\end{aligned}
\tag{14}
$$

Hence, the DFL estimator is an unbiased estimator of $E(Y_1 - Y_0|X=0)$ only if U is independent of X in the weighted population with weights $\omega(\mathbf{v})$ for $X=1$ and constant weights of 1 for $X=0$. However, if U affects intervening variables $\mathbf{V}$, this does not hold because the DFL estimator has a bias of $E(\theta_{1u}(\mathbf{v})u|X=0)- E_\omega(\theta_{1u}(\mathbf{v})u|X=1)$. In Section 2.3, I introduce a method to eliminate this bias.

It is worth examining whether the DFL estimator for explained inequality can be interpreted as inequality that would be eliminated under another counterfactual situation: if women had men's covariate distribution but retained their own value of u. Recall that for such an interpretation, we have already seen in equation (8) that $E(Y_1|X=1) - E(Y_1|X=0)$ requires the ignorability assumption $X \perp U|\mathbf{V}$ to hold. However, we are concerned here with the meaning of the DFL estimator, $E(Y_{obs}|X=1) - E_\omega(Y_{obs}|X=1)$, which can be expressed as

$$E(Y_{obs}|X=1) - E_\omega(Y_{obs}|X=1) = \int_v E(Y_{obs}|X=1,\mathbf{v},u)f(\mathbf{v},u|X=1)d\mathbf{v}du$$

$$- \int_v E(Y_{obs}|X=1,\mathbf{v},u)\omega(\mathbf{v})f(\mathbf{v},u|X=1)d\mathbf{v}du$$

$$= \int_v E(Y_{obs}|X=1,\mathbf{v},u)(f(\mathbf{v}|X=1) - f(\mathbf{v}|X=0))f(u|X=1,\mathbf{v})d\mathbf{v}du$$

$$= \int_v E(Y_{obs}|X=1,\mathbf{v})(f(\mathbf{v}|X=1) - f(\mathbf{v}|X=0))d\mathbf{v}. \qquad (15)$$

Hence, the interpretation holds: the DFL estimate for the "explained" component of inequality can still be interpreted as the extent of inequality that would be eliminated if women had men's covariate distribution.

However, there is an important caveat. There is an inherent ambiguity in conceiving the counterfactual situation at the individual level for the case in which women have men's covariate distribution. This is unlike the other counterfactual situation in which men have women's covariate effects, which can be specified at the individual level as a change of parameters from the set of $\{\theta_0, \theta_{0u}\}$ to the set of $\{\theta_1, \theta_{1u}\}$. The derivation above is based on an implicit assumption that $f(u|X=1,\mathbf{v})$ remains the same when the macrosocial distribution of $\mathbf{V}$ changes. Such a result will be realized under the counterfactual situation in which for each group of women for a given $\mathbf{v}$, their proportion in the population changes from $f(\mathbf{v}|X=1)$ to $f(\mathbf{v}|X=0)$. Then, $f(u|X=1,\mathbf{v})$ will remain the same because we have the same set of women for each value of $\mathbf{v}$. As an example, this implies that for a counterfactual situation in which the proportion of college graduates increases from a factual 40 percent to a hypothetical 50 percent, we are assuming implicitly that the 40 percent of women who actually attained college graduation would occupy the 50 percent of women. This contrasts with counterfactual situations in which women's proportion of college graduation reached 50 percent via other mechanisms: for example, where an additional 10 percent of women, among those who actually did not attain college education, newly attain college graduation. In this case, $f(u|X=1,\mathbf{v})$ may not remain the same because we do not know the joint distribution of U and $\mathbf{V}$ for those additional 10 percent. Hence, if we do not make the assumption that $f(u|X=1,\mathbf{v})$ will remain the same under macrosocial change in the distribution of $\mathbf{V}$, we cannot interpret the DFL component of "explained inequality" as the extent of inequality that would be eliminated when women had men's covariate distribution. Note that if we make a stronger assumption that the covariates are exogenous, and therefore $f(u|X=1,\mathbf{v})=f(u|X=1)$, then the aforementioned qualification for the counterfactual situation in which women have men's covariate distribution becomes unnecessary. In conclusion, the DFL method permits an interpretation of the "explained" component of inequality, even when covariates are endogenous, as the extent of inequality that would be eliminated under the counterfactual situation in which each group of women who attained a distinct set of covariate values occupies the women's population as much as the group of men of the same covariate set does for the men's population. However, the "unexplained" component may not be interpreted as the extent of inequality that would be eliminated if men were treated like women.

2.3. A Method for Eliminating Bias in the Decomposition Analysis

A good thing about the results of equation (14) is that in order to eliminate bias in the DFL estimate of unexplained inequality as an estimate of the direct treatment effect of X on Y, we do not need to eliminate selection bias in all the endogenous intervening variables but rather need only to eliminate the effect of covariance between X and U that may exist when covariates $\mathbf{V}$ are held constant. This is because we already have some methods for handling such a problem. Another merit of equation (14) is that it shows that bias in the DFL estimate arises from a significant covariance between X and U independent of the cause of the covariance between X and U. The covariance may be introduced by holding intervening covariates $\mathbf{V}_I$ constant or may have existed prior to a control for intervening variables because the ignorability assumption $X \perp U(\mathbf{V}_B)|\mathbf{V}_B$ does not hold. Regardless of the alternative cause of the covariance between X and U, we can obtain an unbiased estimate of the direct treatment effect of X if we eliminate the effect of this covariance.

When the methodological issue is the endogeneity of variable X, then a standard econometric method includes the econometric IV method for linear regression. However, we will not use that method, which makes a much stronger assumption than the RCM and, in particular, assumes that the effect of X on Y is homogenous and is represented by a single regression coefficient. Although the reformulation of the IV method from the RCM was made by Angrist, Imbens, and Rubin (1996) as the local average treatment estimator (LATE), this alternative method requires that the single dichotomous IV causally precedes and affects the treatment variable X. Such an IV assumed by the LATE method, however, does not exist when the treatment variable indicates a variable such as sex or race that is not affected by any other variable. A person-specific fixed effects model with panel survey data can be used for the BO decomposition method to handle the issue of endogenous covariates if the treatment variable is time varying (Fortin et al. 2011). A model with person-specific fixed effects, however, cannot be used in the present case in which the treatment-assignment variable is gender or race where no one in the sample experienced a treatment, that is, an observed change in race or gender.

Hence, this paper considers a combination of the method introduced in Sections 2.1 and 2.2 with Heckman's two-step estimation method (Heckman 1979; Heckman and Robb 1986) for handling selection bias in the state of a dichotomous categorical variable by modeling correlated errors, because although it makes additional assumptions about a parametric characterization of the error terms, and about a *distinct* condition described below for IVs to satisfy, we can retain other assumptions described in the preceding sections. The original Heckman method, however, was developed for linear regression models for the outcome. We therefore need a modified derivation of the method with a semiparametric model for the outcome without assuming independence between covariates and the unobserved determinant of the outcome.

Because this method relies on a probit regression that assumes an underlying continuous variable X^*, described below, one may argue that it is not adequate for predicting X, which is a nominal categorical variable such as sex or gender. If we assume the error to be subject to unobserved random variability beyond the binomially distributed random error associated with a dichotomous outcome of a latent probability, probit regression with the normally distributed error seems an acceptable option. However, researchers who are hesitant about this option may use a variation of the Heckman method based on the logistic selection equation (Dubin and Rivers 1989), though such an alternative does not permit the two-step procedure described below.

We consider the weighted population characterized by weights $\omega(\mathbf{v})$, which are defined by equation (4) for $X = 1$ and are constant at 1 for $X = 0$. It is because we are concerned with the elimination of nonindependence between X and U that may exist after this weighting.

We assume that for the weighted population, a set of covariates $\mathbf{W}$ predicts variable X^* as defined below. Furthermore, we require $\mathbf{W}$ to have some interaction effects with variables $\mathbf{V}$ in predicting X^*, because the presence of such interaction effects is crucial in order for the inverse Mills ratio to have variability sufficiently independent of the variability of $\mathbf{W}$. The reason for this requirement is explained later. Note that when the effects of $\mathbf{W}$ and $\mathbf{V}$ on X^* are simply additive, covariates $\mathbf{V}$ are not likely to affect X^* significantly because of statistical independence between X and $\mathbf{V}$ in the inverse probability–weighted population, even though the control of $\mathbf{W}$ may generate some weak association between X and $\mathbf{V}$.

Note that not unlike the estimation of the propensity score $p(X = 1|\mathbf{v})$ in the DFL method, the use of the probit model in predicting X does not imply that the variables $\mathbf{W}$ and their interactions with $\mathbf{V}$ affect X, because we are concerned only with the modeling of covariance of U_x and U_y, where U_x indicates the error term of X^* defined in equation (19) given below and U_y is the unobserved determinant of Y, to eliminate bias generated by covariance between X and U_y. However, variables $\mathbf{W}$ should be IVs for which the following condition must hold:

$$Y_{obs} \perp \mathbf{W}|\mathbf{V}, X. \qquad (16)$$

Note that because $Y_1 = Y_{obs}$ when $X = 1$ and $Y_0 = Y_{obs}$ when $X = 0$, Y_1 and Y_0 are both are functions of $\mathbf{V}$ and U_y. It follows that the condition of equation (16) also implies that $U_y \perp \mathbf{W}|\mathbf{V}, X$ holds. In other words, although we do not make the ignorability assumption of $U_y \perp X|\mathbf{V}$, we make a distinct ignorability assumption for the IVs:

- A-6: $U_y \perp \mathbf{W}|\mathbf{V}, X$ holds for the IVs $\mathbf{W}$.

Given the model in equation (9), assumption $U_y \perp \mathbf{W}|\mathbf{V}, X$ and condition $Y_{obs} \perp \mathbf{W}|\mathbf{V}, X$ are equivalent. It follows that an empirical test of $Y_{obs} \perp \mathbf{W}|\mathbf{V}, X$ also becomes a test of the adequacy of assumption $U_y \perp \mathbf{W}|\mathbf{V}, X$ because $\mathbf{W}$ affecting Y while controlling for $\mathbf{V}$ and X will indicate a violation of the assumption. It may seem difficult to conduct such a test when X and $\mathbf{V}$ are both endogenous variables, but it is feasible as described below.

First, it is worth noting that an important difference exists between the assumption of the standard IV and the ignorability assumption A-6, as depicted in Figure 3. Note that the characteristics shown in the figure should hold controlling for covariates $\mathbf{V}$, though this is omitted for the sake of simplicity.

Case 1 indicates the characteristics of the standard IVs $\mathbf{Z}$ as in local average treatment effects (Angrist et al. 1996). The IVs are assumed to be exogenous and independent of U_y and affect Y only indirectly through

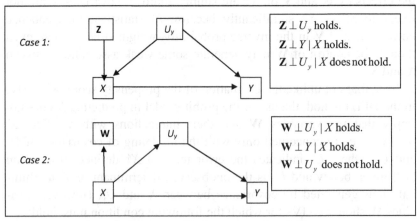

Figure 3. Two causal diagrams with instrumental variables.

the treatment variable X (which is endogenous because of its correlation with U_y). It is important to note that the absence of direct effects of $\mathbf{Z}$ on Y cannot be tested easily in this case. We cannot control for X in a regression to assess the effects of $\mathbf{Z}$ on Y because $E(U_y|X) \neq 0$. On the other hand, fixing a value of X causes $\mathbf{Z}$ to become correlated with U_y, thus preventing $\mathbf{Z}$ from being used as covariates in a regression to predict Y for a given X.

Case 2 indicates the characteristics of the IVs as used in the present case. The group variable X is the common cause of U_y and IVs $\mathbf{W}$, which means that $\mathbf{W} \perp U_y|X$ is assumed to hold instead of $\mathbf{W} \perp U_y$. A nicety about this case is that variables $\mathbf{W}$ become independent of U_y when we fix a value of X; therefore we can test the absence of direct effects of $\mathbf{W}$ on Y separately for each fixed value of X using a regression. However when endogenous covariates $\mathbf{V}$ need to be controlled for, we cannot simply use $\mathbf{V}$ as control variables in the regression to test the effects of $\mathbf{W}$ on Y for each fixed value of X. For the use of a single categorical IV, we can use the semiparametric method described below.

Suppose that we have a single categorical IV W, and let

$$\omega_W(\mathbf{v}|X) \equiv p(W|X)/p(W|X,\mathbf{v}) \qquad (17)$$

for each value of X. It then follows that

$$
\begin{aligned}
\omega_W(\mathbf{v}|X)f(\mathbf{v},w,u_y|X) &= \frac{p(w|X)}{p(w|X,\mathbf{v})}p(\mathbf{v}|X)p(w|X,\mathbf{v})p(u_y|X,\mathbf{v},w) \\
&= p(\mathbf{v}|X)p(u_y|X,\mathbf{v})p(w|X) \text{ since } U_y \perp W|X,\mathbf{V} \\
&= p(\mathbf{v},u_y|X)p(w|X).
\end{aligned}
\qquad (18)
$$

Equation (18) shows that the data of each given X weighted by $\omega_W(\mathbf{v}|X)$ preserve the joint distribution of $\mathbf{V}$ and U_y and that $W \perp (\mathbf{V}, U_y)$ holds for each value of X. It follows that the condition $Y_{obs} \perp W|\mathbf{V}, X$ of equation (16) can be tested with data weighted $\omega_W(\mathbf{v}|X)$ by simply examining whether $E_{\omega_W(\mathbf{v}|X)}(Y|W,X) = E_{\omega_W(\mathbf{v}|X)}(Y|X)$ holds empirically for each value of X. This test is valid regardless of whether covariates $\mathbf{V}$ are endogenous.

We require the assumption $U \perp W|\mathbf{V}, X$ rather than $U_y \perp W|\mathbf{V}$ because only the former is required in deriving a reevaluation of bias in the DFL estimate as given in equation (22) below. For such IVs $\mathbf{W}$, we make the following assumption:

- A-7: Variable X takes a value of 1 if $X^* > 0$ is satisfied for the latent continuous variable X^*, and X^* satisfies the following model:

$$X_i * = \gamma(\mathbf{w}_i, \mathbf{v}_i) + u_{x,i}, \tag{19}$$

where $E(u_{x,i}) = 0$, $V(u_{x,i}) = 1$, and $\gamma(\mathbf{w}, \mathbf{v})$ is a parametric function of $(\mathbf{W}, \mathbf{V})$ that needs to be specified. Note that X^* varies with $\mathbf{V}$ here because interaction effects of some $\mathbf{V}$ with $\mathbf{W}$ are assumed.

Finally, we also make another assumption about the bivariate distribution of U_x and U_y:

- A-8: For given values of $\mathbf{V}$, variable U_y has conditional mean $E(u_y|\mathbf{v})$ and variance $V(u_y|\mathbf{v}) = \sigma_y^2(\mathbf{v})$, and $\{U_x, U_y\}$ are bivariate normally distributed with covariance $COV(u_x, u_y|\mathbf{v}) = \sigma_{xy}(\mathbf{v})$.

Hence, we allow the mean and the variance of U_y and the covariance between U_x and U_y to depend on $\mathbf{V}$. This seems natural, because the covariance between X and U_y can be induced by holding covariates $\mathbf{V}$ constant.

According to Johnson and Kotz (1972; see also Heckman 1979; Maddala 1983), we generally obtain for a bivariate normal distribution $N(u_x, u_y, \sigma_x, \sigma_y, \sigma_{xy})$ with $E(u_x) = E(u_y) = 0$,

$$E(u_y|u_x > c) = (\sigma_{xy}/\sigma_x)\frac{\phi(Z)}{1 - \Phi(Z)},$$

where $Z \equiv c/\sigma_x$, and $\phi(Z)$ and $\Phi(Z)$ are, respectively, the probability density function and the cumulative distribution function of the standard normal distribution.

Because $E(u_y|u_x > c)p(u_x > c) + E(u_y|u_x < c)p(u_x < c) = E(u_y) = 0$, we obtain

$$E(u_y|u_x < c) = - E(u_y|u_x > c)p(u_x > c))/p(u_x < c))$$
$$= - (\sigma_{xy}/\sigma_x)\frac{\phi(Z)}{1 - \Phi(Z)}\frac{1 - \Phi(Z)}{\Phi(Z)} = - (\sigma_{xy}/\sigma_x)\frac{\phi(Z)}{\Phi(Z)}.$$

For the present method, the mean of u_y may depend on covariates $\mathbf{V}$ because of their possible endogeneity. However, because the above characteristics hold for $u_y^* \equiv u_y - E(u_y|\mathbf{v})$ that satisfies $E(u_y^*|\mathbf{v}) = 0$ and $COV(u_x, u_y * |\mathbf{v}) = COV(u_x, u_y|\mathbf{v})$, we obtain from $U_y \perp \mathbf{W}|\mathbf{V}, X$ and $\sigma_x = 1$ that

$$E(u_y|\mathbf{v}, \mathbf{w}, X = 0) = E(u_y|\mathbf{v}, X = 0) = E(u_y|\mathbf{v}, u_x < -\gamma(\mathbf{w}, \mathbf{v}))$$

$$= E(u_y|\mathbf{v}) - \sigma_{xy}(\mathbf{v}) \frac{\phi(-\gamma(\mathbf{w}, \mathbf{v}))}{\Phi(-\gamma(\mathbf{w}, \mathbf{v}))} \qquad (20)$$

$$= E(u_y|\mathbf{v}) - \sigma_{xy}(\mathbf{v}) \frac{\phi(\gamma(\mathbf{w}, \mathbf{v}))}{1 - \Phi(\gamma(\mathbf{w}, \mathbf{v}))},$$

and

$$E(u_y|\mathbf{v}, \mathbf{w}, X = 1) = E(u_y|\mathbf{v}, X = 1) = E(u_y|\mathbf{v}, u_x > -\gamma(\mathbf{w}, \mathbf{v}))$$

$$= E(u_y|\mathbf{v}) + \sigma_{xy}(\mathbf{v}) \frac{\phi(-\gamma(\mathbf{w}, \mathbf{v}))}{1 - \Phi(-\gamma(\mathbf{w}, \mathbf{v}))} \qquad (21)$$

$$= E(u_y|\mathbf{v}) + \sigma_{xy}(\mathbf{v}) \frac{\phi(\gamma(\mathbf{w}, \mathbf{v}))}{\Phi(\gamma(\mathbf{w}, \mathbf{v}))}.$$

Now we can reevaluate bias in the DFL estimate, which is given in equation (14) as $E(\theta_{1u}(\mathbf{v})u|X = 0) - E_\omega(\theta_{1u}(\mathbf{v})u|X = 1)$. We first derive the case where neither $\theta_{1u}(\mathbf{v})$ nor $\sigma_{xy}(\mathbf{v})$ depends on $\mathbf{V}$. We then obtain from equations (20) and (21)

$$E(\theta_{1u}u_y|X = 0) - E_\omega(\theta_{1u}u_y|X = 1)$$

$$= \theta_{1u} \left\{ \int_\mathbf{v} \int_\mathbf{w} E(u_y|\mathbf{v}, \mathbf{w}, X = 0)f(\mathbf{w}, \mathbf{v}|X = 0)d\mathbf{w}d\mathbf{v} \right\}$$

$$- \theta_{1u} \left\{ \int_\mathbf{v} \int_\mathbf{w} \omega(\mathbf{v})E(u_y|\mathbf{v}, \mathbf{w}, X = 1)f(\mathbf{w}, \mathbf{v}|X = 1)d\mathbf{w}d\mathbf{v} \right\}$$

$$= \theta_{1u} \left\{ \int_\mathbf{v} E(u_y|\mathbf{v})f(\mathbf{v}|X = 0)d\mathbf{v} - \int_\mathbf{v} \int_\mathbf{w} \sigma_{xy} \frac{\phi(\gamma(\mathbf{w}, \mathbf{v}))}{1 - \Phi(\gamma(\mathbf{w}, \mathbf{v}))}f(\mathbf{w}, \mathbf{v}|X = 0)d\mathbf{w}d\mathbf{v} \right\}$$

$$- \theta_{1u} \left\{ \int_\mathbf{v} \omega(\mathbf{v})E(u_y|\mathbf{v})f(\mathbf{v}|X = 1)d\mathbf{v} + \int_\mathbf{v} \int_\mathbf{w} \omega(\mathbf{v})\sigma_{xy} \frac{\phi(\gamma(\mathbf{w}, \mathbf{v}))}{\Phi(\gamma(\mathbf{w}, \mathbf{v}))}f(\mathbf{w}, \mathbf{v}|X = 1)d\mathbf{w}d\mathbf{v} \right\}$$

$$= -\theta_{1u}\sigma_{xy} \left\{ E\left(\frac{\phi(\gamma(\mathbf{w}, \mathbf{v}))}{1 - \Phi(\gamma(\mathbf{w}, \mathbf{v}))}\bigg|X = 0\right) + E_\omega\left(\frac{\phi(\gamma(\mathbf{w}, \mathbf{v}))}{\Phi(\gamma(\mathbf{w}, \mathbf{v}))}\bigg|X = 1\right) \right\}. \qquad (22)$$

Note that the first component of $E(\theta_{1u}u_y|X = 0)$ and that of $E_\omega(\theta_{1u}u_y|X = 1)$ that depend on $E(u_y|\mathbf{v})$ are canceled out because $\omega(\mathbf{v})f(\mathbf{v}|X = 1) = f(\mathbf{v}|X = 0)$.

Let H for each person i with $\mathbf{w}_i$ be defined as

$$H_i \equiv \begin{cases} \dfrac{\phi(\gamma(\mathbf{w}_i, \mathbf{v}_i))}{1 - \Phi(\gamma(\mathbf{w}_i, \mathbf{v}_i))} & \text{when } X_i = 0 \\ \dfrac{\phi(\gamma(\mathbf{w}_i, \mathbf{v}_i))}{\Phi(\gamma(\mathbf{w}_i, \mathbf{v}_i))} & \text{when } X_i = 1 \end{cases} . \tag{23}$$

Then, by combining this with equation (14), we obtain

$$E(Y_1 - Y_0 | X = 0) = E_\omega(Y_{obs} | X = 1) - E(Y_{obs} | X = 0)$$
$$- \theta_{1u}\sigma_{xy}\{E(H | X = 0) + E_\omega(H | X = 1)\}. \tag{24}$$

Because the estimates of $E(H|X=0)$ and $E_\omega(H|X=1)$ can be obtained from weighted probit regression with X as the dependent variable and $\mathbf{W}, \mathbf{V}$ and their interactions as covariates, the remaining issue is the estimation of $\theta_{1u}\sigma_{xy}$. The expected value of the observed outcome at the individual level for person i with $X_i = 1$, is given from equations (9) and (21) as

$$E_u(y_{obs,i|x_i=1}) = \phi(\mathbf{v}_i, \boldsymbol{\theta}_1) + \theta_{1u}E(u_y|\mathbf{v}_i, X_i = 1)$$
$$= \phi(\mathbf{v}_i, \boldsymbol{\theta}_1) + \theta_{1u}E(u_y|\mathbf{v}_i) + \theta_{1u}\sigma_{xy}\frac{\phi(\gamma(\mathbf{w}_i, \mathbf{v}_i))}{\Phi(\gamma(\mathbf{w}_i, \mathbf{v}_i))} . \tag{25}$$

Hence, an estimate of $\theta_{1u}\sigma_{xy}$ is given by the coefficient of $\phi(\gamma(\mathbf{w}, \mathbf{v}))/\Phi(\gamma(\mathbf{w}, \mathbf{v}))$, which is Heckman's inverse Mills ratio. Note that $E(u_y|\mathbf{v}_i)$ is a function not of unknown individual $u_{y,i}$ but of $\mathbf{v}_i$ and the parameters of the conditional distribution of u_y, $f(u_y|\mathbf{v})$. Although $\phi(\mathbf{v}, \boldsymbol{\theta}_1)$ and $E(u_y|\mathbf{v}_i)$ are both functionally unspecified, we can linearize the covariate effects in equation (25) in order to obtain an estimate of $\theta_{1u}\sigma_{xy}$. Because we wish this estimate to depend little on the modeling of $\phi(\mathbf{v}_i, \boldsymbol{\theta}_1) + E(u_y|\mathbf{v}_i)$ as a function of $\mathbf{v}_i$, it is desirable to use the categorical expression of covariates, and all significant two-way and higher-order interaction effects among the covariates should be included in the model.

The reason we require $\mathbf{W}$ to have significant interaction effects with some $\mathbf{V}$ in predicting X^* in equation (19) is because the inverse Mills ratio that depends only on $\mathbf{W}$, $H(\mathbf{W})$, will become collinear with $\mathbf{W}$. Because $Y_{obs} \perp \mathbf{W} | \mathbf{V}, X$ holds, $Y_{obs} \perp H(\mathbf{W}) | \mathbf{V}, X$ also holds, which leads to an artificial acceptance of the null hypothesis on the independence between X and U_y.

When either $\theta_{1u}(\mathbf{v})$ or $\sigma_{xy}(\mathbf{v})$ or both depend on $\mathbf{V}$, equation (22) holds for each given set of covariates $\mathbf{V}$, and therefore we obtain

$$E(Y_1 - Y_0|X = 0) = E_\omega(Y_{obs}|X = 1) - E(Y_{obs}|X = 0)$$
$$- E\{\theta_{1u}(\mathbf{v})\sigma_{xy}(\mathbf{v})(E(H|\mathbf{v}, X = 0) + E_\omega(H|\mathbf{v}, X = 1))\}. \qquad (26)$$

We can model and estimate $\theta_{1u}(\mathbf{v})\sigma_{xy}(\mathbf{v})$ by including the interaction effect of covariates $\mathbf{V}$ and the control variable H.

The application should be done in the following steps.

1. We use either a logit or probit regression to obtain a consistent estimate of $p(X = 1|\mathbf{v})$. We need to conduct a diagnosis for an adequate construction of propensity scores to generate a weighted sample for which statistical independence between X and $\mathbf{V}$ should hold.

2. We create weights $\omega(\mathbf{v})$ for the group with $X = 1$, and constant weights of 1 for the group with $X = 0$. We need to re-create $\omega(\mathbf{v})$ when the diagnosis indicates inadequacy.

3. We apply the probit model for X with data weighted by $\omega(\mathbf{v})$, using covariates $\mathbf{V}$, IV $\mathbf{W}$, and their interactions as predictors.

4. We create variable $H_i = \frac{\phi(\gamma(\mathbf{w}_i, \mathbf{v}_i))}{\Phi(\gamma(\mathbf{w}_i, \mathbf{v}_i))}$ for each sample individual i in group $X = 1$, and assign a value of $H_i = \frac{\phi(\gamma(\mathbf{w}_i, \mathbf{v}_i))}{1-\Phi(\gamma(\mathbf{w}_i, \mathbf{v}_i))}$ for each sample individual i in group $X = 0$.

5. With the sample data of $X = 1$ weighted by $\omega(\mathbf{v})$, we run the outcome regression with X, covariates $\mathbf{V}$, and H as predictors to obtain an estimate of $\theta_{1u}\sigma_{xy}$.

6. We should elaborate step 5 by trying various possible interaction effects of H and a subset of $\mathbf{V}$ to identify the best-fitting model.

7. If variable H shows a significant effect in step 5 or 6, then we calculate the adjusted estimate of $E(Y_1 - Y_0|X = 0)$ by using equation (24) and the estimate of $\theta_{1h}\sigma_{xy}$ when no interaction effect of H and $\mathbf{V}$ exists, and by using equation (26) and the estimate of $\theta_{1u}(\mathbf{v})\sigma_{xy}(\mathbf{v})$ when some interaction effects of H and $\mathbf{V}$ exist. If the effect of H is not significant, we retain the DFL decomposition outcome.

Note that if we wish the outcome to reflect an alternative counterfactual situation where women for whom $X = 1$ were treated like men (for whom $X = 0$), we only need to replace the above-described procedure by switching the categories of the dummy variable X.

3. APPLICATION

3.1. *Data and Alternative Hypotheses on the Nature of Endogeneity*

The application presented here uses data from the Comparative Survey of Work Life Balance conducted in 2009 by the Research Institute of Economy, Trade and Industry in Japan for the population of employees in four countries. The survey for Japan includes a nationally representative random sample of white-collar regular employees in firms with 100 or more employees. The analysis that follows uses the sample of married employed men and women ages 23 to 59 years in Japan. The analysis is applied to the sample because we have an effective IV for the population of married people. Excluding 341 samples with missing annual wage/salary (5.8 percent of the total) reduces the sample size to 5,550: 4,449 men and 1,101 women. Although about 41 percent of people in the labor force were women in Japan, regular employment was severely underrepresented by married women, leading to a smaller proportion of female samples than that in the labor force.

The analysis focuses on the decomposition of gender inequality in earned annual income into components that are not explained by the following covariates. Two nested models for covariates are used. The first model employs age (seven categories), education (four categories), and employment duration for current employment (eight categories). The second model adds to model 1 the average hours of work per week (four categories). The two models are used to clarify how much of the proportion of gender inequality in earned annual income is explained by gender difference in the first three covariates and how much more can be explained by taking into account gender difference in hours of work as an additional covariate. Unlike employees in the United States, the majority of white-collar employees in Japan, other than those in managerial positions and certain professionals, are not exempt from payment for overtime work, which therefore means that hours of work strongly affect earned annual income among white-collar regular employees.

For the gender effect, exogenous correlated causes may not exist, because men and women are equally likely to be born into various families. Age, education, and employment duration are major human-capital variables in Japan, where the age-based or duration-based *nenko* wage system is still quite prevalent. Hours of work per week also differ greatly between men and women because married women work fewer hours than married men even among regular employees. The IV used here is a dichotomous distinction about whether the subjects ever took childcare leave. For the present sample, 33.6 percent of women and only 2.5 percent of men ever took such leave. Although this variable has a strong correlation with gender, it has no unique effect on earned annual income for each gender category, as shown later.

Marital status is a strong indicator of gender-specific sample selection because about 60 percent to 70 percent of women quit their jobs during periods of childrearing, and because many Japanese firms give priority for regular employment to recent graduates, many women reentering the labor force after they quit their jobs get employed as irregular employees. Hence, a strong interaction effect of gender and marital status on exit from and reentry into regular employment exists. Hence, sample selection bias in regular employment by the unobserved determinants of income may also exist for the combination of gender and marital status, in addition to the possible induced correlation between latent ability and gender when education is held constant under gender inequality in educational attainment in Japan. The gender-specific selection mechanism associated with marital status may generate an association between the unobserved determinant of income and gender in two ways that predict the opposite direction of association:

- *The opportunity costs hypothesis:* Women whose opportunity costs of leaving their jobs are relatively higher because of their better prospects for future income are more likely to remain as regular employees during the periods of childrearing and are more likely to reenter the labor force. This tendency will generate a positive correlation of marital status (married vs. single) with the unobserved variable that positively affects income among women.

- *The adverse selection hypothesis:* Statistical discrimination against women—which is believed to exist strongly in Japan, especially for married women, because of many employers' reinforcement of the traditional division of household labor—will make women with higher income potential than others more likely to quit during the periods of childrearing and less likely to reenter the labor force. This tendency will generate a negative correlation of marital status (the married versus the single) with the unobserved variable that positively affects income among women.

The theory of the adverse selection mechanism associated with discrimination was introduced by Schwab (1986), who applied the theory of information asymmetry and consequent adverse selection initially theorized by Akerlof (1970) in the context of the commodity market rather than in the context of the labor market. Because selection bias in the unobserved variable occurs mainly for women after marriage, the two hypotheses will yield a significant correlation of gender and the unobserved variable among the married, but in the opposite direction.

3.2. Preliminary Analyses

Two kinds of preliminary analyses were conducted. The first was concerned with the diagnosis of adequacy in the construction of propensity scores. Although the statistical independence of the joint distribution of covariates from gender by weighted data cannot be tested completely, the paper tests (1) the statistical independence of each covariate from gender after weighting by $\omega(v)$ and (2) the absence of significance of all covariates combined for the logistic regression model employed in estimating propensity scores after the weighting.

The second preliminary analysis was concerned with testing the adequacy of the IVs.

3.2.1. Propensity Score Estimation and Its Diagnosis.

A logistic regression is used in the estimation of propensity scores in predicting gender distinction. For model 1 with three covariates, in addition to the main effects of the covariates, significant category-by-category interaction effects between education and age were found by pairwise tests of all possible interaction effects, and they were therefore included. For model 2, two kinds of interaction effects involving hours of work per week were found to be significant in addition to the main effect, and they were included to attain statistical independence between gender and the four covariates. Those interaction effects included in model 2, in their most parsimonious form, are interaction effects between (1) working 49 hr or more and education and (2) working 49 hr or more and linear age (based on the distinction of seven categories). Table 1 presents for each model the test of independence between each covariate and gender, and the significance test of the effects of all covariates, including their interaction effects, in the logistic regression before and after weighting by the propensity-score weights. The results in Table 1 show that although the covariates are strongly associated with gender

Table 1. Diagnostic Tests of Statistical Independence between Gender and Covariates after Weighting

Covariate	L_2	d.f.	p	L_2	d.f.	p
I. Before propensity-score weighting						
1. Pairwise test on independence of the covariate from gender						
(1) Age	192.36	6	.000			
(2) Education	561.83	3	.000			
(3) Employment duration	69.87	7	.000			
(4) Hours of work	558.68	3	.000			
2. Logistic regression to predict propensity scores						
(1) Model 1 with four covariates	879.74	34	.000			
(2) Model 2 with five covariates	1,328.86	41	.000			
II. After propensity-score weighting	Model 1			Model 2		
1. Pairwise test on independence of the covariate from gender						
(1) Age	.10	6	1.000	6.51	6	.369
(2) Education	.04	3	.998	.07	3	.996
(3) Employment duration	4.45	7	.726	7.48	7	.380
(4) Hours of work	—	—	—	6.97	3	.073
2. Logistic regression to predict propensity score	6.56	34	1.000	26.61	41	.960

individually as well as jointly, those associations almost completely disappear for data weighted by propensity-score weights defined by equation (4).

3.2.2. Examinations of IVs. We need to confirm two facts for the IVs to be effective: (1) condition $Y_{obs} \perp W | V, X$ holds, and (2) the IV is strongly associated with gender and this association has some significant variability with covariates.

Table 2 presents results from weighted linear regressions with the weights $\omega_W(v|X) = p(W/X)/p(W|X, v)$, which should attain $W \perp (V, U_y)$ for each sample data of a given gender. The regression on income thus includes the IV as the only covariate. The logistic regression model of $p(W|X = 0, v)$ for men's data to estimate $\omega_W(v|X = 0)$ includes the main effects of age, education, and employment duration for model 1, while model 2 adds the main effects of hours of work per week. No interaction effects of covariates were found in this case. The logistic regression model of $p(W|X = 1, v)$ for women's data to estimate $\omega_W(v|X = 1)$ uses the same main effects as those for men's data, but it also includes interaction effects of linear age and categorical education that were significant only for women. The results of Table 2 for both men and women show that the IV does not affect income significantly when covariates V are controlled for.

Table 3 shows the results of two probit regressions for data weighted by propensity scores obtained for each of the two models for predicting the proportion of women. The first equation includes only the IV to show the strong significance of its average effect. The second equation includes the effects of age and education, both of which had significant interaction effects with the IVs. The second equation is the one used in deriving the inverse Mills ratio to test the possible correlation between X and U_y.

The results for the first equation indicate that women are more likely to take childcare leave and that the effects of the IV in predicting the proportion of women is significant at the .1 percent level for each model. The results for the second equation show that the effects of the IV in predicting gender have significant variability with age and education.

3.3. Main Analyses

I first examined whether gender was correlated with the unobserved determinant of the outcome by testing the significance of $\theta_{1h}\sigma_{xy}$, which

Table 2. Insignificance of the Effects of the IV on Income for Data Weighted by $\omega_W(\mathbf{v}|X)$ (in 10,000 yen)

	Coefficient	S.D.	$|t|$	p
I. Results for men				
1. Model 1 with three covariates for the calculation of $\omega_W(\mathbf{v}|X=0)$				
(1) Intercept	544.84			
(2) IV, "Ever had a childcare leave" (vs. "Never")	18.23	19.95	.91	.361
2. Model 2 with four covariates for the calculation of $\omega_W(\mathbf{v}|X=0)$				
(1) Intercept	566.74			
(2) IV, "Ever had a childcare leave" (versus "Never")	17.97	19.95	.90	.368
II. Results for women				
1. Model 1 with three covariates for the calculation of $\omega_W(\mathbf{v}|X=1)$				
(1) Intercept	354.62			
(2) IV, "Ever had a childcare leave" (versus "Never")	−8.62	10.08	.86	.392
2. Model 2 with four covariates for the calculation of $\omega_W(\mathbf{v}|X=1)$				
(1) Intercept	353.29			
(2) IV, "Ever had a childcare leave" (versus "Never")	−8.22	9.76	.84	.400

Note: IV = instrumental variable.

419

Table 3. The Effects of the Instrumental Variable on Gender for the Inverse Probability–Weighted Population: Probit Regression

	Model 1				Model 2			
	Equation (1)		Equation (2)		Equation (1)		Equation (2)	
	B	|Z|	B	|Z|	B	|Z|	B	|Z|
1. Ever had childcare leave	1.807	26.74	.572	1.61	1.678	24.00	.647	1.77
2. Age (vs. 23–34)								
2.1 main effects								
30–34	—	—	−.021	.20	—	—	−.003	.03
35–39	—	—	−.266	2.68	—	—	−.184	1.84
40–44	—	—	−.236	2.34	—	—	−.197	1.94
45–49	—	—	−.116	1.16	—	—	−.009	.09
50–54	—	—	−.087	.86	—	—	.009	.09
55–59	—	—	−.016	.15	—	—	.063	.60
2.2 Interaction effects with "ever had childcare leave"								
30–34	—	—	−.087	.15	—	—	.494	1.20
35–39	—	—	1.399	3.72	—	—	1.131	2.92
40–44	—	—	1.349	3.54	—	—	1.384	3.53
45–49	—	—	.783	2.04	—	—	.362	.36
50–54	—	—	.847	2.08	—	—	.726	1.73
55–59	—	—	−.077	.16	—	—	.450	.95

(continued)

Table 3. (continued)

	Model 1				Model 2			
	Equation (1)		Equation (2)		Equation (1)		Equation (2)	
	B	|Z|	B	|Z|	B	|Z|	B	|Z|
3. Education (vs. 4-year college)								
3.1 Main effects								
JC/ATS	—	—	−.010	.10	—	—	.087	.92
AVS	—	—	.090	1.33	—	—	.057	.83
High school	—	—	.069	1.49	—	—	.017	.36
3.2 Interaction effects with "ever had childcare leave"								
JC/ATS	—	—	.107	.29	—	—	−1.106	2.89
AVS	—	—	−.690	2.98	—	—	−.729	3.10
High school	—	—	−.244	1.48	—	—	−.134	.77
4. Intercept	−1.058		−.561		−1.019		−.633	

Note: AVS = advanced vocational school after high school; JC/ATS = junior college or advanced technical school (14 years of education).

421

Table 4. The Effect of the Inverse Mills Ratio on Income for Women with Data Weighted by $\omega(v)$

	Model 1				Model 2			
	B	S.D.	$|t|$	p	B	S.D.	$|t|$	p
1. Inverse Mills ratio	−21.21	12.87	1.65	.100	−23.95	16.08	1.49	.137
2. Covariates (parameter estimates are omitted)								
3. Intercept (parameter estimate is omitted)								

is the effect of the inverse Mills ratio derived from the second probit regression equation in Table 3, by using the sample of women as specified by equation (25). For model 1, which has three covariates, the main categorical effects of the covariates, in addition to the inverse Mills ratio, are included as predictors. No significant interaction effects of covariates were found in this case. In model 2, which has four covariates, the main categorical effects of hours of work per week and category-by-category interaction effects of age and hours of work were found to be significant, and they were added. The results in Table 4 show that the effect of the inverse Mills ratio was not significant at the 5 percent level for either model. The interaction effects of the inverse Mills ratio with each of the covariates were also not significant for both models.

Hence, neither the opportunity costs hypothesis nor the adverse selection hypothesis was supported, though it is possible that both hypotheses held but their effects canceled each other out. Hence, in the present analysis, the DFL estimate can be interpreted as the decomposition of gender inequality in income into the direct treatment effect of gender and the effect explained by gender difference in covariate distributions.

Table 5 shows the results from (1) the unweighted regression without covariates (model 0), (2) the weighted regression without covariates (model 1A) and with covariates (model 1B) with weights based on the propensity scores of model 1 with three covariates, and (3) the weighted regression without covariates (model 2A) and with covariates (model 2B) with weights based on the propensity scores of model 2 with four covariates. Models 1A and 2A give the standard DFL estimates, and Models 1B and 2B give doubly robust estimates of them (Bang and Robins 2005). Models 0, 1A, and 2A without covariates do not assume any regression equation, because their coefficients are just the average

Table 5. The DFL Analysis for the Effect of Gender on Income (in 10,000 yen)

	Unweighted Model 0	DFL-1		DFL-2	
		Model 1A	Model 1B	Model 2A	Model 2B
1. Intercept	567.5***	567.5***	402.1***	567.5***	380.4***
2. Gender (vs. men)					
Women	−214.9***	−144.3***	−143.5***	−124.2***	−129.7***
(s.e.)	(6.6)	(6.9)	(6.2)	(7.1)	(6.4)
3. Age (vs. 23–29)					
30–34	—	—	48.7***	—	49.3***
35–49	—	—	99.7***	—	100.4***
40–44	—	—	149.9***	—	152.0***
45–49	—	—	189.5***	—	192.4***
50–54	—	—	210.2***	—	206.0***
55–59	—	—	236.1***	—	239.9***
4. Education (vs. 4-year college)					
JC/ATS	—	—	−58.3***	—	−58.0***
AVS	—	—	−74.6***	—	−65.0***
High school	—	—	−98.4***	—	−101.1***

(continued)

Table 5. (continued)

	Unweighted Model 0	DFL-1		DFL-2	
		Model 1A	Model 1B	Model 2A	Model 2B
5. Employment duration (vs 0–5 years)					
6–10	—	—	29.4**	—	29.3***
11–15	—	—	32.5***	—	31.8***
16–20	—	—	68.9***	—	67.4****
21–25	—	—	70.3****	—	62.5****
26–30	—	—	89.6****	—	95.2****
≥31	—	—	112.5****	—	115.6****
Missing	—	—	53.7***	—	56.8****
6. Hours of work per week (vs. ≤40)					
41–48	—	—	—	—	22.9**
≥49	—	—	—	—	34.7***
Missing	—	—	—	—	−3.5

Note: AVS = advanced vocational school after high school; DFL = DiNardo-Fortin-Lemieux; JC/ATS = junior college or advanced technical school (14 years of education).

**p < .01. ***p < .001. No coefficient attained p < .05

Table 6. A Summary of the Treatment Effects of Gender

Covariates	Age, Education, Employment Duration	Age, Education, Employment Duration, Hours of Work per Week
Percentage explained	32.9	42.2
Percentage unexplained	67.1	57.8

income for men for the intercept and the difference in the average income between women and men for the effect of gender. Agreements in the gender effect between models 1A and 1B and between models 2A and 2B are expected from the statistical independence between gender and covariates in the weighted sample, and they are confirmed here. A comparison of models 0 and 1A indicates that the gender difference in earned annual income explained by the gender difference in the three covariates (age, education, and employment duration) is about 33 percent ($[214.5 - 144.3]/214.9 = .329$). Similarly, a comparison of models 0 and 2A indicates that the gender difference explained by four covariates (the three covariates and hours of work) is about 42 percent ($[214.3 - 124.2]/214.3 = .422$). Hence, by adding hours of work as an additional covariate, the proportion of explained gender inequality increases by about 9 percent. Those decompositions of gender inequality are summarized in Table 6.

4. CONCLUSION

Although decomposition analysis for inequality is quite useful, its assumption may be problematic when we evaluate the method from the counterfactual conception of causality, despite the fact that the decomposition itself implicitly assumes a counterfactual situation. This paper reformulates the DFL method from the viewpoint of RCM and introduces a method to correct its possible bias by combing the DFL method with Heckman's two-step method for the control of selection bias. I consider the use of the method introduced in this paper a complement to the DFL method for examining the possibility of bias in DFL decomposition analysis and for detecting the direction of bias.

This paper also intends to bring gender and race back into the center of statistical causal analysis. As discussed in the introduction, the use of panel survey data for causal analysis seems to have diminished the importance of gender or race in statistical causal analyses because of the lack of a methodological framework to handle such time-constant exogenous variables as the treatment variable in causal analysis. I believe that the discussion and the method presented in this paper will lead to a reconsideration of such trends, and it will be complementary to the experimental audit method, because gender and racial inequality are a major substantive research topic in sociology.

Acknowledgments

I am grateful to Martin Huber and to the anonymous referees of *Sociological Methodology* for helpful comments.

Funding

The author disclosed receipt of the following financial support for the research of this article: This study is partially supported by visiting fellowship of the Research Institute of Economy, Trade, and Industry, Japan.

References

Akerlof, George. 1970. "The Market for Lemons: Quality, Uncertainty, and the Market Mechanism." *Quarterly Journal of Economics* 84:488–500.

Angrist, Joshua D., Guido W. Imbens, and Donald B. Rubin. 1996. "Identification of Causal Effects Using Instrumental Variables." *Journal of the American Statistical Association* 91:444–55.

Bang, Heejung, and James M. Robins. 2005. "Doubly Robust Estimation in Missing Data and Causal Inference Models." *Biometrics* 61:962–72.

Barsky, Robert, John Bound, Kerwin K. Charles, and Joseph P. Lupton. 2002. "Accounting for Black-white Wealth Gap: A Nonparamaric Approach." *Journal of the American Statistical Association* 93:663–73.

Blinder, Alan S. 1973. "Wage Discrimination: Reduced Form and Structural Variables." *Journal of Human Resources* 8:436–55.

Correll, Shelley J., Benard Stephen, and In Paik Source. 2007. "Getting a Job: Is There a Motherhood Penalty?" *American Journal of Sociology* 112:1297–339.

DiNardo, John, Nicole Fortin, and Thomas Lemieux. 1996. "Labor Market Institution and the Distribution of Wages." *Econometrica* 64:1001–44.

Dubin, Jeffrey A., and Rivers Douglas. 1989. "Selection Bias in Linear Regression, Logit and Probit Models." *Sociological Methods and Research* 18: 360–90.

Elwert, Felix, and Christopher Winship. 2014. "Endogenous Selection Bias: The Problem of Conditioning on a Collider Variable." *Annual Review of Sociology* 40: 31–53.

Fortin, Nicole, Thomas Lemieux, and Sergio Firpo. 2011. "Decomposition Methods in Econometrics." Pp. 1–102 in *Handbook of Labor Economics*, vol. 4a, edited by O. Ashenfelter and D. Card. New York: Elsevier.

Heckman, James J. 1979. "Sample Selection Bias as a Specification Error." *Econometrica* 47:153–61.

Heckman, James J., and Richard Robb. 1986. "Alternative Methods for Solving the Problem of Selection Bias in Evaluating the Impact of Treatments on Outcomes." Pp. 63–107 in *Drawing Inferences from Self-selected Samples*, edited by H. Wainer. Mahwah, NJ: Lawrence Erlbaum.

Johnson, N., and S. Kotz. 1972. *Distribution in Statistics: Continuous Multivariate Distributions*. New York: John Wiley.

Jones, Frank L., and Jonahan Kelley. 1984. "Decomposing Differences between Groups: A Cautionary Note on Measuring Discrimination." *Sociological Methods and Research* 12:323–43.

Kim, Chang Hwan. 2013. "Detailed Wage Decompositions: Revisiting the Identification Problem." Pp. 346–63 in *Sociological Methodology*, vol. 43, edited by Tim Futing Liao. Thousand Oaks, CA: Sage Publications.

Maddala, G. S. 1983. *Limited-dependent and Qualitative Variables in Economics*. New York: Cambridge University Press.

Morgan, Stephen L., and Christopher Winship. 2007. *Counterfactuals and Causal Inference*. Cambridge, UK: Cambridge University Press.

Oaxaca, Ronald L. 1973. "Male-female Wage Differentials in Urban Labor Markets." *International Economic Review* 14:693–709.

Oaxaca, Ronald L., and Michael R. Ransom. 1999. "Identification in Detailed Wage Decomposition." *Review of Economics and Statistics* 81:154–57.

Pager, Devah. 2003. "The Mark of a Criminal Record." *American Journal of Sociology* 108:937–75.

Pearl, Judea. 2009. *Causality*. 2nd ed. Cambridge, UK: Cambridge University Press.

Powers, Daniel A., and Meong-Su Yun. 2009. "Multivariate Decomposition of Hazard Rate Models." Pp. 233–63 in *Sociological Methodology*, vol. 39, edited by Yu Xie. Boston, MA: Wiley-Blackwell.

Robins, James M., Miguel Angel Hernan, and Babette Brumback. 2000. "Marginal Structural Models and Causal Inference in Epidemiology." *Epidemiology* 11:550–60.

Rosenbaum, Paul R., and Donald B. Rubin. 1983. "The Central Role of the Propensity Score in Observational Studies for Causal Effects." *Biometrika* 70:41–55.

Rosenbaum, Paul R., and Donald B. Rubin. 1984. "Reducing Bias in Observational Studies Using Sub-classification on the Propensity Scores." *Journal of the American Statistical Association* 79:516–24.

Rubin, Donald B. 1985. "The Use of Propensity Scores in Applied Bayesian Inference." Pp. 463–72 in *Bayesian Statistics*, vol. 2, edited by J. M. Bernardo, M. H. De Groot, D. V. Lindley, and A. F. M. Smith. Amsterdam, the Netherlands: Elsevier.

Schwab, Stewart. 1986. "Is Statistical Discrimination Efficient?" *American Economic Review* 76:228–34.

Yun, Meong-Su. 2008. "Identification Problem and Detailed Oaxaca Decomposition: A General Solution and Inference." *Journal of Economic and Social Measurement* 33: 27–38.

Author Biography

Kazuo Yamaguchi is the Ralph Lewis Professor of Sociology at the University of Chicago and is a former chair in the Department of Sociology. His recent main methodological interests have focused on extending the RCM-type causal analysis to incorporate macrosocial constraints on counterfactual potential outcomes. In addition to his studies on methodology, he is continuing his work on gender inequality and labor markets in Japan, and he is advising the Ministry of Economy, Trade, and Industry of the Japanese government for related policies.